Chef Ron Pirbarki

11/3/20

THE
CLASSICAL
vegetarian
COOKBOOK

"*Chef Ron is a true pioneer and leader through his creative innovative approach to outstanding world-class vegetarian cuisine! The heart of this book reflects his passion, showcasing vegan dietary principles with basic cooking fundamentals along with modern techniques and methods that are dedicated to vegetarian culinary excellence for all to enjoy and savor.*"

STAFFORD T. DeCAMBRA, CEC(r), CCE(r), CCA(r), WCMC, AAC(r)
Chairman, American Academy of Chefs(r)
American Culinary Federation

THE
CLASSICAL
vegetarian
COOKBOOK

For Professional Chefs and Inspired Cooks

RON PICKARSKI

ECO-CUISINE
BOULDER, COLORADO

Copyright 2015 © by Ron Pickarski

Published by Eco-Cuisine, Inc.

P.O. Box 17878

Boulder, CO 80308-0878

303-402-0289

www.eco-cuisine.com

Cover and Interior Design: Ja-lene Clark

Editorial Team: Jo Ann Deck, Ja-lene Clark, Julie Marsh, Joanne Sprott

Photo Credits: 123RF.com on page 170. American Natural Foods Culinary Olympic Team Photographer on pages 17, 31, 105, 151, 160, and 168. Kirsten Boyer on pages 19, 33, 415 and cover. Travis Isaacs on page 67. David Morgenstern on page 152. *New Age Journal* 1990 May/June "Cultured Cuisine" on page 245. Ron Pickarski on pages 169, 177, 187, 194, 201, 207, 208, 229, 231, 242, 258, 274, 290, 293, 315, 325, 332, 334, 349, and 355. Michael Pizzuto Photography on pages 45, 46, 106, 129, 130, 163, 165, 179, 180, 199, 246, 260, 317, 357, 361, and 363. United States Department of Agriculture on page 68.

Color Insert Photo Credits: ANE Team Photographer photos 13, 15, 16, and 31. Army Team Photographer photo 14. Michael Pizzuto Photography photos 1-12, 17-30. Ron Pickarski photo 32.

ISBN-10: 069241536X

ISBN-13: 978-0-692-41536-8

Printed in Canada

1 2 3 4 5 — 20 19 18 17 16 15

DISCLAIMER:

The ideas and opinions expressed in this book by the author and publisher are intended to be used for informational purposes only. Educational insight into the subject matter of vegetarian nutrition is the primary purpose of this book. The reader must seek dietary recommendations from dietary and medical professionals. Diets and nutritional recommendations must be made based on biological individuality which only a health care professional, not a book, can render. Therefore, the author and publisher of this book claim no responsibility to any person for any liability, loss, or damage caused or alleged to be caused directly or indirectly as a result of the use, application, or interpretation of information within this book.

Dedication

To Antonin Carême:
The King of Chefs and the Chef of Kings

 "When we no longer have good cooking in the world, we will have no literature, nor high and sharp intelligence, nor friendly gathering, nor social harmony."

—ANTONIN CARÊME

The Classical Vegetarian Cookbook is dedicated to Antonin Carême, considered the founder of French gastronomy who understood cuisine as both an art and a science. His humble beginnings and his vast knowledge of food and cooking techniques have never failed to inspire me.

Antonin Carême is often referred to as the "The King of Chefs and the Chef of Kings." His life in the kitchen started when he was eleven years old. His parents could no longer afford to support him amidst the French Revolution, telling him he had to leave home and support himself. In 1794 he found a job in a Parisian chop house that would begin the journey defining his life and redefining French cuisine. In 1798 he apprenticed with Sylvain Bailly, a famous French patissier, where his fame began and was further enriched when he embraced savory cuisines.

His major contributions to French cuisine in both savory and pastry realms are immense. He is accredited for his profound contributions to culinary art and the developing of French cuisine, Some of his major contributions are classification of the mother sauces, replacing service à la francaise (serving all dishes at once) with service à la Russe (serving each dish separately as presented on the menu), and the creation of the standard chef's hat, the toque. While Auguste Escoffier deservedly receives much acclaim for his late nineteenth- and early twentieth-century contributions to our culinary trade, it is Carême who created the mother sauces and brought fresh vegetables and herbs back into a cuisine heavily laden with animal foods. I think it is fair to say that he significantly contributed to the development of the first Nouvelle Cuisine that Chef Paul Bocuse resurrected in the 1970s.

As a vegetarian, what stands out so vividly for me is reading how the diplomat Talleyrand, also his culinary mentor, sent Carême a test to create an entire year's worth of vegetable dishes using seasonal produce. And there could be no repetition. He passed the test.

Antonin Carême was a culinary leader whose passion is a blessing to the culinary world and whose talent today seems dimly recognized among foodservice professionals in general and less so among the general public. This book is dedicated to Antonin Carême for his profound contribution to culinary art and to continually honor his work.

Foreword

I was born and raised in France, learning classical French pastry and cuisine working in my parents' pastry shop in Brittany and through culinary education. While traveling the world, continually increasing my knowledge on new cooking techniques, discovering a myriad of new food products, and working along fellow chefs of various ethnic backgrounds, I began to realize that there was an incredible and practically untapped source of natural and complex flavors, textures, colors, available to add to the traditional center of the plate protein that I and others were offering to clients and customers.

However, I did not begin to seriously pay attention to the full potential of a new vegetarian cuisine until my experience at the 1980 International Culinary Olympics, held every four years in Germany. I had heard about but knew very little about this full-fledged vegetarian chef who was going to challenge the culinary old school establishment on a culinary world stage with vegetarian dishes, an incredible feat at the time, by showcasing vegan vegetarian cuisine. It took him many tries and successes until in 1996 when an Olympic vegetarian category was created and Ron and his team took the first gold in that category. This hard won recognition was a signal that the time had come to begin the journey of defining vegetarian cuisine as a universal classical cuisine.

In his book, *The Classical Vegetarian Cookbook for Professional Chefs and Inspired Cooks*, Chef Pickarski presents and emphasizes a culinary philosophy around vegetarianism as cuisine, elevating it from an activist or special diet to a meatless, most interesting cuisine using an extraordinary range of ingredients in imaginative and delicious ways. It is a comprehensive introduction to a cuisine, redefining center of the plate entrées with the likes of complete protein grain loaves and tofu pâtés, translating the five French mother sauces to vegan variations, and making ice cream with only a blender. The challenge is to create a classical vegan cuisine, to develop it, and to educate inspired professional chefs and cooks. This book and an upcoming vegetarian cook certification program move forward that mission. In working with Chef Ron to integrate this cuisine and inspire creative and health conscious individuals, I have seen an urgent need for this cookbook and for such a program.

This book is also a celebration of vegan cuisine, with full tastes, surprising textures, shapes, and colors. It will benefit all of us, because it leads to serving and eating foods that are good for you at work or at home. Flavorful food, beautifully presented, designed to enhance health and well-being of humanity and the sustainability of our overstressed planet—this may be the future of classical cuisine.

CHEF LOUIS PERROTTE, 2015
Former Chairperson of the World Association of Chef Societies (WACS)
Continental Director of the Americas
American Culinary Federation Vice President
Chef Owner, Le Coq au Vin Restaurant, Orlando, Florida

Table of Contents

Acknowledgments

Special Thanks to My Culinary Educators

Growing up in the restaurant business I was fortunate to have attended the Washburne Culinary Institute in Chicago (Washburne Class of 1973). At every stage of my culinary career I was challenged through many culinary ventures to further my skills in the art. After becoming a vegetarian, my decision to compete in the International Culinary Olympics (IKA) was the pivotal moment in my culinary career.

Many chefs helped me arrive at this juncture in my career starting with my culinary instructors at Washburne and ongoing with professional colleagues past and present, especially the chefs who help keep that educational experience thriving. And I am especially grateful to those master chefs who were my teachers during my Culinary Olympic sojourn. Thank you to Master Chef Helmut Holzer, Master Chef Noel Cullen, and Master Chef Alfonso Contrisciani. Amongst the many now helping me, there are three who stand out. Master Chef Hilmar Johansson who was instrumental in encouraging the start of the Certified Vegetarian Cook (CVC) course by introducing it and myself to the World Association of Chefs Societies (WACS). Executive Chef Louis Perrot who is now instrumental in launching the CVC into Latin America. And Master Chef Stafford DeCambra, who is an ardent supporter and Master Chef mentor of the vegetarian cause and the CVC program.

Every cookbook author needs a copy editor and I needed a copy editor who knew both the publishing world and the natural foods industry to copy edit and assemble this book. Jo Ann Deck worked on two of my previous cookbooks with me and took on this monumental task. My spirit is eternally grateful to Jo Ann who passionately pursued this project beyond all of my expectations. And a special thanks to copy editor Julie Marsh and designer and project manager Ja-lene Clark who took the final edited draft and made it into a showcase for my recipes and my dream of a new vegetarian cuisine.

I also want to thank Michael Pizzuto, chef and photographer, and Walter Collins, Bold Productions and major supporter of Eco-Cuisine and American Natural Foods.

One person who continues to be an anchor of support in my culinary sojourn is Nancy Loving, my lovely wife. She is an exceptional macrobiotic natural foods cook who was instrumental in crafting the title of this book. Thank you, Nancy.

Other thanks: I vividly remember the first practice run on the menu my team prepared for the 1996 competition at Boston College where I invited Master Chef Noel Cullen to judge the thirteen course vegan menu. My team met on Friday evening to go over the program. We cooked all day Saturday preparing the food items and plated them on Sunday. Chef Cullen arrived to judge the cuisine. My team was flying high. Chef Cullen judged the presentation severely and at best we would have taken a bronze medal. My team was devastated. I was grateful. Chef Cullen's assessment of the presentation led my team to a Gold in the 1996 International Culinary Olympics.

Chefs have to master the art of cooking, managing, and teaching all while creating menus that traverse global cuisines. It is my culinary education, life experiences that education can't teach, and keeping company with all chefs of diverse talents on my culinary sojourn that have cultivated and enriched my culinary skills.

St. Francis of Assisi said, "Start by doing what's necessary; then do what's possible; and suddenly you are doing the impossible." Competing in the Culinary Olympics, the support of World Association of Chefs Societies (WACS) in developing the Certified Vegetarian Chef program and working with the elite talent of many chefs seemed to me the impossible. And it all started when I was twelve years old (decades ago) by doing what is necessary, washing dishes in my parents' diner in Petoskey, Michigan. It is where I was introduced to the disciplines of a foodservice kitchen: how to wash dishes, properly cook a burger, and start learning how to bake. My culinary education started with the most humble beginnings.

Master Recipe List

Chapter Eleven: Vegan Entrées, Sandwiches, & Smoked Proteins — 245

Chapter Twelve: Vegan Pastries & Desserts

Chapter One

THE VEGETARIAN TWENTY-FIRST CENTURY CULINARY RENAISSANCE OF CLASSICAL CUISINE & SUSTAINABILITY

Classical Vegan Chef Ron Pickarski

On a recent plane ride back from Ecuador, where I gave a presentation on vegan cuisine at the Second Continental Culinary Congress on Food and Culinary Heritage (II Congresso Continental de Copcinas Patrimoniales), I sat next to a man who was curious about why I became a vegetarian. As we discussed my reasons, I had to admit that health and spiritual values were woven throughout them.

Every chef of course has his or her own unique story. My first cooking experiences were in the family diner in Petoskey, Michigan, a coastal resort city of five thousand overlooking Lake Michigan's Little Traverse Bay. At age twelve I flipped burgers and made French fries, already smoking half a pack a day and taking a smoking break behind the restaurant—unknown to my parents.

I was born and raised five miles east of the city in an area surrounded by farmers. My father had a half-acre organic garden when organic farming was the standard along with farm to table. We picked corn and an hour later it was going through a biological transmutation in my stomach. We picked wild blackberries, which my mother canned along with tomatoes and various other foods for the winter months. We were so poor we could not afford sugar to can the berries so they were canned without sugar. And my father had a root cellar loaded with root vegetables to help us through the winter months when produce was expensive or unavailable.

The air was clean, we drank from the nearby streams where I loved to fish for brook trout that I brought home, dressed out, and fried in butter (stream to kitchen). My spirit was at home in the country. During the summer months I went to town with my father to pick up my mother when she finished as the chef at a local restaurant and on Sunday to go to church. I was more at home helping my classmate Barney and his family haul hay, milk cows, and plow the fields where we occasionally lost control of the tractor causing some collateral damage. Then I had to hurry home to weed my father's garden. We had chores to do while he was working, and when he returned, he headed straight for the garden to check on my work. From working in my parents' garden and restaurant to picking wild berries and fishing, I was constantly involved with food beyond the dinner table.

As a shy person I liked the solitude of nature where I would often find a quiet place to sit and watch the natural world come alive. It feeds my spirit to this day in the same manner. While still not an extrovert, I now enjoy meeting people and hearing their uniquely wonderful stories, and I love the immediate gratification of serving them my food.

I also fell in love with art and was number painting at around ten years old. In high school I

took up oil painting after school with a personal instructor. My parents gave me a studio room in their apartment house not far from the restaurant, and I often painted until two in the morning during the summer. My parents chided me because I had a summer job driving a truck for Pepsi Cola and had to be up at 7 a.m. for work. I was commissioned by a North American Indian community to paint a picture of their country church with fall colors and it was received very well.

My mother was overweight and my father a chain-smoker. I suffered from bronchial pneumonia as a baby and in fourth grade; this didn't stop me from smoking half a pack a day at age eleven. An awakening a few years later began my transformation. In tenth grade I remember walking out the back door of our country home to have a cigarette, and while smoking it, I realized that I was killing myself and stopped, but that did not stop a chronic lung condition.

A tug toward a deeper spirituality, a love for all living things, drew me to the Franciscans. Educated in a Catholic school (St. Francis Xavier) and Franciscan parish, I realized in third grade that I wanted to join the Franciscan order. I am a "country boy" at heart and St. Francis is the patron saint of the environment and a most beloved saint among all spiritual people. In life we are often compelled to do something that we don't fully understand. In retrospect, it now all makes sense. My love of art, sense of spirit, state of my personal health, and desire for better health led me to the Franciscans and eventually into the kitchen.

At age nineteen, weighing two hundred pounds (at least sixty pounds overweight), I entered seminary and eventually realized I needed to change my diet. Upon returning home on a holiday, I was given a book entitled *Food Is Your Best Medicine* by Henry Bieler, MD. This classic health book prompted me to think of food as a solution. This philosophy has been a beacon of light and a guiding principle on how I approach culinary art.

The Franciscans allowed me to attend Washburne Culinary Institute after completing my seminary studies. Loving art and with an interest in food and nutrition, I was intrigued and fascinated by the culinary arts. When I was told the program would take two years, not understanding the immensity of culinary art, I thought to myself, "How can it take that long to learn this art?"

Upon starting school I was introduced to classical cuisine, the basis of the school's culinary curriculum. I also learned words I had never heard: napoleons, profiteroles, tortes, marzipan, galantines, wellingtons, and so much more. I instantly became passionate to learn this new cuisine. Each new culinary discipline learned was like pouring gas on a fire, fueling my passion to learn more. My instructors told me that what I learned in this two-year culinary program of the new world of classical training was the equivalent of twenty years of on-the-job training. Many years later I remain a passionate student of this amazing art form.

While in school I was invited by the chairman of Washburne to visit the Drake Hotel in Chicago to view the Culinary Olympic Gold Medal pastry presentation in the lobby of the hotel.

When I viewed the amazing pastry presentation, I told myself, "Someday I am going to compete with a new form of classical cuisine in the Culinary Olympics." Culinary innovation is one of the judging criteria in the competition.

So when I graduated from Washburne Culinary Institute in Chicago a few years later, this new culinary chapter was incubating. I also completed a two-year apprenticeship in meat cutting, never expecting that my life would do a complete turnaround as I became a vegetarian two months after graduation. The Franciscans were as shocked as I was when I became a vegetarian and six months later a vegan.

When I became a vegan, I discovered that this entirely new culinary world was entirely void of classical cuisine. My life's culinary mission instantly blossomed before me. Classical cuisine had not been translated to vegan cuisine and vegan cuisine had no classical representation. And no chef had ever competed in the International Olympics as a vegan. Classical vegan cuisine was, at that period in time, an undiscovered culinary world. Like a positive and negative charge, these two elements electrified my passion for classical cuisine when I made the connection. It was undiscovered in the vegan world and what better place to introduce it than the Culinary Olympics.

Would the great French masters have been shocked? More likely pleased!

In the introduction of the 1996 edition of *Escoffier: Memories of My Life*, Julia Child writes: "I think when you read Escoffier's introduction [to *La Guide Culinaire* and *Ma Cuisine*] you see he had very contemporary ideas. When he was writing about sauces such as Espagnole and demi-glace, he said that there would probably be simpler ways of doing things in the future. I think his idea was that cuisine has to adapt to the times…He also believed in cooking for the customer. Giving them what they wanted."

Child also says, "I think chefs have to bow to people's tastes, as Escoffier realized he had to do."

The new customer was vegan. Translating classical culinary techniques would raise the taste level while vegan ingredients would also make this a cuisine about health.

I had adopted a vegetarian lifestyle after reading *Diet for a Small Planet* (Frances Moore Lappe) and after being encouraged by fellow seminarians. But attending a lecture put on by the International Association of Cancer Victors and Friends (IACVF) convinced me that vegetarianism was an essential element in improving my chronic lung condition, which I believed was related to meat consumption. I stopped eating meat and it went away. I started eating more cheese and it came back. So I went from being vegetarian in February to vegan in September and began my journey of translating my professional skills into vegan cuisine. When I read *Diet for a Small Planet* it also made me aware of the food supply issues with a diet high on the food chain (animals). My health was the compelling motivator but I saw the big picture.

Several decades later, I take no medications and have no chronic diseases. I watched both my parents suffer with cancer. Our health care system thinks I am hardwired for cancer. What they don't realize is that I rewired myself to prevent it. I spent more on preventative medicine (healthy foods) realizing that food is my body's best medicine.

As I moved into a career in culinary education and spent considerable time training in locations far from the Franciscan monastery, I was being challenged by my culinary call within my religious calling, and I had to make a choice between being obedient to a religious order or my spirit's calling. With immense gratitude for my twenty years as a Franciscan, I changed course. It was the right choice.

The culinary sense of mission that emerged from my life as a Franciscan has only grown stronger over time and is abundant with knowledge gained from my vegetarian experience in preparing this book. *The Classical Vegetarian Cookbook for Professional Chefs and Inspired Cooks* is the result of both my culinary experience and my passion for vegan cuisine. This book comprehensively addresses the center of the plate (vegan proteins) and sauces in both a classical and modern format like no other cookbook ever has. Vegetarian cuisine is about the center plate protein and dairy- and egg-free desserts and pastries. But this book will also give you a unique perspective on vegetarian history and evolution as a cuisine as well as our relationship with it as omnivores. Often considered a special diet, vegetarianism has evolved into a cuisine; now veganism is the new cuisine emerging within vegetarianism. This book recognizes its dynamic history from animal rights in its Greek origin to sustainability and human nutrition in our modern age. Health is only one part of the new vegan cuisine. The other part is taste and flavor. The food must taste good. Techniques developed by the French master chefs also play a role here. Tofu pâtés, translations of the mother sauces into vegan cuisine, and new innovations that transform classical desserts, these are some of the offerings to be found in *The Classical Vegetarian Cookbook*. Whether you are a professional chef or an inspired cook, let me guide you through this modern dairy-free and animal-free cuisine, in a way of eating that will support us—in our new twenty-first century cuisine.

Every passionate culinary artist seeks to master some element of his or her art form and contribute to the art. It's in all artists' DNA. Their passion for perfection is an eternal driving force. With many years of learning about and developing vegan cuisine, both philosophically and in the culinary realm, and continually learning new techniques and developing new recipes for plant proteins, I realize that I, and all culinary artists, have more to learn and contribute to this dynamic international cuisine and that it is entering into its culinary renaissance. How we now develop classical vegetarian cuisine, like classical French cuisine, will live for the ages.

VEGETARIAN AND/OR VEGAN

This is a vegetarian cookbook with vegan recipes. While the concept of not eating animal flesh seems to be as old as recorded history, the word "vegetarian" dates only to the nineteenth century, and the word "vegan" to the 1940s.

The use of milk and eggs has always been controversial with vegans who don't consume animal products. This vegetarian cookbook addresses the original intent of this emerging cuisine, and the word "vegan" is used to designate products without any animal by-products. As this cookbook explains, we can receive all the protein we need from plant-based foods.

THE OMNIVORE

Whatever our culinary preferences, our biological makeup tells us that we are omnivores. As human beings we are physically created as omnivores, with the ability to eat both plant life and animal protein. Before civilization, anthropology tells us that we were much more dependent on animal protein and needed that animal protein for our brain growth. Since the dawn of civilization, most people have depended primarily on plant foods with animal protein as a supplement. Today we overindulge in animal protein, especially meat, and skimp on the necessary fresh produce and plant protein, all to the detriment of our personal and planetary well-being. This is changing as vegetarian cuisine emerges among health-conscious consumers who want chefs to deliver nutrition, innovation, texture, and taste on their vegetarian menus.

According to John McArdle, PhD, whose article "Humans Are Omnivores" can be found on the vegetarian resource group website (vrg.org), "Humans are classic examples of omnivores in all relevant anatomical traits. There is no basis in anatomy or physiology for the assumption that humans are pre-adapted to the vegetarian diet. For that reason, the best arguments in support of a meat-free diet remain ecological, ethical, and health concerns." Humans have canine teeth for tearing flesh and molars for grinding grains. We now have the intelligence, possibly gained through thousands of years of meat consumption, to thrive on an herbivore's diet.

Human health and the global food supply are motivational survival factors that are driving vegetarianism. The simple point is that we now can live a healthy life without meat.

Protecting animals from the cruelties of industrial animal farming, while a worthy cause my spirit supports, isn't the appropriate platform for me to market or promote vegetarianism. I skipped from the activist approach to appealing to the health-conscious consumer, realizing that embracing vegetarianism would also reduce animal consumption and related suffering of animals. From a health perspective, rather than protect the animals from ourselves, we need to protect ourselves from the animals at the dinner plate.

The omnivore's challenge is to strike a balance between two major food groups: protein used to build body tissue and complex carbohydrates to fuel the body's work. Striking that balance, in addition to the others issues I've discussed such as food supply, environmental health, and personal health, have led me to become a vegan. My love of French classical cuisine also defines my culinary sojourn.

THE VEGETARIAN COMMUNITY

The diverse vegetarian community includes activists, vegans who encourage us to dine on meat analogues simulating meat or anything but meat, esoteric vegans who distain meat analogues stating they would eat meat if they wanted the taste of meat, and environmental, macrobiotic, raw foods, hygienic, and health-conscious vegans and omnivores embracing vegetarianism as part of a healthy dietary lifestyle. Understanding the roots of the vegetarian movement in ancient Greek, Indian, and Chinese Buddhist and Taoist cultures will help you understand the different vegetarian consumer groups that emerged out of its intent to protect all living things.

Vegetarianism is a cuisine that emerged from a positive community movement against animal cruelty. It is primarily a universal, plant-based protein cuisine that in its pristine form eliminates all animal ingredients. For chefs and inspired cooks, it is today a journey into a new world of culinary discovery. We have learned about and used animal proteins in nearly every culinary application possible, while plant proteins are in their culinary infancy. We have landed in this new culinary world and are on a journey to explore it. *The Classical Vegetarian Cookbook* supports that journey and bears the fruits of my life's several decades-long journey developing the cuisine.

VEGAN PROTEIN

We may all know militant vegans and staunch carnivores and the tension they bring to the table. *The Classical Vegetarian Cookbook* moves beyond the disagreements between herbivores and carnivores with the acknowledgment that our Earth cannot sustain the feeding of its current population with a diet high in animal protein. Today we know scientifically that our physical bodies can receive all the nutrients they need, including protein, from plant sources.

Not only can we now move beyond eating meat, we recognize that a diet with an excess of animal protein is high on the food chain and unsustainable in feeding the billions of people now inhabiting our planet. We need to consume more plant proteins, not more animal protein; I will share more about this with you in Chapter Three: Vegan Protein & Nutrition.

Conversely, being vegetarian isn't always synonymous with being healthy. The balanced diet principles are universally applicable. I would suggest that there is probably need for an enhanced awareness of balance as a vegetarian because insufficient carbohydrate consumption can result in a protein deficiency even if one is consuming sufficient protein. Treat meat analogues in the same manner you would treat meat. Meat analogues are plant-based proteins that simulate the taste and texture of traditional meats. Meat analogues are concentrated protein, generally higher in sodium and lower in fat.

Meat analogues are addressed in the ingredient section of this book along with both ancient proteins and modern. They provide good nutrition but quantity undermines quality in all food categories. My position is that meat analogues should not represent more than 50 percent of your daily dietary protein. A mix of beans, tempeh, tofu, and seitan are the ancient proteins that could be 100 percent of your daily protein. And a mono diet is an unhealthy diet.

My position on vegetarianism is that of the omnivore with the belief that one can go vegan upholding our natural biological design in a healthy manner by consuming a balanced diet of plant-based proteins. At the end of the day, it is the quality of vegetarian and vegan cuisine that will be the determining factor in winning public opinion and acceptance. It has already started as evidenced by vegetarianism's popularity. Society will not sacrifice the pleasure of plate for health, nor should they have to. Taste and health can be synonymous.

THE CERTIFIED VEGETARIAN COOK (CVC) CERTIFICATION COURSE

Consumer demand from the privacy of our homes to foodservice professionals has laid the foundation for offering the Certified Vegetarian Cook (CVC) course. Professional chefs are compelled to learn this emerging but undefined cuisine, and passionate cooks and consumers are realizing the need for this cuisine as part of a balanced diet.

Already being introduced in professional foodservice conventions, the Certified Vegetarian Cook (CVC) is a certification course that will be offered by American Natural Foods, Inc. to culinary professionals. It is a core competency certification on vegetarian cuisine and the emerging vegan cuisine within vegetarianism. This cookbook is a synopsis or overview of the CVC course, introducing the core principles of vegetarian cuisine with classical context.

The CVC will be taught online, culminating with an intensive seminar in the kitchen with me or a certified CVC instructor before the student can graduate from the course. Educated foodservice professionals will be taught the dynamics of vegetarian cuisine, vegan protein innovation, and cuisine innovation within the disciplines of foodservice operations.

I appreciate Julia Child who said, "I wouldn't consider a [culinary] program to be serious if it didn't teach Escoffier or classic French technique."

Please visit americannaturalfoods.org for more information on the CVC certification program.

SPEED SCRATCH

Before leaving for Germany for my fifth and final Culinary Olympic competition, the *Boston Globe* interviewed me for their September 4, 1996, issue regarding the upcoming competition. In the article I was quoted as saying, "I want to take what I have done at the Olympics and put it on the American plate." That is how Eco-Cuisine's "Speed Scratch" line of dry blended savory and dessert products emerged. As I traversed the country starting in 1980, before, during, and after my Culinary Olympic sojourn, consulting and cooking vegan dinners for conventions and special events, the major comment from chefs was that the food is expensive and labor intensive. And their position was correct for a number of reasons too long to briefly address here. With my culinary experience, I started working on a number of solutions. What if a line of vegan speed scratch dry mixes could be created that could be integrated into existing meat-based menus, converting meat entrées and dairy/egg-based desserts to vegan? And what if those products reduced both labor and food cost while delivering on nutrition, taste, and menu innovation? The menu dynamics where, in short, both the vegan and non-vegan menus were designed to be interactive using the ancient proteins (beans, tofu, tempeh, and seitan).

Since there was no vegan culinary speed scratch line of savory or pastry products in the market, I took it upon myself to create the line with Eco-Cuisine, the first vegan foodservice company in the United States. And since Speed Scratch is in the CVC as an integral component of twenty-first century cooking, I have briefly presented it in this book as an option to deliver plant-based vegan cuisine in an innovative and cost-effective manner. It will be extensively addressed in the CVC curriculum.

The American Natural Foods nonprofit was created to support vegan culinary education and the American Natural Foods Culinary Olympic team. All Culinary Olympic chef competitors compete out of a passion for their art form. But my spirit had a mission to give vegan cuisine respect on the international stage, and I knew that winning gold would further that goal. Were that not the case, I doubt I would have ever competed. Sure, I won Olympic Gold with vegan cuisine and it surely helped its image, which was my original intention. But what difference does that make to the way Western cultures embrace vegan cuisine as part of a healthy diet and lifestyle? That comes with putting the cuisine on America's plate. Taste sells. The speed scratch vegan mixes evolved to complement scratch cooking and help chefs achieve that goal. No other company had created a menu concept-driven line of vegan speed scratch mixes that one can actually innovatively cook and bake with using fresh raw ingredients so I took up the task.

The mixes are part of the Certified Vegetarian Chef (CVC) certification program and are primarily mentioned in the appendix of this cookbook with a few recipes for interested chefs and inspired home cooks. Speed Scratch is a necessary option to foodservice operators and can only help time-constrained cooks prepare healthier options with less time and lower food cost.

At a time in both professional and personal kitchens when so much food is brought in precooked, it is important to find a bridge back to the basics of preparing food with high quality plant-based ingredients in a manner that resonates with twenty-first century life. Speed scratch mixes are a step back into cooking in a way that allows the foodservice professional to cook, using fresh produce and regional foods. This to me is another important evolution in the new emerging vegetarian cuisine.

Vegetarianism from the Ancient World to Today

Vegetarianism's history has its roots (both moral and dietary) in the ancient civilizations of India and Greece. At that time vegetarianism was the voluntary nonconsumption of animal flesh while enjoyably dining on animal byproducts such as eggs and dairy. During that time in history, industrial farming was nonexistent and there was no animal cruelty associated with dairy or egg consumption.

With the introduction of Buddhism and Jainism in the sixth century BCE, vegetarianism took root in India. People of the early Indus Valley were agriculturists, and the later arriving Aryans were a pastoral society that slaughtered cattle for food. India, as a country, has a strong vegetarian population, and many Hindus do not consider people who eat eggs to be vegetarians. Of course the cow is sacred to Hindus, who do not eat beef, but they do use cow's milk in cheeses and cooking.

The irony is that while the Buddha believed in *ahimsa* or nonviolence, he was not himself a vegetarian. It is believed that his last meal contained pork. This is where the moral and practical aspects of vegetarianism come to bear on all of us omnivores. Is it possible that nonviolence means avoiding unnecessary violence? I share this because many modern-day vegans are primarily driven by nonviolence, while part-time vegetarians tend to be interested in health.

Historically speaking, Pythagoras, a Greek philosopher at the end of the sixth century BCE, is considered the first modern vegetarian. Around 490 BCE his vegetarian diet became a philosophical morality focused on nonviolence as reflected in the avoidance of consuming meat. He is probably the founder of the moral or ethical vegetarian movement driven more by values than cuisine and nutrition. Vegetarianism was first referred to as the Pythagorean Diet due to his influence on the cuisine.

The irony of vegetarian moral values is its heretical roots. In the early first centuries CE, a driving force of vegetarianism was the Manicheans, members of a heretical sect with vegetarianism at the center of their beliefs. Of course, they were reviled by local Christians, which is why they were called vegetarian demon worshipers. Colin Spencer titled his book *The Heretic's Feast: A History of Vegetarianism* for this reason.

During the Renaissance, meat consumption was considered the affluent diet in Europe, despite some Christian monastic groups who sought spiritual enlightenment by abstaining from meat. With the proliferation of religious groups abstaining from meat and fewer dangerous carnivorous animals, the moral objection to meat consumption continued to grow. In his book

Man and the Natural World, Keith Thomas takes the position that our need to kill animals should decrease with the reduced threat of wild animals. Thomas Tryon, a prominent seventeenth century vegetarian, promoted the cuisine and strongly influenced the Quakers. Going into the eighteenth century, the killing of animals remained controversial. The debate continued into the nineteenth century when Dr. William Lambe, Fellow of the Royal College of Physicians, recommended the vegetarian diet as a cure for certain diseases. Animal welfare started gaining momentum on the ideological side, and vegetables and grains became more readily abundant, helping further the practice of vegetarianism. Out of this period emerged all of the moral and dietary arguments we now use in supporting a vegetarian diet.

In 1847 the Pythagorean Diet was officially changed to Vegetarianism at a meeting in an English seaside town called Ramsgate. This diet was spartan as reflected in one of its first members, George Dornbusch, who ate his food without salt or condiments because they were considered as bad as alcohol. Vegetarianism was considered a moral diet and equated with purity. As Spencer writes in *The Heretic's Feast,* "Meat was considered a generator of lust." Wealthy English who made their money off British beef relegated vegetarianism to satire and jokes. Vegetarianism has always been seen as a threat to the financial interests of the meat industry. Because vegetarianism was considered a virtuous diet or moral movement, it did not develop as a cuisine. Auguste Escoffier, the founder of modern French cuisine, developed the first vegetarian Espagnole (Brown) Sauce that was originally made by roasting animal bones. This is an indicator that culinary professionals were aware of the vegetarian movement. Further evidence rests in *The Heretic's Feast:*

> *In 1847, the Manchester branch of the Vegetarian Society held their first annual meeting and a banquet. At this banquet they ate macaroni omelette, onion and sage fritters, savoury pie, plum pudding, moulded rice, flummery [fruit pudding], and several other dishes. In the early 1880's, membership in the Vegetarian Society rose until it reached over 2,000. In 1889 there were estimated to be 52 vegetarian restaurants in England, 34 of them in London. In 1889, Gandhi became a member of the London Vegetarian Society.*

Thus England was the cradle of vegetarianism in Western civilization.

During the nineteenth century, vegetarianism struggled to organize, find its social voice, and continue to formulate a message. Pacifism, nonviolence, and animal rights seemed to be the driving forces propelling the movement. At the beginning of the twentieth century, at the outbreak of World War I, pacifism and vegetarianism became intertwined. Refusal to fight was viewed as treason, causing a social backlash. Vegetarians were sent to prison for refusal to fight, and some died in prison as a result of harsh treatment and poor diet. After World War II, vegetarianism continued as a culinary activist movement. In struggling to refine and put forward its message, the vegetarian movement focused on the moral issues of killing animals and consuming meat. Unfortunately the culinary side of vegetarianism continued to be neglected and recipe development was limited. More acceptable were the ethnic cuisines of which vegetarianism was a part of their cultures. Indian, Asian, and Italian are three cuisines that stand out in this area.

The twenty-first century driving force behind the vegetarian movement is primarily health, with 35 percent of Americans becoming part-time vegetarians for health reasons. Yet this market segment will not sacrifice taste for health. Animal rights and the environmental movements will always have a prominent place as the activist side of vegetarianism. But it is the cuisine that is currently driving the vegetarian movement. According to the Vegetarian Resource Group, 6 percent of Americans are vegetarian and 5 percent of that category are vegan. The vegans are the active, vocal, and influential segment of the marketplace that is driving the ethical values of vegetarian cuisine. It is not significant within America's foodservice industry or homes but these vegetarians and vegans are vocal—rightly so I might add—about having their dietary preferences met. The popularity of the vegan diet goes beyond the vegan market segment due to its perceived value as a healthy diet, especially in addressing lactose intolerance and heart disease, which collectively encompass over 60 percent of the U.S. marketplace. The vegan segment is inconsequential as a market segment, but important as caretakers of the cuisine in that they set the culinary integrity and do not compromise.

A secondary force that received considerable attention in Frances Moore Lappe's book *Diet for a Small Planet* in the 1970s is the massive global growth of the human population (now about seven billion) and our ability to feed those numbers with food high on the food chain. Our planet will not be able to feed a rapidly expanding human population by eating high on the food chain, and meat is at the top of the chain. Because it's a cuisine that is low on the food chain and a healthy diet, vegetarianism will become a prominent twenty-first century cuisine. Subliminally, if not consciously, all who dine on vegetarian cuisine are supporting the vegetarian activist movement. Further, those who successfully develop a superior vegan cuisine and retain its health benefits are supporting all of the vegetarian activist movements. However, a cuisine cannot be sold on ideology, worthy though it may be. Cuisine must be sold on the merits of the cuisine. The chef must learn the art of marrying the vegetarian disciplines of health and nutrition with culinary disciplines of taste, texture, and presentation. This goal is achievable and worthy of every inspired foodservice professional and cook.

FOUR DIFFERENT TYPES OF VEGETARIAN CUISINES

Today we recognize four different types of vegetarian cuisine:

- ↻ Lacto-ovo vegetarian cuisine includes dairy and eggs.

- ↻ Lacto vegetarian cuisine includes milk and no eggs.

- ↻ Oval vegetarian cuisine includes eggs of living beings but not milk. For example, fish roe or caviar is technically an egg or by-product of the living being and would be included in this category.

- ↻ Vegan vegetarian cuisine avoids all animal by-products; all food ingredients are plant based.

FUSING TASTE & NUTRITION

Vegan vegetarian cuisine is the new evolving cuisine, and healthy dining is driving its popularity. It is motivated by numerous values of which the current one is nutrition. The activist values are responsible for the emergence of the vegetarian movement but will eventually take a second position to the cuisine and human nutrition. Moral virtue, in general, is not a strong culinary marketing tool. Nor is "mock" or "fake" used as descriptors for vegetarian proteins as those terms do not belong in this new evolving cuisine's vocabulary. We tend to be extreme in seeking a balanced diet. But what we need is a prudence in our diet so that extremity does not sacrifice the pleasure of the table for nutrition or other agendas, noble though they may be. Fusing taste and nutrition is an imperative strategy in the acceptance of any emerging cuisine.

Humanity wants to enjoy the pleasures of the plate while improving or sustaining their health on vegetarian cuisine. In the professional or home kitchen, this is the only culinary and menu development strategy that will succeed. It is vegetarian nutrition that is starting to drive the cuisine and will be the primary driver into and beyond the twenty-first century. Its success is directly related to culinary innovation delivering on taste.

When a person dines on vegetarian cuisine, for whatever reason, they are supporting all of the values the cuisine stands for and the rich history from which it emerged. Vegetarianism is the Nouvelle Cuisine of the twenty-first century. I dare call it the twenty-first century Renaissance Cuisine.

"If the divine creator has taken pains to give us delicious and exquisite things to eat, the least we can do is prepare them well and serve them with ceremony."

—FERNAND POINT

Chapter Two

HOW TO USE
THIS BOOK

Food is an inspirational and dynamic art form.

This cookbook has a special mix of both meat-alternative dishes and ancient plant protein techniques and recipes to help you grasp and define the possibilities of an emerging ancient art form called vegetarianism. In honor of the eighteenth century culinary master Antonin Carême and my love of classical cuisine as an art form, I have incorporated some French cooking techniques and a number of French-inspired recipes, such as different tofu pâtés and vegan forms of the great French classical sauces. This cookbook translates or reinvents the culinary classics of the past into vegetarian cuisine for the health conscious and vegan consumer of today and the future. Vegetarianism is now a twenty-first century global cuisine embracing every nation's culinary treasures and identity.

Without eggs or dairy products, the recipes in this cookbook offer a culinary platform for vegan cuisine. It is my hope that you, the reader and cook, will take the recipes and own them, make them yours by creating original interpretations. Build on them. Mix and match your own variations, using different sauces with different proteins, and changing dessert sauces into pie and crepe fillings. Each recipe in this cookbook has numerous cross-utilization options and in many cases options within the recipes. All together this book offers 1,200+ variations, and you can create many more to call your own.

Learning about the history of vegetarianism puts the cuisine into perspective and helps one understand how to cook for vegetarians. The nutrition piece on protein and fatty acids helps the chef or cook find plant protein in the ingredients section. And the technique sections demonstrate how to prepare the recipes. All of this is achieved without any animal products or animal by-products. This cookbook lays a solid foundation to build your knowledge of the basics of vegan cooking and includes some advanced material explaining the chemistry of a dairy-free and plant-based cuisine.

DIET DEFINED

Diet is defined in the twenty-first century as a restrictive group of foods one consumes to nurture the human body or reach a biological end result. The word "diet" actually comes from the Greek word *diatia,* meaning a manner of living or *diaitasthai,* to lead one's life. In culinary terms it is a lifestyle choice of food consumption based on ethnicity, culture, season, and geography. Diatia is an inclusive term embracing all food consumption for the purpose of biological nutrition. Vegetarian cuisine includes all cuisines using plant-based and animal by-product ingredients such as eggs or dairy. This cookbook only deals with the vegan aspect—no animal by-products, with recipes that can be used as is or modified to meet your ethnic or special diet request of your family or guest. This book caters primarily to healthy diets as a vegan cookbook and has many special diet applications (lactose-free, heart-healthy, and some gluten-free diet options).

THE RECIPES & THE COOK'S EVOLUTION

The recipes are the key to any cookbook's success. But these recipes are meant as launching pads for one's creative culinary inspiration to take form and evolve as recipes by modifying the ingredients, flavors, textures, and cooking techniques. A well-constructed recipe should have only the essential ingredients or as few ingredients as possible, sound cooking technique, and a simple, elegant flavor profile designed to enhance the primary ingredients in the recipe. With vegan recipes the number of ingredients is sometimes higher when replacing eggs since multiple ingredients are often used or when combining proteins to make a complete protein. The upside is vegan proteins often cook in shorter periods of time and unlike meat can be salvaged if overcooked.

Prepare the recipe and follow the directions to understand the recipe. Then you can modify or customize it to meet the needs of your guest or family member. Classical cooking using the vegan mother sauces and pastry cream, for example, shows how one basic recipe is used to efficiently create numerous recipe applications.

All the recipes in this cookbook come from my many years as a vegan culinary professional and some are revised versions from recipe collections no longer in publication. Many were modified, making them simpler and easier to prepare. Other recipes, like making a one-step ice cream in a blender, are original recipes—new to this book.

FOOD PREPARATION

To effectively prepare vegetarian cuisine, professional cooks should understand the cuisine, vegan ingredients, specifically vegan proteins, plant protein nutrition, and the cooking techniques.

Using French cuisine as the culinary foundation is ideal since French cuisine is essentially a melting pot of ethnic cuisines. It is also the cuisine that developed modern culinary technique. Going "French" also moves vegetarian cuisine into innovative Western cuisines where it isn't as well represented as in Asian and Indian cuisines. Learning how to translate traditional recipes into egg-free and dairy-free vegan cuisine will allow professional cooks to explore an entire new world with vegan ingredients.

Vegetarianism, as a cuisine, includes both vegetables and vegetarian proteins (tempeh, tofu, seitan, beans, and analogues such as ground beef or chicken). Seitan is one of the ancient proteins. The focus of this cookbook will be plant proteins. While making a quiche with eggs and milk is easier than cooking without them, I will show how this dairy-free and egg-free cuisine can work for many traditional recipes, including the French mother sauces.

The recipes in this cookbook are designed to work off your existing menus and inventory with minimal addition to food preparation labor. If one is inspired to be creative, the recipes can easily be modified to work with your existing recipes, allowing you to make them original signature menus for restaurant guests and family members.

DIFFERENT VEGETARIAN GROUPS

When crafting a vegan menu it is necessary for the chef to understand the vegetarian consumer. Various types include:

- ○ **Vegetarian consumers** who are 6 percent of U.S. consumers with 5 percent of that market as vegan. Vegan is definitely a niche market if focused on the vegetarian category.

- ○ **PETA vegetarians** who advocate consumption of meat analogues to appeal to non-vegetarians. They are a strong activist group.

- ○ **Esoteric vegetarians** who are activists and will not consume vegan meat analogues.

- ○ **Health-conscious part-time vegetarians** who are approximately 35 percent of the U.S. population.

- ○ **Medical diet consumers** on restricted diets (such as high-cholesterol or lactose-intolerant diet).

VEGAN MENU DEVELOPMENT

In menu development, the restaurant operator or home cook doesn't need to reinvent their menu or create new vegan dishes to address their guest demand for vegetarian cuisine. Using the menu dynamics concept with one or two vegan ingredients, one can address their vegetarian patron or family member. The recipes in this book are designed to create infinite options. The sauces can be used with an array of proteins to create a variety of entrées. For instance, the Piccata Sauce can be served with tempeh, breaded tofu, Tofu Pâté, seitan, chicken analogue, and cannellini beans. The Tofu Pâté mixture can be used as a loaf, Thanksgiving Tofu, smoked for a rustic flavor, or a grain burger can be made with an infinite option of grains. The Lemon Cheesecake filling can be used as a crepe filling and the vegan pasty cream in pudding or mousse. Or the recipes can be modified to meet the vegetarian's request.

SUGAR & SALT

I use organic, bone-char free sugar in addition to other sweeteners such as agave syrup, rice syrup, and barley malt syrup. I also use a high quality sea salt. In this cookbook I just call it salt.

DAIRY-FREE CHEESES

I present recipes for several vegan cheeses and vegan sour creams. These recipes should be a springboard into creating an infinite variety of nut and/or soy cheeses with a variety of flavors. Combined with commercial products available, there is no shortage of vegan dairy options.

DAIRY-FREE DESSERTS

The vegan pastry cream converts to puddings and into innovative pie fillings such as holiday nog pie and custards. Sugar dough can be used as a torte dough with layers of fillings or as cookies, filled or plain. Crepes can be used for savory or dessert recipes, for appetizers or entrées. Kanten Cake filling can become a type of vegan "jello." One of my favorite desserts is the Ice Cream Cake using the chocolate cake recipe and chocolate ice cream (or variety of choice) and glazed with the rich Chocolate Ganache. That is decadent health (nutritious and delicious).

GLUTEN FREE

The Classical Vegetarian Cookbook for Professional Chefs and Inspired Cooks has many gluten-free recipes, some labeled and some not labeled. Since gluten free is a growing market segment and with many gluten-free recipes I decided to bring them to your attention. Many chefs have asked me if I or Eco-Cuisine have vegan gluten-free products or recipes and the answer is yes to both. But they are not certified gluten free by FDA standards. The FDA standard for certified gluten free is 20 parts per million (ppm) with 10 ppm being the industry standard. Fifty ppm is the highest threshold for gluten-free ppm. No product can be 100 percent certified gluten free because the gluten-free standards can only test up to 5 ppm.

Tempeh, tofu and beans are, in their pristine form (no additional ingredients added), gluten free. The Basic Tofu Pâté is a gluten-free protein that, as a vegan product, has many innovative recipe entrée possibilities with gluten-free beans, seeds, nuts, and seasonings.

Note: Practice ingredient awareness. Make sure ingredients being used in recipes are gluten free. For instance, there are commercial gluten and gluten-free versions of tamari. When a gluten-free recipe calls for tamari, it has to be a gluten-free tamari. Cross-contamination is a major concern in preparing gluten-free products. That is the most volatile aspect of cooking gluten free in a gluten environment. Wheat dust can remain in the air for around 30 minutes, contaminating everything under it.

There is a gluten-free index in this book and there are many recipe spin-offs from each recipe (such as the Basic Tofu Pâté). There may be more gluten-free recipes that I missed and many that could easily be converted to vegan gluten free. If cooking for celiac guests or family members this cookbook can assist your culinary efforts. My lovely wife is celiac and has enjoyed many of the gluten-free recipes in this cookbook.

CLASSICAL & MODERN SAUCES

Sauce Renaissance (roasted red bell pepper puree) is an example of a vegetable sauce and foundational concept used to create vegetable coulis such as parsnip coulis. Fresh basil or Cajun Hollandaise prepared with vegan butter or an Asian Five Spice with coconut butter would completely transform the traditional Hollandaise. The speed scratch Bolognese sauce renders itself to a Caribbean or Indian Bolognese sauce, lasagna "meat" sauce, or taco/burrito filling. Different fruit bases are options for the Bigarade Sauce.

Mac and cheese made with Béchamel Sauce is a good example of making an original recipe from recipes in this cookbook. I use ⅓ ratio each of vegetable(s) of choice (carrots, peas, red bell peppers, leeks, etc.), ⅓ cooked pasta, and ⅓ Béchamel Sauce with vegan shredded cheese (or American Melting Cheese in this book), and seasonings to taste. Or combine the Niçoise Sauce with any of the proteins (tempeh, tofu, beans or the chicken analogue) for a hot entrée or a cold salad combined with a pasta of your choice.

SAVORY ENTRÉES

In addition to mixing and matching plant-based proteins and sauce recipes, different grain and bean combinations are interchangeable in grain loaf recipes. The versatile Tofu Pâté can be infused with different flavors and textures, combined with numerous grains for loaves, vegetable cakes, crusted tofu patties, forcemeat fillings, and used in making an infinite variety of quiches and pâtés. Any of the ethnic or classical entrées can be modified with use of any of the ancient or modern proteins.

Vegan meat-style analogues (pre-cooked, frozen, or dry speed scratch) can also be used interchangeably with any of the proteins used in entrées. Tofu Cacciatore can become a chicken-style or seitan-style cacciatore. Vegan ground beef can be partially substituted for some of the bulgur in the Bulgur Walnut Loaf or included in a seitan steak. Tofu, tempeh, seitan, and chicken-style proteins are all interchangeable.

Fried Corn Mush flavored with Chinese Five Spice, Fried Green Tomatoes using breading or batter and served with the Sauce Renaissance and Bok Choy—I call this vegan fusion cuisine. Creative salad options could include a barley sea vegetable salad (1½ cups cooked barley, ½ cup French Vinaigrette, 1 cup grilled vegetables, a few tablespoons soaked and chopped wakame, and sugar, salt and pepper to taste). Any grain can be combined with any dressing that works and served hot or cold.

I also list a number of smoked vegan protein dishes, including tofu. Smoking adds a rustic flavor. Smoked Seitan is one of my favorites and many vegan proteins can be smoked.

COMMERCIAL VEGAN PRODUCTS

Another unique feature in this cookbook offers the choice to either work off the recipe ingredients or substitute commercial products. The distributor/retailer resource section at the back of the book lists a good number of vegan products. The cook has the option of using different commercial dairy-free products or creating them in their kitchen.

This resource section also lists meat analogues (with the exception of seitan which is considered an analogue but is actually an ancient protein) that can only be purchased as commercial products. The speed scratch dry vegan protein analogues are cost effective and allow for many creative options. The cook has to prepare the proteins and with the right cooking techniques can create a diverse line of savory recipes. All of the vegan bakery mixes offer new choices for the busy chef and harried cook.

Any new ingredient I bring into my kitchen needs at least three menu or recipe applications or I will not use it. One should not have to reinvent their menu to cook vegan.

INGREDIENTS, PREP TIME, & RECIPE ANALYSIS

All ingredients used in this book are vegan. Recipes have many variables in terms of quality ingredients, prep time, and cooking time.

Preparation times given are general due to numerous variables. Does the cook have their *mise en place* before starting to cook? Knife skills play into how fast the ingredients are prepped. Can some of the ingredients be run through a food processor, etc.? Were some of the vegetables prepared pre-cut? Prep time for a given recipe is often based on sub-recipes being prepared in advance. Is the recipe being upscaled to cook for a larger number of guests?

In the final analysis of a recipe, impeccably high-quality ingredients could have been used in the recipe, techniques executed to perfection, and the result was mediocre. Why? The cook didn't taste the food before serving it. A minor detail can make a major difference. Just a touch of salt to bring up the flavor or cooking the food a little longer. Perhaps the vinegar was a little too acidic and the dressing needed a touch of sweetener to neutralize it. The final discipline in food preparation is to always taste the food before serving it to adjust flavor, if necessary.

Your Continuing Culinary Education

Culinary education isn't just about teaching how to cook, it is about exploring new ideas and rethinking traditional culinary beliefs. Vegetarianism is a complex cuisine that can test the skills of seasoned culinary professionals and apprentices alike, offering them an opportunity to vibrantly grow in their trade. And you will be exposed to the culinary, nutritional, and activist ideologies associated with the cuisine. All cuisines have their culinary heritage but vegetarian cuisine also has an activist history and heritage.

The evolution of ingredients, cooking techniques, recipes, animal rights, human nutrition, environment, and sustainability of our food supply have all emerged in the philosophical discussion on the doctrine of vegetarian cuisine. I am not here to pass judgment on my diners. My position is simple—human nutrition and our need for protein as omnivores. If humanity embraces vegetarian cuisine based on human nutrition, the positive ripple effect will be felt across a wide spectrum of issues which probably would not exist today if we were more in line with a balanced omnivore's diet.

While giving instruction to a culinary student on how to make a Hollandaise sauce in a blender with half tofu and half butter using a totally different technique, he said, "That isn't a classical hollandaise sauce." I said, "Correct, and this isn't the nineteenth century." Overconsumption of cholesterol is impeding our health, and we need to find innovative ways through culinary technique and recipe innovation to deliver on flavor while reducing cholesterol. The sauce wasn't vegan but it was consistent with improving an omnivore's diet. Now I would simply create one of my vegan versions.

As a chef and culinary artist, my personal philosophy is in embracing and supporting vegetarian cuisine as an essential part of an omnivore's diet while respecting everyone's dietary choices. We must all choose the diet that is right for us and cooks, both professional and personal, must honor the choices of those for whom they cook. Balance is the operative word in diet and what should be the common denominator in all social dialogue on the subject. The facts are in—we can fulfill all our protein needs with plant proteins. Nutrition science, the evolution of the human body, animal cruelty, our omnivore nature, and environmental concerns suggest that we should embrace vegetarian cuisine but not that we need be vegetarians. In the twenty-first century vegetarian cuisine is the essential part of the omnivore's diet that seems to be lacking in human nutrition.

LET THE BUYER BEWARE

When I hear or read of an ingredient being marketed with health claims touting scientific data to back those claims, or the opposite with claims that a product is dangerous for human consumption, I am not sold. I need to see double blind studies that affirm the claim by a credible institution and know that the study wasn't funded by the company manufacturing the product to believe the data credible. Don't believe any nutritional claims, positive or negative, at face value. With a number of decades of study on this subject, I have observed a great deal. The FDA doesn't have a definitive policy or regulation on the policy of what is natural in the food arena. They have stated what isn't natural but not what is natural, leaving much grey area on the subject. The GRAS standard (Generally Recognized As Safe) is a good example. The government states that it thinks the food is safe for human consumption but may not have scientific proof to verify its position. Food is considered safe though you may read controversial claims. All of the food ingredients used in this cookbook are FDA-approved ingredients safe for human consumption. I have been dining on them for decades.

"Advice to young chefs: Young people who love your art; have courage, persistence...always hope...don't count on anyone, be sure of yourself, of your talent and your probity and all will be well."

—ANTONIN CARÊME

Measures & Scaling

We measure by volume. Sixteen tablespoons equal one cup with any dry ingredient. When converting a volume measurement to liquid or cooked ingredients, there are many variables.

DRY MEASUREMENTS

Dry ingredients, which include flours, sugar, different commercial mixes (bakery, breading), whole versus ground spices and herbs, and dried vegetables and fruits (whole or chopped), all have different weights for the same measurement. This is referred to as the density of the ingredient. Solid mass ingredients such as granulated sugar will weigh more than dry beans or textured vegetable protein that have significant small air pockets between the granules.

LIQUID MEASUREMENTS

The density of liquids also varies. Water is heavier than oil which is why oil floats on water. Minced fresh onion will weigh more than large diced onions on the same per cup measurement.

DRY-TO-COOKED EQUIVALENTS

The conversion ratio for each dry ingredient to its cooked form is different for each food ingredient. Dry grains, when cooked, significantly increase in volume and weight by absorbing water. Fresh ingredients such as onions or zucchini, when cooked will generally lose weight due to moisture in the vegetable evaporating in the cooking process. As examples, one cup raw long grain brown rice is equal to approximately three cups cooked brown rice, and one cup raw chopped onions becomes half a cup sautéed onion.

MEASUREMENT EQUIVALENTS FOR DRY OR LIQUID

MEASUREMENT	EQUIVALENT	WEIGHT MEASUREMENT	EQUIVALENT
3 teaspoons	1 tablespoon	28.35 grams	1 ounce
16 tablespoons	1 cup	16 ounces	1 pound
2 cups	1 pint	1,000 grams	1 kilogram
2 pints	1 quart	1 kilogram	2.2 pounds
4 quarts	1 gallon		

WATER MEASUREMENT	EQUIVALENT
1 cup	8 ounces
2 cups	1 pound
1 quart	2 pounds
1 gallon	8 pounds

A SCALE FOR EVERY CHEF

The best and only solution is to take a measured unit of the ingredient and weight it on a scale. That way you have an accurate volume to weight ratio. Keep a record of the volume to weight yields and once you have the equivalents, you have the option of using weight or measurement in your recipe. Weight is always one hundred percent accurate and generally the preferred method in the baking industry while volume measurements are preferred in personal cooking.

For about thirty dollars one can purchase a scale that measures in grams or ounces for personal use. Accurate measuring is essential to the success of a recipe and understanding the different measurement equivalencies, such as tablespoons to cups, can help in accurately changing the yields of a recipe.

Because cooking is an art and raw ingredients vary, the cook must use his or her intuition to make any adjustments in measurements to change the flavor or texture.

"Cookery is not chemistry. It is an art. It requires instinct and taste rather than exact measurements."— MARCEL BOULESTIN

Food Plating & the Art of Presenting Vegetarian Cuisine

Like all cuisines, vegetarianism is heavily influenced by presentation. The plate presentation is a reflection of the chef's culinary skills and the foodservice operation's marketing statement. Diners eat with their eyes and are heavily influenced by a dish's elaborate presentation, which will also garner media attention. Food presentation depends on the courses being properly prepared and ingredients and flavors that work. Overcooked green vegetables lose their color and loose sauces have no drape. Numerous elements in culinary art must merge on the plate to create elegant eye appeal in a flavorful plate presentation.

An integral component of culinary art, plate presentation depends on fresh herbs, vegetables, fruits, and plant-based foods that enhance all cuisines. With vegetarian cuisine, instead of meat being center plate with vegetables relegated to side dishes, vegetables can be elevated to entrée status with plant proteins integrated into the vegetables to increase protein content and perceived value.

When a plated culinary creation is presented, 90 percent of acceptance is presentation and 10 percent taste. Once tasted, acceptance is 90 percent taste and 10 percent presentation. Presentation is part of the pleasure of the plate that takes second place only to taste, the ultimate culinary pleasure. Less is more in taste and simplicity is elegance in presentation.

THREE-DIMENSIONAL PLATING

In plating food, make it three dimensional to give the food life. The cuisine must speak to the patron. In that sense it must be animated in a way that makes the patron's mouth salivate. In simple terms, the cuisine must be appetizing in presentation (color, texture, animation). Taste is the seal of approval. Before the culinary experience is complete, the patron will have experienced the cuisine with his or her sight, smell, taste, and texture. The experience starts with presentation. Ever notice how a patron lights up when being served a stunningly beautiful entrée?

SELECTING THE APPROPRIATE PLATE

The norm in choosing a plate is directly related to the course or entrée being served. If the entrée is complicated, choose a plate with a simple design, and if the menu item is simple, choose a complicated plate design for service. Imagine a very colorful and intricate plate design with a colorful entrée. Too busy. The reverse is a plain white plate with a brown piece of seitan on brown rice, sauce, and green vegetable. Somewhat dull. Selecting a plate for your cuisine is like selecting a frame for a picture. They must complement each other.

NATURAL VERSUS ARTIFICIAL HEIGHT

If you have to crash the food presentation to consume it, the presentation is inappropriate. Focus on the natural height of the food emerging from the components on the plate. Cut a baked potato into wedges and stack them center plate, laying the entrée against it and topping it with a simple sautéed green. Stacking ingredients Napoleon Style is using natural height as a means of experiencing a stratum of flavors and textures with one gentle swipe of the fork as it cuts through the presentation. I would not go higher than three inches unless using simple garnishes like fried pasta or fresh thyme sprigs which can go higher. Scale the presentation as if it were a landscape.

Creating a tight plating allows the evolution of natural height and also helps hold in the food's heat. To put height to a pasta dish, the bird's nest is one option and a second is deep frying linguine or fettuccine and implanting the strands center plate for natural height. It creates interest, is practical, the guest can consume it, and it takes seconds to plate. If it takes more than a minute to plate your creation, it is too complicated.

THE ORGANIC LOOK

The organic look uses many natural ingredients in their pristine state as part of the plate presentation. Contrived foods like a vegetable loaf, or a barley loaf wrapped in polenta, add a degree of culinary sophistication and technical eye appeal, but it is whole foods that give a presentation a natural organic look. Focus on plate. Everything flows into or out of center of plate. A well-thought-out presentation uses a balanced combination of stunning technical food components in combination with whole natural ingredients. The food should look natural, bringing out its pristine beauty with colors and textures.

SUFFICIENT SAUCING

Use sufficient sauce to complement the entrée, not excessive. It should be draped on the surface or food where the protein will be laid. A small amount drizzled on the protein, especially if there is a color contrast, acts as an accent on the plate. Vegan sauces function in the same manner as a meat-based sauce. They should drape (coat the food). In entrées like a pepper seitan steak, the ingredients should be covered, not floating in the sauce. Vegetable sauces add significant color and flavor, with colorful components highlighting the color contrast.

THE ART OF GARNISHING

There are two schools of thought in the way I garnish a presentation. One is to build the garnish into the course or entrée with sufficient eye appeal and not need a separate garnish. The second is to garnish a simple entrée with lack of eye appeal. The sauce can and should act as a garnish when used. One additional garnish is standard and that is sufficient and it must work with the entrée. Remember, less is more.

While visual aspects of presentation are perhaps overemphasized in the media, understanding effective principles of composition are an important part of culinary artistry. When understood and created, magic happens and the cuisine is elevated to the level of gourmet—elegant culinary art.

"I want order and taste. A well-displayed meal is enhanced one hundred percent in my eyes."— ANTONIN CARÊME

Chapter Three

VEGAN PROTEIN & NUTRITION

The first question I hear is "where do you get your protein?"

This chapter is in response to that question. Protein nutrition, underexplored in most vegetarian cookbooks, is a necessity for all chefs and cooks who are concerned about the health of their guests, friends, and families. This chapter is written by a chef to distill the bare bones basics of what you need to know in order to deliver proper nutrition in a vegan diet. Nutrition takes second place to taste in culinary art but is essential for the well-being of all at the table, many of whom seek vegan food as an answer to health issues.

From my decades of experience, major nutrition issues for vegans are protein nutrition, salt, oils and essential fatty acids, and the elusive necessary vitamin we call B-12. This chapter will look at all these issues and offer a good number of recommendations. This chapter also sets up the rest of the book and reminds us that health is true wealth. Understanding some key principles will help assure us of vegan health.

Unlike cooking with meat, which in itself is a complete protein, the professional chef and passionate cook must understand vegan protein nutrition and be able to deliver complete plant proteins because singled out, plant proteins individually are not complete. They must be combined to create complete proteins. This section explores plant proteins, the definition of a balanced diet, nutritional density, plant-based protein combination, charts to compare various vegan protein sources, and a simple formula to calculate adequate protein consumption.

Understanding plant protein and nutrition is the foundation for the rest of this book. In the ingredient section you will learn the culinary characteristics of plant proteins; in the technique section, how to cook with them; and in the recipe section, some innovative culinary applications. All of these components are brought together in the recipes.

PLANT PROTEINS

Plant proteins are the centerpiece of vegan cuisine. Modern nutrition science and the American Dietetic Association now recognize that when properly combined, animal-free proteins can supply all of the essential amino and fatty acids necessary for human growth and maintenance. This chapter also will address the basics of vegetarian protein nutrition and the advantages they hold over animal proteins. Understanding vegetarian protein nutrition is essential to effectively cooking the cuisine in a balanced manner.

Plant proteins are derived from vegetation or plants. Plant proteins contain no animal or animal by-products. They are vegetable-based and are categorized, in nutritional terms, as incomplete proteins because unlike animal protein, they don't contain all nine essential amino acids. Proteins contain twenty-one amino acids but only nine of them are essential, which means our bodies cannot produce them. They must come from the food we consume. If the body doesn't receive them, it will begin breaking down its tissue to supply them.

A combination of beans and grains will supply the nine essential amino acids. Nutritionally speaking, plant proteins can meet all our protein needs while providing additional health benefits. They are often more concentrated. According to the United States Department of Agriculture National Nutrient Database (ndb.nal.usda.gov), a cheeseburger, (regular patty/115 grams) contains 15.02 grams of protein, and cooked tempeh (100 grams) contains 18 grams of protein. One cup of cooked lentils (198 grams) contains 17.86 grams, of protein, one cup of cooked black beans (172 grams) contains 15.24 grams of protein. One cup of cooked quinoa (185 grams) contains 8.14 grams of protein and one cup of cooked millet (174 grams) contains 6.11 grams of protein.

Meat is high in water and can be 20 percent fat. Plant proteins are concentrated, containing significantly less moisture (such as nuts, seeds, and beans) and tend to be osmotic, absorbing water when exposed to moist heat whereas meat dehydrates when cooked.

We receive our carbohydrates from a variety of beans, grains, seeds, nuts, and vegetables as part of a balanced diet. We should do the same with vegetable proteins using nuts, beans, and grains as the primary sources of protein. The controversy over plant protein versus animal protein is finished. We know that plant protein can sustain human life as part of a balanced diet. As twenty-first century omnivores, humanity can thrive on a vegan diet. We don't have to, but we can. Vegetarian ingredients (beans, grains, nuts, seeds, and many vegetables) contain protein. We don't need and should never rely on animal proteins for 100 percent of our protein intake under normal conditions.

WHAT IS A BALANCED DIET?

Cooks and chefs should be familiar with this term because it is the basis of developing a healthy menu. Complex carbohydrates should be at the center of the menu, however, many chefs would say the menu should be protein-centered because they don't understand the meaning of the term. The only healthy diet is a balanced diet.

Generally speaking, it means choosing a wide variety of foods from all the food groups and consuming them in moderation as this approach serves your biologically individual needs. Specifically, a balanced diet is a high complex carbohydrate, low protein, and low fat diet. Complex carbohydrates include whole grains (whole foods) with sufficient carbohydrates to fuel the body and provide dietary fiber. This fiber adds bulk giving the satiated effect while acting as an intestinal brush to allow the intestinal track to absorb nutrients. Fats provide essential fatty acids, support organs, and carry some necessary vitamins. And low fat suggests calorie suppression. Refined pure fat has 9 calories per gram, protein 4 calories per gram, and carbohydrates 4 calories per gram. Our bodies convert carbohydrates into fuel. If we don't receive sufficient carbohydrates, our metabolism will convert protein into fuel and deprive our body of protein needed for brain and cell functions.

Eating too many simple carbohydrates like sugar with a high dextrose equivalent (DE) can create sweet blood or high blood sugar, which is a perfect environment for diseases to incubate and excessively burn (deplete) nutrients from one's body to digest the carbs. Part of a balanced diet is ingesting sufficient nutrients in our food (nutritional density) to replace those same nutrients burned in our body's daily effort to maintain itself and to replace nutrients lost through the consumption of the empty calories of junk food.

NUTRITIONAL DENSITY

Just as dining should be a pleasurable experience, it must also nurture one's body. Chefs and cooks should know which foods are of high nutritional value. Nutritional density is defined as the ratio of nutrient content in grams to the total energy content (in calories). Caloric-dense foods, like white sugar, are quite different and often called "empty calories" because they have been stripped of their nutrition in the refinement process. The 2010 USDA Dietary Guidelines for Americans (cnpp.usda.gov/Dietary Guidelines) states that nutrient-dense foods are those foods that provide substantial amounts of vitamins and minerals and relatively few calories. Fruits and vegetables are nutrient-dense foods, while products containing added sugars, processed cereals, and alcohol are not.

Is the body getting what it needs? This really shows the difference between processed and refined foods. Tempeh and whole wheat flour are processed foods made from the whole bean or whole wheat grain. White flour and TVP (Textured Vegetable Protein) are refined foods that have lost some of their intrinsic nutritional value. Processed foods will always retain more of their intrinsic nutritional value. Refined foods can be nutritionally fortified but generally lose intrinsic nutritional values.

PROTEIN'S FUNCTION IN THE HUMAN BODY

Sixteen percent of our total body weight (muscle, hair, skin, and connective tissue) is primarily made up of protein. It plays a major role in cell metabolism and fluids in our bodies. Many of our body's important chemicals (such as enzymes, hormones, neurotransmitters, and DNA) contain protein. We also need to continually replace protein lost through the energy we use for daily activities. It is speculated that our bodies completely regenerate themselves every seven years.

AMINO ACIDS

Proteins are made up of smaller units called amino acids, the building blocks of our bodies. Our bodies cannot manufacture nine of the amino acids, so we must include all these essential amino acids in our diets. If these amino acids are in the vegetarian diet, the protein component of the diet is satisfied. The essential amino acids are phenylalanine, valine, threonine, tryptophan, isoleucine, methionine, leucine, lysine, and histidine.

Here are more important facts about protein:

- Protein stabilizes blood sugar.
- Protein is needed to build body mass and to repair injured tissue.
- Weight-loss diets like the Atkins diet (based on higher protein and lower carbohydrate consumption) are effective because protein takes more energy to burn than simple carbohydrates.

HOW MUCH PROTEIN DO YOU NEED?

For a balanced diet we need to know where to find healthy sources of proteins, fats, and complex carbohydrates. Teaching basic human macro nutrition is essential in culinary art for it is the core essence of cuisine.

According to the American Dietetic Association, the recommended daily allowance (RDA) of protein is about 50 to 70 grams per person. That works out to about 3 to 4 grams of protein per 100 calories of food consumed. The Center for Disease Control also lists similar RDAs and suggests that protein intake be between 10 percent and 35 percent of calories consumed:

RECOMMENDED DIETARY ALLOWANCE FOR PROTEIN/GRAMS OF PROTEINS NEEDED EACH DAY

Children ages 1–3	13	Girls ages 14–18	46
Children ages 4–8	19	Boys ages 14–18	52
Children ages 9–13	34	Women ages 19–70+	46
		Men ages 19–70+	56

Source: cdc.gov/nutrition/everyone/basics/protein.html

NOTE: Although people are often concerned that vegetarians may not eat enough protein, we should remember most meat eaters consume as much as twice the protein as really needed.

Here are some vegan examples of protein-rich food:

BEANS set themselves apart in grams of protein per cooked cup portion. Garbanzos are 14.5 grams, lentils 17.9, and soy beans 28.6 grams of protein. It's interesting to note that 43 percent of the calories in cooked soy beans is from fat and 21 percent from carbohydrates. Garbanzo beans are only 14 percent fat.

GRAINS: 1 cup of cooked quinoa has 8 grams of protein, 1 cup of cooked millet has 6 grams of protein, with complex carbohydrates making up a bulk of the calories. Many grains can supply a reasonable amount of protein.

NUTS: ¼ cup almonds has 7.4 grams of protein, 74 percent fat calories and 13 percent calories from carbohydrates. Seeds generally have similar protein/fat/carb calorie ratio to protein as nuts.

VEGETABLES: Some vegetables do have a high-protein content, such as 2 cups of chopped raw broccoli have 5 grams of protein, a 10-ounce package of raw spinach has 8.12 grams of protein, and 100 grams of dried shiitake mushrooms have 9.58 grams of protein. The protein content differs in raw, dried, or cooked vegetables.

Source USDA National Nutrient Database (ndb.nal.usda.gov.)

On a protein per calorie ratio, some vegetables could be viable source of protein. For example, one would need to consume about 1,500 calories (approximately 75 percent of their total daily

calories) from broccoli, but it is not a complete protein. Beans have a similar protein per calorie ratio but 4 to 5 times the protein per portion of other vegetables. With the exception of soybeans, the percentage of fat is in single digits. All sources of vegetarian protein are viable sources.

The general source for plant protein should be beans as the anchor food. With the exception of high-protein soy, they are low in fat and a strong source of complex carbohydrates when combined with grains. They complete the protein's essential amino acids and deliver on complex carbohydrates, assuring that one's body will not revert to protein as a fuel source. Aside from soy milk, I think of nuts as the dairy side of vegan cuisine as you will see in the recipe section. They have great value in the human diet, along with seeds. Nuts usually have a high oil content and, like dairy, should be consumed in moderation.

When Frances Moore Lappe wrote her first edition of *Diet for a Small Planet* in 1971, she emphasized that we needed to receive the complete essential amino acids each time we consumed the equivalent of an entrée. The American National Research Council and ADA became concerned, cautioning vegans to combine their proteins at each meal. In her 1981 edition of *Diet for a Small Planet*, she changed her position and wrote:

> *In 1971 I stressed protein complementarity because I assumed that the only way to get enough protein ... was to create a protein as usable by the body as animal protein. In combating the myth that meat is the only way to get high-quality protein, I reinforced another myth. I gave the impression that in order to get enough protein without meat, considerable care was needed in choosing foods. Actually, it is much easier than I thought.*
>
> *With three important exceptions, there is little danger of protein deficiency in a plant food diet. The exceptions are diets very heavily dependent on fruit or on some tubers, such as sweet potatoes or cassava, or on junk food (refined flours, sugars, and fat). Fortunately, relatively few people in the world try to survive on diets in which these foods are virtually the sole source of calories. In all other diets, if people are getting enough calories, they are virtually certain of getting enough protein.*

Because protein is in virtually every food, if one is consuming a balanced diet of grains, legumes, nuts, and fresh produce one should be receiving sufficient amounts of protein. After all, the beef protein consumed by humanity comes from an animal that lived on plant protein.

We don't have to combine plant proteins at each meal, but we should combine the proteins within our daily diet. That is a great deal easier.

Here are five factors to consider when following a vegan diet:

- ↺ Vegetable proteins must be combined in a way that makes them "complete" within the daily diet to meet the individual's protein requirements. Combining beans and grains are the simplest means of receiving all of the essential amino acids needed in one's diet.

- ↺ If vegan meat analogues generally have both soy and wheat protein, they are complete, concentrated sources of protein that is more easily digested.

- ↺ The vegetarian must consume sufficient calories, protein consumption excluded, to sustain one's body weight. If not, protein will be converted to energy, depriving one's body of the protein necessary for self-maintenance.

- ↺ Strict vegans must pay close attention to the essential B-12 vitamin found in fortified nutritional yeast, B-12 fortified soy milk, or B-12 tablets. B-12 is discussed later in this chapter.

The following charts show examples of the four primary sources of vegan or plant-based proteins. We will explore grains, beans and legumes, nuts, and seeds, and also look at vegan meat analogues.

FOUR PRIMARY SOURCES OF PLANT-BASED PROTEINS

GRAINS	BEANS & LEGUMES*	NUTS	SEEDS
Amaranth	Black-eyed Peas	Almonds	Chia Seeds
Barley	Chickpeas (Garbanzos)	Brazil Nuts	Flaxseeds
Bulgur (Cracked Wheat)	Lentils	Cashews	Pumpkin Seeds
Corn	Peanuts**	Pecans	Sesame Seeds
Millet	Peas	Pine Nuts	Sunflower Seeds
Quinoa	Soybeans	Pistachios	
Rice		Walnuts	
Wheat			

*All beans include Edamame (soybean), Great Northern, Kidney, Pinto, Lima, Navy, White, and Black Beans

**A peanut is a legume even though it is generally looked upon as a nut.

Source: *Becoming Vegan: Express Edition* by Brenda Davis, RD, and Vesanto Melina, MS, RD (Book Publishing Company: Summertown, TN, 2013)

NUTRIENT PROTEIN DENSITY OF PLANT PROTEINS

On July 3, 2009, the American Dietetic Association (ADA) drafted a position paper on vegetarian and vegan diets (2009 Jul: 109/7: 1266-82). In the abstract the ADA stated: "…appropriately planned vegetarian diets, including total vegetarian or vegan diets, are healthful nutritionally adequate, and may provide health benefits in the prevention and treatment of certain diseases. Well-planned vegetarian diets are appropriate for individuals during all stages of the life cycle, including pregnancy, lactation, infancy, childhood, and adolescence, and for athletes."

I believe beans are the perfect food. They contain all the macro nutrients (complex carbohydrates, many of the essential amino acids, fiber, and the preferred, healthy fats) and many micro nutrients (vitamins and minerals such as B vitamins, folic acid, vitamin E, calcium, potassium, and iron). They have a high soluble-fiber content, which may help reduce cholesterol levels because fiber acts as a brush to limit absorption into the blood stream. The protein helps stabilize blood sugar. Per serving, beans have twice as much protein as cereals.

USDA research revealed that the skin of beans contains the same heart-healthy flavonoid compounds found in many fruits, vegetables, and red wine. These flavonoids are antioxidant compounds that protect the cells from free radicals (compounds that can alter DNA, protein molecules, and enzymes, and damage cells, cancer, and premature aging). Beans are a nutrient-dense and balanced macronutrient protein, an essential food for good health.

HOW TO CALCULATE PROTEIN AS A PERCENT OF CALORIES

One way to count protein requirements is as a percentage of calories. The USDA's My Pyramid plan suggests that protein makes up between 17 percent and up to 21 percent of total calories. The CDC and the National Institute of Medicine recommend we get at least 10 percent and no more than 35 percent of calories from protein.

Protein is 4 calories per gram. 10 percent of 2,000 calories in a daily diet is 200 calories divided by 4 calories per gram of protein = 50 grams of protein.

In *Becoming Vegetarian,* Vesanto Melina RD, Brenda Davis RD, and Victoria Harrison RD state that the recommended protein intake as a ratio or percentage of total calories is 10 to 15 percent, fat is 15 to 30 percent with 15 percent being the ideal, and carbohydrate is 55 to 75 percent. I'm pleased to see that the ADA, the National Institute of Health, and serious scholarly vegetarians/vegans find some common ground about the recommended protein intake.

PROTEIN VARIETIES AND NUTRITIONAL DENSITY FOR PROTEINS, CARBS, AND FATS (CHART)

PROTEIN VARIETIES	PROTEIN GRAMS	% PROTEIN FROM CALORIES	% CARBS FROM CALORIES	% FATS FROM CALORIES
Traditional Proteins				
Beef, ground, 2 ounces	14.3	33%	0%	67%
Salmon, baked, 2 ounces	15.5	52%	0%	48%
Chicken, roasted, 2 ounces	15.3	52%	0%	48%
Bean Protein				
Black beans, cooked, 1 cup	15.24	27%	69%	4%
Lentils, cooked, 1 cup	17.9	30%	67%	3%
Tofu, firm, 1 cup	8.3	40%	11%	49%
Nut Protein				
Almonds, ¼ cup	7.4	13%	13%	74%
Sesame Butter, 3 tablespoons	7.83	11%	11%	78%
Grain Protein				
Whole wheat cereal, ¼ cup	4.8	15%	80%	5%
Quinoa, ¼ cup	8.14	14%	72%	14%
Vegetable Protein				
Broccoli, raw, 1 cup	2.6	33%	58%	9%
Sun-dried Tomato, 100 grams	7.62	22%	87%	1%
Recommended % Calories		10% to 15%	55% to 75%	15%

*Percentages were derived using values of 4 calories per gram for protein and carbohydrates and 9 calories per gram of fat.

USDA National Nutrient Database (ndb.nal.usda.gov.) and inspired and modified from *Becoming Vegan* by Vesanto Melina, RD, Brenda Davis, RD, and Victoria Harrison, RD, (pages 46 and 47)

The "Protein Varieties and Nutritional Density" chart shows the calorie to protein, carbohydrate, and fat ratios for macro nutrient foods. Total calories of macro nutrients (i.e., protein) are divided by total calories of food item. Our bodies need a certain amount of protein, carbohydrates, and fat within the limited number of calories allotted our body type to deliver on all nutrients. The chef or cook must know where to find high yielding sources of plant proteins and how to build calorie-efficient proteins into their menus while limiting high-calorie fat.

The chart reveals how each ingredient delivers on protein to calorie percentage ratio. Nuts, while nutritious, have a poor ratio of protein to fat calories. The chart demonstrates three factors. First it compares the percentage of protein calories in a food item to the amount of protein calories required in a food item to meet an individual's minimum daily requirement of protein within their allotted daily caloric intake (such as 2000 calories). Here is another way of explaining this concept. If 10 to 15 percent of our calories must be from protein, one must consume in a 2,000 calorie daily diet a minimum of 200 or maximum of 300 calories of protein. Second, the chart compares the percentage of protein calories from animal proteins to the percentage of protein calories in plant proteins. All plant proteins exceed the minimum 10 percent of proteins to calories. Animal proteins of 8 or more ounces are usually in excess of the protein to calorie ratio which the body will convert to energy to cover its deficiency in complex carbohydrates. Finally, the chart demonstrates how each individual food item compares to a balanced diet high in complex carbohydrates and low in fat and protein. When you look at the beans' profile you will see why beans are the perfect food for a balanced diet.

HOW TO CALCULATE PROTEIN BY BODY WEIGHT

The American Dietetic Association recommends that most active adults consume 0.8 gram of protein per kilogram of body weight per day. (A kilogram is 2.2 pounds.) So a person who weighs:

- ○ 130 pounds needs 45 to 57 grams of protein in a day.
- ○ 175 pounds needs 63 to 68 grams of protein in a day.

The equation is to use your weight (such as 130 pounds.) as the base number:

130 pounds divided by 2.2 pounds (1 kilogram) =
59.09 kilograms x .8 gram per kilogram = 47.27 grams per day

This example shows how easy it is to add up the vegan proteins for your day. One cup of cooked navy beans, for instance, provides 15 grams of protein (almost 25 percent of the recommended daily allowance for the 175 pound person).

NUTRITIONAL PROFILE OF COOKED BEANS

The humble bean is the actual king of health foods. Bean varieties are basic to vegan cooking.

NUTRITIONAL VALUES BASED ON 1 CUP COOKED BEANS WITHOUT SALT

BEAN VARIETY	CALORIES	PROTEIN (GRAMS)	FAT (GRAMS)	CARB (GRAMS)
Adzuki	294	17.30	.23	56.97
Black Beans	227	15.20	.90	40.80
Garbanzo	269	14.50	4.20	45.00
Great Northern	209	14.70	.80	37.30
Kidney	225	15.30	.90	40.40
Lentils	230	17.90	.80	39.90
Navy	255	14.00	1.00	47.41
Pinto	245	15.40	1.10	44.80
Soybean	254	22.20	11.50	19.90

Source: USDA National Nutrient Database (ndb.nal.usda.gov.)

NUTRITIONAL PROFILE OF WHOLE GRAINS

Whole grains add fiber and nutrients such as B vitamins, and selenium and magnesium.

NUTRITIONAL VALUE OF 1 CUP COOKED GRAINS WITHOUT SALT

GRAIN	CALORIES	PROTEIN (GRAMS)	FAT (GRAMS)	CARB (GRAMS)
Amaranth	251	9.3	3.9	46.00
Barley	193	3.5	.69	44.31
Brown Rice	218	4.5	1.6	45.80
Bulgur (Cracked Wheat)	151	5.60	.40	33.80
Corn	143	5.8	2.24	31.26
Millet	207	6.10	1.70	44.30
Quinoa	222	8.10	3.60	39.40

Source: USDA National Nutrient Database (ndb.nal.usda.gov)

NUTRITIONAL PROFILE OF RAW NUTS

Nuts are essential to a balanced vegetarian diet for their macro- and micro-nutrients. Nuts are high in fat and moderation is encouraged.

NUTRITIONAL VALUES BASED ON 1 OUNCE OF RAW NUTS WITHOUT SALT

NUT VARIETY	CALORIES	PROTEIN (GRAMS)	FAT (GRAMS)	CARB (GRAMS)
Almonds	163	6.0	14.0	6.1
Brazil Nuts	186	4.1	18.8	3.5
Cashews	157	5.2	12.4	8.6
Macadamia	204	2.24	21.5	3.9
Pecans	196	2.6	20.4	3.9
Pistachios	159	5.75	12.87	7.80
Pine Nuts	159	5.8	12.9	7.8
Walnuts	185	4.3	18.5	3.9

Source: USDA National Nutrient Database (ndb.nal.usda.gov.

PROTEIN PROFILE OF SEEDS

The simple seed offers an abundant protein source. Great for snacks and sprinkling on cereals and vegetables. I also use seeds in recipes to add to texture and flavor.

PROTEIN VALUE BASED ON ¼ CUP OF SEED

SEED VARIETY	CALORIES	PROTEIN (GRAMS)	FAT (GRAMS)	CARB (GRAMS)
Chia	196	6	12.66	17.35
Flaxseed	224	7	17.71	12.13
Pumpkin	180	10	15.82	3.34
Sesame	206	6.38	17.88	8.44
Sunflower	210	7	18.01	7.0

Source: USDA National Nutrient Database (ndb.nal.usda.gov).

Using Meat Analogues

Meat analogues are vegetarian proteins generally formulated with a combination of soy and a second protein (such as gluten or pea protein). Their function is the direct replacement of meat. The analogue generally has a texture, form, color, and taste similar to that of meat. They are different from the ancient proteins (beans, tofu, tempeh, and seitan) in that the ancient proteins are not trying to resemble the standard of meat proteins and they are not flavored. Textured soy proteins are generally used in meat-style analogues along with gelling agents and flavoring systems to give the analogue the taste and texture of meat. Vegetarian burgers, hot dogs, and sausages are examples of prepared meat analogues. There is a relatively new protein called mycoprotein, which is made from a special fungus. And there are gluten-free meat analogues, which are primarily soy-based.

Today analogues are available in prepared frozen form and also in dry mixes. Health food stores carry many frozen brands, and dry mixes can be ordered online.

NUTRITIONAL VALUE OF ANALOGUES BASED ON GRAM COUNT

ANALOGUE (COOKED)	GRAM	CALORIES	PROTEIN (GRAMS)	CARB (GRAMS)
Chicken Strips	67	100	19.00	3.0
Ground Beef	56	60	8.00	7.00
Hot Dogs	76	100	13.00	4.00
Meatballs	90	150	17.00	10.00
Sausage	56	60	7.00	7.00
Seitan	57	57	15.00	7.00
Veg Burger	85	130	16.00	7.00

Resource: Author research on product declaration information.

Analogue Nutrition

Analogues are generally a great source of protein but not necessarily because vegan proteins are formulated differently. Some brands use more starch or lower quality proteins with less protein, which both drops the quality of the protein and gives it a baby food texture. Burgers can be as low as 3 grams of protein per 2 ½ ounces to as high as 16 grams. The low protein analogues are generally higher in carb fillers, which can increase calories from starch.

Soy meat proteins generally contain concentrated amounts of proteins close to that of meat and generally no fat because Textured Soy (Vegetable) Protein (TVP) is the byproduct of extracting oil from the soy bean. Soy has high oil content. The absence of oil significantly reduces the caloric content. Meat analogues are generally healthier in that they are concentrated forms of protein with little fat and no cholesterol if the protein is vegan. TVP comes fortified and nonfortified and there is the option of fortifying the protein with a supplement. If there is B-12 in the mix, it was probably fortified.

Carrageenan is a sea vegetable with the gelling properties of gelatin and is generally used in analogues adding dietary fiber to the protein and as a binder. And dry meat analogues allow the cook to integrate beans, nuts, whole grains, and vegetables into them, which intensifies the nutritional density of the protein.

While plain soy has a consistency and texture similar to real meat, it is flavorless and needs a great deal of help. There are natural meat-type flavors and HVP flavors that create a strong meat-type flavor. They are generally based on yeast extracts and are fermented to develop their unique flavors, some of which taste like meat.

These flavors are used in meat analogues and the higher quality ones are expensive, adding significantly to the cost of the analogue. The flavors generally have a high sodium content, which is why the analogues are generally higher in sodium. Reduced sodium ingredients are emerging as options as reflected in the new wave of reduced sodium proteins on the market. While plain TVP is inexpensive, the analogues are expensive due to the gelling and flavor ingredients used in them.

For part-time health conscious vegetarian consumers, meat analogues are very appealing in that they resemble meats and therefore can be used to replicate meat entrées on menus. Meat loaf, steaks, and cutlets, etc., are examples of protein options not available with the ancient proteins (seitan is the exception). While many of the ingredients in analogues are refined, they are concentrated forms of protein and can meet our dietary protein requirements. While protein requirements may be filled by a combination of beans, grains, and vegetables, meat analogues add another level of culinary innovation and excitement to vegan cuisine. Meat analogues are the new world of culinary innovation eventually to become the global standard bearer of protein innovation in the twenty-first century.

FINAL THOUGHTS ON PROTEIN

The nutritional profiles of vegan vegetarian protein ingredients and the above protein mathematical calculations show that the vegan diet can meet the basic human daily protein needs. These are essential culinary tools designed to help you understand the nutritional protein component of animal-free dining and integrate it into menu and recipe development. Health is a major driver, and as culinary professionals serving vegetarian cuisine, we should know how to meet the dietary and culinary expectations of those patronizing our foodservice operations.

We don't have to meet the recommended daily allowance in our hospitality operations, but we should be contributing to that nutritional goal with innovation, taste, and eye appeal.

SODIUM

The reviews in the nutritional community are mixed with one universal truth. We need a certain amount of sodium in our diets. Too little or too much and our health is negatively impacted. According to The Dietary Guidelines for Americans, 2010 (cnpp.usda.gov/DietaryGuidelines), recommend that everyone age 2 and up should consume less than 2,300 milligrams (mg) of sodium each day. Some groups of people should further limit sodium intake to 1,500 mg per day, including:

- ○ Adults age 51 or older.
- ○ All African Americans.
- ○ Anyone who has high blood pressure, diabetes, or chronic kidney disease.

While there is a debate about whether the sodium amount recommended is too low, more research should be done before we raise our sodium intake. I applaud all the current efforts to lower sodium intake in processed foods and I encourage you to take advantage of low sodium options. We must stay within the realm of a balanced sodium diet to maintain our quality of health.

OILS AND FATS

This brief overview of oils and fats is essential to vegetarian cuisine. In cooking healthy vegetarian/vegan cuisine, choosing the right oil for the recipe is essential for optimum flavor and nutritional value. Understanding the basic nature of oils is crucial to selecting the appropriate oil for the cooking technique and recipe application. In cooking vegetarian cuisine, we should be choosing the right oil for the culinary application (for example, use high heat-tolerant oils for high heat applications such as deep frying). Going vegan and overconsuming saturated fats, hydrogenated, or excessive fats create a flawed diet and will probably result in health issues.

Like protein, fats are an essential part of human nutrition. We need the essential fatty acids (EFAs) for skin, brain, and organ health. Fat tissue is a major component of the human brain and is important in the function of neuron transmitters. Fats are energy intense, containing 9 calories per gram versus protein and carbohydrates, which contain 4 calories per gram. Low-fat diets are essential to losing and controlling one's weight, but that does not cancel the need for healthy fats in one's diet. Dieting on nutrient=dense quality fats is as essential to human health as are dieting on high quality proteins and complex carbohydrates. If we get these three macro nutrients right and the right mix within each category, we will probably be safe from many diet-related diseases.

This is not a scientific statement—my personal intuitive position on Alzheimer's disease is that diet may have a significant impact in impeding the disease. This is a scientific statement—as a primarily fat organ, the brain needs healthy fats to sustain the human body's biological functions. Your brain is the fattest organ in your body and may consist of at least 60 percent fat.

OMEGA-3 FATTY ACIDS

The omega-3 fatty acids keep the dopamine levels in your brain high, increase neuronal growth in the frontal cortex of your brain, and increase cerebral circulation.

The human brain requires fatty acids, antioxidants (found in fruits and vegetables), B-complex vitamins, and protein. The human body cannot produce omega-3 and omega-6 fatty acids. Those fatty acids must be present in our diet. Fortunately flaxseed oil is a primary vegan source. Essential fatty acids (EFAs) cannot survive in high heat; they can only come from unheated oils.

Chefs and cooks need to understand which oils are appropriate for each cooking technique. Cold-pressed oils with EFAs should never be used in cooking as it can destroy the EFAs and possibly create free radicals that disrupt cell metabolism. When using high heat, use an oil designed to hold up in high heat. If it breaks down, peroxides (free radicals) are created that destroy cell metabolism and can be potentially carcinogenic. Free radicals can also have a negative effect on brain health.

TRANS FATS

Trans fats can minimally but naturally occur in natural foods. However, industrially produced artificial trans fats are detrimental to human health as they can gradually build up to create chronic conditions. Trans fats could increase the risk of heart attack if consumed on a regular basis in sufficient quantities. While many trans fats have been removed from refined foods, we should always be vigilant and read those labels.

CHOLESTEROL

Cholesterol is a waxy, fat-like substance that's found in human blood and all cells of the body. If poor eating habits allow it to accumulate, it could ends up in one's bloodstream, attach to arterial walls and cause a heart attack. For some people, high cholesterol levels could be caused by an overactive liver (genetics). Avoiding excessive consumption of dietary cholesterol, consuming whole grains, and exercising are means to ensure the maintaining of healthy levels of cholesterol.

Our body's liver manufactures cholesterol to create hormones and Vitamin D, to protect our arteries, and to help our bodies digest food. It is essential to maintaining our health, but we don't need to consume it because our liver will produce it if we are not consuming sufficient quantities.

Dietary cholesterol is only found in animal foods and in excessive amounts in highly processed meats. Aside from its presence in fat, it is especially high in egg yolks and organ meats (brains, liver, and kidneys). Pollution can also turn good cholesterol bad. New studies are showing that that environment is as important to our health as the food we ingest because the air we breathe and water we drink carry elements that can inhibit or enhance human health. Researchers have found that exposure to diesel exhaust led to the loss of the antioxidant and anti-inflammatory properties of HDL (high-density lipoprotein, a type of cholesterol). Biological health is not purely a dietary issue.

It is worth noting that cholesterol does exist in vegetables and other plant-based foods. The percentage is so low that the FDA and ADA software average it out of the nutritional panels with a false positive, meaning it is present in such low percentages that it doesn't register on the nutritional data sheet. I was mystified when cholesterol showed up in vegan products I developed for the foodservice industry, knowing all ingredients were vegan.

SATURATED, MONOUNSATURATED & POLYUNSATURATED FATS

Saturated fats are found in animals and plant-based foods such as palm shortening and coconut milk. The RDA for saturated fat is 20 grams or less per day. It is a type of fat that remains solid at room temperature because it is fully saturated with hydrogen atoms. It is also a primary source of LDL (low-density lipoprotein), which can raise your cholesterol level and why it is referred to as bad cholesterol.

Monounsaturated fat is often called the "healthy" fat in that it lowers LDL or bad cholesterol and raises HDL or good cholesterol when consumed in moderation, thus lowering the risk of heart disease and strokes. This fat differs from saturated fats in that it is liquid at room temperature. The most common sources of monounsaturated fats are olive oil, peanut oil, canola oil, sesame oil, nuts, seeds, peanut butter, and avocados.

Polyunsaturated fat differs from other fats in its molecular makeup and is found in foods such as soybean oil, corn oil, sunflower seeds and oil, walnuts, and flaxseeds. It is considered a healthy fat.

B-12 VITAMIN

Becoming vegetarian isn't necessarily synonymous with health. Like any cuisine it can be healthy or unhealthy depending on dietary application. A person consuming a little meat with a balance of vegetables and whole grains will be healthier than an activist vegan living on refined grains, sugars, and vegan meat analogues with little or no fresh vegetables, fruits, or whole grains. Vegetarians are not exempt from consuming a balanced whole foods diet. One primary challenge in a vegan diet is supplementing the B-12 vitamin because it isn't naturally occurring in most plant foods.

B-12 is the most complex vitamin known to humanity and the most difficult to find in any plant. It is primarily found in animal foods such as red meat, seafood, dairy products, and organ meats. It can only be manufactured by living bacteria. Short-term deficiencies can lead to fatigue, depression, and anemia. Long-term deficiencies can lead to permanent brain and central nervous system damage.

Fortunately, there is a synthetic B-12 that is supplemented in many vegan foods from soy milk, grains/cereals, and silken tofu to nutritional yeast. B-12 supplements are also available.

Many people believe B-12 naturally occurs in nutritional yeast. It could but doesn't because the bacteria is deactivated in production to prevent yeast-type infections. Two tablespoons of fortified nutritional yeast generally contain 130 percent of the RDA for B-12. Not all nutritional yeast is fortified. The nutritional yeast I use meets the 130 percent standard. Because B-12 is available in many fortified foods, one only has to read the label to make sure they are receiving the needed amount. I use nutritional yeast in recipes for flavor and nutrition. It is a flavor enhancer in dairy-type and savory dishes.

With the options of supplements and fortified food, we should be able to supply all our needs for B-12. People older than fifty who are not vegans have been recommended to take B-12 supplements since the body's ability to absorb Vitamin B from animal products diminishes with age.

ECO-CUISINE BALANCED DIET PYRAMID CHART

While I am not a dietician, I have often felt that the food pyramid charts presented to us have been rigid and have not easily explained vegan protein nutrition. I have taken the liberty as a chef and citizen concerned with health issues to offer you a flexible and balanced diet pyramid chart.

The Eco-Cuisine Food Pyramid Chart (following page) reflects the balanced diet concept (high complex carbohydrates, high fiber which exists in complex carbohydrates, low protein, and low fat) explained in this book. All of the lines are in curves to remind us that our biological individuality needs within each food group will vary. We can diet heavily on any one category in a given day but when averaged out, our food consumption should look like this pyramid chart.

High consumption of complex carbohydrates is the foundation of a balanced diet and of this pyramid. I separated root vegetables from grains, legumes, and beans because the grain/bean category has a higher protein to carb ratio, (protein stabilizes blood sugar), and the grain/bean combination creates complete proteins. Nudged in on the left are sweets (referring to sugary sweets) and on the right are junk foods. Indulging "a little" is okay and is put into perspective in this chart. On the left are fresh fruits and on the right fresh vegetables. These two categories,

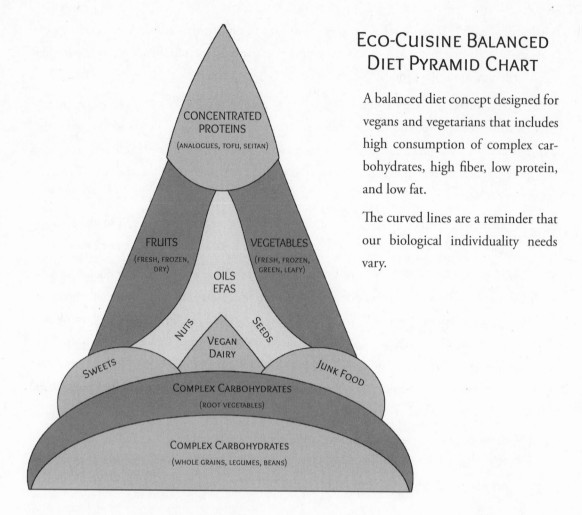

ECO-CUISINE BALANCED DIET PYRAMID CHART

A balanced diet concept designed for vegans and vegetarians that includes high consumption of complex carbohydrates, high fiber, low protein, and low fat.

The curved lines are a reminder that our biological individuality needs vary.

along with the complex carbs of the grain/bean combination, are the triad of a healthy diet. Beans do contain EFAs. At the heart of the pyramid chart are the Essential Fatty Acids (EFAs) we need to maintain our health.

While they are whole foods and nutrient dense, seeds and nuts are placed in a special section to remind us that they are fat concentrated and should be consumed in small amounts as reflected in the chart. I put vegan non-dairy (often created with nuts) in this category for the same reason. Concentrated proteins are at the top and are generally essential to balance out our protein needs. Tofu, soy powders (i.e., soy flours, concentrates, and isolates), and seitan are concentrated proteins in that they are refined to remove fiber and/or carbohydrates. The analogues are concentrated proteins that simulate meat. Concentrated proteins, or refined such as seitan and tofu where the protein is separated from the carbs and fiber, should be used to supplement our protein needs if not acquired from the complex grain/beans category.

This pyramid chart takes a commonsense approach to a balanced diet, not an arbitrary prescriptive one. This chart, for instance, doesn't work for diabetics who probably need a higher protein diet. See your health care provider for advice in how to implement these food categories into your diet.

THE FUTURE OF VEGAN PROTEIN NUTRITION

As I look into the future, I see only more interest in a vegan diet based on protein nutrition. More frequently as government agencies and health-related organizations examine the facts of vegan protein nutrition, they are realizing that it is essential to human nutrition and is sorely lacking in our diets. Earlier this year, the Dietary Guidelines Advisory Committee, a federally appointed panel of nutritionists created in 1983, concluded that a diet lower in animal fat is not only healthier but has less of an environmental impact. This committee made a strong statement for the vegan lifestyle. Who are these people? The health.gov website states:

The Dietary Guidelines for Americans encourages individuals to eat a healthful diet—one that focuses on foods and beverages that help achieve and maintain a healthy weight, promote health, and prevent chronic disease. The U.S. Department of Health and Human Services (HHS) and the U.S. Department of Agriculture (USDA) jointly publish the Dietary Guidelines every 5 years... . The 2015 Dietary Guidelines Advisory Committee (Committee) submitted the *Scientific Report of the 2015 Dietary Guidelines Advisory Committee* (Advisory Report) to the Secretaries of the U.S. Department of Health and Human Services (HHS) and the U.S. Department of Agriculture (USDA) in February 2015. The purpose of the Advisory Report is to inform the Federal government of current scientific evidence on topics related to diet, nutrition, and health. It provides the Federal government with a foundation for developing national nutrition policy. However, the Advisory Report is not the *Dietary Guidelines for Americans* policy or a draft of the policy. The Federal government will determine how it will use the information in the Advisory Report as the government develops the *Dietary Guidelines for Americans*. HHS and USDA will jointly release the *Dietary Guidelines for Americans, 2015* later this year.

On April 5, *The Hill*, a Washington D.C. newspaper and website reported:

The 571-page report says the average U.S. diet has a larger environmental impact in terms of increased greenhouse gas emissions, land use, water use and energy use than the healthy dietary pattern it suggests—one that's rich in vegetables, fruit, whole grains, seafood, legumes and nuts; moderate in low- and non-fat dairy products and alcohol; and lower in red and processed meat, sugar-sweetened foods and beverages, and refined grains.

In its review of scientific studies, the committee highlighted research concluding that a vegan diet had the most potential health benefits:

The organically grown vegan diet also had the lowest estimated impact on resources and ecosystem quality...Though consumers have never been known to strictly follow the final guidelines, NAMI's spokesman Eric Mittenthal said the recommendations do impact federal programs like school lunches, WIC, the special supplemental nutrition program for women, infants and children, and military rations.

While many may debate the actual meaning of this report, I am convinced that this is one step in many steps to come that will continue to support vegan protein nutrition.

Another positive sign is the recent industry interest in "alternative" proteins as shown in the December 2014 Lux Research (luxresearchinc.com) private report titled, "WhooPea: Plant Sources Are Changing the Protein Landscape."

> **This food and nutrition report suggests that:** "Growth of alternative protein sources posed to accelerate, potentially claiming up to 33 percent market share by 2054."
>
> **Lux lists the key takeaway as:** "Alternative proteins set to rise dramatically, representing 33 percent of the 940 MMT protein market by 2054. Although soy dominates in 2024, nascent alternatives like second-generation proteins and algae will aggressively enter the market and could represent significant portions of the alternative protein market by 2054. (...) Increasing demand for plant protein sources causes a distribution shift in agricultural land, resulting in increased production of various second-generation protein sources such as peas, rice, and canola."
>
> **The Lux Research website also states:** "Protein is one of the fundamental building blocks of the human diet, and powerful factors are shifting demand and driving the development of novel sources. The current dominance of meat and seafood will wane in the coming decades, and several alternative protein sources will fill the gap....As demand for protein grows more rapidly than conventional meat sources can supply, the food industry will respond by supplying non-meat-based proteins. How much? We predict a possible 9 percent potential annual growth for the alternative protein sources over the coming 40 years, a growth level sufficient to cause a shift in agricultural production towards protein-heavy crops."

So with government and nonprofit policy centers intersecting with new agricultural concerns, vegan protein nutrition may soon become a way of life for many more people. I am confident that vegan protein nutrition will eventually be the major protein source for our future.

LAST NOTES FROM A HEALTH CONSCIOUS CHEF

From reading this section and referring to the scientific data supporting the position, everyone should comfortably agree that humanity can thrive on a vegan vegetarian diet receiving all of the essential amino acids necessary for a balanced diet. Protein is available in almost every plant food. This chapter has presented the basics of vegan protein nutrition, salt, oils and fats, and the elusive B-12 vitamin as tools to effectively achieve vegan health. Being a vegetarian is a walk in the park but creating vegan complete proteins requires a little more attention. Nutrition is an essential element of all cuisines and protein nutrition is center stage with vegan cuisine.

For cooks learning how to cook vegan vegetarian cuisine, you have all of the basics to effectively prepare entrées with complete plant-based proteins. You also now have a basic understanding of some nutritional challenges surrounding vegan proteins, oils and fats, and how to supplement the essential B-12 vitamin. Now you have some basic information ready to provide for the health and well-being needs of those who sit at your table. For more study on nutrition, I recommend the work of Brenda Davis, RD, and Vesanto Melina, MS, RD. Their books *Becoming Vegetarian* and *Becoming Vegan* belong on the bookshelf of every concerned chef and diner.

Chapter Four

VEGAN
INGREDIENTS

REAL SW
PL
$4

When I became a vegetarian in 1976, vegetarian and vegan natural foods ingredients were virtually nonexistent in foodservice and in their infancy stage in retail.

Soy milk was available from local producers but quite frankly not fit for human consumption. I had to make tempeh from a starter kit. Silken tofu, if it was available, wasn't easy to find, and I purchased tofu from a local producer in Milwaukee. I remember bringing it back to the Renaissance restaurant in Milwaukee at 6 a.m. and dipping it, while still warm, in a fresh ginger dressing. For myself that was the breakfast of champions.

Now there is a myriad of vegan ingredients (different styles of tofu, soy milk, meat analogues, etc.) in retail and emerging in foodservice. I will focus on the ingredients that, with rare exception, are available through natural food distributors, co-ops, and retail stores. Rather than get lost in the minutia of options, this section will address the core ingredients of vegetarian cuisine.

The building blocks of vegetarian cuisine will be addressed in this section: the center plate vegan proteins, including meat and seafood analogues; sea vegetables; flavoring systems; oils; dairy and egg options/substitute ingredients; gelling; and sweeteners. There are many options to milk and butter that are superb.

As a professional or personal cook you do not want to significantly expand your pantry with numerous specialty food ingredients—nor should you have to. Any ingredient purchased should have common use in your cooking, and as I recommend in this book, at least three applications.

Rotate specialty vegan ingredients with the season, and spin your vegan menu off your traditional cooking using the vegan ingredients in your kitchen. A good place to start is with your more popular menu items.

This section reviews many ingredients and discusses foodservice pack sizes for a number of items. It does not address brands. Some of the ingredients may not be available through retail outlets, but if they are not, they are definitely available through online website store fronts. If the ingredient is presented in this cookbook, the reader, whether personal or professional cook, will have a purchasing option. The resource section at the back of this book lists vegan ingredient companies. Many of them have both retail and foodservice pack sizes. You can check with the companies for their packaging options.

Finally, culinary professionals often ask if a vegetarian ingredient is certified vegan or vegetarian. The answer is simple. There is no U.S. Department of Agriculture (USDA) or Food and Drug Administration (FDA) standard for certified vegan or vegetarian so vegan ingredients cannot be certified vegan. Let common sense prevail and refer to the vegetarian categories in Chapter One (see "Four Different Types of Vegetarian Cuisines" on page 30). Vegan ingredients must be free of all animal ingredients. It is that simple.

Vegan Proteins for Today

The special ingredients that differentiate vegan cuisine are the core common vegan proteins used in the preparation of vegetarian entrées. Vegetables and pilafs do not constitute nutritionally balanced entrées, have little or no perceived value as an entrée, and are not satiating.

An essential part of mastering vegan cuisine is learning how to work with plant proteins. That may sound simple; in fact, they actually are easier to cook than meats, as described in the chapter on savory cooking techniques. Combining a wide variety of these proteins in recipe and menu development is crucial to both creating innovative entrées and assuring that all the essential amino acids are achieved in the dining experience.

WHAT ARE PLANT PROTEINS?

Plant proteins are derived from vegetation or plants. Plant proteins contain no animal products or by-products. These vegetables are categorized in nutritional terms as incomplete proteins, as already discussed in the previous chapter on vegan nutrition, because they don't contain all the essential amino acids.

Meat has a high water content and can be 20 percent fat. Plant proteins, as in nuts, seeds, and beans, are concentrated, containing significantly less moisture, and tend to be osmotic, absorbing water when exposed to moist heat while meat dehydrates when cooked. Plant proteins are generally shelf stable in their dry raw natural state.

TYPES OF VEGAN PROTEINS

The two types of vegan proteins are ancient plant proteins and modern plant (meat analogue) proteins. Vegetarian animal by-product proteins such as eggs and cow or goat milk are not featured in this book, only vegan proteins.

Ancient plant proteins are broken down into two categories—whole foods proteins and processed proteins.

1. Whole food proteins are the beans, seeds, nuts, and grains. Many other vegetables also contain protein but not in such concentrated forms.

2. Ancient plant processed proteins are tofu, tempeh, and seitan. Tofu and tempeh are derived from soybeans, seitan from wheat. Tofu and tempeh are concentrated proteins with most of the fiber of the soybean removed through the manufacturing process. My favorite soy product is tempeh, a whole food ingredient that is fermented to create a very versatile protein.

Soy is the white meat of vegan proteins. In ancient vegetarian cuisine tofu and tempeh were the central types of soy proteins. Seitan, made from high-protein wheat, is the red meat of vegan proteins.

TOFU

Tofu is often called soy curd and is made from soybeans, water, and a coagulant or curdling agent and then pressed into white blocks. There are many varieties of tofu dependent on the curdling method, pressing technique, and flavor infusions that I will explain in this section. It is a very versatile culinary ingredient as its flavor ranges from savory to sweet, depending on the manufacturing process. Tofu is used in the cuisine of many East and Southeast Asian countries. It originated in ancient China about two thousand years ago; legend ascribes its invention to Prince Liu An (179–122 BCE). It is an ancient protein whose production techniques migrated to Korea and Japan during the Nara period. Its spread into Asia is associated with rise of Buddhism whose diet is primarily vegetarian. Yuba is a by-product of making soy milk. It is a thin film that forms on soy milk during the cooking process and is skimmed off after cooking. It can be used in its fresh state or dried to use later as a protein.

Two different manufacturing methods create the two basic types of tofu available to us today. *Fresh pressed tofu* is an ancient version. *Fresh* refers to freshly pressed and refrigerated tofu. The chemical curdling/pressing process of making fresh tofu starts with grinding soybeans with water, cooking the mixture, and draining/pressing the milk from the solids. A curdling agent (calcium sulfate, magnesium chloride, or calcium chloride) is added to the soy milk to start the coagulating process, which lasts about twenty minutes. Once the curds form, the mixture moves through an industrial strainer into a forming box where the remaining water is pressed out using an industrial or personal mechanical tofu press. The process, similar to pressing olive oil, forms a bean curd called tofu. Fresh tofu has a gritty texture regardless of the firmness and carries a defining soy flavor. It is the ideal tofu for dishes with strong savory flavors that overpower the soy taste. In Korea and Japan, fresh tofu is sometimes made with sea water.

Silken tofu, the second form, starts by adding a coagulating agent to the soy milk, thickening it without the curdling and pressing. The solution is dispensed into an aseptic or sterile container or into blocks and allowed to set. If poured into large blocks, it is cut into cubes similar to traditional curdled tofu. It is more delicate than fresh-pressed tofu and has the highest moisture content of all tofu. The result is a soft silky tofu with a custard texture and very mild flavor. This tofu works well in desserts and in savory and dessert sauces.

The two manufacturing methods create different textures of tofu: *extra firm, firm,* and *soft.* For professional chefs and inspired cooks, extra firm tofu can be used for all applications by adjusting the culinary technique or recipe.

- ○ Fresh pressed tofu is the ancient traditional curdled/pressed tofu.

    a. *Extra firm* is pressed very hard by a mechanical tofu press to extract as much water as possible, resulting in a product exceptionally firm with more protein and less water.

    b. *Firm* is pressed less and is relatively firm, with less protein and more water than extra firm.

    c. *Soft* retains the largest amount of water so is very soft and breaks apart easily. It has the least protein and maximum water of the pressed tofu.

Silken tofu has a custardy texture. It comes in a firm or soft texture and has a very delicate flavor useful in desserts and delicate sauces like Hollandaise. I also use it in cheesecakes and quiches. Silken tofu is the most diverse tofu with uses in both dessert and savory recipes because of its mild flavor. The recipe sections in this book shows the diversity of silken tofu.

Silken tofu is considered a staple in Japanese supermarkets, somewhat like cheese in American markets. The Japanese manufacture numerous varieties of artisan tofu, which is starting to gain popularity in the United States. Many Japanese markets have dedicated entire sections to both plain and artisan tofu. Japan also has tofu shops where you can purchase fresh, warm tofu off the manufacturer's floor. As yogurt went through about a hundred-year transformation from a foreign food product to an American breakfast, snack, and health food staple, now tofu needs to evolve to a culinary form the American consumer will embrace by integrating it into classical and American cuisine.

ORIGINAL SOY MILK

Many vegan foods are fortified with vitamin B-12, but the most common source is soy milk. For foodservice operators it is sold in a half-gallon containers and larger three- to five-gallon disperser bags for milk machines. (Foodservice packs are 6 units of 64 ounces or a half gallon.) There are several brands, a few of which are in foodservice distribution. The major brands offer soy milk in both sweetened and unsweetened versions. The many varieties include vanilla, chocolate, coffee, and fruit flavored soy milks, among others.

There are only two that you should consider for the kitchen, and I would actually choose only one. The two are "unsweetened" and "sweetened" soy milk. The unsweetened is the preferred version because it can be used in both savory and dessert applications. The sweetened version can work in savory applications like whipped potatoes and béchamel sauce, if not too sweet. Sweetened soy milk is excellent for pastries, dessert sauces, puddings/pastry cream, etc., and for making a sweet yogurt. You can use unsweetened for the same applications by adding perhaps 2 to 3 percent more sweetener, such as sugar or agave to the soy milk. The sweetener, beyond sweetness, must have a neutral flavor.

One 8-ounce cup of soy milk has approximately 50 percent of the daily value (RDA) for vitamin B-12 and 45 percent of calcium. As for culinary applications, it functions similarly to regular milk with perhaps a few nuances in some cooking techniques/recipes.

Cheaper brands, using a lower quality soy bean, will add an excessive amount of sugar and use vanilla flavor as a resolver to override the soy flavor.

SOYBEAN TEMPEH

Tempeh is an ancient soy protein originating in Indonesia. It is one of my favorite proteins and the only processed soy protein that is a whole food (remember how nutritional density is amplified in whole foods). Four ounces of plain tempeh contains 24 grams of protein (this ranges from almost half to one third protein needed on a daily basis). Tempeh is made by cooking whole soybeans, removing the husk and mixing a culture of Rhizopus spores with a substrate of either soybeans or rice into the warm beans. The beans are then pressed into a cake about half an inch thick and put into the equivalent of a proof box for a natural and controlled fermentation/culturing process that lasts about twenty-four hours. A white mold forms binding the beans together. The flavor and scent of tempeh is mild when the mold is white. If tempeh is overfermented, the mold will turn black or intensely dark and have a slight to strong ammonia scent, which means you must discard it because the mold is toxic. In Indonesia a few people die each year from eating toxic tempeh. That isn't the case in the United States because the tempeh is pasteurized when the fermentation process is complete to prevent overfermentation.

Tempeh was invented on the island of Java in Indonesia where it is a staple source of protein.

It is a soy-based product with the unique feature that it is made from whole soybeans that are processed but not refined like Textured Vegetable Protein (TVP). Tempeh has a higher protein/vitamin/mineral density and more dietary fiber because it is a whole bean. It has a firmer texture than tofu and a soft textured mouthfeel similar to a burger. In fact, it could be cut into squares and served as a burger. It is a universally accepted ancient protein for vegetarian cuisine. It is not a meat analogue because it was not created to simulate meat. Tempeh manufactured in the United States is vacuum packed in eight-ounce pieces in a plastic pouch, frozen and shipped into retail stores where it is commonly sold.

Like all original ancient foods, there are many versions of tempeh. Three of those available commercially are:

- ○ *Flax tempeh*—flaxseed is mixed with soybeans to add more nutrition, texture, and flavor to tempeh

- ○ *Three-grain tempeh* with a subtle blend of brown rice, barley, and millet

- ○ *Sea vegetable tempeh* with cooked and chopped sea vegetables mixed into the beans before fermentation

SEITAN

Seitan (pronounced SAY-tahn) is the red meat of ancient vegan proteins. While similar to meat analogues, it doesn't replicate animal protein in taste or texture. It is a concentrated wheat protein with approximately 24 grams protein in 4 ounces. It is a meat alternative that is often called wheat gluten, wheat meat, or mock duck. Seitan is produced by washing all starch out of high-protein flour. The original process for making it is labor intensive, which was the method I was introduced to. Dough is made using a high-gluten flour (about 13 percent protein) and water. Next the dough is washed with water until the water is clear (all starch is washed out). The result is an insoluble mass of elastic gluten (protein), which is then cooked until it is firm. At that point it is ready to be used in a recipe as a center plate protein. If making it from scratch, the starch can be saved for use in soups and sauces or as you would use a cornstarch.

The history of seitan is sketchy. The truth probably lies embedded somewhere in Buddhist culinary history. It does make sense, combined with knowledge about Buddhist cuisine, that in the seventh century Buddhist monks were looking for a meat alternative besides tofu. As they were making a dough, they somehow washed or rinsed all of the starch out of the dough, and they had what we today call "wheat meat." It is also called "Buddha's Food." It was a plain flavorless protein for which the Japanese developed the process of simmering it in soy sauce and seasonings, known as the macrobiotic method of production. Like all of the ancient proteins, the flavor has to be added to the protein. I was first introduced to seitan while working with macrobiotic cuisine around 1982. At that time the product was commercially available in a few retail natural foods stores but not in foodservice.

There is no commercial market quality standard for seitan. The protein's texture can vary depending on the cook's knowledge of the protein medium. The ideal texture is the mouthfeel of meat (soft but firm bite). If the protein is spongy or tough and chewy, it is poorly prepared. If purchased commercially, the chef is at the mercy of the manufacturer. The soggy version could be ground and used in a filling or chili. The tough version can be salvaged by cooking it in water. As the seitan absorbs more moisture it softens.

Today some cooks use vital wheat gluten flour and water to make seitan. That form is generally quite tough, but it can work if one is knowledgeable in making seitan. There are dry mix and prepared seitan products now available through foodservice providers. You will learn how to make it from a dry mix and from scratch (washing the dough) to have culinary understanding of this protein.

Unlike tofu, seitan comes in one style. The pieces, texture, and flavor may have minimal variance. It comes in small or perhaps eight-ounce pieces, but there is generally no consistency in the weights. Foodservice product is packed in a pail with brine. I have made it into New York strip steaks, marinated it in papaya enzymes, grilled it and served it with a vegan Bordelaise sauce, baked potato, and vegan sour cream. The six ounce steak costs about ninety cents.

A finished frozen product will cost about twice that of a dry mix speed scratch protein. It is freeze-thaw stable once prepared. Seitan is a versatile vegan protein that the chef can make fresh or work out of the freezer with á la carte menus.

Beans

Today the world produces 500 billion tons a year of all varieties of beans or 70 pounds for every person on Earth. It is the world's oldest crop. The United States produces 180 billion pounds of soybeans on 70,000 acres of land. It is the number-one bean crop in the United States and a sustainable form of protein. One acre of land will produce 356 pounds of soybean protein, while it takes 18 acres of land to produce 356 pounds of beef protein. Beans are a major source of protein in poor countries and a secondary form of protein in industrial countries. Chickpeas (garbanzo beans) are the most widely consumed bean in the world; the pinto bean holds that honor in the United States.

Beans are at the core of healthy vegetarian cuisine. They may be purchased in three forms: instant, canned (or processed), and dry. They are members of the legume (Facabeae) family, which includes pulses (lentils, soybeans, lupins, peanuts, and peas), and are an important human food crop for their high protein and essential amino acids. Beans are a very diverse ingredient in menu development whose culinary potential, soybeans aside, has more to offer in vegetarian menu development. They are a good source of protein, complex carbohydrates, and dietary fiber.

This text discusses the most popular beans we use today. These include black beans, black-eyed peas, dark red kidney beans, garbanzo beans, great northern beans, white kidney beans (cannellini beans), navy beans, pinto beans, soybeans, and lentils (red, green, brown, and yellow).

I recommend working with those beans available in your region. Pinto, navy, black, kidney, and garbanzo are the more universally common ones. Cooking with beans is deemed as being a bit trivial. Boston baked beans, chili, burritos, beans and rice, and bean salads are the general perception of bean cuisine. Beans don't, but should, have a significant place in modern cuisine as a desirable medium of culinary significance because their culinary potential has not yet been tapped to develop innovative menu items with great perceived value.

CANNED BEANS

Varieties include black beans, garbanzo beans (low sodium option), dark red kidney beans (low sodium option), pinto beans (low sodium option), vegetarian baked beans, and great northern beans. They're available in six number 10 size cans for foodservice and approximately sixteen-ounce cans for retail.

DRY BEANS

Varieties are generally packed in one pound, five pound, and twenty-five pound cases for food-service cooking. In converting ethnic meat dishes to vegetarian, I generally use the popular bean of the culture.

INSTANT DRY BEANS

Instant beans are a specialty item that is not readily available from broad line foodservice distribution centers. Natural foods and specialty foods distributors may carry one or more dried beans. E-commerce is another option. The more common types are the instant refried pinto or black beans, which are designed for ease of use. Add water, mix, and use in your recipe.

While one can cook creatively with instant dry beans, I don't often use them. Seasoned Vegetarian Black Beans (six 26.9-ounce pouches per case) is an example of an instant dry bean mix ready for use in a foodservice application. Lentils and peas, in the legume family, are much easier to cook and not in sufficient demand to commercialize as an instant product.

ADZUKI BEANS

The adzuki bean is a small reddish bean with a nutty, sweet flavor and is used in Asian cuisine as both a savory and dessert course. An ancient protein source, the adzuki has been cultivated in Asia for more than four thousand years. The Japanese use the bean primarily in dessert cooking. Macrobiotic cuisine uses the adzuki in both savory and dessert. In vegetarian cuisine, this bean is used primarily as a bean entrée (stew) served on rice and in salads. Because this is a rare bean used in both entrées and desserts, I chose to give it special attention. On the savory side, it can be substituted for any bean in recipes calling for beans.

EDAMAME

Edamame are cooked green immature soybeans distributed in two forms: in or out of the soy pod. Foodservice packaging varies but is similar to frozen vegetables. Unlike traditional soybeans, edamame beans are green and hydrated, requiring significantly less time to cook (about twenty to thirty minutes in total). The pods or beans are boiled or steamed and served with salt. Considered a healthy food item, they are a popular bean in Japan and China. While used as a side dish in traditional Asian cuisines, they contain 12 percent protein. The earliest recorded history of the bean dates to 1275 CE in Japan. This bean could easily be included with the dry bean category except that it is a fresh bean.

Seeds

Both ancient and modern cuisines include many traditional uses of seeds. The focus here is to utilize seeds as part of a center plate protein/entrée. Whether used as a condiment or in a side dish, the seed is adding a complex of protein, oil, carbohydrates, and fiber to one's diet. In entrées seeds add fat and protein, which should be considered in the formulation of the entrée. I enjoy using them together with beans, nuts, and grains to create a complex and complete protein.

SUNFLOWER SEEDS

Sweet, nutty sunflower seeds are an excellent source of calories, essential fatty acids, vitamins, and minerals. Culinary applications are primarily in condiments, vegetarian meat-style loaves, salads, and pastries.

SESAME SEEDS

There are two types of sesame seeds. One is the plain (white) sesame seed and the second is the dark (black) sesame seed. The dark is a specialty item. If your distribution center doesn't carry the black seed, you will probably find them at an Asian foodservice distribution company or at an Asian supermarket or online.

One of the oldest oil seed crops known, sesame seed was domesticated over five thousand years ago. Because it is drought tolerant, it has been called a survivor crop. It has one of the highest oil contents of any seed, with a rich, pleasant nutty flavor, and is a common ingredient in international cuisines. Sesame seeds are traditionally used as condiments (such as gomasio);

in breads, pastries, and confections such as halvah; in sauces, dressings, salads, glazes on entrées, and protein spreads like hummus. Because of the seed's significant oil content, I use them as part of the oil in recipe development and not as a primary source of protein.

Sesame Tahini or Roasted Sesame Butter

Sesame seeds are soaked in water and then crushed to separate the bran from the seed kernels. The crushed seeds are soaked in salt water, causing the bran to sink. The floating kernels are skimmed off the surface, toasted, and ground to produce an oily paste.

Sesame butter uses the raw seed. Culinary applications for both raw and roasted sesame butter are primarily in condiments like gomasio, which can be served on grains or proteins, vegetarian meat-style loaves, sauces, salads, pastries and confections (such as halvah).

Flaxseed

The seed is both tiny and mighty, carrying one of the biggest nutrient payloads on Earth. They have a pleasantly sweet, nutty taste. It is not technically a grain even though it has a similar vitamin and mineral profile. The fiber, antioxidants, and omega-3 fatty acids in flax leave grains in the dust.

There are two types of flaxseed: dark and golden. Culinary applications are primarily in baking, structural emulsification in both savory protein loaves and sweet pastries, and emulsifying sauces and dressings. Roasted, salted, or sweetened flaxseeds are enjoyed as snacks. Typical uses are ground seeds as toppings on yogurt, desserts, and cereal dishes. Flax meal is also used in confectionery, biscuits, muffins, and cakes. Sprinkling the seed on a food item is a traditional practice in ancient cuisine. Both modern and classical cuisines should take advantage of the seed's culinary value.

Pumpkin Seeds

Pumpkin seeds have a high caloric content first from fat and second from protein. On the positive side, they are rich in monounsaturated fatty acids (MUFA), like oleic acid that helps lower bad LDL cholesterol and increase good HDL cholesterol in the blood. Pumpkin seeds can generally be used to replace any seed in this book.

Chia Seeds

Now a popular snack, chia seeds have a similar nutritional profile to flax and sesame seeds. Often sprinkled on top of cereal, vegetables, and other foods, chia seeds have not yet become popular recipe ingredients and I currently haven't created any recipe applications, but it is a seed worthy of addressing as a healthful ingredient in vegan cuisine.

Nuts

Nuts are a nutrient-dense food ingredient with approximately 5 to 20 percent protein.

Unlike beans, they are 40 to 50 percent fat. When using them as an entrée, their fat content must be taken into consideration in recipe formulation. The nut also contains about 20 percent carbohydrates and 10 percent fiber. With the high fat profile, I recommend utilizing nuts as a complementary protein with beans and/or grains. Protein is protein regardless of the menu item contributing to one's diet.

With rare exception I prefer working with whole raw nuts and processing them for the desired savory or dessert application as mentioned in the cooking technique sections. I am presenting some of the more common nuts available through foodservice distributors. They are best refrigerated to maintain their integrity unless using them within a few weeks of purchase. I did not address hazelnuts or macadamia nuts as they are primarily specialty ingredients (nuts) available through bakery suppliers and specialty food distributors. Coconut is a "nut" with only 3.3 percent protein, and should be utilized like a nut in recipes.

ALMONDS, RAW WHOLE, BLANCHED

I recommend two purchasing options for almonds. The blanched slivered are recommended as a garnish or to add more protein to an entrée with other vegan proteins. Second is blanched whole. Blanched almond pieces may be available but are not a common option. Any form of blanched almonds (whole or pieces) can be used in ice creams, cheeses, and sauces.

ALMOND PASTE (PASTRY)

Almond paste is a combination of ground almonds and sugar that is sold commercially in eight-ounce tubes and is used in pastries for making items like Hippen Masse (page 335) or frangipane tarts.

CASHEWS—RAW PIECES

This nut is readily available throughout the year. I use only one form of cashew in the kitchen—raw pieces. Raw leaves me the option of using the nuts in dairy-style recipes without the roasted flavor. I choose pieces for the price point. Quality is the same as whole nuts. Because they are always broken or pulverized into dairy-style recipes, it makes no sense to use whole nuts at a premium price. I use them as a textural ingredient in entrées and in dairy-style products (cream sauces, cheese, etc.).

PEANUTS

Peanuts are legumes, which grow on the ground and not on a tree, and they have almost identical macronutrient qualities of almonds. They can be purchased in a variety of pack sizes. Always choose unsalted for culinary applications. If stuck with salted nuts, rinse and dry. Peanuts are used in Asian foods adding crunch to stir fry recipes and sauces. I use the butter form in desserts (icings, mousses, ice cream, and cream glacés). Though I have not used peanuts in pilafs, polentas, and loaves, I know they work, adding flavor and texture to the entrées.

PECAN PIECES

Nuts are generally harvested from October through December and are then subjected to the dehydration process, which is essential to remove moisture to improve the nut's shelf life. Again, I use pecan pieces, which are less expensive in entrées and savory recipes. Whole pecans are often used in pastries (pecan pie or Swiss Burnt-Pecan Torte, page 351).

PINE NUTS

Pine Nuts are 68 percent fat, which means they should be considered a nutrient-dense fat ingredient with emulsification properties and not a protein in recipe development (only 13 percent). You would do much better with beans. The cost per pound of pure protein extracted from pine nuts is approximately 50 times more expensive than the same pound of protein extracted from beans. But pine nuts do very well in condiments. I use them in ravioli fillings, and they are common in pesto. They can become the fat basis for a sauce or dairy-style product.

PISTACHIOS

I enjoy the exotic flavor of pistachios, especially with grains. Originally from the Middle East, pistachios are a member of the cashew family and have been cultivated for at least 7,000 years. Enjoyed by ancient royalty, rich in nutrients like other nuts, pistachios remain a special treat.

WALNUTS—RAW, PIECES, WHOLE

Culinary applications include Bulgur Walnut Loaf (page 298) and Sautéed Brussels Sprouts with Walnut Oil (page 197) and as an inclusion to tofu pâtés in the form of a classical forcemeat. Pieces are less expensive if available. I use whole, pieces, or ground walnuts for garnishes depending on the food item.

Grains

Grains are often ineffectively used in entrées in vegetarian cuisine. I believe they're ineffectively used because they are not combined properly to offer a reasonable measure of protein, perceived value, or satiety. Using grains as a pilaf or polenta can work elegantly if innovatively created. Adding a roasted nut to a pilaf with Kalamata olives, molded, served with a complementary sauce and gremolata on top would be an incredible entrée. Grains can contain considerable quantities of protein. Vital wheat gluten is an almost pure source of dietary protein, which is the primary ingredient in seitan and used in many vegetarian meat-style protein analogues. I will focus on the few grains that are generally higher in protein, which renders them more suitable for entrées. In developing vegetarian menus, the chef must consider how most of the food items in the entrée course contribute to the total protein necessary for a balanced diet.

QUINOA

This nutritious grain-type seed (pronounced KIN-wah) is obtained from the goosefoot family plant growing in the highland plains of the South American Andes. Cultivated by Incas, they believed quinoa was the "mother grain" (*chisaya mama*) and that eating it would grant them health and longevity. The crop was an Inca staple food until the Spanish explorers forced them to abandon its cultivation. Technically speaking, quinoa is not a cereal-class grain. It is a seed similar to other dicotyledons, such as amaranth, and legume family plants. Because, as a seed, it contains significantly less fat content than oil seeds, it is categorized as a grain. It has approximately 14 percent protein per 100 grams, making it a high-protein grain that works well in meat-style loaves, Peruvian Pot au Feu (page 290), casseroles, pilafs, and burgers. It is also a great hot breakfast cereal with soy milk and fruit for a sweet protein-rich breakfast or with miso and roasted seeds for a savory high-protein breakfast. It comes in natural shades of white, red, and black varieties. Find quinoa in five-pound bulk bags and one-pound retail bags.

HARD WINTER WHEAT

The use of wheat in human nutrition dates back to about 9000 BCE. It was one of the first domesticated grains on the Fertile Crescent and the Nile delta. Wheat is available in many varieties, described online. For vegan cuisine I recommend three versions of wheat: hard winter wheat, bulgur, and vital wheat gluten. Hard winter wheat has about 12 to 13 percent protein. My use of it in vegan cuisine ranges from egg replacer in grain loaves to textured protein ingredient in entrées. Entrée applications are infinite. Buy wheat in bulk and retail in one-pound and twenty-five-pound bags.

BULGUR

Bulgur is a cereal food made from the groats of several different wheat species, most often from *durum* wheat. It is of Turkish origin, making it common in Middle Eastern and South Asian cuisines. It is also commonly used in Europe.

Bulgur used for human consumption is usually sold parboiled and dried with a small amount of the bran partially removed. Bulgur is recognized as a whole grain. It is sometimes confused with cracked wheat, which is crushed but not parboiled. I use bulgur in grain loaves because it has the texture of ground beef and a natural dark color. It works well as a mixed medium with a variety of either grains with beans or with a meat analogue, tofu, tempeh or seitan, pilaf and as a polenta and in casseroles. Bulgur is available in bulk and retail in one-pound and twenty-five-pound bags.

VITAL WHEAT GLUTEN FLOUR

Vital wheat gluten flour is a refined wheat flour with all of the bran and starch removed, creating a concentrated protein that is approximately 95 percent protein, To make seitan, wheat meat, mock duck, and gluten meat in different cultures, the cook combines water and seasonings and then adds that to the flour and mixes. Traditionally made from gluten, the main protein of wheat, vital wheat gluten flour is made by washing wheat flour dough with water until all the starch is washed out, leaving insoluble gluten as an elastic mass, which is then cooked before eating. This flour is used in vegan breading recipes for its binding power and in loaves as the binding protein.

Vital wheat gluten flour is a specialty ingredient that can be purchased through natural or specialty foods distributors or online in 25-pound and 50-pound bags or through retail natural food distributors in 22-ounce packages. It is expensive as a retail product. I would purchase either the prepared product, the foodservice seitan dry mix (see Appendixes A and B) or make your own seitan (page 276).

BARLEY

Barley is a member of the grass family. Wild barley dates back to 10,000 BCE. It is a popular European grain, produced mainly in Russia, Germany, and France. It is 9.9 percent protein, a delicious way to boost the protein in an entrée.

I use barley in combination with soy proteins for numerous entrées ranging from loaves and burgers to pilafs and polentas. I like to use barley in developing entrées because it's a grain that holds its firm texture after cooking. It adds nutrition and a satisfying mouthfeel to the entrée. Barley is available in bulk and five-pound and twenty-five-pound bags.

CORNMEAL

While cornmeal is a low-protein grain, contrary to my original intent of working only with high-protein grains, it is commonly used in both ethnic and modern cuisines and is a superb carrier of proteins. You could say all grains can carry proteins, but cornmeal specifically has texture to complement mouthfeel and renders itself perfectly for polenta-type entrées that can be infused with proteins like beans to create a complete protein for human nutrition.

The three different types of cornmeal are white, blue, and yellow. White cornmeal is made from white corn and is commonly used in parts of Africa and the southern United States for making cornbread. It is also produced in Italy in small quantities. Blue cornmeal is actually light blue or violet in color, has a sweet flavor, and is made from dried corn kernels that have been ground into a fine or medium texture. Blue corn has been cultivated in the American Southwest for at least a 1,000 years.

Steel-ground yellow cornmeal is commonly used in the United States. To make it, the husk and germ of the maize kernel are almost completely removed. It has a shelf life of about one year if stored in an airtight container in a cool and dry place. Stone-ground yellow cornmeal retains some of the hull and germ, lending a little more flavor and nutrition to recipes. It is more perishable, but will store longer if refrigerated.

I use only yellow cornmeal as it is most common and can be interchanged with the white and blue. It can be used to make entrées centering on loaves, protein infused polentas, and duxelles or fillings. The challenge is thinking outside the box on how to use grains as complete protein entrées. Cornmeal can be purchased in bulk or retail 4 packs of 24 ounces each and 25-pound bags.

MILLET

Several varieties of millet from highly variable small-seeded grasses are widely grown around the world as cereal crops for both human nutrition and animal feed. It is a popular grain in India and Nigeria and an important crop in the semi-arid tropics. Millet has been cultivated in East Asia for the past ten thousand years and was said to be Michelangelo's favorite grain. It is also one of mine. Yellow pearl millet is the popular version in the United States, and the one used in vegetarian cuisine to make loaves, croquettes, and duxelles, and added to quinoa for a popular breakfast porridge. Puffed millet has numerous dessert applications. You'll find millet in bulk, 2-pound bags, and 25-pound bags.

RICE

Rice comes in white, brown, short grain, long grain, wild (wild rice is actually a seed from a grass), sushi, and sweet varieties. This grain contributes to dietary protein, complements beans as a complete protein, and does this primarily as a side dish.

Brown rice cooks differently than white rice, and cooking methods determine water to rice ratios and cooking times. If pressure cooking short grain brown rice, the water ratio is 3 cups water to 2 cups rice and once up to pressure, 35 minute cook time. One cup of white basmati rice boiled in a pot requires 1 ½ cups water for 20 minutes in a covered pot. Rice comes in a wide variety of pack sizes from bulk and retail pack sizes to 25-pound bags.

AMARANTH

When cooked, this grain has a gelatinous effect, rendering it an ideal grain for using in grain loaves and center plate proteins. It also works in puddings similar to a tapioca and in polentas and is an ideal breakfast cereal. The flavor is slightly nutty and texture is similarly to caviar with a sort of burst or pop when eaten. It is a good source of plant protein with about 9.3 grams or more of protein per cup of cooked amaranth according to the U.S. Department of Agriculture. I have worked with it minimally, and it is a grain that I will be developing into future recipes. It's available in a wide variety of pack sizes from 1-pound and 5-pound to 25-pound bags.

Modern Processed Plant Proteins

Modern processed plant proteins are the modern meat analogues, derived from the ancient proteins. These proteins are designed to simulate meat and often made with textured soy protein, pea protein, and wheat gluten. They are generally highly refined and concentrated proteins that are the result of the industrial revolution and food science. While they generally attempt to resemble meat for the healthy dining consumer, they can take a non-meat ethnic or innovative flavor profile as in a black bean veggie burger. Textured soy protein (also known as textured vegetable protein/TVP), soy protein flour, isolates, and concentrates are the modern versions of soy protein in twenty-first century vegetarian cuisine.

TEXTURED VEGETABLE PROTEIN (TVP)

A versatile form of the soybean, TVP is also known as textured soy protein (TSP) and is the by-product of extracting soy oil from soybeans. You'll find soy TVP in many meat analogues on the market today.

TVP comes in two forms: soy protein flour and concentrate, with the concentrate having a higher protein percentage and better mouthfeel. It's available in twenty-five-pound bags in a foodservice pack, bulk, and four 10-ounce packs in retail. The defatted protein is extruded into ground pieces, strips, or chunks and dried. Originally, the by-product was used up to 15 percent in meats as an excellent high-protein extender.

Soy TVP has as much as 50 percent protein and is generally rehydrated at two to three parts water to one part TVP. After extruding, the protein is heated to 150°C to 200°C, which denatures it to a fibrous, insoluble porous protein. Upon exiting the extruder, the pressurized protein expands to a puffy solid and is then dried. The oil in soy is generally extracted through the use of a solvent called hexane. It is impossible for the trace amounts found in TVP to be harmful. And there is a non-hexane version of TVP on the market. Unlike cooked beans, TVP has a firm structure, with a texture similar to that of meat. TVP comes in caramel color and off white and also has a fortified option. I use it in casseroles, loaves, burgers, and taco-type fillings.

MEAT SUBSTITUTES TODAY

Meat substitutes are often called imitation, faux, mock, or analogue proteins. The appropriate name for a vegetarian protein simulating meat is *analogue* because it suggests that it is similar to something else. I also use the word *style* and would call a vegetarian chicken protein *chicken-style* protein. *Style* is a marketable suffix to an analogue suggesting positive images of the protein. When I read mock, faux, or imitation as the descriptors of a protein, my first impression is that the food item is cheap, not original, and has no perceived value. Naming your vegan entrée properly is very important, along with how it is described on the menu.

A well formulated meat analogue will have the texture, flavor, and eye appeal of the meat it is replicating. While some may argue the point that tofu, tempeh, and seitan are meat analogues, they are not because they don't taste like meat nor were they developed to replicate meat. They are ancient protein sources. They could be integrated into a meat analogue but of themselves, they are not meat analogues.

There are three types of vegetarian meat analogues that are vegan, lacto, and ovo. Whey and egg proteins are sometimes added for structure. Egg will add significant mouthfeel and is generally used as the easier means to develop texture. Quorn is an example of an egg-based vegetarian protein made in combination with micro proteins. Because it is an egg-based protein, it is not a vegan protein, which is why I don't address it in detail.

Extrusion is a mechanical compressed shear process used in the manufacture of vegetarian proteins to give the foods their texture. Textured Vegetable Protein (TVP) is a primary protein in many ground meat analogues to intensify the protein and add the texture needed to simulate meat. There are many forms of protein extrusion depending on the protein. A second version of extruding is layering of protein through the compressed and shear stresses with the emerging analogue having the texture of a muscle meat. When pulling it apart, it is like pulling a piece of chicken breast apart with the stringy looking effect. Extruded meats have little if any oil in them because oil impedes the extrusion process. The natural meat-style flavors are addressed in the vegan seasoning ingredients section.

Meat analogues come in refrigerated/frozen, dried protein, or dry protein mixes. The frozen/refrigerated proteins I recommend are the vegan hot dogs and burgers for concession stands and the plain frozen proteins such as chicken-style and beef-style strips that can be used in recipe applications. The preferred least expensive proteins that a foodservice professional or personal cook can actually cook with are dry speed scratch protein mixes. See the ingredient distribution sources in the back of the book.

There are the specific varieties of meat analogues that can be used in a foodservice operation. These include a variety of sausage chubs, cold cuts (ham, bologna, and turkey), BBQ ribs, Canadian bacon, chorizo, breaded seafood-style fillets, scallops, and seafood cakes, etc. They are primarily available in retail and some in foodservice packs and tend to be very expensive. A broad line distributor will either have a drop ship program in place for frozen and dry or direct you to a natural foods distributor who supplies these unique products.

The ingredient declarations for each item include the unique ingredients to give you an approximate idea of what makes a meat analogue. Unlike meat, there are carbohydrates and fiber in the proteins. Extruded proteins will always have little or no oil because oil inhibits the extrusion process. Please note: Food companies do change their ingredient listing so it's important to always read the label for the most up-to-date information.

FROZEN MEAT ANALOGUES

Extruded frozen meat analogues are all, with rare exception, pre-formed and pre-cooked. The only exception that I know of is the frozen ground beef chubs and sausage chubs, which are raw vegan products.

Vegan Chicken Strips are extruded to simulate pre-cooked chicken cut into strips and are used in stir fries, sandwiches, and salads.

> **Ingredients:** water, soy protein, Canadian wheat protein, natural flavors, yeast extract, canola oil, sugar, sea salt, organic ancient grain flour (kamut, amaranth, millet, quinoa), onion powder, garlic powder, pea protein.

> *Sold at retail in approximately 8-ounce package and 10-pound case.*

Vegan Sausage Chub is good for sausage patties, meatballs, and savory pastry fillings. It can easily be formed to a specific shape and additional seasonings can be added to customize the flavor.

> **Ingredients:** water, textured soy protein concentrate, textured soy protein, tapioca starch, natural flavor, soy sauce, soy protein concentrate, cellulose gum, soy protein isolate, dried onions, salt, vital wheat gluten, yeast extract, molasses, sea salt, dried garlic, xanthan gum, wheat starch.

> *Sold in retails stores as 12 (14-ounce) chubs per case.*

Vegan Ground Beef Chub is used for meatballs, burgers, loaves, tacos, and savory pastry fillings. The flavor can also be customized by adding additional spices and herbs.

Ingredients: textured soy protein, tapioca starch, natural flavor, soy sauce, soy protein concentrate, soy protein isolate, barley malt extract, dried onions, salt, soy milk powder, vital wheat gluten, torula yeast, yeast extract, molasses, sea salt, dried garlic, xanthan gum, soy flour, wheat starch.

Sold at retail as 12 (14-ounce) chubs per case.

Vegan Hot Dogs sans meat look, feel (texture), taste, and cook like traditional hot dogs and are used in the same manner.

Ingredients: water, soy protein isolate, oil, sugar, pea protein isolate, tapioca starch, salt, potassium chloride, yeast extract, carrageenan, dried garlic, natural flavor, natural smoke flavor, xanthan gum, fermented rice flour, oleoresin paprika (color).

Sold at retail as 12 (11-ounce) units per case (8.25 pounds per case) and 64 (2.5-ounce) hot dogs in a 10-pound case.

Vegan Burgers vary with some having the texture and flavor of a traditional beef burger and some going more vegetarian. Some vegetarian burgers vary in texture and taste with generally a weaker texture (less protein) and a vegetable flavor profile in the vegetable-based burgers.

Ingredients (vegetable burger): cooked brown rice, broccoli, carrots, onions, whole kernel corn, rolled oats, water, brown lentils, red bell peppers, green peppers, oat fiber, ground flaxseed, canola oil, salt, methylcellulose, soy sauce, yeast extract, hydrolyzed wheat gluten, sugar, spices, caramel color, garlic powder and natural flavors.

Sold in retail stores as 6 (12.8 ounce) units per case (4.5-pounds per case) and for foodservice as 64 (2.5-ounce) burgers in a 10-pound case.

Vegan Meatballs can be used just like traditional meatballs. Even a few will give a pasta dish perceived value, additional flavor, and a hearty dose of protein.

Ingredients: water, textured soy concentrate, textured vegetable protein (soy flour, caramel color), oil, seasoning blend, bread crumbs, paprika, salt, pepper, garlic, parsley, wheat gluten, sea salt, methylcellulose.

Sold in a 10-pound case in retail packs.

Seitan, an ancient protein, is listed in the analogue section because it is positioned as such by retail and foodservice companies. It comes in different shapes (strips, and large pieces) and some companies make a chicken-style version. A good quality seitan will have a firm bite. If spongy or like shoe leather, it was not properly prepared.

Ingredients: vital wheat gluten flour, tamari, ginger, and garlic.

Sold in a 10-pound pail or as 12 (8-ounce) units per case.

Vegan Prawns/Shrimp, and other vegan seafood-type proteins, vary radically in the amount of protein they contain. The ingredient declaration is the indicator. If soy isn't used in the protein, then it is generally going to be low in protein. There is usually only 1 gram of protein in an 80 gram portion of vegan prawns.

Ingredients: water, curdlan gum, refined konjac powder, modified tapioca starch, potato starch, raw cane sugar, sea salt, white pepper powder, onion powder, garlic powder, yeast extract powder, seaweed extract, sesame oil, fermented ice vinegar, calcium carbonate, sodium tripolyphosphate, oleoresin paprika.

Sold as 9 (8.8-ounce) units per case.

Other vegan seafood analogues include: vegan seafood, calamari, crab cakes, fish fillets, vegan scallops, and vegan shrimp, and all come in 9 (8.8-ounce) packages per case. The retail packs listed above, and many more varieties of vegan seafood, are available through natural foods distributors and retail stores. As a center plate entrée protein, the vegan seafood analogues are generally not a good deal for protein. You are better off working with sea vegetables and soy proteins (tofu pâtés) to make your proteins using different ethnic ideas. You will learn more about these proteins in the cooking technique and recipe sections.

DRY MIXES

Meat analogue dry mixes allow the foodservice cook or personal cook to be creative and innovative. The ground beef, for instance, can be used to make a meatball, burger, Salisbury steak, or Bolognese sauce. The mixes, when rehydrated, are about 50 percent less expensive than frozen meat analogues and have about a two-year shelf life in dry storage.

Ground Beef-Style Mix

Ingredients: soy protein concentrate, wheat gluten, maltodextrin, carrageenan, natural flavors, autolyzed yeast extract, dehydrated garlic, hydrolyzed soy protein, caramel color (contains sulfites), salt, potassium chloride, sodium phosphate, dextrose, dehydrated onion, lactic acid (vegetable-based), spice, and no more than 2 percent calcium silicate added to prevent caking.

Sold by the 10-pound case for foodservice needs.

Chicken-Style Mix

Ingredients: wheat gluten, soy protein concentrate, maltodextrin, natural flavors (yeast, spices, garlic and onion powders, turmeric), carrageenan, salt, potassium chloride, turmeric, and 2 percent or less silicon dioxide added to prevent caking.

Sold by the 10-pound case for foodservice needs.

Sausage-Style Mix

Ingredients: soy protein concentrate, vital wheat gluten, maltodextrin, spices, yeast extract, carrageenan, potassium chloride, salt, natural flavors, sodium phosphate, dextrose, lactic acid (vegetable-based), caramel color, and 2 percent or less silicon dioxide added to prevent caking.

Sold by the 10-pound case for foodservice needs.

Seitan Dry Mix

Ingredients: wheat gluten, flour, whole wheat, sauce, soy, tamari, flaxseed meal, ginger.

Sold by the 10-pound case for foodservice needs.

Vegan Bacon Bits

The popularity of vegan bacon bits gives them a special category. These bits are good as salad toppings, pasta entrées, loaves, casseroles, and burgers. They are generally high in sodium. This product goes by different names but the ingredient declaration is similar.

Ingredients: textured vegetable protein (soy flour and caramel color), soybean oil, salt, natural flavors.

Sold only in 16-ounce foil bags.

Sea Vegetables

Sea vegetables are a superior nutritionally dense food containing many minerals, vitamins, some protein, high fiber, and a modest amount of carbohydrates. The red sea vegetables like dulse and laver (also called nori) generally contain most (no plant protein contains all of the essential amino acids) of the essential amino acids providing a quality of protein that supports our daily protein intake. Because sea vegetables grow in mineral-rich ocean waters, they can provide about fifty-six minerals and trace minerals needed in the human body.

Certain varieties are used to create gelling agents for commercial food products. I use sea vegetables to simulate the flavor of seafood in vegan entrées, soups, appetizers, and salads, etc. Nori, wakame, arame, kombu, and hijiki are my favorite choices for savory seafood-style recipes. Dulse and kelp are commonly used as condiments.

Sea vegetables like arame and wakame grow closer to the surface of the ocean and therefore have a delicate flavor. Hijiki grows deeper in the ocean and has a stronger flavor that may need to be neutralized in the cooking process. I don't find it to be an offensive flavor, but it takes over the recipe's flavor profile unless tamed.

Using several different methods of analysis, vitamin B-12 or an analogue has shown up in many sea vegetables. The key is that the analogue is a molecule that looks like B-12 but the human body isn't able to assimilate it, rendering it useless. And sea vegetables may or may not contain actual B-12, rendering it an undependable source. It is best to rely on fortified vegan foods like soy milk and nutritional yeast for B-12. No final clinical decision has been made on this subject.

Glutamic acid, the basis for synthetic MSG, is one of the amino acids found in sea vegetables like kelp and kombu. That is why I cook my beans with a stick of kombu. It is a traditional cooking technique used by macrobiotic cooks because glutamic acid enhances the flavor of the food it is cooked in.

The pack sizes on sea vegetables vary by distributor. I am using standard 8-ounce and one-pound packs. There are also 2- and 4-ounce options. Asian stores and natural foods distributors are regional sources, or sea vegetables can be purchased online. As dry products sea vegetables can be shipped via ground and have an infinite shelf life.

The many nutritional mysteries of sea vegetables remain to be explored. It's possible that consuming sea vegetables can help fight obesity. A *Science Daily* article titled "Seaweed to Tackle Rising Tide of Obesity," dated March 22, 2010, reported:

> Seaweed could hold the key to tackling obesity after it was found it reduces fat uptake by more than 75 per cent, new research has shown. Now the team at Newcastle University are adding seaweed fibre to bread to see if they can develop foods that help you lose weight while you eat them. A team of scientists led by Doctor Iain Brownlee and Professor Jeff Pearson have found that dietary fibre in one of the world's largest commercially-used seaweed could reduce the amount of fat absorbed by the body by around 75 per cent. The Newcastle University team found that Alginate—a natural fibre found in sea kelp—stops the body from absorbing fat better than most anti-obesity treatments currently available over the counter.

These findings were presented at the March 3, 2010 meeting of the American Chemical Society in San Francisco. I expect that future research will show great benefits to adding sea vegetables to one's diet.

NORI

The Japanese name for the red alga version of edible seaweed, nori is called laver in Wales and English-speaking countries. Originally it was processed into a paste. Later it was made by shredding and rack drying similar to Japanese paper making, which is why it looks and feels like a sheet of paper. Its history goes back to about the seventh century CE. The name first appeared in 1867 in an English dictionary and Asian grocery stores brought it to the western United States to serve the Japanese. In 1960 it took off in popularity with the emergence of the macrobiotic movement. It is primarily used in sushi as most culinary professionals know. It is used the same way in vegan cuisine but I expand on it for salad rolls as in Tempura Vegetable Nori Salad Roll (page 166), pâtés, and polentas. Nori is available retail in a 20-sheet pack, 50-sheet pack, and case with four 50-sheet packs.

WAKAME

Wakame is an edible sea vegetable with a subtly sweet flavor that is most often served in soups and salads. It is my favorite sea vegetable because it has a delicate sea-type flavor that resonates with seafood but has no harsh flavor notes. It is, in macrobiotic terms, a yin sea vegetable, because it grows closer to the surface. It is very diverse in culinary applications and functions exceptionally well as a New England Sea Vegetable Chowder (page 240) and Sea Vegetable Cakes, similar to crab cakes (page 261). Sea-farmers have grown wakame in Japan from the seventh century. In the 1960s wakame began to be imported in dried form from Japan. In the 1970s, the growing number of Japanese restaurants and sushi bars further drove its popularity. Today, due to the macrobiotic movement, it is widely available at natural food stores and Asian-American grocery stores. Purchase wakame in retail outlets in 50 gram and 1-pound packages.

ARAME

Arame is a sea vegetable harvested off the coast of Japan that typically comes in small angel hair–like strips. It is a yin, delicately flavored sea vegetable due to its growing close to the surface of the ocean. It is especially good for those who are first trying sea vegetables. It goes well with tofu, sushi, and other Asian ingredients. I integrate it into Sautéed Arame with Leeks and Cranberries (page 192), pâté inclusions, soups, and salads. It's available at retail stores in 50 gram and 1-pound packages.

Kombu

Kombu is a long sheet of dense, hard, dry sea vegetable with a salty dark grey color. It does come in powder form, but I have never used it in that way. I always cook dry beans with a 4-inch stick of kombu as a natural form of MSG to enhance flavor. In Japanese cuisine, kombu is one of the three main ingredients used to make dashi, a Japanese broth. It is also shredded and pickled. I use it primarily as a natural nutrient-dense seasoning containing many of the minerals and trace minerals found in sea vegetables. It is not a high-protein ingredient but does significantly enhance flavor and add texture to a recipe. I use it in Lentil Pâté (page 293) and Pecan Nut Loaf (page 297), It also can be served as a condiment. It is delicious when pickled with mirin and soy sauce. You can purchase kombu in 50 gram or 1-pound packages.

Hijiki

Recent studies have shown that hijiki may contains potentially toxic quantities of inorganic arsenic, and food safety agencies of several countries (excluding Japan) have advised against its consumption. I do think this matter will eventually be resolved and we will be able to again consume it. If you are purchasing sea vegetables from China, ask for their arsenic report to check for contamination. Hijiki is supposedly harvested in limited amounts where water isn't contaminated. Hijiki has been a popular Japanese sea vegetable for centuries. It is rich in dietary fiber and nutrients. Hijiki is a black, thick stringy vegetable that grows deep in the ocean and has a strong flavor, like other sea vegetables grown at depth. It has been sold in the United Kingdom for thirty years; the macrobiotic diet helped establish it in the United States. Purchase it in 50 gram and 1-pound packages.

Other Sea Vegetables

Additional sea vegetables used today in culinary application include bladderwrack, digitata kelp, dulse, dulse-applewood smoked, Irish moss, kelp, wild Atlantic kombu, European laver, wild Atlantic nori, sea lettuce, and Pacific Coast sea palm fronds. I encourage you to experiment and enjoy these alternative fruits of the sea in creating innovative recipes, especially integrating them into the tofu pâté concept, as in Sea Vegetable Tofu (page 267).

Vegan Seasonings

Aside from plant-based proteins, vegetarian flavor systems are the second most important ingredient in vegetarian cuisine. One of the major hurdles in both meat-based and vegan flavor systems is the high salt content in the ingredients. Meat analogues and any meat-like flavoring systems generally have high sodium autolyzed yeast or high sodium meat-like ingredients. That is changing as I write this, Dieticians are pressing the chefs and cooks to lower the sodium in their cuisine because sodium is related to hypertension and/or heart attacks. New flavor technology is bringing down the sodium. Look for the reduced-salt flavorings, and when seasoning a food, don't salt if using miso, tamari, or a meat-style flavor until tasting the food.

Vegan seasonings work off the same platform of spices, herbs, ethnic spice blends, and flavor concentrates that are used in traditional meat-based fare. The primary difference is that no animal or animal by-products are allowed in the flavoring systems. Flavoring ingredients like Worcestershire sauce contains anchovy paste, which isn't vegan. There is a vegan version but you must read the label. All flavoring ingredients must be vegan to cover all categories of vegetarian cuisine.

Vegan flavoring ingredients discussed in this book include

- ☼ Vegan meat-style broths and vegetable flavoring broths, powders, and pastes
- ☼ Common ancient flavoring ingredients, primarily Asian—miso, soy sauce, tamari, and umeboshi paste
- ☼ Specialty modern seasonings that enhance flavor

VEGAN MEAT-STYLE BROTHS & VEGETABLE FLAVOR SEASONINGS

A number of brands are available through retailers and foodservice distributors nationwide that include reduced and low-sodium options. If you have access to a distributor's catalog, search for vegan ingredients. The ingredients for these items continue to be refined, so study the ingredient declaration carefully.

VEGAN MEAT-STYLE BROTH POWDERS

I prefer vegan meat-style broth powders in that they have a stronger menu diversity. For example, they can be used in breading an ingredient like tofu or tempeh. Both paste and powdered flavor bases work well in soups, sauces, and deglazing in a sauté and may help in emulsifying a pan-glazed sauce.

Meat-style broth powders include reduced sodium chicken-style broth mix and reduced sodium beef-style broth mix, usually available in 1- and 5-pound units and smaller packages. Low-sodium vegetable broth powder is also available. Low sodium and reduced sodium broth powder cannot exceed 140 mg per serving, and reduced sodium has to be at least 25 percent less than the standard sodium in a food item. No sodium is less than 5 milligrams per serving. The claim on the label will verify the sodium level and is verified by FDA standards.

VEGETABLE BROTHS & PASTES

Vegetable broth powders and pastes come in a variety of flavors—roasted mirepoix, Herb de Provence, roasted onion, and many more. Always check the ingredient declaration. Low sodium is often the right choice.

ANCIENT FLAVORING SYSTEMS

While every cuisine has its own flavoring system, I am often drawn to Asian ingredients to complement vegan food. I have also used these ingredients in other ethnic vegan dishes whenever I am in the mood for fusion cooking. Once you are familiar with all of these ingredients, I encourage you to experiment.

MISO & ITS DIFFERENT TYPES

Miso is an ancient Japanese seasoning ingredient dating to the third century BCE used in entrées, sauces, spreads, and soups and as a condiment. It is a whole foods fermented flavor paste/concentrate ingredient that is enzymatically active.

I would be skeptical of many of the different flavor concentrates/pastes produced and sold under different national brands because they consist of about 50 percent sodium. The customer must check out the label—let the buyer beware! I have successfully used a non-miso mirepoix base. Some flavor concentrates produced by national brand companies are adequate, meaning cleaner labels using natural ingredients to produce stronger flavor profiles with less sodium.

Different misos have a broader sodium range from 90 milligrams for light sweet miso to 180 milligrams for darker misos for the same ¾ teaspoon. Light misos contain about 50 percent less sodium than dark misos. And they are a natural product with a natural flavor. Some are custom flavored with spices. It belongs on your shelf, especially if cooking macrobiotic vegetarian (light miso for poultry and seafood-style recipes and dark miso for red meat-style entrées).

Miso is a superior substitute for flavor concentrates. The lighter versions are superb with tofu, bean, and tempeh proteins. The darker misos are a superior option to concentrates for beef and dark meat-type products, and they complement vegan proteins like adzuki beans, seitan, grain loaves, and hearty beef-style soups. The darker the miso, the stronger and perhaps more earthy the flavor. Different types of miso have been described as salty, sweet, earthy, fruity, and savory. The darker color indicates it has been fermented longer and the flavor is stronger. Miso is enzymatically active; if added to a starch-thickened sauce, it will break down the sauce, as long as it has not been added to hot liquid first (which neutralizes or incapacitates the enzymes). When used in marinades or dressings, the miso doesn't have to be heated.

I use a lighter miso in savory recipes requiring a delicate flavor and a darker miso in entrées with strong flavor profiles that can stand up to the darker miso. Also miso is a nutrient-dense processed whole food and adds a little protein to one's diet.

Miso is available in numerous variations—mellow white or sweet, yellow, red, brown or black—that have different flavors and culinary applications. Many varieties of miso can be broken down into two types: ancient miso and the modern varieties, which are spin-offs of the original versions. One example found in my refrigerator today is chickpea miso, which includes chickpeas and water, and has no soy. Modern misos, in some cases, have spices added for additional flavors.

Mellow White and/or Sweet Miso is made from soybeans that have been fermented with a large percentage of rice. The color will vary from white to light beige, and this miso has a sweet savory flavor.

    Ingredients: soybeans, rice koji, sea salt, water, and koji spores.

Yellow Miso is a combination of soybeans that have been fermented with another grain like barley and/or rice; it is light brown and has a mild, earthy flavor. It is best used in marinades, soups, and glazes.

    Ingredients: soybeans, rice koji, sea salt, water and koji spores.

Red Miso is also typically made from soybeans fermented with barley or other grains, usually with a higher percentage of soybeans and/or a longer fermentation period. It can range in color from red to dark brown. The deep umami flavor of red miso can overwhelm mild dishes, but is perfect for hearty soups, entrées, and glazes.

    Ingredients: soybeans, rice koji, sea salt, water and koji spores.

Brown Rice or Black Miso has a bit of mystery about it. Some sources say this paste is made entirely from soybeans, others say that it's made from soybeans fermented with hearty dark grains like buckwheat. It is a dark miso because it uses brown rice and black soy beans which give it a stronger flavor profile. Regardless, this sounds like the strongest flavored miso around (the descriptions remind us a bit of the British marmite!).

    Ingredients: soybeans, rice koji, sea salt, and water.

SOY SAUCE

Soy sauce or soya sauce is made from fermented soybeans, roasted grains, brine, and a mold such as *Aspergillus sojae*. Once the fermentation process is complete, the paste is pressed to remove the soy sauce. The cereal residue is used for animal feed. Soy sauce originated in China around the second century BCE. This brown liquid has a basic salty umami flavor and is commonly used in Asian savory recipes of every kind. The flavor and color varies between Chinese, Taiwanese, Japanese, Indonesian, Burmese, and Vietnamese soy sauces with Indonesian being sweet. The variations are based on the recipe and/or fermentation process.

There are reduced sodium soy sauces, which I recommend in place of full sodium soy sauce. Those soy sauces allow the cook to have more control over the sodium in the recipe.

Tamari

Tamari is similar to soy sauce but different in its higher concentration of soybeans. It is fermented differently than soy sauce, which gives it a richer, milder sodium, and smoother heat-stable flavor that does not burn under high heat. It is used in stir-fry recipes, dipping sauces, salad dressings, sauces like Espagnole sauce, and soups, and for grilling vegetables and vegetarian proteins. It is preferred to soy sauce in natural foods cooking. Tamari comes in reduced sodium and gluten-free versions. One tablespoon of reduced sodium tamari has 710 milligrams of sodium (29 percent of the RDA, which is high) and only 2 grams of protein. Diluted over four servings, it is modest in sodium.

Ingredients: water, soybeans, salt, and alcohol.

Umeboshi

Umeboshi paste is used in sandwich wraps, nori rolls, sauces, and salad dressings. It leans more to Asian-style cooking; as a paste this would be categorized with miso and other flavor concentrated pastes. I use it in dairy-style recipes like vegan sour cream and cream cheeses for the souring acidity effect. I also use it in macrobiotic cooking and as a home remedy for nausea and nausea-related illness. I make a hot cup of bancha tea and add a teaspoon of tamari and one ume plum. Let it set for 10 minutes, drink the liquid and eat the plum. This is NOT a medical prescription—see your doctor. But food is our best front line medicine.

Ingredients: ume plums, sea salt, shiso.

Modern Specialty Flavorings

Several modern flavorings hold an important place in my kitchen. Each one adds a special touch to the right vegan dish and stimulates a unique flavor.

Nutritional Yeast

Nutritional yeast is nutrient dense, with a natural flavor profile similar to cheese. It works well in a cream sauce or in delicately flavored recipes to give them a dairy-style flavor note. As a dry ingredient, nutritional yeast has an indefinite shelf life and doesn't need to be refrigerated. Two tablespoons of nutritional yeast contain 130 percent of the RDA for B-12 and 8 grams of protein. Nutritional yeast is sold in flakes and powder. It is generally available in one pound packages.

Ingredients: dried yeast, niacin, pyridoxine, hydrochloride (B-6), riboflavin (B-2), thiamin hydrochloride (B-1) folic acid, vitamin B-12.

Old Bay Seasoning

Old Bay Seasoning complements sea vegetables in developing seafood-style vegan entrées. My favorite applications are the Sea Vegetable Cake (page 258), which simulates the crab cake, and New England Sea Vegetable Chowder (page 240). A teaspoon of Old Bay Seasoning has 740 milligrams of sodium (28 percent of RDA), which is high. This ingredient is traditionally used in seafood, poultry, seasonings, and meats. It has the same crossover applications in vegan cooking.

Ingredients: celery salt (salt, celery seed), spices (including red pepper and black pepper), and paprika.

Liquid Smoke

Liquid Smoke is manufactured by collecting the smoke from burning wood (hickory, maple, apple, etc.) in a condenser and cooking it until it forms a concentrated liquid smoke flavor. It is a natural flavor and is concentrated so should be used with caution in order to not overly flavor the food item. If you are unable to smoke a food, this is a second option to come close to the same flavor. Some brands of this ingredient are available in different wood flavor profiles.

Let the Buyer Beware!!!

Always read the ingredient declaration to confirm the contents of the product, and to make sure the product is vegan or even vegetarian for that matter. Several years ago I was given a tasty Thai snack food of sea vegetable chips. I did not know that the sea vegetables had been sprinkled with cuttlefish and shrimp powder. The flavor was so subtle that I did not recognize it but decided to read the label to find out what made the chips taste so good and ended that culinary delight.

Oils & Shortenings

An oil's smoke point indicates how high a heat the oil can take before, literally, beginning to break down and start smoking. When an oil smokes, it releases carcinogens into the air and free radicals within the oil that disrupt cellular metabolism. For the healthiest approach, discard any oil that has gone beyond its smoke point. Each oil has a different use and smoke point, and each performs best within a certain range of temperatures. Some are made for high heat cooking, while others have intense flavors that are best enjoyed by drizzling directly onto food. The guide below shows the smoke point for each type of oil. This is the essence of what everyone working in the kitchen needs to know about fats and oils from a vegetarian culinary perspective.

OILS REFINED FOR HIGH HEAT

Avocado	510°F
Canola	460°F
Sunflower	460°F
Safflower, High Oleic	445°F
Almond	495°F
Safflower	460°F
Palm Fruit	450°F
Sesame	445°F

BAKING & SAUTÉING— MEDIUM-HIGH HEAT OILS

Canola	425°F
Walnut	400°F
Safflower, High Oleic	390°F
Coconut	365°F
Soy	360°F

UNREFINED OILS FOR LIGHT SAUTÉING & SAUCES—MEDIUM HEAT OILS

Sesame	350°F	Olive	325°F
Peanut	350°F	Corn	320°F
Toasted Sesame	350°F	Coconut	280°F
Extra Virgin Olive Oil	325°F		

UNREFINED OILS FOR FLAVOR

Each oil listed below has a different smoke point. When you want the flavor of the oil to be part of the final dish, use unrefined oils such as:

Peanut Oil	350°F
Toasted Sesame Oil	350°F
Extra Virgin Olive Oil	325°F
Corn Oil	320°F
Coconut Oil	280°F

OILS BEST USED IN NO-COOK COLD RECIPE APPLICATIONS

Never use the following oils in cooking because the heat will destroy the essential fatty acids when present and will break down the oil's structure, which could create peroxides that can be pre-carcinogenic. These oils are best served cold as in salad dressings.

Flax Oil	225°F
Wheat Germ	225°F

In general, oils are a poor substitute for a saturated fat (plant or animal). Oils can be combined with vegan saturated fats (palm or coconut oils) to reduce their saturated fat.

SHORTENINGS

Hydrogenated (trans fat) shortenings are vegan but not a healthy fat. Butter is used a great deal in traditional cooking and pastries. Avoiding it in cooking means we need another shortening to replace it. Butter is generally used for lacto cooking and baking. Vegan "butter spreads" are the vegan option and bring more flavor to a vegan recipe but are generally slightly higher in sodium, so wait to salt the dish until after adding the butter spread.

There are two types of shortening generally used in vegan cooking: palm shortening and vegan butter spreads. They are readily available through foodservice, distributors, and retail stores. Coconut oil also works but isn't as readily available.

PALM SHORTENING

A mechanically processed palm oil, this ingredient functions in exactly the same manner as butter or hydrogenated shortenings but without the cholesterol or trans fats. Available in a 24-ounce tub.

VEGAN BUTTER SPREADS

Vegan Butter Spreads have a butter-like flavor. They work well in light sautéing but in high heat applications the flavors break down, ruining the flavor of the product. However, it is a superior vegan product for baking. Butter spreads can contain palm shortening, vegan dairy-style flavors, water, and/or soy and other ingredients. The sodium in vegan butter spreads is usually at 4 percent, the same as dairy butter. Again, read label for sodium information and current ingredient listing. Available in 15-ounce mini-tubs in retail and in larger cubes for foodservice or industrial food production.

Non-Dairy & Egg Substitutes

Cooking and baking vegetarian cuisine with dairy and eggs is relatively easy. Cooking and baking vegan without dairy and eggs can be a bit more challenging, especially if we don't know the ingredient substitutes and cooking techniques to apply them.

Some ingredients are ancient and some are modern inventions. Like eggs, the vegan substitutes can be used in both savory dishes and desserts. Earlier in this chapter the high-protein qualities of vital wheat gluten and flax meal were discussed. In some recipes these both also work as vegan egg replacement. Vegan cuisine uses a variety of egg replacement ingredients depending on the recipe application. No one item works in every recipe or cooking technique.

DAIRY SUBSTITUTES

Vegan dairy substitutes are available in the form of soy milk, coconut products, non-dairy cheeses including cream cheeses, sour cream, butter spreads, yogurt, ice creams, and whipped toppings. Options for most of these categories are in the recipe sections. Soy milk and butter spreads for cooking are the two that I did not try to replicate since these ingredients are readily available to either foodservice or the retail markets. Vegan dairy substitutes, brands, and specific items are presented in the resource section at the back of this book.

SOY MILK

As already discussed, the two basic soy milks for cooking are sweetened and unsweetened. Unsweetened is the one I recommend because it can be used in both savory and dessert items. Some sweetened soy milks will work in savory recipes. Generally speaking, vanilla sweetened soy milks could contain a lower quality bean with more flavor off-notes (strong unappealing soy-type flavors that have to be overridden). Sugar and vanilla added to unsweetened soy milk perform superbly in dessert or pastry recipes. But a neutral flavored soy milk is essential in savory recipes.

COCONUT MILK

Containing 22 percent fat, coconut milk is used as a milk or light cream in recipe applications. Coconut milk works well with ice cream recipes where additional fats and/or nuts are added to give the ice cream sufficient fat.

Ingredients: coconut milk, water, and guar gum (a stabilizer).

COCONUT CREAM

With a higher fat profile, coconut cream whips up well for whipping cream and ice cream without the addition of nuts. It contains 31 percent fat (½ cup contains 95 percent of the RDA for saturated fat).

Ingredients: 70 percent coconut extract with water.

NON-DAIRY CHEESES

Vegan dairy ingredients can be made to taste like cheese, but they don't *have* to taste like cheese. They do need to physically perform like cheese and bring a rich lubricity to the recipe and melt in the manner of cheese. I provide a recipe for American Melting Cheese (page 172) Just as different milks (such as goat milk) define the dairy cheese, different nuts define different vegan cheeses. Check out the recipes in the non-dairy section (starting on page 169).

There are many options in the retail market. New technology now enables a vegan cheese to melt under dry heat. Previously soy cheese needed casein to facilitate melting. Without casein these commercial cheeses can work well in casserole type dishes and to flavor sauces.

Ingredients: primarily starch and gums with flavors.

Non-dairy cream cheese alternative is as versatile as traditional cream cheese. I present several recipes for making non-dairy cream cheeses in your kitchen. Nut Cream Cheese (page 175) is an ideal substitute for traditional cream cheese on a bagel.

A few different brands are available through natural foods distributors. They can be purchased in both foodservice and retail packs.

Ingredients: water, palm fruit oil, soy oil, soy protein, agave syrup, salt, rice starch, lemon juice, natural flavors and xanthan gum.

Cashew Sour Cream (page 175) functions similarly to dairy-based sour cream. It also works well in recipes like Szekely Goulash (page 282) to create a savory cream sauce.

Whipped topping concentrates are available in a few different versions from foodservice distributors. One is natural and contains casein, which is not a vegan product. The second has a little hydrogenated (trans fat) shortening and is vegan. I haven't consumed trans fats, with rare exception, since 1977. If I am cooking for vegetarians, I prefer the natural version. If cooking for vegans, I use the vegan version. A vegan whipped soy topping is available from many natural foods stores. I offer a Coconut Whipped Cream Topping (page 345).

Butter spreads were covered in the oils and shortenings section. Current variations are: original butter spread, olive oil butter spread, and coconut butter spread. Only the original "butter spread" is currently available in foodservice pack sizes.

EGG SUBSTITUTES

The egg is a very dynamic ingredient in cooking. There will never be a universal ingredient to replace an egg because it is multifunctional. The egg contains two ingredients that can act as one or be separated to act as two unique ingredients. Egg whites are whipped into meringues or together for a chiffon cake. Egg yolks act as an emulsifier in hollandaise. Whole eggs are used in quiches and custards or to bind a meat loaf. In vegan cuisine, specific ingredients are used to replace eggs according to their specific functions. For instance, I use starch and agar to create the same custard effect created by an egg in a dessert. Or I combine vital gluten flour with white flour to create a binding ingredient for savory grain meat loaves. Tofu is used as an emulsifier in making mayonnaise. And these ingredients are all, generally speaking, dry egg replacements without oil (tofu is one exception). Therefore water and oil have to be adjusted into the formula. It is a complex formula that can be explained by studying the recipes.

A number of commercial egg replacement ingredients have been created for the food manufacturing sector. They are not available to the general public but could be eventually if a demand arises for them. In my kitchen I often use egg replacement powder, flax meal, and vital wheat gluten.

EGG REPLACEMENT POWDER

Egg replacement powder creates a gelling effect when hydrated and heated. Potato starch is one of its ingredients because it is a binder. But this powder doesn't aerate when whipped.

FLAX MEAL

Flax meal performs three functions as a binder, structure builder, and emulsifier in pastries and savory recipe applications.

VITAL WHEAT GLUTEN

Vital wheat gluten is primarily a structure builder in both savory and dessert applications. If an excessive amount is used in vegan proteins, seitan being the exception, the end product can become stringy.

MOCHI

A hard refrigerated paste, mochi when baked will puff up like *pâté choux*. I use this rice paste to make mini cream puffs (profiteroles).

Agar for Gelling

One type of gelling ingredient available to both foodservice and personal cooks has my approval: agar. Agar (also called agar agar) is derived from a red purple sea algae that was discovered by the Japanese several hundred years ago. In Japan it's called kanten; agar is a Malaysian term. Red bean paste from adzuki beans and agar make a popular Japanese dessert. Agar is the primary vegan gelling ingredient commonly available both in powder and flake form. I work exclusively with powder. Both the savory and pastry technique chapters will explain cooking and baking with agar. It isn't clear like gelatin and can have a slight flavor note that can be neutralized in the recipe by overpowering flavor profiles of other recipe ingredients. Fruit juices, sweeteners, and dessert flavors easily overcome the slight off-note. In savory recipes, the strong savory flavors easily override agar's flavor. It is also different from gelatin in that it will set at room temperature. It is an excellent gelling option to gelatin, an animal by-product.

Additional gelling ingredients in the marketplace claim to be vegan but are controversial and tests counter the manufacturers' claim. Until those claims are cleared, I am withholding my recommendation for the use of those ingredients. There should be no controversy around the authenticity of a vegan ingredient. Agar is sufficient as a vegan gelatin for now.

Sugars

For a vegan, sweetening a food can be complicated and desserts may require some extra thought. Even white sugar may not be a vegan product, honey is actually a by-product of a living creature, and different alternative sweeteners have different dextrose equivalents.

Is White Sugar Vegan?

Is white granulated sugar vegan? Well, not all white granulated sugars are vegan. Some are whitened through a refinement process using bone char from animals.

One of the first questions I'm asked when selling my company's bakery mixes to a foodservice operation looking for vegan bakery mixes is whether the sugar is bone char free. That is how I learned about the issue. When choosing a white granulated sugar, know your source and be sure the sugar is bone char free if you are a declared vegan since there is no physical way to distinguish between the two sugars.

- ○ Cane sugar has to use bone char to get the white color. It is expensive to use bone char.
- ○ Beet sugar processors do not use bone char. They don't need it to get the white color so why use it if you don't need it?

White granulated sugar and honey are the only two vegan sugar concerns. Using beet sugar and eliminating honey place your bakery item in the vegan category.

Say No to Honey

Honey is derived from a living insect (bee) and corporately harvested in a manner that can rip the hind legs off a bee. Because it is a by-product of a living insect, it cannot be considered vegan. But it is vegetarian, the equivalent of milk from cows.

Sucanat

Sucanat (Natural Sugar Cane) is a brand name for a variety of whole cane sugar that retains its molasses content. It is essentially pure dried sugar cane juice with a distinctive brown sugar color and flavor.

Dextrose Equivalent for Replacing Sugar

When using an alternative sweetener to replace sugar, there are two factors to consider. First is the dextrose equivalent (DE) to determine the equivalent amount of sweetener needed. There are many technical explanations but the simplest one is to use 100 as the value of glucose (sugar) on a dry basis, which is technically referred to as the "reducing power" of sugar. Each alternative sweetener may have a different equivalent (i.e., 70 DE is 70 percent of sugar).

Coconut Sugar

Coconut sugar is made from the sap of flower buds from the coconut palm tree, not from coconuts themselves. The sap is boiled over moderate heat to evaporate most of its water content.

I mention coconut sugar because it may become a popular alternative sweetener in Western cuisine. Coconut sugar is mildly sweet with a mild caramel flavor. Because it isn't highly processed, the color, sweetness, and flavor can vary depending on different factors from the coconut species used, the season it was harvested, and the way it was reduced. While the quality isn't consistent, the variance is subliminally different. It is primarily a sucrose syrup with a glycemic index of 35 and is used in all recipes on a 1-to-1 basis, coconut sugar to white granulated sugar. Coconut sugar is best used in place of brown, not white sugar, because it has a brown sugar/caramel flavor.

Agave Nectar

Produced from the agave plant, agave nectar or syrup can vary from 92 percent fructose and 8 percent glucose, depending on the vendor, plant, and processing variations. It is the perfect substitute for honey in vegan cuisine. Agave nectar is 1.4 to 1.6 times as sweet as sugar. That is 140 to 160 DE compared to 100 for sugar. The moisture content is 22.4 percent. If you are using agave nectar, adjust the amount by adding more to equal the sugar content and cut the water to equal the water in the agave. It dissolves quickly into hot or cold food items. In baking it can be used in place of a stock syrup.

Rice Syrup

Rice syrup is my favored syrup in vegan pastry development. It isn't very sweet, adding a delicate sweet backnote to whatever the application. Rice syrup has a dextrose equivalent (DE) of 26. Substitute rice syrup in place of sugar, honey, corn syrup, maple syrup, or molasses. To replace sugar, use 1 ¼ cup rice syrup for 1 cup sugar, and decrease another liquid in the recipe by ¼ cup. While rice syrup has a DE that is ¼ of sugar, because sugar is dry and syrup has a high water content, water (moisture) in the recipe would need to be removed to balance the syrup with the sugar.

ALTERNATIVE SWEETENERS

Vegan cuisine allows for a number of alternative sweeteners. In modifying traditional recipes, always check for the dextrose equivalent, and remember that some of these alternative sweeteners are quite sweet and others carry a more delicate sweetness.

MAPLE SYRUP

Maple syrup is popular in natural foods cooking and baking. With a distinctive maple flavor, it only works in recipes calling for a maple flavor. The "A" grades are lighter in color and flavor rendering them better for direct use on delicately flavored desserts, while the "B" grades, which are generally darker in color and stronger in flavor, are better for baking and cooking.

Photosynthesis creates carbohydrates in a maple tree, which are stored as starch. This starch is converted to sucrose (sugar), which mixes with groundwater to make sap. The sap is mostly crystal clear water with about 2 percent sugar. It takes forty gallons of sap to make each gallon of maple syrup with a sugar content of 66.9 percent (DE). In a recipe calling for ⅔ cup sugar, use 1 cup maple syrup and decrease water by ⅓ cup. Because there are maple flavored corn or high fructose corn syrups, verify that you are purchasing a 100 percent maple syrup.

BARLEY MALT SYRUP

This is a commercial syrup sold in natural foods stores. It is made from barley and has a DE structure similar to rice syrup (low) and is a very dark color. It has a strong malted flavor. It is good as a flavored syrup for specific recipe applications, and I would not recommend it for light colored and delicate flavored pastries because of its darker color and stronger flavor. If using, I would apply it to a recipe as I would rice syrup. As I mention throughout this book, each ingredient must have at least three applications to justify its existence in one's inventory, so any alternative sweetener must have multiple applications on one's menu. Barley malt syrup isn't as diverse as rice syrup. It is used primarily in desserts, especially macrobiotic desserts where white sugar is frowned upon, and is a superior finishing glaze for tortes like the Swiss Burnt Pecan Torte or a pie with a top crust. Diluting it with equal parts water and brushing it on a crust about 15 minutes before baking is complete will give the crust a beautiful shining glaze similar to egg wash.

MOLASSES

Molasses is used primarily as a flavoring ingredient and generally doesn't exceed 10 percent in a recipe. One tablespoon (20 grams) of molasses contains 58 calories, 15 grams of carbohydrates, and 15 grams of sugar. That is a DE of 55.5. As a flavoring agent the DE should not be a factor as the use is minimal and the DE is modest. I add molasses into white granulated sugar to make brown sugar. Add 5 percent molasses to 95 percent granulated sugar and mix until evenly dispersed.

Chapter Five

GENERAL SAVORY COOKING TECHNIQUES

This section is a basic overview of the classical cooking techniques

related to vegan ingredients and specific savory recipe applications. Vegan cuisine uses traditional and modified versions of classical cooking techniques, applying them to vegan ingredients, specifically to proteins and sauces. All cooking programs designed for professional cooks mandate that the culinary professional understand classical cooking techniques. A comprehensive study of classical and modern cooking techniques will also enrich the home cook.

Recipe, ingredients, and technique are the foundation of superior cuisine. The chef or home cook brings together these three elements to create incredible dishes and a unique dining experience, whether in the home or in a restaurant setting. Technique is the final and determining factor in creating memorable cuisine and bringing pleasure to the plate. Good technique develops and showcases ingredient characteristics and flavors while marrying the ingredients into a memorable recipe that is the fusion of technique and ingredients. Any protein can be ruined with poor cooking technique or the wrong sauce, and a poor quality protein can be improved with sound culinary technique and the appropriate sauce. Escoffier said the only reason a protein is covered with a sauce is to cover a mistake. This holds true with vegan cuisine. Vegan proteins should be presented in the same manner as animal proteins. From a presentation perspective, I agree that a protein not cooked in a sauce should not be drenched in sauce when plated.

A note on flavoring: There is one simple rule to seasoning a food: *Less is more.* The flavors and cooking techniques can add and enhance flavor. There are exceptions in vegan proteins where the protein becomes the flavor carrier. Tofu is a good example. It is bland and flavorless and takes on the flavors of the other ingredients used in the recipe. Tofu is a flavor vacuum protein and Pâté Français on page 254 is a good example of using a flavoring system to override the ingredient.

It is easy to overseason, leaving the diner with a confused palate and wondering what was tasted. Sugar and salt are used often in place of sound cooking techniques to give the food a cheap flavor shot in place of developing the flavor through the cooking process and complementary seasonings. Salt, used minimally, will bring out the flavor in a recipe. And the sauté method can be used on low heat to develop the sugars in onions, carrots, and starch vegetables with caramelization. Caramelization equals flavor. A red pepper can be grilled to create the grilled/caramelization effect or slow roasted in the oven to develop the sugars. The recipe application determines the technique.

Cooking Proteins & Vegetables

The techniques for vegan cuisine will work with all recipes. Some techniques are modified, and a few I created over years of experimentation.

BROILING

Broiling is using direct heat under the food item as in a grill or over the food item as in an oven. It is generally high heat and a relatively fast cooking process used to brown animal proteins and caramelize vegetable sauces or gratin topping.

In vegan and vegetarian cooking, broiling is generally used to brown a protein food item and to finish off the cooking process, not cook the protein. A vegan quiche, casserole, or frittata is placed under the broiler to give the entrée additional color if it is insufficiently browned after baking. Exceptions are raw vegan protein analogues and vegetables. Instead of broiling, I often sauté (or brown) the vegan protein and cover to cook pot roast-style for a vegan protein that requires prolonged cooking. This technique is to maintain the protein's moisture.

I use the term "browning" protein because caramelization occurs only with carbohydrates and sugars. The Maillard reaction, first described by French chemist Louis-Camille Maillard, is a culinary phenomenon similar to caramelization but instead occurs only in sugars and proteins (a chemical reaction between amino acids and reducing sugars) that are heated to temperatures of 310°F or higher, causing them to turn brown. Broiling and grilling will both activate the chemical reaction in food.

CARAMELIZATION

Caramelization is a culinary phenomenon that occurs when carbohydrates like sugar are heated to temperatures of 300°F or higher, causing the food medium to turn brown.

Caramelization equals flavor, and the technique is liberally and successfully used in vegetarian cuisine to develop flavors in all foods and particularly vegetables, grains, brown sauces, and bakery products. Proteins don't caramelize, they brown, taking on the Maillard effect.

There is a distinction made between the Maillard and caramelization effects in chemistry terms, but in flavor I don't taste a difference between a caramelized or maillardized food.

CONFIT FOR VEGETABLES & FRUIT

An ancient form of preserving food, confit is the process of slow cooking in oil (generally fat of the animal for meat recipes and vegetable and nut oils for vegan cuisine) to preserve the food by cooking out most of the moisture. Temperatures range from 175° to 225°F., and the food is cooked for extended periods of time. In this slow cooking on low heat, the food medium is covered with oil and cooked until the oil stops emitting bubbles, a sign that most, if not all, of the moisture is cooked out of the food. In early days before refrigeration, the food was then left covered in the cooking oil to preserve it and stored in a cellar/basement. With the invention of refrigeration, the confit technique lost its edge as a preservation technique.

While confit foods don't have to be refrigerated, I recommend it regardless of the food medium. For oil, it is best to use a high-heat oil such as canola or safflower to assure it does not break down during cooking or later when used in a recipe as an infused oil.

The confit technique creates infused oils when an herb, like fresh basil, is blended into an oil and left for 8 hours or more to be absorbed into the oil. Or a vegetable like garlic can be slow cooked or infused into an oil to make a confit.

While some culinarians believe that confit is a term and technique related only to duck, I believe this technique is not restricted to any one food. I use the term extensively with vegetables. But the technique also works using a simple syrup with fruits. Recently I experimented by mixing sugar with fresh peaches in a sauté pan and slow-cooked the peaches into a confit. No moisture was used.

Proteins excluded, the confit technique has many applications with vegan cuisine in vegetable and fruit applications. Its primary applications include:

- ♻ Preserving firm flesh vegetables in oil (such as carrots, garlic, onions).

- ♻ Creating a confit of fruit by using a simple syrup to cook firm flesh fruits.

- ♻ Slow sautéing inclusions to bleed out most of the moisture to prevent a steam out in the protein. Inclusions are ingredients such as diced carrots, garlic cloves, and bell pepper that are cooked into a confit, drained of oil, and added to a grain or meat analogue loaf.

- ♻ By cooking moisture out of the food item (inclusion) before adding to the protein, the inclusion will stick to the protein when sliced into portions. If it isn't cooked into a confit, it will steam out in the cooking process.

CONFIT INFUSED OILS

The by-product of confit of vegetables is flavor-infused oil. Oil will take on the flavor of the ingredient being cooked. Slow cooking, as in confit, significantly infuses flavor into the oil. For example, oil from confit of garlic, when used in a recipe, may replace the need for additional garlic because the oil has sufficient flavor. Infused oils render themselves to seasoning for use as plate garnishes, marinades, or salad dressings and mayonnaise. Recipe development is an open door to your culinary genius.

SAVORY & SWEET INCLUSIONS

A good example of inclusions in savory cooking is using a confit of vegetable in a meat analogue or tofu pâté. Inclusions are ingredients (savory or sweet) added to a food medium for numerous reasons (flavor, texture, color, and nutrition). A savory inclusion would be confit of garlic, pistachio nut, or a pitted Kalamata olive added to an Italian tofu loaf made with a tofu pâté base. For example, on the dessert side an inclusion would be chocolate chips and walnuts added to a cookie dough to make a chocolate chip cookie.

POT ROASTING

Pot roasting is a technique to caramelize starchy root vegetables and vegan proteins. It is the easiest way to impart the roasted caramelized flavor into a food item without drying it out in the oven. With rare exceptions, this is the technique you want to use in cooking vegan proteins because they are generally less moist than meats.

In this technique the food medium is oiled, seasoned, and caramelized at high heat on the top of the stove or under the broiler, then covered and pot roasted in the oven on a lower heat. This caramelizes the food up front and allows it to develop its flavors in the slow oven.

Pot roasting is my preferred means of roasting root vegetables because it develops a delicate vegetable flavor, light caramelization, and mild sweetness. No water is needed. Root vegetables have sufficient moisture, which flashes off in the cooking process to create steam in the covered pot and aid in the cooking.

Any vegetable composed of a solid mass can be roasted in dry heat, but I don't recommend it. Tossed with oil and seasoning and put straight into the oven at high heat, vegetables will eventually develop some caramelization, but it is a lot harder to get the caramelization without dehydrating the vegetables and the caramelization will not be as intense. The vegetables will dry out and the sweetness will not be as pronounced.

The technique for roasting vegan meat analogues or the ancient proteins is different from roasting meats for a number of reasons. Vegan proteins generally have no or significantly less fat in them. Analogues will reabsorb moisture if overcooked in dry heat, and they are very forgiving of abuse in the cooking process. Meats are irreparable if overcooked.

- ↻ Pot roasting is the technique that works best with vegetarian proteins because they have little or no oil and are a dry protein compared to animal proteins.

- ↻ Extruded frozen analogues (seitan, chicken, seafood-style proteins) are pre-cooked and pre-cut. With the exception of items like seitan roast or chicken-style breast, they cannot be roasted because they are in cubes or strips of protein weighing about one half to one ounce each.

○ Breast and roast of vegan chicken or seitan can be browned in a roasting pan with the recipe ingredients and pot roasted with moist heat. These proteins need only enough roast time to develop the recipe's flavors. Both breast and roast come in commercial products and can be made from scratch or speed scratch (from dry mixes). Vegan breasts are generally three to four ounces and vegan roasts range from eight ounces up to two pounds.

○ Cooking time is relative to the protein's size.

○ The same principles apply to working with tempeh and tofu.

○ There are two types of dry proteins. One is the extruded cutlets and strips, etc., and the second is the powdered protein (mixes). The extruded and dried version, especially the cutlets, are like soggy bread dough (I do not recommend). The TVPs (textured vegetable proteins) are different—available in particle size pieces, not a portion of dry meat, and used in meat analogues and recipes to offer protein and texture. Like Tofu, TVP doesn't have flavor and is plain protein, flexible enough to be used in any recipe application.

○ Dry powdered protein mixes are quite different and will create a modest challenge to one's cooking skills.

   ○ The cook can control the amount of oil added to the protein ranging from 5 percent to 15 percent or more to simulate the texture of meat.

      ◊ After mixing and seasoning, ground beef and sausage-style proteins must reach 170°F to set the protein and sanitize the meat. Vegan proteins are subject to cross contamination from the same contaminates that threaten all foods.

      ◊ *Instant marinating* Dry protein blends have an advantage—they can be custom flavor infused. The flavor seasoning is mixed into water and then added to the protein. This eliminates the marinating step.

      ◊ *Inclusions* Adding inclusions, specifically whole grains, is another unique advantage. Whole grains give a dry blended meat analogue additional color, texture, flavor and nutrition.

○ To roast a vegan protein, oil the roasting pan. Place the formed meat analogue as a loaf or desired shape in the pan. Lightly coat with oil. Place the protein in the pan under the broiler until lightly browned. Cover and pot roast until the recipe is developed. That should take about an hour but is relative to the recipe.

○ After a dry protein mix product is finished cooking, it is best to let the protein sit for about 30 minutes to allow the protein to "set" or firm up as it cools down. If it becomes too cool simply reheat in a sauté pan, steam, or microwave.

PRESSURE COOKING

Pressure cooking is a cooking technique in which a reinforced pot constructed of steel or aluminum is used to cook a variety of foods quickly in pressurized moist heat above the boiling point. Cooking time is dependent on the food ingredient or recipe and is generally half that of regular cooking. Crucial to successfully cooking with a pressure cooker is getting the timing correct. Modern pressure cookers have safety values that will relieve excess pressure if the heat is too high. Once the pressure cooker comes up to pressure, the indicator on top of the cooker will rise halfway on the pressure gauge (about two notches up the gauge). Reduce heat to low to keep pressure consistent for the duration of the prescribed time. Take off the heat and let it cool down naturally. If cooking a vegetable, put the cooker under cold water to release the pressure and stop the cooking immediately lest the vegetables overcook.

Pressure cooking is traditionally used to cook grains and dry beans. It is also a fast way to cook squash or hard vegetables. With vegetables it is the equivalent of pressure steaming. It is a quick process with vegetables taking 10 to 15 minutes to cook.

For example, to pressure cook butternut squash:

1. Peel and slice butternut squash 1 inch thick. (The skin can be tough and the thickness of the squash has to do with cook time. If cut too thin and pressure cooked, the squash will be mush. If cut too thick and pressure cooked for the same time, the squash will be raw.)

2. Place in pressure cooker with ¼ inch water, sprinkle with salt, and bring up to pressure.

3. Pressure cook for 8 to 9 minutes and immediately release pressure as described above (so as to not overcook the squash). The release of pressure cools the chamber causing the steam (pressure) to condense.

SAUTÉING

The literal translation means "to jump," as to jump in the pan. Sautéing allows the cook to quickly fry foods in a little fat in an open skillet over medium-high to high heat, turning or tossing often, until tender and lightly browned, as dictated by the recipe. Sautéing also pulls the flavor out of the food medium and allows it to develop slowly using a low to medium heat. I use it to develop the sweetness in starchy vegetables. Slow cooking in any form is the key to developing the flavor/sweetness. Onions are a good example. The cook can start out caramelizing the vegetable and turn down the heat, reverting to a sauté method which will develop the sweetness. I also sauté with high heat for a very brief period (one to two minutes) to brown the vegan pre-cooked proteins.

Vegan butter spreads must be drawn to work in the sauté method. These vegan butters are often expensive so I use them only when the flavor is essential. They work best as emulsions in sauces or in slow sautés where the solids will not burn. Instead of a vegan butter spread, I use high-heat refined oils for sautéing and frying.

SAUTÉ/STEAM

Sauté/steam is a unique method of first sautéing the vegetable or protein with a little oil and salt on medium to high heat for about 3 to 5 minutes while stirring to bring out the food's flavor. Add water, cover, and steam for about 3 to 5 minutes. For about 2 cups of vegetable, add ¼ cup water. This method combines two basic cooking methods to develop the flavor in a nutrient-dense manner.

VEGAN PROTEIN GRILLING

Pre-cooked refrigerated or frozen vegan proteins (burgers, sausage, seitan, etc.) should be brushed with oil and grilled on direct heat until the temperature of the protein reaches 165°F. The burgers should have grill marks and develop a grilled flavor. On the grill the heat is usually on the left side for cooking and on the right side a lower heat for holding or slow-cooking proteins.

To barbecue vegan proteins on a grill is a two-step process. Brush proteins with oil, briefly grill (1 to 2 minutes on each side) on high heat on both sides to create grill marks and flavor. Next generously brush protein with barbecue sauce on both sides. Brush oil onto the lower heat side of the grill, place protein on indirect heat, and brush the top with barbecue sauce. If you have a grill cover, close it and give the protein 5 minutes or until they reach an internal temperature of 165°F. Open, brush again with sauce and serve.

Because vegan proteins generally do not contain a great deal of oil or moisture, they cannot be slow grilled or barbecued on dry heat as this will cause them to dry out. If a vegan protein dries out on the grill, make a solution of half water and half barbecue sauce in a shallow pan and place the proteins in the solution. Set the pan on the grill, bring sauce to a simmer and move to indirect heat. In about 15 minutes the protein will fully rehydrate. Vegan proteins, unlike meat, are salvageable. To barbecue a protein, brush protein with oil, briefly grill on high heat on both sides. Oil the pan and pour a thin layer of BBQ sauce into the pan. Place proteins in the pan, brush with BBQ sauce and a few tablespoons water. Cover and pot roast for about 1 hour in a 325°F preheated oven. This will give the protein a grilled flavor and develop the barbecued flavor in a moist cooking environment.

SMOKING TECHNIQUES

Smoking is a superb flavoring and/or cooking technique that gives a robust flavor to vegan protein where the flavor enhancer (fat) is missing. Smoking adds a tremendous flavor punch to soy marinated tofu, tempeh, or seitan ingredients, giving these protein mediums the simulated flavor of smoked animal protein.

While animal protein often only needs a little salt for the omnivore diner, smoking takes vegan protein to another level of interest, giving it a stronger position in traditional cuisine. With the focus on consuming healthy low-fat menu items, the smoker is an ideal flavor enhancer. Coupled with the caramelization technique, smoking allows for a delicious robust flavor profile to emerge.

In this section I offer a variety of smoking techniques and smoking equipment options. Since vegan proteins are, with a few exceptions, generally precooked, the smoking technique creates the intensity of flavor desired. I have successfully smoked tofu, tempeh, nuts, seitan, black beans, and the chicken-style analogues. Liquid smoked flavor or smoked yeast are alternatives to smoking, but I prefer the authentic smoked flavor. But if you just can't smoke a protein, the smoked yeast is the better of the two options. I do use liquid smoke in a number of vegetable and sauce recipes or when smoked yeast isn't available.

As in all cooking and flavoring techniques, smoking time, smoking heat, and the right wood chip are crucial to a successful smoked item.

Cold Smoking is the quick method with vegan proteins in which the food is smoked at a cooler temperature so as not to cook the food ingredient. It is the preferred method for vegan proteins because they are generally pre-cooked and don't have significant moisture or fat to hold their texture. The key in cold smoking is keeping the heat away from the food product to prevent the food item from cooking. Cold smoking is using enough heat to cause the chips to burn/smoke, generally at the bottom of the smoke chamber. The smoking chamber is cold and the food product is well above the heat and consumed by smoke.

Dry Smoking is the cold smoking method using no water to wet the chips or smoke steam the food.

Hot Smoking or *Cook Smoking* is a method in which the food medium is smoked and cooked at the same time. The length of time is generally longer than either alone. Because plant proteins are generally pre-cooked, this method isn't necessary. It can be used to give food an intense smoke flavor and to preserve the protein. Where plant proteins generally last a few weeks in refrigeration, they can last up to 6 to 8 weeks using a hot smoke. The protein has to be sufficiently smoked and dried to succeed.

Wet Smoke uses the hot smoking technique. Chips are spread in a smoke pan. The tray is placed in the smoke pan and hot water lightly sprinkled into the tray; place the rack in the tray and the food on the rack. For beans, use a fine steel mesh on the rack.

Indirect Smoking can cook and/or smoke the protein. The smoke is created in a separate area of the smoker and circulated into and out of the cooking or smoking chamber. The smoke is generated independent from the smoking chamber.

Direct Smoking is generally a cold smoking technique but it can also be used to cook the protein. The chamber temperature is controlled. Unlike indirect smoking where the smoke is circulated, the source of the smoke sits directly under the food, which is smoked with direct heat.

SMOKING TEMPERATURES TO COOK FOOD

- ↻   180°F is slow and low

- ↻   180–220°F is good for BBQ

- ↻   Medium low is 250°F; it's called the "gold smoke" because it gives the food a golden color.

NOTE: Higher temperatures than 250°F are not recommended because this would cause the food to be cooked before it is fully smoked.

SMOKING CHIPS

Big chips take more heat to smoke and the heat must remain high to continue smoking. Smaller smoking chips don't require the same amount of time or high heat and will smoke and burn sooner. When smoking a food, if a black smoke appears the chips are impure and may leave a bitter flavor on smoked foods. If the smoke is black, it is recommended that food not be placed in the smoking chamber. When white smoke starts to emerge, it is time to place food in the chamber.

You can change the flavor of your smoked foods with chips made of different woods. It is important to use only commercially purchased chips. Some woods are toxic when smoked making it dangerous to select chips from the wild.

- ↻   *ALDER* Very delicate with a hint of sweetness. Good with tofu, tempeh, beans, and any mild-flavored vegan proteins.

- ↻   *APPLE* Very mild with a subtle fruity flavor, slightly sweet. Good with seitan and tempeh.

- ↻   *CHERRY* Mild and fruity. Good with tofu, tempeh, seitan, and intensely flavored proteins. If the cherry wood comes from choke cherry trees, the chips may produce a bitter flavor.

○ *HICKORY* Most commonly used wood for smoking—the king of smoking woods. Sweet to strong, imparts a heavy bacon flavor. Good with seitan, tofu, and chicken analogues. This is my preferred wood.

○ *MAPLE* Smoky, mellow, and slightly sweet. Good with vegan cheeses, tofu, tempeh, and nuts.

○ *MESQUITE* Strong earthy flavor. Good with seitan, meat analogues, and beans. It is one of the hottest burning woods, which makes it a good choice for hot smoking.

○ *OAK* has a heavy smoke flavor making it good for seitan and intensely flavored vegan proteins like vegan ground beef and beans. It has a long smoking time.

STOVETOP SMOKING

If you would like to engage in smoking foods in your own kitchen, a stovetop smoker in the Appendix B (page 398) to help you get started. As for equipment, there are both foodservice and retail equipment options.

SMOKING BEANS

I smoke beans using a stovetop smoker. Use the directions. Note that I prefer to use the wet smoking method.

I also smoke portabella mushrooms, tomatoes, and potatoes. Many foods can be smoked. Please see "Smoked Protein & Produce" section on page 314 for more ideas.

Egg Replacement Formulas/Techniques for Savory Foods

In vegan cuisine there is no one universal egg replacement system. One irony in many of the vegan egg replacers is that they don't contain, in general, any significant amount of protein essential to bind and give the food a pleasing texture. The major challenge, especially with vegan proteins, is sufficient texture to create a firm bite. The vegan entrée should have the pleasing texture of firm meat loaf, not one of baby food.

The egg replacers used to bind vegan proteins are:

○ 50 percent vital gluten flour and 50 percent unbleached white flour. This combination creates a high-protein binder. Using straight vital gluten protein would create a stringy protein bind in a savory recipe. Vital gluten needs to be softened to work in recipes like grain loaves, burgers, etc.

○ For vegan custards and quiches, I generally use a combination of a cornstarch or arrowroot starch and agar powder to create the custard gelling effect. This creates a similar gelling effect of the egg in a custard. The ratio is about 4 parts cornstarch to 1 part agar powder. The recipes in this book use both the agar powder and agar flakes in specific recipe applications.

○ Starches ranging from potato to arrowroot are common binding ingredients. Kudzu, a root powder, is a more popular starch used in macrobiotic cooking. Any of these starches work as egg replacers in combination with agar to give the gelling effect of an egg yolk in recipes to create a custard or quiche. Any non-pre-gelatinized starch will work in combination with agar to create a custard effect.

○ Flax meal is an option to using starch/agar in a quiche, custard, or meat loaf–style product. If using with a starch, I would use approximately 75 percent starch and 25 percent fine ground flax meal. Flax meal has a strong gelling effect similar to agar.

When making a savory entrée using grains, the grains must be cooked dry and minimal water added to activate the starch and agar or flax meal to activate the egg replacement system.

○ If a vegan grain, nut, seed, and vegetable combination doesn't have sufficient water to activate the egg replacement protein, the protein will not bind. Water is necessary to activate the vegan gelling ingredients.

○ In quiches where moisture is the key to activating the egg replacer to set or gelatinize the quiche, lack of moisture will cause the texture to become tight and rubbery. A vegan quiche should have a wet, savory lubricity with a firm mouthfeel as in a standard quiche.

VEGAN BREADING TECHNIQUE

The egg replacement for eggless breading is pure vital gluten flour. The second option is a combination of 50 percent vital gluten flour and 50 percent unbleached white flour. The third option is the use of unbleached white flour. Vital gluten flour has a strong binding quality and is the number-one preferred method. It will hold breading in place similarly to eggs and can take a lot of abuse while holding the breading to the food medium. The only tool needed aside from the traditional cooking tools is a spray bottle full of water.

1. Dip food medium in water, quickly removing it.

2. Dip food medium in flour medium of choice.

3. Spritz food item with water to activate the binding qualities of the protein or quickly dip into the water.

4. Drench in finely ground bread crumbs or flour and lightly press the crumbs. The moist

flour acts like an egg causing crumbs to bind to the protein.

OPTION: Season breading (crumbs or flour) to enhance the flavor of the proteins or vegetables. Choose ethnic seasoning blends or specific dry herbs, spices, or vegan broth powders. Initially the medium being breaded has to be wet to activate the flour's protein.

The one exception is breading a raw protein analogue prepared from a dry mix vegan meat analogue. The protein need only be moist to activate the breading.

Techniques for Non-Dairy Products

Vegetable spreads can be used for light sautés with medium heat but are not preferred for high heat (burner turned to maximum heat). Unlike dairy butter where the milk solids burn to create a different but pleasant taste, vegan butter spreads have flavors and gelling ingredients that are not designed for high heat, may emit a burnt smell and will definitely ruin the flavor. They are designed for moderate short-term heat. These butter spreads substitute well for a vegan mounted butter added to a hot sauce or puddings. They also work well in bakery goods.

VEGAN COMPOUND BUTTER-STYLE SPREADS

Vegan compound butter-style spreads are condiments meant to be used on breads and sandwiches and in appetizer applications. They are stabilized emulsions like hummus and generally made in a food processor. However, butter-type spreads can be as high as 50 percent oil, which distinguishes them from a hummus spread, which is around 25 percent or less oil.

- ○ Compound vegan butters are primarily vegetable solids, fat, and a flavoring system with sufficient moisture to bind the ingredients together.

- ○ The technique is simple. Ingredients such as onions, squash, bell peppers, and eggplant may be sautéed and caramelized before going into the blender and puréed until smooth.

- ○ A butter-style spread or palm shortening are oil options if the desired spread is to function like a compound butter such as Squash Butter (page 176) or Greek Potato Butter (page 177). If using a commercial vegan spread, melt it and add to vegetables in food processor. Adjust water after adding the spread. Spreads may have a higher percentage of water, eliminating the need for additional water.

- ○ When you need butters and spreads for cold applications, for use as a spread on bread, or for sandwiches, Greek Potato Butter and Squash Butter perform and spread like butter when made with saturated fats.

○ Because pure olive oil will set in the refrigerator, it is the preferred healthier option. Some vegan butter spreads use olive oil in the formula.

○ Confit of vegetable and infused oils make exceptional compound butters. The infused oil can be a saturated palm shortening.

VEGAN CHEESES AND YOGURT

Neither the foodservice professional nor the home cook have to rely on commercial vegan dairy-style products to develop their vegan menus. When vegan cheese options are not available through the distribution center or local stores, if they are cost prohibitive, or if you want to use your creative skills, these in-house produced options are a good alternative.

In vegan cuisine the objective isn't to mimic any specific cheese. It is to bring the qualities of cheese (mouthfeel, lubricity, and savory notes) into the recipe. In conventional cooking the cheese often carries the recipe as the dominant flavor. The vegan cheese product is added to support the culinary objective in the recipe with its unique flavor. Vegan cheeses made from nuts have a higher nutritional density and are healthier. Their unique flavor adds a different cheese-like flavor. Several techniques are used in making vegan dairy-style products:

○ To make a yogurt-style product, heat soy milk and add a mixture of starch and water or white wash to thicken it. Once thickened, add vinegar, lemon juice, or other acidifying agent to make the stabilized soy milk form a curd. Ideally the curd should set about 8 hours or overnight. The product will have a yogurt texture and slight acidic/sour taste associated with yogurt but without the strong dairy notes. (See Soy Yogurt on page 172.)

○ If making the yogurt for a pastry dessert, you can use a sweetened soy milk or add sugar to a nonsweetened soy milk.

○ When making cream cheese-style products, I blend cashew nuts and water until smooth (no grit in the mixture when rubbed between your fingers) and creamy. (See Nut Cream Cheese on page 174.)

   ◌ When the texture is smooth, add the acidifying agent (lemon juice or vinegar) and blend to thoroughly mix. For a milder acidic flavor use rice vinegar.

   ◌ Nutritional yeast is a flavoring option to give the mixture a subtle cheese note. It will also fortify it; nutritional yeast is high in many vitamins and minerals, especially in B-12.

   ◌ Vegan cream cheese recipes use about twice as much water as traditional cream cheese to blend nuts into a heavy cream. The nuts draw moisture and may continue drawing moisture from the liquid in the recipe until the nuts have reached their maximum absorption capacity. Should the texture be too stiff, add very small amounts of water incrementally to make a softer texture.

○ Do not use silken tofu to make yogurt as it will not work with the curdling process. Silken tofu can be used for a cheese-style product by adding a dash of lemon juice with the option of nutritional yeast.

○ As in traditional cheeses, herbs and spices can create a unique or ethnic flavor profile.

○ To give an innovative Parmesan cheese-like flavor to pasta, coarsely grind toasted pine nuts and add a touch of salt and nutritional yeast.

○ Some casein-free cheeses melt and some do not. If the cheese doesn't melt under dry heat, use moist heat or place it in direct heat and cover it to let the moisture in the recipe steam-melt the cheese. For a vegan melting cheese, see American Melting Cheese (page 172). Also see vegan cheese brands in the ingredient and resource section.

Techniques for Plant-Based Sauces

Both classical and modern sauce techniques have a place in twenty-first century cuisine. In this book the intention is to give modern and classical sauces a vegetarian overhaul. Modern sauces are generally an interpretation of classical French or ethnic sauces that evolved over time. The traditional technique for producing mother sauces is replaced with efficient production techniques and new innovative applications. One unique technique that stands out is the use of the vegan mother sauces to deglaze vegan protein entrées that are sautéed to order. Using the ancient and modern vegetarian broth powders and concentrates will define the quality of your cuisine. The commercial flavor systems are meant as platforms to build your sauce program, not to be the program, for both the commercial chef and the home cook.

Many vegan and specialty seasonings such as vegan meat-style broths, miso, and Old Bay Spice are generally high in sodium. When seasoning a food, use the specialty seasonings first, and if that isn't sufficient, then adjust with salt because specialty seasonings may be high in sodium. Salt's primary role is to bring out flavor in a recipe, not to be the predominate flavor. This principle applies to all food preparation.

Sodium's flavor disperses instantly, without heat, when mixed into a recipe. Many vegan meat-style broth powders have reduced their sodium and are superb ingredients in developing meat-style flavors.

VEGETABLES TO DEVELOP FLAVOR

Caramelizing, sautéing, and roasting vegetables are the primary techniques, as in classical and traditional cooking, to develop the flavors. This is a quicker process than the traditional stock, which depends on extracting flavor the slow way from animal bones, especially beef bones.

- ○ For sauces based on vegetable stocks, medium sautéing the vegetables for light sauces (Velouté) or caramelizing for darker sauces (Espagnole-style) is the preferred method of creating the stock.

- ○ Lightly caramelizing the vegetables and finishing them off in the oven—pot roasting—is the preferred method for vegetable puree-style sauces such as the Sauce Renaissance (page 227) where the vegetable solids become the roux.

- ○ For brown sauces, give vegetables a strong caramelization and add the spices and herbs toward the end of the caramelization process.

VEGAN STOCKS

Mirepoix stocks are often prepared by adding for flavoring a mirepoix (meer-pwa), which is a combination of approximately 50 percent onions, 25 percent carrots, and 25 percent celery by weight. Since vegetables are one of the strengths of vegetarian cuisine, I open mirepoix up to vegetables that will complement the recipe. The traditional approach is to boil the vegetables to death to extract all flavor and nutrients that are heat stable, strain the stock, and then discard the vegetables. Basil, thyme, garlic, parsley, salt, bay leaves, and pepper are generally used. The vegan approach: If making a chicken-style stock, add a vegan chicken-style broth powder, and a beef-style broth powder if making a beef-style stock, to the stock after straining. If making a seafood-style stock, I prefer using wakame very loosely tied in cheesecloth for later use in the sea vegetable sauce. Two tablespoons per quart of water is a good starting point. More or less can be added based on desired flavor.

High quality vegan meat-style broth powders are the equivalent of making a concentrated meat stock from bones. The only difference is these stocks are instant with no cooking time required, and they are higher in sodium because they are made with reactive or autolyzed flavor concentrates. My recommendation is to use them as flavor platforms on which to build flavors through the use of whole foods and cooking techniques.

These stocks become the foundation of developing soups using the traditional recipes. Cooking time for the soup, depending on the recipe, uses a one-step approach: to sauté the vegetables and seasonings, adding water to make the stock. The sauté step releases the vegetables' flavor quickly without overcooking, essential in making a vegan soup with the integrity of the vegetables intact.

Consommé is a clear soup slow cooked in either the traditional or vegan approach. In the traditional approach an egg float is created and room-temperature-to-cold stock added to the float (mixture of meat, eggs, seasoning, and vegetables). The float sinks to the bottom of the broth and slowly rises as the stock temperature rises. The stock should cook at a very low temperature for several hours. With vegan stocks, the key is to sauté vegetables and seasonings in oil, add stock or water, and slowly cook so as to not cause the stock to become cloudy.

Roux & Other Thickeners

The history of roux (pronounced "roo"), the major thickening agent in sauces and soups, goes back about three hundred years in French cuisine. It is traditionally cooked using pure oils, animal fats, or clarified butter. There are four types of roux: white for white sauces, blond for Velouté-type sauces, brown for brown sauces, and dark roux for Cajun cuisine and specific recipes calling for a dark roasted flavor. As a traditional thickening agent in the classical mother sauces, the vegan roux has one major difference: no animal fat is used. Vegan roux functions in the same manner as an animal fat–based roux. In traditional roux the animal fat adds flavor. In vegan cuisine, I build a stronger stock with the flavor concentrates, miso, or reactive meat-style flavors from the vegan broth powder, achieving the same result. Traditional roux ratios apply to vegan sauces. Roux ratio is 8 ounces flour and 8 ounces oil to make 1 pound of roux, and 1 pound of roux thickens 1 gallon of stock to create the sauce.

In classical preparation, a roux is first cooked or baked. Cooking is the simplest technique. Bring roux to a bubbly simmer while stirring the flour and oil and simmer for 5 minutes. Whether you want a blonde (light brown), brown, or dark brown roux, increase the heat while constantly stirring until you can smell a light roasted flour scent. Cook to a desired darkness. Cooked roux thickens sauces quicker than raw (uncooked flour and oil). I use a raw roux in white sauces and in dark sauces where the roux's flavor isn't a factor. The cooking time in the recipe application is about the same in both raw (when adding the roux to the recipe instead of making it) and cooked roux with flavor being the only difference.

I don't use roux very often in vegan cuisine because I make the Espagnole and Velouté sauces using the modern stock to sauce technique where the roux is prepared in the sauté step of the sauce. The Béchamel sauce is the one exception. Gravy is prepared by adding flour to the remaining oil in a pan used to sauté a protein, making a roux to which water or stock is added. It is the exact method used in the modern sauce technique.

White Wash is a slurry of flour and water that produces a very dull, matte finish and diminishes flavor due to no oil. That can be overcome with the addition of a cold vegan butter spread or oil, which will emulsify into the sauce. I use white wash primarily to reduce fat, and if I want to use an oil, I can significantly reduce the amount and/or use a flavor concentrated oil (infused oil or butter spread).

Beurre Manié traditionally consists of equal parts butter and flour blended together cold and added at the end to finish a sauce. For vegan cuisine, use the same ratio as in a roux (50 percent vegan butter spread or shortening and 50 percent flour) that complements the sauce.

Vegan Liaison, a thickening agent, is traditionally a mixture of cream and egg yolks to thicken liquids. Popular in certain high-end restaurants, this mixture must be added at the end of the cooking process and whisked or sheared. Once added, the sauce must not boil or simmer, or you'll end up with scrambled eggs. Cream and yolks give a very silky texture and rich profile and mouthfeel. The vegan version is a smooth viscous cashew cream, which will add more body and sheen to the sauce. The cashew cream can be cut half and half with a vegan butter spread for more lubricity.

Monter au Beurre (Mounted Butter) is made with cold butter whipped into a sauce to give it a rich texture and flavor. This technique works with vegan butter spreads.

DEMI-GLACE

Demi-glace literally translated, "half glaze," is a rich, brown sauce generally made with one part Espagnole sauce and one part veal stock cooked down to the desired consistency of the sauce. For example, one quart of brown sauce and one quart of veal or meat stock is reduced (cooked down) to one quart of demi-glace with the consistency of light syrup. A meat stock that is reduced will thicken because of its collagen or gelatin. Demi-glace is also considered one of the "small sauces" created from the mother sauces. The term comes from the French word *glace*, which, used in reference to a sauce, means "icing" or "glaze." The term *demi-glace* by itself implies that it is made with the traditional veal stock but is often made from beef stock. If making a demi-glace concentrate, a reduced sodium base or miso must be used or the demi-glace will be too salty.

In the following recipes I am using the quick vegan method to make the demi-glace, combining the mother sauces with a demi-glace base (concentrate). This is the vegan version and a quick modern method.

Quick Beef-Style Demi-Glace (Demi-Glace au Boeuf)

In classical cuisine the stock had to be prepared and reduced into the Espagnole sauce. Today, with flavor concentrates, especially with vegan cuisine, a customized concentrate (Demi-Glace Base below) can be added directly into the sauce. That works but is a compromise in technique and flavor. The ideal technique is cutting the water in half, adding a full measure of the base equal to 2 cups broth. This cuts cook time in half but it gives enough cook time to allow the flavors to develop. The important factor is to use at least a reduced sodium concentrate or broth powder or the sauce may become too salty. The lower the sodium the better.

YIELD: 2 ¼ cups sauce
TIME: 5 minutes prep and 15 minutes (or more) cooking

2 cups vegan Espagnole Sauce (page 209)
3 tablespoons Beef-Style Demi-Glace Base
1 cup water

1. Combine the Espagnole Sauce and Demi-Glace Base. Whip to incorporate and bring to a simmer in a heavy-bottomed saucepan.

2. Reduce heat to low and let simmer until the sauce is reduced to 2 ¼ cups. Remove from heat and serve or containerize and refrigerate.

Beef-Style Demi-Glace Base

YIELD: 7 tablespoons base
2 tablespoons reduced sodium beef-style broth or mirepoix roasted vegetable base
3 tablespoons cashew butter or cream
4 tablespoons water or red wine

Mix the three ingredients together until evenly dispersed. Store and refrigerate until ready to use. Can store for three months.

Reductions are concentrates similar to a demi-glace but made from animal or plant-based foods. Balsamic vinegar is an example. This technique concentrates flavor through the evaporation of water. It can be reduced to a syrup, which will increase sweetness and reduce acidity.

SAUCE-COLORING TECHNIQUES WITH TAMARI & PORTABELLA MUSHROOMS

In dark sauces such as Espagnole-style sauces, I started out by using a reduced-sodium tamari to both flavor and to color the sauce. Several Japanese tamari products could also be used as a combination flavoring and caramel color. Later I discovered that portabella mushroom gills are a superior coloring agent and give the sauce a rich earthy flavor note that I prefer. Using mushrooms in a sauce will impart the rich umami (the fifth taste) and will give a stronger, more complex flavor. The gills also infuse a dark color into the portabella's membranes when cooked. Because the gills inhibit a duxelle or filling from adhering to the mushroom, I remove them and dry the gills, storing them in an air-tight container and using them as needed for coloring and flavoring sauces. The gills will store indefinitely if in an air-tight container at room temperature.

STOCK TO SAUCE TECHNIQUE

This technique combines making the stock and the sauce into one process. Without the need to simmer animal bones, a sauce can be made using a slow sauté or caramelization to enhance the extraction of flavor from the ingredients. If making a Velouté sauce, sauté vegetables on medium to medium-low heat to develop flavor without caramelizing. If preparing an Espagnole or brown sauce, caramelize the vegetables and mushroom gills to give the sauce a darker richer color and flavor.

Add seasonings, herbs, spices, and flour per the recipe, and cook the mass into a roux. Slowly add water in ¼-cup increments with wine being the last addition.

VEGETABLE PUREE BLENDED SAUCES

Vegetable purees are made from 100 percent vegetable solids. In vegetable blended sauces, the vegetable mass is used as a natural thickener and basic flavor. Broth or seasonings and a small amount of water or wine are added to thin the puree and convert it to a sauce. A small amount of oil or vegetable spread can be added (emulsified) into a vegetable-based sauce to enhance it, such as the Sauce Renaissance (page 227). I use roasted, caramelized, or confit of vegetables for making sauces to intensify the flavor.

CREAM SAUCES

The simplest and better option for a cream sauce is using a cashew cream to achieve the same effect in creaming out a soup or making a Supreme Sauce (page 213). Before decent soy milks with an acceptable flavor profile were on the market, I would use a combination of 50 percent soy milk and 50 percent cashew milk to make a Béchamel sauce. They are combined to become the milk and are generally thickened with a white roux. Cashew cream made from raw nuts is equal to a traditional heavy cream when used in the mother sauces in vegan cuisine. It works as the cream in the sauce in both savory and dessert items and may need to be thinned out with water or the roux in a sauce may need to be reduced. A properly thickened sauce should drape the back of a spoon at about $1/16$ inch thick.

VEGAN-STYLE BEURRE BLANC

The traditional beurre blanc sauces are lacto vegetarian with butter in them, but they contain animal fat, are high in cholesterol and saturated fats, and not vegan nor heart healthy. Beurre blanc is a French culinary term literally translated as "white butter." It is a hot emulsified butter sauce made with a reduction of vinegar and/or white wine and grey shallots into which cold, whole butter is blended off the heat to prevent separation. The small amounts of lecithin (found in egg yolks and soybeans) and other emulsifiers naturally found in butter are used to form an oil-in-water emulsion. It is different from the traditional Hollandaise sauce with egg yolks adding significant emulsification properties. The beurre blanc is considered a compound butter. Vegan hot butter-style sauces are similar in technique and different in that they don't use butter.

- ○ I use vegan butter spreads, which include what I would call enhanced emulsifiers from the lecithin in soybeans. With the reduction of wine or vinegar, the butter spread will emulsify. Bean puree, smooth cashew butter, or potato puree will also enhance emulsification, binding the oil and liquids together.

- ○ Unsaturated oil such as canola oil with no emulsifiers will work with either bean, cashew, or potato as the emulsifier.

- ○ Roasted hazelnut or almond butter will work with additional oil sufficient to thin the butter into a sauce consistency. The ratio is approximately 25 percent oil to 75 percent nut butter and reduced liquid to simulate a Beurre Noisette (a browned or roasted nut butter). I recommend adding a 35 percent ratio vegan butter (moisture) spread to the sauce to give it a butter flavor.

Use the traditional method of making a beurre blanc with a vegan butter spread; I use wine, lemon juice, shallots or onions, and cashew cream. The cashew cream will act as the super emulsifier with vegan beurre blancs, and little if any reduction is necessary.

HOLLANDAISE-STYLE SAUCES

One of the five French mother sauces, Hollandaise sauce is lacto oval vegetarian. As an emulsion of warm butter, egg yolks, lemon juice, and salt, it is not heart healthy nor does it appeal to health-conscious consumers. The vegan version is a blended sauce that uses a different and easy cooking technique. The technique for making a vegan Basic Hollandaise Sauce (page 220) begins with a warm vegan butter spread that is poured into a combination of silken tofu and lemon juice. Blend until smooth. Remove from the blender and heat in a bain-marie (double boiler) or on a low direct heat, scraping the bottom with a spatula until the consistency has the drape of a Hollandaise. A few unique features of the vegan sauce are:

- It does not have to be periodically stirred to prevent separation.

- It can be refrigerated and reheated, unlike the traditional Hollandaise sauce.

HOW TO CONVERT A SAVORY MEAT/SEAFOOD RECIPE TO VEGAN

The key to converting meat and seafood recipes to vegan is to identify four primary ingredients and find their replacements:

- The obvious first ingredient is the protein.

- The second is the flavoring system used to enhance the recipe. Is this a meat-flavored system or a vegetable system?

- The third is the egg or binder system used to hold the protein together. Is this another animal product or a grain or vegetable product?

- The fourth is any dairy ingredient such as milk, cheese, cream, or butter that would need to be replaced.

This is a simple discipline, so obvious that a cook may miss it. Substituting a flavoring system, an egg replacement, and/or dairy products is fairly straightforward depending on the recipe's directions. At this point, protein replacement is center stage. Protein options should be based on the type of protein used in the original recipe.

- For chicken: tofu, tempeh, seitan, white beans, and chicken-style analogue

- For beef: tempeh, seitan, dark beans, grain loaves, and beef-style analogues

- For seafood: tofu, tofu pâté served with sea vegetables, tempeh served with sea vegetables, seitan made with soy milk and served with sea vegetables, and white beans served with sea vegetables

The cooking techniques for the vegan protein may be similar and may also require pre-preparation such as making a tofu pâté or seitan. The cook can build upon these recipes.

Vegetarian Macrobiotic Cooking Techniques

I studied macrobiotics in 1985 to improve my culinary skills and learn how to cook macrobiotic vegetarian cuisine. George Ohsawa, the founder of the macrobiotic diet, incorporated the Taoist principles of yin (expansive) and yang (contractive) to create an energetic balance and harmony in our bodies through food choices, cooking techniques, and lifestyle.

The principle of yin and yang is relative to all foods and cuisines. When I asked my instructor at the Kushi Institute if a carrot is yang (contractive), she said, "Compared to what? It is yang compared to a parsnip, which is lighter in color and sweeter. It is yin (expansive) compared to burdock, which is darker in color and bitter."

Cooking techniques are classified into yin and yang methods. Steaming, poaching, and boiling are yin methods of cooking because they use water, which is yin (expansive). Roasting, frying, and baking use dry hot heat, which is yang (contractive).

Macrobiotics doesn't use most spices and herbs in the belief that such seasonings are too yin and disruptive to the body. Eastern principles espouse that balance is created in a cuisine by using a mixture of yin and yang cooking techniques with yin and yang foods. On the other hand, garlic is occasionally used in macrobiotic cooking.

Ingredients are also classified as having yin or yang properties. Yin ingredients like bok choy, sweet fruits, bean sprouts, eggplant, and tofu, are said to have a cooling nature. Yang ingredients like burdock, carrots, lamb, garlic, and ginger have a warming nature.

In order to balance the yin and yang, ingredients are traditionally cooked together as in a stir-fried bok choy and ginger, or an eggplant in garlic sauce, or in the summertime a purely yin dish like spinach and tofu. Yin and yang seasonings include salt, yang, and sugar, yin.

Dark Miso is yang because it is dark colored and salty. White miso is yin because it is sweet and lighter in color. Miso is a finishing flavor that is added toward the end of the cooking process in any recipe. The easiest way to incorporate it into a broth-type recipe is to place the miso in a strainer and place the strainer in liquid. Using a spoon press the miso against the strainer to dissolve the miso into the broth.

Whole grains of all types are popular in macrobiotic cuisine, which overall is quite simple to prepare.

Some of my favorite dishes are

- ↻ Macrobiotic Lyonnaise Tempeh (page 271) with a Miso Mustard Onion Sauce (page 237) on a whole grain or polenta

- ↻ Kasha (buckwheat) porridge with steamed kale served with seared tempeh, smoked seitan or tofu with a light miso sauce

- ↻ Basic Millet Quinoa Polenta (page 184) for breakfast

- ↻ Tempeh Reuben Sandwich (page 308)

Macrobiotic consumers usually stay away from spicy foods, and the strict ones forbid the use of microwaves. My goal here is to give the cook enough knowledge to minimally address a macrobiotic vegan should they dine at your restaurant or in your home. In the reference section are three macrobiotic books for those interested in the philosophy, diet, and cuisine.

"Cooking demands attention, patience, and above all, a respect for the gifts of the earth. It is a form of worship, a way of giving thanks."

—JUDITH B. JONES

Chapter Six

VEGAN PASTRY
TECHNIQUES

To understand vegan pastry techniques is to understand vegan baking chemistry, primarily how to cook and bake with egg replacements.

Baking is an exacting science in food preparation with eggs. Egg substitution in vegan cuisine is for myself an incredible challenge. The egg is universal, but there are many different techniques for its application. The whites are separated to make an angel food cake, but the whole egg is used in a chiffon cake. Only the egg yolk is used in hollandaise. Whether the whole egg or a component of the egg, eggs are ubiquitous in pastry.

With vegan cuisine and pastries, there isn't—and I seriously doubt there ever will be—one vegan ingredient used universally to replace the egg. Different recipe qualities call for different replacements. I use starch and agar to replace the egg in a custard. Structure is needed in pastries like muffins, so a replacement with protein, other than gluten, is required. Gluten can be used to replace eggs in proteins like meat loaf, but it must be tempered to make it less stringy. The dessert chapter will show how to use these ingredients in various recipe applications.

The irony of vegan pastries is their similarity to traditional pastries, while their unique difference is that eggs and dairy are eliminated from the cuisine. The technique of making a buttercream icing, creating the fissure in a cookie, or causing lift in a cake is the same. Where eggs are traditionally used is where the challenge arises. Egg replacement is a complex subject, as previously addressed, with each pastry category having different egg replacement ingredient formulas. The primary or essential element to know is that an egg is a high-protein, moist ingredient with emulsification properties (the yolk). Translated, use a high-protein ingredient to replace a high-protein ingredient and build the emulsification component into the recipe when the properties of a whole egg are needed.

Vegan Egg & Dairy Replacements

The chemistry of egg replacement is both complex and simple. It is simple because the protein replacement is relative to the recipe application. Vegan egg replacement in a custard is quite different from vegan egg replacement in a cake or cookie. Egg replacement is a precise science—the dry vegan protein replacement must have the exact amount of moisture and protein to replicate the egg's function in a recipe. I'll say this again: Unlike an egg that works across all sorts of pastries, there is no one egg replacement system that functions comprehensively as a vegan egg replacement ingredient.

There are three types of egg replacement relative to the egg's function:

- ○ *Aeration,* the whipping of air into the egg white, creates the gelling effect as in a custard or pastry cream,
- ○ *Emulsification* as in making a mayonnaise, and
- ○ *Building structure* into a pastry like a muffin or brownie.

BAKERY EGG REPLACEMENTS

Bakery egg replacement options must both stabilize and give lift to a pastry in the same manner as an egg. A number of different ingredients facilitate these processes.

The Ener-G Egg Replacer is a vegan gluten- and wheat-free egg replacement that has been around for decades. I started using it shortly after becoming a vegetarian in 1976. This ingredient has no lecithin to create an emulsification in a recipe nor does it have sufficient protein to give lift and hold structure. What it does have is starch (from potatoes and tapioca) and leavening agents (vegan calcium lactate, calcium carbonate, and citric acid) to give lift to the starch structure, and cellulose gum to give it a gelling property. This egg replacement is a good substitute for eggs to bind ingredients together, such as grains in vegan loaves, and to cause quiches to set. It does not have the protein properties to replace the egg as in an angel food cake. Compared to an egg, which has moisture and is very high in protein, the two are night and day different.

VEGAN CUSTARD EGG REPLACEMENTS

Custard egg replacements do not need a protein structure to attain a custard consistency. What is needed are a gelling ingredient and osmosis to achieve the custard effect. In creating the egg effect to gel a custard, I use approximately 75 percent starch from corn, potato, wheat, etc., and 25 percent agar for gelling. Oil can be added after the starch and the agar have been dissolved in the liquid according to the recipe. The agar combined with the starch imparts a custard texture. Adding oil is acceptable but must happen quickly and be emulsified into the recipe with rapid mixing.

An example of an osmotic custard is the Chocolate Cream Filling (page 362) It calls for warm chocolate to be added to a warm silken tofu, which is then blended until smooth. Moisture from the tofu migrates into the chocolate causing it to solidify to a cheesecake texture. Loss of moisture in the tofu causes it to become firmer. When warm chocolate cools, it becomes firm. Using two basic ingredients and basic chemistry, one can create a vegan cheesecake or pie filling.

WHIPPING CREAMS

Vegan whipped creams are available as commercial products, and recipes from scratch are relatively easy to produce with a mixer. Whipping cream requires a simple but exacting recipe to create the aeration or specific gravity of a whipped cream. Scratch versions have a heavier texture. The technique is universal—whip air into the cream or liquid. You can determine the aeration, for example, by measuring the volume of the cream mixture before and after whipping. If you have 7 cups of cream before whipping it and 10 cups after whipping, you have a specific gravity of 70 percent. When making a whipping cream from coconut cream, I add a few tablespoons of palm shortening because it is firm at room temperature and gives additional stability.

Unlike dairy whipping cream, the vegan version isn't quite as delicate to handle and cannot be overwhipped. If overwhipped, dairy whipping cream curdles, separating the water from the fat, which is the foundation of butter. Commercial vegan whipped toppings, without any additional ingredients, cannot be overwhipped. The topping will simply become stiffer.

For one example, try the Coconut Whipped Cream Topping (page 345). Made with coconut cream, this whipped topping aerates or whips to a lighter texture when whipped like whipped cream. The psyllium husk binds the water in the coconut cream to help stabilize it when whipped. It has the richness of whipped cream and is a slight bit heavier with a delicate coconut flavor.

VEGAN MOUSSES

Traditional mousses are made in two stages with pastry cream and whipping cream. Gelatin is warmed, mixed into warm pastry cream, which is then mixed with cool pastry cream and then whipping cream is folded into it. Very technical and labor intense. Too often, in vegan cuisine the term mousse is loosely used with a dessert that is smooth and creamy but not light. It is usually a combination of whipping cream folded into pastry cream; however, it is possible to use a vegan whipping cream and fold it into a vegan pastry cream. (See Peanut Butter Mousse on page 323.)

- ○ *Scratch method* may not give as light a mousse but would be a light-textured cream. Here the pastry cream (stiff pudding) is prepared and the soy or coconut cream is whipped and folded into the pastry cream. Agar is used in place of gelatin.

- ○ *Speed scratch version* is where a vegan Instant Soy Pudding (page 387) with additional water is mixed with a commercial vegan frozen whipped cream topping concentrate to create a mousse. In the whipping process, the pastry cream sets while the whipping cream is aerated.

- ○ *Flavor variations* are infinite, ranging from simple extracts to inclusions such as minced dry fruits, coconut, nuts, or nut butters. Note: The inclusion must be added in a manner that doesn't break down the aeration in the mousse.

- ○ Extracts such as lemon, orange, mint, or vanilla can be added at any point.

- ○ Nut butters and other inclusions must be added to the pastry cream before folding in the whipped cream. One exception for the nut butter is the speed scratch version where the nut butter is whipped into the mousse at the end of the whipping process for about 10 to 15 seconds on high speed.

The commercial ingredients I use are listed in the ingredient/distribution resource section. Two options are presented in this cookbook that allow the pastry cook to choose the one best suited for their operation or kitchen. For example, the scratch method using the vegan pastry cream and coconut whipped cream in the dessert section compared to the time saved with products such as the Eco-Cuisine® Instant Soy Pudding and the commercial Rich's Whipped Topping (see Appendix B).

VEGAN ICE CREAMS

Three factors in ice cream formulas are universal: Brix scale (sugar density), overrun (amount of air infused into the ice cream), and emulsification (the binding of fats and water or fat and dry ingredients such as nuts). Emulsification applies only to oil and water and needs an emulsifier which can be a dry oil laden ingredient such as nuts. Depending on the aqueous/fat relationship, an emulsifier may be needed to bond the ingredients. Lecithin (found in soybeans) and egg yolks are emulsifiers. The yolks also create the custard effect and explain why the French call ice cream "frozen custard."

While vegan ice creams are readily available, but expensive, in retail markets, they are generally not available in foodservice packaging for the foodservice market. However, make-your-own vegan ice cream is easy to make, is significantly less expensive, and has a long shelf life. It may be feasible for a foodservice operation or to make at home. Making it for personal use is a practical option to save money and develop original flavors.

Sugar is the antifreeze in both sorbets and ice creams. Not enough and ice cream is like a rock. Too much and it will not freeze to desired consistency. Sugar is measured in two ways. One is the *Brix scale* or "Degrees Brix," which is the measure of the sugar content in an aqueous (liquid) solution. One degree Brix is 1 gram of sucrose in 100 grams of solution and represents the strength of the solution as a percentage by weight. If other solids are in the aqueous solution, the Brix measurement accounts for those solids in its reading. The second measurement is the *Baumè scale*, which also measures the density in liquids. A one-to-one ratio of water to sugar is B28. A two-to-one ratio of water to sugar is B18. Sorbet has a B12 to B20 rating on the Baumé scale. If there is too much sugar, the water cannot absorb it and the sorbet will not freeze.

TWO BASIC TYPES OF ICE CREAM AND OVERRUN

Two basic frozen custard types of ice cream are French ice cream and Philadelphia style or American ice cream. French ice cream is made with eggs which give it a silky custard texture. Philadelphia ice cream is made with sugar, milk, and cream.

Overrun is related to preparation techniques, not formulations (recipes). Overrun is basically how much air is whipped into the ice cream. An overrun reading of 50 means the product is 50 percent air and 50 percent ice cream. The texture will be lighter and smoother, readily and effortlessly melting on one's palate. The overrun can be mechanically set on commercial soft serve machines. Cutting frozen ice cream into large pieces and, in a frozen mixing bowl with a frozen whip, whipping air into the product for about 3 to 8 minutes and immediately returning to the freezer, may aerate the ice cream depending on the formula.

One of my favorite ice creams is banana ice cream (technically speaking it is a frozen fruit puree). I call it ice cream because it has the rich creamy mouthfeel of ice cream. The process is simple. Freeze overripe bananas and, using the nut butter mechanism on a Champion juicer or nut butter machine, run the frozen bananas through it. Nut butter can also be beaten into ice cream using the overrun technique for a different flavor. But it will always have the defined banana flavor and must be served immediately.

My favorite vegan ice cream recipes are included in the dessert section. They are a sample of the vast possibilities of ice creams that can be created in a home or commercial kitchen with a blender.

SORBETS

Sorbet is sugar and fruit puree. Sorbet is sometimes made with a liqueur such as chocolate instead of a fruit puree, but that isn't as common. The challenge in making sorbet is that the water and sugar content in the puree will alter the final sorbet product.

Two different sorbet techniques include the cooked method using sugar, fruit juice, and fruit juice concentrate, and the uncooked technique using fruit puree and a syrup. Where whole fruit is used as in the uncooked Mango Sorbet (page 343), the blender is needed to pulverize the fruit. Where fruit is used as in the cooked Cranberry Sorbet (page 344), a food processor is used to convert the ice-type texture to a sorbet texture.

- ↻ Some sorbet recipes allow for the use of whipping cream as an optional ingredient to give the sorbet richness and lubricity.

- ↻ The general classic proportion of sugar in the Brix scale for frozen desserts is 65 percent sugar and 35 percent water.

- ↻ Sugar is what keeps sorbets and ice creams from freezing solid as in ice. If your sorbet has the texture of ice, it doesn't have sufficient sugar; if too soft, that indicates excess sugar.

- ↻ Use Cashew Cream (page 175) as a whipped cream substitute and cut the amount in half to give the sorbet a richer creamier texture.

Sorbets are easy to make and are generally vegan. But dairy whipping cream could be used, so ask if the sorbet is vegan if you are a vegan or lactose intolerant. In making your sorbet, you can add a little cashew cream to the sorbet in the blender (puree uncooked version or into the cooked version when it has cooled to room temperature or when put through a food processor). The cream will give it a smoother mouthfeel.

PASTRY CREAM, PUDDINGS, CUSTARDS, & ICINGS

These four items are all interrelated as pastry cream is the foundation for the other three. Pastry creams are traditionally made by making a slurry of egg yolks, sugar, and flour that is added to warm milk and heated to thicken. It is the consistency of a thick pudding with a light vanilla flavor. For vegan pastry creams (see Vanilla Pastry Cream on page 321):

⟳   Thin out with soy milk to convert to a pudding by using approximately ½ cup soy milk
to 1 cup pastry cream. (Vanilla Pudding page 322)

⟳   Thin out with additional soy milk to convert to crème glacé (additional ½ cup soy milk
to 1 cup pastry cream). (Lemon Crème Anglaise page 323)

⟳   Add agar powder as a gelling agent to convert to a custard. (Diabetic Coconut Custard
page 322)

The techniques for preparing pastry cream and its recipe variations are very close to traditional cooking techniques. Supplementing liquid lecithin for egg yolks is one minor change in the technique. Another is the use of nuts in the blender scratch method where the nuts become the emulsifier.

As already mentioned, there are two options to making a pastry cream: the traditional scratch method and the speed scratch instant pudding mix. Nuts act as the emulsifier in the scratch method, and oil acts as the emulsifier in the speed scratch method for vegan pastry creams and pudding mixes.

Options for vegan milk ingredients in pastry cream are:

⟳   Original (unsweetened) soy milk

⟳   One part coconut milk and two parts soy milk

⟳   One part original (unsweetened) and one part cashew milk. I created this soy milk
to cashew nut ratio back in 1981 before there was a decent soy milk on the market
and it performed exceptionally well in creating neutral to dairy-style flavored milk
for a Béchamel sauce and I realized it would also work in a pastry cream recipe.

Vegan Oils & Butter Spreads

CASHEW MILK, CREAM, & SOUR CREAM

The milk version ratio of cashew nuts to water is ¼ cup raw cashew pieces and 1 ½ cups water. Combine half the water with the cashew nuts (blanched almonds optional). Blend until the mixture is smooth and creamy with no grit when you rub the mixture between your fingers. Add remaining water and mix until evenly dispersed.

⟳   Cashew Cream (page 175) is half water and half cashews.

⟳   Cashew Sour Cream (page 175) is ¾ cup water and 1 cup cashew pieces.

The ratio of water to nuts can be adjusted based on the density sought.

SHORTENINGS AND OILS IN PASTRIES

The primary function of oils and shortenings in dessert pastries is to tenderize the texture, which creates flakiness, intensifies flavor, and adds lubricity. (Creating shortness or tenderness in a pastry or cookie is like flakiness in a pie crust.) Oils and shortenings have the same function in both traditional and vegetarian pastries. Flavor is a major difference when departing from the use of butter in vegan pastries. The vegan spreads have a butter-like flavor and are a modest replication of butter, but they are not butter.

Whether the objective is for flavor or for function, there are three shortening options:

○ *Mechanically pressed palm oil.* This is a saturated fat, white, and neutrally flavored shortening that functions exactly as a traditional hydrogenated shortening. I like this shortening because it is neutral in flavor and is functional in all pastry applications calling for shortening.

○ *Vegan butter spreads.* They function in the same manner as a margarine and work well in recipes that call for the shortening to deliver a butter-type flavor in icings, short dough, cookies, and pastry creams.

○ *Unrefined corn oil.* If a saturated fat isn't necessary, unrefined corn oil works in muffins, cookies, and pastry creams to give a subliminal butter-like flavor.

Flavor aside, vegan palm non-hydrogenated shortening functions in the exact manner as hydrogenated shortenings or saturated animal fats.

ICING TECHNIQUES

Icing techniques for vegetarian or vegan desserts are similar to those that use butter and milk in that sugar and a little milk are whipped with a paddle or whisked into a light creamy icing. If a vegan meringue is desired, I recommend whipping cream that is not browned, as you can with a traditional meringue, because whipping cream is oil based. With icings, addressing vegan is the easy part; the challenge is health, keeping in mind that healthy dining is the driver behind vegan cuisine. The solution is to reduce the amount of sugar used by at least 10 percent and to use less icing. Icing should complement, not dominate, the pastry.

BUTTERCREAM TECHNIQUES

Buttercream icing techniques are vegan options found in the icing recipes starting on page 327.

○ Use a combination of vegan butter spread and palm shortening to make a butter cream-style icing with a light yellow hue and subliminal butter flavor.

○ If using granulated sugar, the creaming time to dissolve granulation is longer. To cut down on creaming time, add liquid as stated in the recipe directly into the sugar and dissolve it before adding to shortening.

○ If using a creamy nut butter to make, for example, a Peanut Buttercream Icing (page 327), use a half measure of water for every measure of nut butter.

GANACHE ICING

Loaded with saturated fat, cholesterol, and sugar, a traditional ganache icing is made by heating butter, sugar, and heavy cream until warm enough (about 120°F) to melt chocolate, then bittersweet or milk chocolate chips are added to the warm mixture. For a vegan chocolate ganache (page 328), the technique and core ingredients (soy milk, butter spread or shortening, and chocolate) are the same. I heat soy milk to about 120°F before adding chocolate which will melt quickly. The osmotic principle in the vegan ganache is at work here. The chocolate takes up the excess moisture and, when combined with the saturated fat, will set firm when refrigerated and cut like cheesecake when cold. When hot, it pours and drapes. If it's not pourable and doesn't have a drape (coating effect), the recipe will need to be adjusted.

○ With the vegan version, heat soy milk, bittersweet (dairy-free) chocolate chips, and vanilla extract. Remove from heat and mix until the chips have dissolved. The icing should create a drape on the back of the spoon.

○ Additional sugar can be added to milk in the warming stage to dissolve it. If added at the end, use powdered sugar. Granulated sugar will not easily break down in fat. You will have to mix (agitate it) to break down granulation.

○ Additional shortening (palm shortening, coconut butter, butter spread, or vegan shortening of choice) can be added at any time (with the soy milk or at the end as a sort of mounted butter).

○ If the icing is too stiff, add a little more soy milk to bring it to a pourable consistency. If too thin, add more chocolate chips to tighten the consistency.

Crusts

Different types of crust are all easily converted to vegan, if dairy is the exclusive animal product used in the recipe. There are four basic styles of crust, and each works best with different types of fillings.

CRUMB CRUST

Similar to a graham cracker crust, a crumb crust is easy to make and doesn't require a rolling pin. The crust can be made with dried out plain cookies with inclusions (such as chocolate chips or nuts) but they must be ground fine. The cookies must be vegan if making the claim. Crumb crust is dry and has a weak structure. It's pressed into an oiled pie plate or tin of your choice. Because the crust is dry with little structure, it must be used with a filling that is firm (such as a cheesecake-type filling). The Gluten-Free Crust (page 336) without the water is similar to a crumb crust. It can be made in a food processor or mixer with a paddle.

- ○ Mixing 5 to 10 percent unbleached white flour into the mix and spritzing with water will give the crust more structure.

- ○ Second option is to cut back on shortening to give the crust additional structure.

- ○ Any nuts that are used must be ground fine.

- ○ The reason the crumb crust has no structure is that normally the moisture from shortening and water bind the ingredients. Lightly spritzing the crust with water in a spray bottle before pouring in the filling will help activate the ingredients giving this crust more sturdy binding structure.

CROÛTE CRUST

This crust has a stronger texture making it the better choice for wetter fillings such as moist fruit fillings and custards. It is often used for nonsweet dishes like savory pies, *pâté en croûte*, and quiches. The crust is prepared in the same manner as a traditional pie crust by cutting the oil ingredient(s) into the flour with sugar and salt. Unlike the flaky crust, this one has minimal texture and sufficient fat to hold off water migration into the crust. It is a carrier for fillings. If the dough is made with cold shortening, it can probably be rolled out and used immediately. If the shortening is room temperature, it's best to let it cool for 3 to 4 hours in the refrigerator so it will not stick to the floured surface when rolling out. It is an easy-to-handle dough when rolling out and crimping. The crust can be made in a mixer with a paddle or small amounts can be assembled in a food processor.

FLAKY PIE CRUST

Flaky pie crusts (Basic Pie Crust on page 336) require attention to the technique of cutting the shortening into the flour. The flakiness results when fat is dispersed into the dough in layers in the first preparation step. Similar to a mealy crust, the fat has to be evenly blended into the dry ingredients. It works well with all but wet fillings such as custards and fruit fillings.

- ○ Use either palm shortening or a vegan margarine/spread. Palm shortening can be used at room temperature, and the vegan spread should be refrigerated to create a better flake.

- ○ Refrigerate dough until cold and roll out when cold. This will reduce the dough's shrinkage in the pan.

- ○ To cut saturated fat in the crust, use a combination of 25 percent canola oil or oil low in saturated fat and 75 percent shortening/saturated fat and refrigerate the mixture until cold. I recommend refrigerating the flour to keep the shortening cold in the mixing process.

Sweet Crust or Sugar Dough

This is strictly a dessert crust similar to a shortbread cookie (Sugar Dough on page 333). It has a very tender structure (high fat), causing it to tear easily when rolling. But it is also easy to pinch back together and patch. While it has a wide range of pastry applications, I recommend using it for individual tarts. Like a flaky pie crust, it can be used in both single and double pie crusts, but is most frequently used as a single crust. The texture is shorter because of both the sugar and shortening.

This dough can be used in a traditional pie pan, but also works well pressed into a tart pan (you will need less dough).

Other notes on sugar dough:

- ○ When using liquid lecithin, it must be mixed into the shortening to give it an even dispersion into the food. Shortening must be cold to roll out crust.

- ○ For a shortbread-type cookie, add flavor and inclusions.

- ○ To use as a cookie mix or as a short dough crust, increase the oil and, if too wet, reduce the water to create a dough that can be rolled out when cold.

In formulating and baking vegan cookies, as with all vegan dessert items, the challenge is to find appropriate substitutes for eggs and dairy. Substituting non-dairy ingredients for dairy for the same function is easy. Egg replacements are more challenging.

Cookies, Cakes, Pastries, & More

Cookie Mixing Technique

The technique is as important as the ingredients and the recipe. Creaming sugar and shortening is the crucial first step. It encapsulates the sugar with fat. When baking a Toll House chocolate chip cookie, you will notice, as the cookie bakes, it begins to puff up. When the cookie reaches about 275°F, the sugar, which is encapsulated in oil, breaks down, collapsing the cookie, creating the fissure. If using a syrup or powdered sugar, the cookie will not fissure.

- Mixing sugar and oil will give the same effect as the creaming method. This is one option that delivers on functionality and taste without the saturated fat.

- After creaming, immediately add the wet ingredients and the dry ingredients.

- If adding dried foods (such as dried fruit), it is a good idea to dip the fruit quickly into water and immediately pull it out. Dry ingredients will draw on the moisture in the cookie dough, which will cause it to become stiff and to not function as desired. Thus the dough will become a hockey puck as opposed to a cookie.

INGREDIENT RATIOS

I am submitting basic cookie ingredient ratios to give you an idea of how to build a vegan cookie. If you are a pastry chef or inspired home cook and want to test your ability to create vegan pastries, these ratios and substitution options will give you a platform to get started. I don't have salt in these ratios. It should be added as needed but the cookie will need a little to bring out flavor.

In the ratios I state "egg" and that is to be substituted by a vegan egg replacement. A common egg replacement is 1 tablespoon flax meal (defatted or full fat) mixed with 3 tablespoons water. This is a "general" egg replacement system.

One replaces an egg in vegan cooking by first looking at the breakdown of an egg, which is about 85 percent water, 11 percent concentrated protein, and 4 percent fat. About 80 grams whole flax meal with oil combined with 80 grams water will address the protein in 100 grams whole egg. The fat in the recipe will have to be reduced by 38 grams. The osmotic effect of flax will compensate for the gelling effect of the egg white, which can absorb water in the cooking process. That is how eggs make custard with milk.

Flax is about 19 percent protein and has significant emulsifying properties that, when combined with the protein, function similarly to an egg. Not exactly the same but in the ball park. The ingredients in the recipe have to compensate for the lack of protein in the egg substitute. And that reverts back to the egg's function in the recipe. Obviously, the flax meal does not whip up like an egg white. What we need are ingredients that work in specific instances, and flax meal does work for cookies. There are numerous others like chia seed that also function as binders with vegan entrées and pastries.

EGG REPLACEMENT IN COOKIES

Building the flaxseed model for an egg into the following ratios is a solid platform in developing vegan cookies.

Standard Cookie Ratio

6 ounces sugar

12 ounces shortening

18 ounces flour

*Egg replacement equivalent to 1 egg

¼ cup inclusions, such as chocolate chips (optional)

Baking powder or baking soda (optional depending on the formula)

This is the drop cookie dough that will spread during baking. If the dough doesn't have enough structure, it will become a wafer. If it has too much, it will impart a cake-type texture.

*1 egg = 1 ½ teaspoons Ener-G Egg Replacer plus 2 tablespoons water

Sample Sugar Cookie Ingredient Ratio	**Sample Toll House Cookie Ingredient Ratio**
8 ounces sugar	8 ounces sugar
8 ounces shortening	8 ounces shortening
12 ounces flour	8 ounces flour
*Egg replacement equivalent to 1 egg	*Egg replacement equivalent to 1 egg
2 teaspoons vanilla	¼ cup chocolate chips
1 teaspoon baking powder	

The vegan egg replacement selected is relevant to the cookie type. Liquid lecithin and flax meal work in bakery items as an emulsifier to replace the egg yolk. Since the egg's function as a protein is to give structure, a wet protein is needed to replace it. Soy protein isolate is a viable egg replacer. For items like crepes, I use Ener-G Egg Replacer not because of its protein but because it has the binding qualities needed to make a crepe. The amount of egg replacement will vary depending on the recipe. In cookies protein is needed, not aeration. This will vary but about 2 teaspoons of egg replacement per 1 ½ cups flour is an average.

CALCULATING EGG SUBSTITUTE OR REPLACEMENT IN RECIPES

Choosing a vegan egg replacement ingredient for a recipe is determined by the function of the egg in the recipe. Angel food cake uses egg whites. Chiffon cake uses the whole egg with the egg whites separated, whipped, and folded into the cake batter. Whole eggs are used in custard for their gelling properties and meat loaf to bind the protein together. Egg yolks are used raw in mayonnaise and cooked in hollandaise sauce. Egg wash is used to glaze pastries giving them their golden tan, glazed appearance and to bind breading to a food item. As I've already noted, there is no one simple vegan egg replacement with universal applications because recipes and applications vary and use the whole or separate components of the egg. There is no one unique formula or chart to determine how to substitute a vegan egg replacement in a recipe. To shed some light on this subject, I will approach the subject from the perspective of an egg's function in a recipe and match vegan ingredients to that function.

One of the primary functions of the egg is that its protein binds or gives structure to a recipe. When a binder is needed, look to the protein content as a factor. Unfortunately, this is not universal. Starch can act as an egg replacement in certain recipes like custard or lecithin in sugar dough to emulsify. Study the recipes and you will learn how each works.

The technical equation to calculate an exact vegan egg replacement starts with breaking down primary ingredients in an egg, which is 4 percent fat, 11 percent protein, and 85 percent water. Here is the formula to replace 100 grams of egg in a pastry with flaxseed:

- ○ 100 grams flax meal is 18 percent protein, 42 percent fat, and 28 percent carbohydrate with no water.

- ○ The conversion to flax is achieved by using 80 grams flax to deliver on the protein, 80 grams water to replace moisture, and reduce the shortening in the recipe by 38 grams to compensate for the flax's fat contribution.

- ○ If using defatted flax meal, leave the fat unchanged in the recipe, and reduce the flax and water needed because the protein content is higher in defatted flax.

This is the scientific means of conversion and isn't 100 percent foolproof because the proteins are different. Trying to create an egg white would be a quite different challenge involving eliminating flax meal. Again, because eggs have multifunctional applications there is no simple equation.

This is a brief overview and ideal starting point to wrap your mind around vegan egg replacements in vegan pastries and desserts.

CULINARY FUNCTION: VEGAN EGG PASTRY REPLACEMENT

Gelling	*Starch and agar powder combination:* Corn, arrowroot, potato, or starch of choice combined with agar powder to give the custard effect.
Structure	*Chia meal, flax meal, and vital wheat gluten flour:* These are the primary structure builders and emulsifiers in pastries. Silken tofu will also work where a pound cake texture is the objective.
Emulsifier	*Lecithin, tofu, flax meal, xanthan gum, and nuts (smooth nut butter):* Work well as emulsifiers.
Aeration	*High-protein soy powder* dissolved in a small amount of water can be whipped or aerated. A cold set option for a meringue is to use puffed rice with a vegan whipped cream. This recipe builds aeration into a cream giving it the effect of a raw egg white. It is light, moist, and creamy.

It is not just ratios of the ingredients that determine the cookie's outcome. The quality and specifications of the ingredients also affect its quality.

- ♻ In vegan pastries when removing eggs, I immediately revert to a high-gluten (bread) flour to give the cookie more structure. As in savory cuisine and in pastry, protein is a key ingredient. Think of formulating a cookie like building a house. The house frame is built to hold up the house and then walls and roof are assembled. Without the house-frame structure, the cookie will collapse to a flat wafer-like consistency with no crumb or texture.

- ♻ Oil tenderizes and breaks down structure. If the cookie crumbles too easily, it either has excess oil or not enough protein to hold the product together. The oil-to-protein ratio is critical. You should never exceed the oil ratio in vegan products; meeting the protein ratio in a vegan product is somewhat more challenging.

- ♻ Sugar breaks down structure. Use the appropriate ratio to produce the desired quality. If using a liquid sweetener, reduce your water by about 25 percent to account for the moisture in the syrup. This is a rough estimate. There are too many variables in the ingredients to give an exact ratio.

  - ♨ White granulated sugar creates a crispy sugar wafer-type cookie. Brown sugar (not white sugar with caramel color) will absorb moisture creating a chewier cookie. The molasses, which is naturally occurring in sugar cane, is left in brown sugar and removed in white sugar.

⬧ Use ¾ cup maple syrup to replace ½ cup sugar and reduce water by ¼ cup. If no water is called for in the formula, increase the amount of flour in the recipe starting at about 1 percent. If the recipe calls for 16 ounces (454 grams) flour, that is 4.54 grams increase or roughly 1 ½ teaspoons. This small percent does make a difference. Continue adding flour, if necessary, until reaching the appropriate dough consistency. Keep in mind that each formula is unique—the percentage is a moving target.

⬧ Use ⅔ cup agave syrup per cup of flour and reduce water by about ¼ cup. If no liquid is called for in the recipe, increase flour by 1 percent increments until dough consistency is reached. Again, if the recipe calls for 16 ounces (454 grams) that is 4.54 grams increase or roughly 1 ½ teaspoons.

↻ If dough is too stiff, add water, and if too thin, add more flour.

↻ Always adjust recipe in small increments. Overcompensating will cost you the loss of the recipe.

↻ Baking powder and baking soda will also shorten the structure of a cookie. You should not exceed 1 teaspoon baking powder per cup of flour. If using baking soda, use ½ teaspoon per cup of flour. Note that there should be an acidic ingredient in the formula such as vinegar or lemon juice to activate the baking soda.

↻ Eggs—In substituting ingredients for eggs, remember that eggs are primarily liquid protein (egg whites). Two-thirds of the egg's total net weight out of its shell is egg white, with nearly 92 percent of that weight coming from water. A raw U.S. large egg white weighs 33 grams with 3.6 grams or 11 percent protein. When replacing eggs with vegan substitutes, these ratios must be followed: using a vegan egg replacement, the ratio would be approximately 85 percent water, 4 percent fat, and 11 percent concentrated protein powder.

CREPES

For most baked goods, there are ratios that give you the best results. For the crepe, 1 part flour, 2 parts egg, and 2 parts water. This is the traditional ratio. Keep that ratio and let your imagination run free by using different liquids, spices, or flavors in the batter. The 1 part flour and 2 parts water are easy with vegan crepes. The challenge is the egg replacement and one of the rare times where I use Ener-G Egg Replacer. To compensate for the loss of moisture from the egg, increase to 3 parts water to 1 part flour. The protein and moisture provided in the egg must be equalized in the vegan crepe batter, keeping it wet enough to spread paper thin and hold together when heated. The Ener-G Egg Replacer and the increased water help to compensate for the protein as well as the moisture.

The crepe must be so thin that you can see a shadow through it. My Vegan Crepes recipe (page 337) functions as a traditional crepe but it is, at first, a challenge to prepare, and once a feel is developed for the consistency of the batter and technique, the process is much easier. Vegan crepes will tear easier than traditional crepes so handle delicately.

Vegan stews, pepper steak, and any hot relatively thick fillings can be used in crepes for an elegant savory entrée. For any savory filling that is loose, simply heat and thicken it more or add dried whole wheat bread crumbs to the mixture, and let it set in the refrigerator until it firms up and then heat for crepe filling. To serve, microwave crepes for about 30 seconds or longer depending on how many are being microwaved at one time or cover crepes so no moisture gets in and steam them for about 5 minutes or until hot. Or gently sauté in oil in a covered sauté pan to lightly crisp and cook. Choose an appropriate sauce for the crepes if desired. Good choices are Classical Tomato Sauce (page 216) thinned out with a cabernet red wine or Sauce Renaissance (page 227).

HIPPEN MASSE AND TUILES

The German *hippen masse* and the French *tuiles* are simple, healthy, thin cookie wafers that are often used as a shell to carry a food item or as a garnish on a dessert. I have used tuiles primarily as a savory garnish and hippen masse as a dessert garnish. Vegan tuiles and hippen masse bring another level of sophistication to vegan cuisine.

Tuile is a French word meaning "tile" and the cookie is supposed to resemble the curved tiles on tops of buildings. It is a flat, thin cookie-like wafer. The dough is spread on an oiled and floured surface of a sheet pan or on parchment paper and baked. It will be soft coming out of the oven and will harden within minutes, if not immediately shaped. If it is to be shaped, it must be laid into or over the mold to create the specific form. Tuiles are made into a variety of shapes from cigarette (rolled) tuiles to cups for holding berries. Tuile batter is also called tulip paste.

Hippen masse, also called hippen paste, is the German version of the French tuiles. This is a thin wafer cookie similar to a plain tuiles. The batter can be spread or piped or molded to create a specific shape or design. It is generally piped over a template and baked. The difference between a traditional tuile and hippen masse is that Hippen Masse (page 335) uses almond paste in the formula. In these vegan formulas, an egg replacement gives body to the tuile and the hippen masse. Flour is the primary structure in vegan tuiles or hippen masse, and high-protein bread flours are needed to hold the structure in the vegan version.

Cakes, Tortes, & Brownies

Like all other vegan pastries and desserts, the ultimate challenge in making a vegan cake is replacing the egg. It is the protein from the egg that creates the structure to hold the cake's structure intact as it rises. Without protein, the cake will collapse to a dense consistency similar to fudge. Baking, unlike cooking, is an exacting science. If the rough ratio in a sauce is a little off either way, it can be adjusted. Once a vegan cake goes into the oven, if it isn't right, it is a failed product. The mistake may be recycled into another recipe but its original objective is lost.

How does one replace eggs in a cake? Start out by looking to the breakdown of the egg. What is the water to protein/fat ratio in an egg? As stated earlier, substituting a vegan egg replacement, the ratio would be approximately 85 percent water to 4 percent fat and 11 percent concentrated protein. Flaxseed, per 100 grams, is 18 percent protein, 42 percent fat, and 28 percent carbohydrates. To replace 100 grams of egg in a recipe, use about 80 grams of flax to deliver on the protein. An additional 80 grams of water and a reduction of oil or shortening by 38 grams would create the exact percentages in the recipe with the egg replacement. Flax meal is osmotic so it will definitely draw on the excessive moisture.

The egg replacement equation for vegan cakes:

1. Calculate from the cookie ingredient specifications the amount of protein, fat, moisture, and carbohydrate needed in the egg replacement ingredient.

2. Calculate the amount of protein, water, and fat in the eggs in the cake formula.

3. Compare the two and use enough of the egg replacement ingredient to meet the protein percentage called for in the recipe. Adjust the fat, carbohydrate, and water up or down to fall in line with the percentage of each called for in the traditional recipe.

This may seem simple but every ingredient called for in the recipe must be compensated with substitutions.

Here's another example: If the eggs provide 40 grams of egg protein, 180 grams of water, and 8 grams of fat, those ingredients must be replaced for the recipe to perform to specification. Gluten flour, soy protein, pea protein, and flax meal are a few examples of substitutes. Depending on the recipe application, different combinations of ingredients can deliver as a substitute for eggs. Understanding the role of eggs in baking and their role in the specific recipe is crucial to creating a substitution.

The type of cake or torte being prepared will determine the type of egg replacement needed to succeed. Some items like meringue, where the egg white increases in volume eight-fold, don't have an exact replacement. There are options; I have successfully used them but they are not cost effective in any kitchen and the flavor needs help. In time better substitutes will emerge.

GLAZING PASTRIES

Egg wash is generally used to glaze a pastry before placing in the oven. The purpose is to give it a richer light brown color as the crust bakes. The glaze bakes into the crust though the entire baking process. Vegan pastry glazing uses the same principle but a different technique. Use 2 parts syrup to 1 part water and mix until incorporated. Eight minutes before the pastry is completely baked, remove from the oven, glaze with the syrup mixture and return to the oven to finish baking. The syrup will bake into the crust creating a glaze.

My preferred syrup for glazing is barley malt syrup. It has a darker caramel color. Rice syrup is my second option. Any similar syrup will work. The dextrose equivalent (DE) or sucrose concentration in the syrup will determine how fast the pastry browns. Barley malt and rice syrups have a lower DE, which will cause them to caramelize slower.

If a syrup with a high concentration of sugar is used, it will cause the pastry to brown quicker. Give the pastry the same eight minutes but check it in four. If it is browning too quickly, cover it with foil to finish baking. Time and temperature are the factors to consider. It is a simple technique and the simplest ones are the easiest to fail at.

Vegan Gelling

AGAR TECHNIQUES

Derived from a sea vegetable and usually available in either flakes or powder, agar is used as a gelling agent in foods such as pastry creams and fruit jellos. Powder is a concentrated form and therefore can absorb more liquid than the flakes. A similar example would be comparing egg meringue to a raw unwhipped egg white. One would need significantly more volume to equal one raw egg white. For example, agar flakes are like bread cubes versus agar powder which is like flour. Agar powder is three times more concentrated than flakes. Agar flakes must also be cooked slowly to dissolve; agar powder instantly dissolves in warm water.

APPLICATION TECHNIQUES AND RULES

1. Ratios: Use 1 teaspoon agar powder or 1 tablespoon agar flakes per cup of water or juice.
2. I use agar powder, in foods like the pastry cream, by blending it into the solution and cooking it. I would not use agar flakes in the pastry cream. Agar flakes must be cooked first until they are completely dissolved and no specks of undissolved agar are present. It takes more time to dissolve agar flakes than to dissolve agar powder.

3. The process of dissolving the agar flakes takes about 10 minutes at a simmer. Agar powder dissolves instantly and only need be heated to about 170°F. Less agar powder is needed than agar flakes because agar powder is concentrated. The result is less evaporation so less liquid is needed in the process.

4. If using agar flakes in place of agar powder, it helps to grind the agar flakes in a coffee grinder for 3 minutes, if you have one, to break down the agar for use in any of the recipes in this book. Note: For a more accurate amount, measure the agar flakes before placing in the coffee grinder, since after grinding the flakes will be condensed.

5. When using agar flakes in recipes that call for agar powder as a binder (such as the tofu mixtures where agar is mixed with arrowroot), it is best to blend the flakes with a water-based medium first, especially if oil is needed because oil will bind agar thus not allowing it to gel or bind the food medium.

6. If using agar flakes in place of agar powder in a recipe that calls for blending the agar into a food, blend the mixture about three times longer than specified to help break down the agar flakes.

MORE NOTES ON AGAR

1. Agar breaks down after cooking if blended.

2. Unlike gelatin, agar sets at room temperature.

3. Gelatin is clear when set and agar is cloudy when used as a gelatin for a jello-style dessert. Agar works better as an aspic than gelatin since it doesn't have to be cooled to set. The downside is it creates a cloudy effect in the liquid.

4. Agar has a slightly off flavor, which is lost when it is used in fruit juice, pudding, or savory food.

SOME FINAL BAKING TIPS

↺ Overbaking an item in the oven for 1 minute will cause it to lose 1 hour of shelf life.

↺ If a bakery item isn't performing to specification, first check time and temperature.

↺ To strengthen all-purpose flour for use in vegan pastries, add ½ ounce (14 grams) of vital gluten flour.

↺ To weaken a bread flour to the functionality of an all-purpose flour, add 1 ounce of cornstarch to 1 pound of bread or high-gluten flour.

To Master the Cuisine

To master the technique of a cuisine is to master the cuisine. And vegan cuisine is the "New World" of cuisine. Vegan bakery techniques are one key to mastering the cuisine. Unlike classical pastries with hundreds of years in development, classical vegan cuisine techniques are in their infancy stages. Vegan egg and gelatin replacement are the keys to mastering vegan pastries. There is no one vegan egg replacement used in egg-free pastries, and there are additional vegan sea vegetable options to agar that are not yet available to retail or foodservice operators. This chapter lays the foundation for you to better understand the chemistry behind the recipes in this book as a means of experimenting with vegan pastries. As Chef Guy Fieri wrote: "Cooking is like snow skiing: If you don't fall at least ten times, then you're not skiing hard enough." Falls are teachable moments to be cherished for the learning they impart.

Chapter Seven

VEGAN SALADS & DRESSINGS

Salads by their very nature are vegetarian so why address them in this book?

The answer is simple. Many components used in salad recipes are not vegan. Salads are an area where vegan should be the standard and not the exception. In this salad section I focus on salads that are generally not vegan or even vegetarian in order to show the alternative.

This section includes my favorite creamy dressings and side salads, such as Dijon Potato Salad and Asian Coleslaw. Another favorite, Vegan Chicken Cranberry Salad, is found on page 378. These dressings and salads complement a protein to become a complete meal. The Tofu "Egg" and Asian Chicken-style salads can be integrated into a luncheon sandwich menu. A few salads, like the Pineapple Raisin Waldorf, are traditional salads that, with minor changes, become vegan. Some salad recipes are vegan replications of classical salads. Making a vegan salad isn't complicated but converting some of the classical salads can be challenging. There are two versions of the carrot salad; the traditional or classical version and the natural foods version. I have presented the classical version in this section. The natural is made with tahini.

The salad dressings in this chapter can be refrigerated for up to three months.

While I have kept dressings in the refrigerator for longer, three months is a safe number.

All the dressings can be used with pasta salads. The pasta salads can incorporate the various vegetarian proteins (beans, tempeh, seitan, and analogues) to make the salad a complete meal. I will leave it to your imagination to creatively utilize the vegan proteins in salads. Included here are a variety of the salads that can become entrée salads or accompany a protein as a balanced meal.

NOTE: The Sauce Niçoise (page 231) with its Mediterranean flavors also makes a superb salad dressing for hot or cold pasta salads.

SALAD DRESSINGS

Soy Mayonnaise

    Variation: Sweet Mayonnaise

Thousand Island Dressing

Yellow Pepper Vinaigrette

Tofu Herb Dressing

Basic French Vinaigrette Dressing

    Variation: Lorenzo Dressing

Creamy Ginger Dressing

Tahini Dressing

Lemon Tahini Cream Dressing

Cranberry Port Vinaigrette

PROTEIN & TRADITIONAL SALADS

Penne Pasta Salad with Tempeh or Chicken-Style Protein

Lentil Salad with Olives

Roasted Vegetable Salad

Sea Vegetable Bean Salad

Salad à la Russe

Quinoa Bean Salad with Sundried Tomatoes

Tofu "Cottage Cheese"

Tofu "Egg" Salad

Carrot Salad

Dijon Potato Salad

Pineapple Raisin Waldorf Salad

Salad Beatrice with Artichokes

American-Style Potato Salad

Tempura Vegetable Nori Roll Salad

Asian Coleslaw

    Variation: Asian Coleslaw with Tempeh

    Variation: Asian Chicken-Style Salad

Pasta Salad Niçoise

Salad Dressings

SOY MAYONNAISE

The vegan mayonnaise I prefer to make is essentially an oil, emulsified with tofu. It is high in fat. The blending of oil with tofu gives this dressing a rich, smooth, creamy texture with a little protein.

YIELD: About 1 ½ cups
TIME: 10 minutes prep

1 (12.3-ounce) package firm silken tofu
¼ cup canola oil
1 tablespoon lemon juice
1 teaspoon yellow mustard
½ teaspoon salt

1. Place all of the ingredients in a blender, and blend until smooth.

2. Use immediately, or place in a covered container and refrigerate.

VARIATION: *Sweet Mayonnaise*

Replace the mustard with 2 tablespoons sugar.

THOUSAND ISLAND DRESSING

YIELD: 4 ½ cups
TIME: 25 minutes prep

2 ½ cups Soy Mayonnaise or commercial vegan mayonnaise
¾ finely diced cup onions
¾ cup chili sauce
2 tablespoons chopped capers
6 tablespoons chopped dill pickles
¾ finely diced cup tofu
¾ cup finely diced green bell peppers
1 tablespoon finely chopped parsley
¾ cup catsup

Mix all ingredients together until evenly dispersed. Refrigerate until ready to use.

YELLOW PEPPER VINAIGRETTE

YIELD: 1 ⅓ cups
TIME: 10 minutes prep and 5 minutes blending time (add 20 minutes to roast the pepper)

½ cup chopped roasted, yellow bell pepper
½ cup canola oil or oil of choice
½ cup rice vinegar
½ teaspoon salt
2 teaspoons sugar
½ teaspoon fresh minced garlic
¼ cup firmly packed fresh cilantro

Put all ingredients in a blender and blend until smooth.

TOFU HERB DRESSING

A very popular dressing in all of the restaurants where I have worked, this high-protein dressing gives a rich robust flavor.

YIELD: 1 quart
TIME: 15 minutes prep

¾ pound tofu, drained for 15 minutes

1 ⅛ cups water

1 ¼ cups canola oil or oil of choice

¼ cup chopped onion

5 tablespoons cider vinegar

2 tablespoons agave syrup or sugar

1 ⅛ teaspoons salt

1 ⅛ teaspoons dill weed

¾ teaspoon dried basil

1 ⅛ teaspoons yellow prepared mustard

⅔ teaspoon cayenne pepper

1. Blend all ingredients together until smooth.

2. Refrigerate until ready to serve.

3. Pour over the fresh vegetable salad of your choice and enjoy.

BASIC FRENCH VINAIGRETTE

This dressing is a vegan modification of a French vinaigrette. The oil, vinegar, and salt are the essential ingredients. The remaining ingredients give the dressing character with flavor, texture, and eye appeal that stand out if used in a simple pasta or grain salad. It combines well with roasted vegetables for a superb salad or side dish.

YIELD: 2 ½ cups
TIME: 30 minutes prep

1 ½ cups canola oil or oil of choice

¾ cups cider vinegar

2 teaspoons minced garlic

2 teaspoons chopped basil (or 2 tablespoons fresh chopped)

1 ⅛ teaspoons black pepper

1 ½ tablespoons minced red bell pepper

1 teaspoon sugar (optional for lighter acidity)

¼ cup finely chopped scallions or chives

1 tablespoon chopped pitted black olives

2 teaspoons salt

Mix all the ingredients together and refrigerate until chilled. Mix well before using.

FRENCH VINAIGRETTE VARIATION:

Lorenzo Dressing

YIELD: 2 ½ cups
TIME: 10 minutes prep

1 ½ cups Basic French Vinaigrette

¾ cup vegan chili sauce

¾ cup catsup

¼ cup horseradish

¼ cup chopped fresh parsley

To the Basic French Vinaigrette, add chili sauce, catsup, horseradish, and parsley. Place all ingredients in a blender and blend until smooth. Refrigerate until cold.

CREAMY GINGER DRESSING

This dressing also works well with pasta.

YIELD: 2 ½ cups
TIME: 20 minutes prep

1 ½ tablespoons peeled, chopped fresh ginger
½ peeled, chopped carrots
¼ cup chopped celery
½ cup peeled, chopped onion
½ cup canola oil
½ cider vinegar
¼ cup sweet white miso
2 tablespoons tomato paste
1 tablespoon sugar
3 tablespoons lemon juice
¾ teaspoon dried basil
¼ teaspoon peppercorns

Place all ingredients in blender and blend about 5 minutes or until smooth.

TAHINI DRESSING

YIELD: 6 cups
TIME: 10 minutes prep

2 cups water
2 cups tahini
1 cup apple cider vinegar
½ cup rice syrup
½ cup white miso
1 cup chopped parsley, loosely packed

Pour water, tahini, vinegar, syrup, and miso into the blender and blend until smooth or whip in a bowl until smooth. Add parsley, mix, and refrigerate until ready to use.

LEMON TAHINI CREAM DRESSING

YIELD: 2 ¼ cups
TIME: 10 minutes prep

½ cup tahini
8 ounces firm or silken tofu
1 lemon, zested and juiced
¼ cup cider vinegar
1 clove garlic, minced
¼ cup brown rice syrup or agave syrup
2 tablespoons white miso
½ cup water

Place all ingredients in a blender and blend until smooth. Chill then serve.

CRANBERRY PORT VINAIGRETTE

YIELD: 1 ½ cups
TIME: 10 minutes prep and 1 hour refrigeration

¼ cup cranberry concentrate (not juice)
¼ cup balsamic vinegar
¼ cup port wine
¼ cup water
¼ cup olive oil
1 ½ tablespoons (6 leaves) fresh basil
1 tablespoon agave syrup
2 teaspoons Dijon mustard
1 teaspoon minced garlic
¼ teaspoon sea salt

Put all ingredients into a blender and blend until smooth. Transfer to a covered container and refrigerate for 1 hour. Serve cold.

Protein & Traditional Salads

PENNE PASTA SALAD WITH TEMPEH OR CHICKEN-STYLE PROTEIN

This salad was created as a bean salad and has a strong balanced flavor profile. Numerous vegan proteins would work well in this salad. It was originally developed with beans and can easily be converted to a tempeh/analogue salad for variety. Seitan or tofu can also be used but if using tofu, I recommend an infused tofu pâté with an intense flavor. Plain tofu is a flavor detractor because it is bland. The same is true with tempeh unless it is flavor infused via sautéing. Seitan would be the exception because it is flavored in the cooking process.

YIELD: 6 cups (5 servings)
TIME: 30 minutes prep and 30 minutes cooking

2 cups dry or fresh penne pasta

1 cup diced eggplant

½ cup extra virgin olive oil

Pinch of salt

1 ½ cups of ½-inch diced tempeh or chicken protein analogue*

1 tablespoon tamari

2 tablespoons canola or sunflower oil

1 cup sliced shiitake mushrooms (option to use fresh or rehydrated mushrooms of choice)

½ cup thinly sliced scallions

1 cup diced fresh tomatoes or drained diced canned tomatoes

¾ cup rice vinegar

1 teaspoon fresh minced garlic

1 teaspoon sugar

½ teaspoon salt

1. Cook pasta and sauté eggplant in two tablespoons olive oil on medium heat with a pinch of salt until soft.

2. Brush or toss tempeh with tamari, and sauté in two tablespoons of canola oil for 3 minutes on each side. Add ¼ inch water, cover, and cook until water is completely evaporated.

3. Toss mushrooms, scallions, tomatoes, rice vinegar, garlic, sugar, remaining olive oil, and salt together. Add pasta, tempeh, and eggplant. Mix until evenly distributed.

*OPTIONS: 1 (15–ounce) can garbanzo beans, drained; 15 ounces sliced or diced seitan; cooked tofu pâté; or half nuts and half beans. Kalamata olives are an option for extra flavor and color.

LENTIL SALAD WITH OLIVES

This salad can be served at room temperature or warm on a cold day on a bed of spinach.

YIELD: 4 servings
TIME: 1 hour prep and 40 to 60 minutes cooking

Cooking Lentils

Cooking grains and beans is both art and chemistry. One of the key factors is heating the ingredient until it is cooked but still holds its shape. This is achieved by soaking lentils in a saltwater brine for 60 minutes during which the salt removes the calcium and magnesium ions from the skin and breaks down the pectin to soften the skin, allowing it flexibility to prevent bursting. The lentils are drained. Water and salt are added, but now the salt's role changes. The sodium ions work into the lentils, preventing the starch from absorbing too much water.

French green lentils, or *Lentilles du Puy*, are our preferred choice for this recipe, but it works with any type of lentil except red or yellow. Brining helps keep the lentils intact, but if you don't have time, they'll still taste good. The salad can be served warm or at room temperature.

For Brining Lentils

1 cup black, Beluga, or French green lentils, rinsed

4 cups warm water, 110° to 120°F

1 teaspoon salt

For Cooking Lentils

4 cups additional water

¾ teaspoon salt

1 tablespoon minced garlic

2 bay leaves

To Mix with Lentils for Salad

6 tablespoons extra virgin olive oil

¼ cup white wine or golden balsamic vinegar

½ cup coarsely chopped pitted Kalamata olives

½ cup grilled and finely diced eggplant

⅓ cup chopped fresh mint leaves

¼ teaspoon salt

⅛ teaspoon black pepper

1. Mix lentils, warm water, and salt together and let stand for 60 minutes. Drain.

2. Pour lentils, water, salt, garlic, and bay leaves into a 2-quart saucepan. Cover and bring to a simmer. Reduce to very low heat and cook covered for about 45 minutes or until lentils are soft but not bursting (check in 35 minutes and cook until lentils are tender but remain intact, 40 to 60 minutes overall).

3. While lentils are cooking, whisk oil and vinegar together in a large bowl and prep remaining ingredients for salad.

4. Drain lentils and remove bay leaves. Mix lentils with oil, vinegar, olives, eggplant, chopped mint, salt, and black pepper.

ROASTED VEGETABLE SALAD

For this salad, you can substitute a different type of root vegetable for any of those listed. In making substitutions, use the same amount as for the original vegetable.

YIELD: 4 to 6 servings
TIME: 25 minutes prep and 45 minutes cooking and mixing

Squash

Half of large butternut squash or 1 small acorn squash
1 tablespoon olive oil or oil of choice
Sprinkling of salt

Other Vegetables

4 tablespoons olive oil
1 ½ cups carrots, peeled, cut in half lengthwise, and sliced
1 ½ cups parsnips, peeled, cut in half lengthwise, and sliced
1 ½ cups sliced Jerusalem artichokes or another root vegetable
2 cups peeled and diced rutabaga
1 ½ cups Spanish onion, peeled and diced
1 tablespoon fresh, minced garlic
½ teaspoon salt
½ teaspoon black pepper
1 ½ cups Brussels sprouts
¼ cup water
2 cups Basic French Vinaigrette Dressing (page 155)
1 head leaf lettuce
2 tomatoes, for garnish

1. If you are using a whole squash, cut it in half lengthwise and scrape out the seeds and the stringy part.

2. Rub the inside of the squash with 1 tablespoon olive oil and sprinkle it with a little salt.

3. Bake uncovered in the oven while the other vegetables are roasting. The squash should take 30 to 45 minutes to bake. It should be tender but still fairly firm.

4. Allow the squash to cool. Then peel and dice it. Measure out about 1 ½ cups for the salad.

5. While squash is baking, pour 2 tablespoons olive oil in a large sauté pan on medium high heat and add prepared carrots, parsnips, artichokes, rutabaga, onion, and garlic. Lightly caramelize vegetables.

6. Place the caramelized vegetables in a roasting pan, add salt and pepper and shake well to make sure all of the vegetables are well coated. Cover the pan with a lid or aluminum foil and place it in a preheated oven at 375°F. Roast the vegetables for about 25 minutes or until soft but firm. Remove from oven and set aside to cool.

7. Meanwhile cut stems off Brussels sprouts and slice in half. Lightly oil sauté pan with 1 tablespoon oil. Turn heat to medium high. Pour Brussels sprouts into pan and lightly brown. Add ¼ cup water, cover, and cook for about 5 minutes. Uncover and let cool.

8. When all the vegetables are cool, toss them gently with the vinaigrette and refrigerate. Serve the salad cold on a bed of lettuce garnished with wedges of tomato.

SEA VEGETABLE BEAN SALAD

This entrée salad is a complete protein and balanced meal.

YIELD: 11 servings (11 cups)
TIME: 40 minutes prep

Dressing	Salad
½ cup canola oil	¾ cup hydrated ocean greens or wakame
½ cup rice vinegar	1 ½ cups shredded red radishes
¼ cup roasted sesame oil	1 cup shredded carrots
¼ cup creamy peanut butter	1 medium cucumber
¼ cup water	5 cups cooked spiral pasta (about 2 ½ cups dry)
¼ cup tamari	1 ¼ cups cooked garbanzo beans (or 1 [15–ounce]
2 tablespoons agave syrup	can)
2 teaspoons granulated garlic	Salad greens (optional)
2 teaspoons ginger powder	

1. Cut cucumber in half, seed, and slice to get 2 cups' worth.

2. Mix all dressing ingredients together until evenly dispersed. Place in a container and refrigerate until ready to use.

3. Soak dry sea vegetables in enough water to cover the vegetables for 10 minutes. Drain and coarsely chop. Toss dressing with vegetables, pasta, and beans.

OPTION: Shred or very thinly slice lettuce and use as a bed to serve salad. Or serve on several lettuce leaves.

Modification of the Quinoa Bean Salad (opposite page) using fresh tomatoes in place of sundries tomatoes and Nut Cream Cheese.

SALAD À LA RUSSE

It is best to let the salad set overnight to let the onions mellow out the flavor.

YIELD: 5 servings
TIME: 30 minutes prep and 20 minutes cooking

2 medium potatoes, washed, unpeeled and ¼ inch diced
1 cup peeled and julienned carrots
1 tablespoon high-heat safflower oil or preferred oil
1 ½ teaspoons minced garlic
¼ teaspoon black pepper
1 cup frozen green peas
½ cup Soy Mayonnaise (page 154) or commercial vegan mayonnaise
1 cup peeled and diced onions
5 medium tomatoes
Lettuce leaves for serving
5 pitted black olives

1. Boil potatoes on medium heat 20 minutes or more until soft; cool and peel the potatoes. Cut them into thick strips. Set aside.

2. Sauté the carrots in the oil with the garlic and pepper over medium heat for about 5 minutes. After 2 minutes add the peas, which will continue to cook in the hot mixture for another 2 minutes.

3. Mix the potatoes with the mayonnaise and the carrot mixture. Add the diced onions.

4. Slice the top off each tomato and hollow out the centers. Fill the tomatoes with the mixture and serve on a plate lined with lettuce leaves. Garnish the salads with the olives. Refrigerate until ready to serve.

QUINOA BEAN SALAD WITH SUNDRIED TOMATOES

This salad is loaded with protein and flavor coming from the simple, natural flavors of the ingredients.

YIELD: 4 ¾ cups
TIME: 30 minutes

1 ½ cups cooked kidney beans, drained (or 1 [15-ounce] can)
1 ½ cups cooked black beans, drained (or 1 [15-ounce] can)
1 ½ cups cooked quinoa
½ cup whole kernel corn, frozen, thawed
½ cup roasted walnuts
½ cup chopped sundried tomatoes
½ cup extra virgin olive oil
½ cup rice vinegar
½ cup fresh stemmed, chopped cilantro,
1 tablespoon agave syrup or sugar (to cut the acidity)
2 teaspoons fresh minced garlic
1 teaspoon salt

Prep all ingredients. Mix all ingredients in any order. Best to refrigerate the salad for at least an hour to let the ingredients fuse.

TOFU "COTTAGE CHEESE"

This strongly resembles regular cottage cheese. It has a delicate flavor accented by the dill weed.

YIELD: 3 servings
TIME: 10 minutes prep and 15 minutes cooking

½ cup finely chopped onion
1 ½ teaspoons canola oil or olive oil
¼ teaspoon salt (optional)
1 cup firm tofu, crushed by hand
¼ teaspoon dill weed
½ Soy Mayonnaise (page 154) or commercial vegan mayonnaise
2 tablespoons chopped chives

1. Sauté the onion in the oil and salt until the onions are translucent. Add the tofu and dill weed and sauté another 4 to 5 minutes or until mixture is simmering.

2. Remove from heat and let sit for 3 to 4 minutes to cool down a little. Note: The heat allows the flavor to develop more quickly than when cold. Mayonnaise can be added during the last few minutes of cooking if desired but if it overcooks (becomes too hot) it will separate.

3. When tofu mixture is cool, add mayonnaise and chives and mix into tofu mixture.

TOFU "EGG" SALAD

YIELD 4 portions (2 cups)
TIME: 10 minutes prep and 15 minutes cooking

2 cups tofu, extra firm, crumbled
½ cup chopped onions
½ teaspoon minced garlic
1 tablespoon canola oil
½ teaspoon salt
Dash of annatto or turmeric for color
½ cup Soy Mayonnaise (page 154) or commercial vegan mayonnaise
¼ cup finely diced celery (optional)
1 teaspoon yellow mustard
2 tablespoons chopped parsley

1. Rinse and drain tofu (wrap in towel and press to remove excess water). Crumble.

2. Sauté onion and garlic in oil on medium heat.

3. Add crumbled tofu, salt, and annatto or turmeric. Sauté until heat reaches 160°F.

4. Remove from heat. Add mayonnaise, celery, and yellow mustard. Stir to coat. Finish with parsley.

NOTE: Mayonnaise must be added at the end of the cooking process to prevent it from separating since the mayo will break down under intense heat.

CARROT SALAD

This is the vegan traditional version of carrot salad. Raisins or any dry fruit can be used in place of cranberries. Walnut pieces are an option for more crunch.

YIELD: 2 cups
TIME: 15 to 20 minutes

2 cups carrots, peeled and grated
½ cup cranberries, dried, sweetened
½ cup shredded sweetened coconut
¾ cup Soy Mayonnaise (page 154) or commercial vegan mayonnaise
½ teaspoon pure vanilla extract
1/16 teaspoon salt

1. Combine all ingredients and mix well.

2. Refrigerate until cold. It is best to let the carrot salad set overnight to allow the flavors to mellow.

Dijon Potato Salad

DIJON POTATO SALAD

YIELD: 6 servings
TIME: 15 minutes prep and 25 minutes cooking

5 medium potatoes, red, new potato, or Yukon Gold
3 tablespoons Dijon-style mustard
1 ½ cups Basic French Vinaigrette (page 155) (hold ¼ cup for vegetable sauté)
1 cup finely diced, peeled onions
1 cup finely chopped carrots
1 cup finely diced celery
½ teaspoon salt
¼ teaspoon black pepper
1 tablespoon arame, dry crumbled fine (optional)
1 cup broccoli stems and florets

1. Peel and dice the potatoes and place them in a saucepan with water to cover. Bring to a boil, then simmer the potatoes, half-covered, for 20 minutes, until the potatoes are tender. Drain and set aside.

2. Mix the mustard into the vinaigrette. Sauté the onions, carrots, and celery in ¼ cup of oil from the Basic French Vinaigrette dressing (the oil separates from the other liquids in the dressing) with salt and pepper, over medium heat for 5 minutes.

3. Add the cooked potatoes and arame and sauté for another 2 minutes. Remove from heat, add the remaining 1 ¼ cup dressing, and let cool. Then refrigerate until the potatoes are cold.

4. Blanch the broccoli and set aside to cool. To prevent your broccoli from being discolored by the vinegar, add just before serving.

Pineapple Raisin Waldorf Salad

YIELD: 8 servings
TIME: 30 minutes

Dressing

YIELD: 1 ⅔ cups

1 (10 ½ ounce) package silken tofu, extra firm
¼ cup Soy Mayonnaise or commercial vegan mayonnaise
3 tablespoons agave syrup
1 tablespoon lemon juice
¼ teaspoon nutmeg
¼ teaspoon vanilla extract

Place all of the dressing ingredients into a blender and blend until smooth. Check the flavor and adjust the seasonings to taste if necessary. Cover and refrigerate until ready to use.

NOTE: Add the dressing to this salad just prior to serving. Adding it too far in advance will cause the salad to go limp.

IMPORTANT: The lettuce must dry thoroughly after washing or any remaining water will thin out the dressing.

Salad

YIELD: 6 cups

½ cup chopped walnuts, raw or roasted
2 cups red delicious apples, diced
2 cups fresh or canned pineapple chunks, drained
1 cup diced celery
½ cup raisins
2 heads lettuce, shredded (or 8 whole lettuce leaves)
6 mint leaves
6 strawberries, fanned

1. If you are roasting the walnuts, preheat oven to 325°F. Spread the walnuts on a baking sheet and roast them in the oven until lightly browned and aromatic, between 5 and 15 minutes. Immediately remove them from the sheet and transfer them to another container to cool. Once cool, chop the nuts coarsely into ¼ inch pieces.

2. Mix the walnuts, apples, pineapple, celery, and raisins together, cover, and refrigerate until chilled.

3. When ready to serve, combine the dressing with the salad ingredients and arrange the mix on a bed of lettuce, shredded or whole, on each of the serving plates. Garnish each serving with a mint leaf and fanned strawberry, then serve immediately.

SALAD BEATRICE WITH ARTICHOKES

YIELD: 6 servings
TIME: 20 minutes with the Tofu "Egg" Salad and dressing prepared

1 ½ pounds green beans, fresh or frozen
12 whole artichoke hearts, canned or cooked if fresh (2 per salad)
1 ½ cups Basic French Vinaigrette (page 155)
3 medium to large tomatoes, ripe
2 bunches watercress
¼ pound firm tofu, finely diced or ¾ cup Tofu "Egg" Salad (page 162)

1. Halve green beans. If using frozen beans, blanch in hot water. If using fresh green beans, cook for about 5 minutes in simmering water and dip into ice water to stop the cooking process.

2. Mix the cold cooked green beans and artichoke hearts with the dressing. Turn onto a serving dish.

3. Slice the tomatoes, place the slices on small bunches of watercress, and arrange them around the beans. Sprinkle with finely diced tofu or tablespoon-size dollops of Tofu "Egg" Salad (page 162). Refrigerate and serve cold.

AMERICAN-STYLE POTATO SALAD

YIELD: 6 servings
TIME: 15 minutes prep and 25 minutes cooking

5 medium new potatoes
1 cup finely diced peeled onions
1 cup medium-diced celery
1 ½ cups Soy Mayonnaise (page 154) or commercial vegan mayonnaise
2 tablespoons yellow mustard
1 tablespoon pickle relish
½ teaspoon salt
¼ teaspoon black pepper

1. Peel and dice the potatoes and place them in a saucepan with water to cover. Bring to a boil, then simmer potatoes, half-covered, for 20 minutes, until potatoes are tender. Drain and set aside.

2. Mix vegetables with potatoes and add mayo, mustard, relish, salt, and black pepper. Refrigerate until the potatoes are cold. Serve salad cold.

TEMPURA VEGETABLE NORI ROLL SALAD

This salad is anything but traditional. I could not resist the temptation as it is one of my favorite decadently healthy salads. It is a tempura raw vegetable salad that received a silver medal in the International Culinary Olympics. I lined the nori with a tofu pâté for the competition.

YIELD: 2 servings
TIME: 45 minutes

¼ cup tamari

2 cups hot water

½ cup dry arame

1 ½ cups shredded red cabbage

¼ cup cider vinegar or red wine vinegar

1 ½ cups peeled and julienned carrots

1 ½ cups watercress

3 nori sheets

2 cups tempura batter (page 198)

4 cups high-heat cooking oil in a 2-quart sauce pan or 10-inch skillet

2 cups salad greens of choice

SERVING OPTIONS: Either a traditional Asian dipping sauce or a Balsamic Orange Marinade (page 231) can be used. The Asian BBQ Sauce (page 235) would also work by diluting the recipe with 2 tablespoons water. The Five Spice Asian Dressing (page 167) or Grilled Vegetable Marinade & Citrus Dipping Sauce (page 236) would complement these rolls as a delicious salad or appetizer.

1. Mix the tamari in hot water and soak the arame in this mixture for 30 minutes. Drain and press dry.

2. Meanwhile dip the shredded cabbage in a small amount of vinegar and rub the cabbage by hand. Let it sit for a few hours. Drain and press dry.

3. Combine the carrots and watercress.

4. Lightly toast the nori sheets by holding them about 6 inches over medium heat for 5 to 10 seconds on each side. Place a nori sheet on a flat surface. Lay all the vegetables in a row along the nori sheet. Roll up the vegetables tightly in the nori sheet, squeezing hard to eliminate as much juice as possible. Roll up this nori roll in the second sheet. Wet the ends of the second sheet with water and seal the edges. Repeat with the third nori sheet.

5. In a deep skillet heat the cooking oil to 375°F. Dip the whole roll into the tempura batter. (Leftover tempura batter can be used immediately or refrigerated for future use.) Then fry the roll in the hot oil until lightly brown (30 to 60 seconds). Remove and drain.

6. Serve slices of the nori roll on a bed of greens with a sauce of your choice.

ASIAN COLESLAW

YIELD: 4 cups (8 servings)
TIME: 30 minutes

Five Spice Asian Dressing

YIELD: ¾ cup

3 tablespoons rice wine vinegar

3 tablespoons vegetable oil

3 tablespoons creamy peanut butter (4
tablespoons for a creamier texture)

1 ½ tablespoons tamari (gluten-free) or soy
sauce

1 ½ tablespoons brown sugar

1 tablespoon minced fresh ginger

2 ½ teaspoons minced fresh garlic

½ teaspoon Chinese five spice powder

Coleslaw

2 ½ cups thinly sliced green cabbage

1 cup thinly sliced red cabbage

½ cup thinly sliced red or yellow bell pepper

½ cup julienned carrots

½ cup chopped green onions

¼ cup fresh chopped cilantro

Mix together the dressing ingredients. Toss
cabbages, pepper, carrots, green onions, and
cilantro to blend. Add dressing to vegetables
and serve or refrigerate until ready to serve.

VARIATION: *Asian Tempeh Salad*

2 tablespoons tamari

2 tablespoons water

12 ounces tempeh

2 tablespoons oil canola or oil of choice

1. Mix tamari and water.

2. Slice tempeh into 12 pieces, approximately
    1 ounce each and place in pan. Coat with
    tamari mixture.

3. On medium heat, pour oil into sauté pan
    and lightly brown tempeh.

4. Add 3 ounces tempeh to each serving of
    slaw.

VARIATION: *Asian Chicken-Style Salad*

Use 12 strips of a pre-cooked chicken-style
protein (analogue) in place of the tempeh.

PASTA SALAD NIÇOISE

YIELD: 4 (1 cup) servings
TIME: 20 minutes prep and 20 minutes cooking

2 cups dry penne or rigatoni pasta*
Pinch of salt
2 teaspoons olive oil
1 cup Sauce Niçoise (page 231)
¼ cup diced green bell pepper
¼ cup diced red bell pepper
2 tablespoons extra virgin olive oil
¼ teaspoon ground black pepper
¼ teaspoon salt
¼ cup crumbled tofu
¼ cup shredded vegan mozzarella cheese (optional)
½ gallon mixed field greens or salad greens of your choice

1. In a 2-quart sauce pan pour 1 quart of water, a pinch of salt, and 2 teaspoons olive oil and turn heat on to medium. When water is simmering, add pasta and stir to keep from sticking together. Stir about every minute for the first few minutes. Continue cooking for 15 to 20 minutes or until pasta is cooked yet firm.

2. Drain, rinse in cold water, pour into a mixing bowl, and add sauce, peppers, oil, pepper, salt, and tofu and mix well.

3. Serve salad immediately at room temperature or refrigerate until ready to serve. (The pasta mixture will keep in the refrigerator for a week if the salad greens are not mixed into it.) To serve, arrange 2 cups salad greens on a salad plate and top with one cup pasta mixture.

4. The vegan cheese can be mixed into the pasta salad or used to garnish the tops of the salads.

*2 cups raw pasta yields 4 cups cooked pasta

From Culinary Olympics: American Bounty

Chapter Eight

VEGAN NON-DAIRY CHEESES, SPREADS, & CONDIMENTS

Humanity, at the onset of existence as hunter-gathers, discovered nuts.

We shelled and consumed them. Perhaps some processing, such as roasting, took place. With the evolution of vegetarian cuisine, nuts have risen to an enviable position as a "dairy" ingredient in dairy-free cuisine.

When animals were domesticated, we began drinking their milk. Then we discovered how to convert it into cheese. We also created coconut milk with coconut (classified as a fruit) and soy milk with soybean (classified as a legume). Soybeans, coconuts, and nuts are the sustainable dairy replacements of the twenty-first century; they have the capability of feeding a larger portion of the billions of inhabitants of our planet.

Vegan cheeses are a dairy-style ingredient that replicates the function of cheeses in traditional and new recipes, but they are not a mimic of dairy cheeses. They create a light curd and add lubricity (fatty flavor) with mild plant-based flavors. They give the recipe a richer flavor and creamy texture. A number of decent vegan cheeses are now sold in supermarkets; these brands are listed in the resource section in the back of this cookbook.

Like dairy cheeses, adding a curdling agent such as lemon juice or vinegar to the vegan cream mixture will cause it to curd. Vegan cheeses develop their firm texture between the curd and osmosis. Nuts or tofu absorb the moisture to help solidify the vegan cheese, and lemon as the souring agent causes the soy milk to curdle. The handcrafted versions are made with whole foods with a higher percentage of protein and nutritional value, unlike vegan commercial cheeses, which contain more highly refined ingredients. Whole foods cost more, which is why the foodservice industry doesn't often use them in vegan cheeses.

Another desirable property of dairy cheeses is their ability to melt and stretch due to the milk protein casein. Vegan cheeses can't take advantage of casein. But scientists are coming close to replicating that function of cheese, which will provide a better mouth-feel to vegan cheeses. There are some excellent vegan cheeses available to both foodservice and retail consumers that do a better job of melting without the casein.

If these commercial vegan cheeses are not available or you want to make your own signature cheese, here are a few basic formulas made with nutrient-dense whole foods.

Following the vegan cheese recipes are a few examples of vegan spreads and condiments to complement either a menu course or to add to crackers or breads. Spreads are often related to cheeses and most likely used on sandwiches. Essential to all cuisines, spreads and condiments will continue to evolve with the evolution of global cuisines.

NON-DAIRY CHEESES

American Melting Cheese

Soy Curd "Cottage Cheese"

Coconut Lemon Cream Cheese

Lemon Nut Cheese

    Variation: Italian Lemon Nut Cheese

Smoked Cream Cheese

Cauliflower Sour Cream

Nut Cream Cheese

Soy Yogurt

Cashew Cream

Tofu Cashew Sour Cream

    Variation: Cashew Sour Cream

SPREADS & CONDIMENTS

Rosemary, Thyme, & Sage Squash Butter

Squash Butter

Greek Potato Butter

Cranberry Apricot Chutney with Port Wine

Mushroom Confit

Gremolata

Non-Dairy Cheeses

American Melting Cheese

This cheese simulates an American-style cheese that will melt. While the flavor is "basic," the cook has the option to adjust the flavor using nutritional yeast and/or herbs, spices, and souring flavors. This cheese was designed to be scooped when cold, spread on a protein like a veggie burger, and melted under dry heat similar to American or mozzarella cheese or it can be used in dishes like a chili mac.

YIELD: 2 cups
TIME: 10 minutes

6 tablespoons vegan butter spread
1 (12.3 ounce) package extra firm silken tofu
2 tablespoons arrowroot or cornstarch
½ cup raw cashew pieces
$1/16$ teaspoon annatto or turmeric
2 teaspoons nutritional yeast

1. Warm butter spread.

2. Pour all ingredients into blender and blend until smooth and creamy. Chill until ready to use.

Soy Curd "Cottage Cheese"

YIELD: 6 servings
TIME: 10 minutes prep and 10 minutes cooking

2 cups (1 ¼ pounds) extra firm tofu, crushed by hand
1 cup finely chopped onion
1 tablespoon canola, olive, or oil of choice
¼ teaspoon salt
1 cup Soy Mayonnaise (page 154) or commercial vegan mayonnaise
½ teaspoon dill weed
4 tablespoons chopped chives or parsley

1. Drain, rinse, and dry the extra firm tofu. Wash hands and then crush by squeezing through hands 2 to 3 times.

2. Sauté the onion in the oil with salt on medium heat until onion is translucent.

3. Add tofu and continue sautéing until tofu is hot. Note: Do not brown tofu or onions because this is a dairy curd–style food and caramelization isn't part of the flavor.

4. Set aside to cool. Add Soy Mayonnaise, dill weed, and chives. Store in container and chill in refrigerator.

COCONUT LEMON CREAM CHEESE

YIELD: 1 ½ cups
TIME: 15 minutes and 24 hours incubation

1 cup whole almonds, blanched
¾ cup coconut milk
¼ teaspoon salt
2 tablespoons lemon juice*

1. Pour all ingredients into a blender and blend on high speed for about 5 minutes (until smooth with no grit when rubbed between your fingers).

2. Refrigerate for 24 hours to let flavor, osmosis, and curdling develop.

*For a lighter lemon flavor, use 1 tablespoon lemon juice and 1 tablespoon water.

LEMON NUT CHEESE

This cheese will be firmer than a sour cream and have a strong cream cheese note. Using or roasting different nuts creates unique flavors. Try walnuts, peanuts, or pecans.

YIELD: 2 cups
TIME: 15 minutes and 24 hours incubation

1 cup whole cashews
1 cup whole almonds, blanched
¾ cup hot water
6 tablespoons canola oil
3 tablespoons lemon juice
3 tablespoons nutritional yeast
½ teaspoon salt
1 tablespoon rice vinegar

1. Pour all ingredients into a blender and blend until smooth.

2. Place in a lightly oiled container, cover, and steam until the mixture begins to curdle.

3. Remove from steamer and stir to form a paste. Wrap in plastic in a cylindrical form or containerize and cover. Refrigerate.

VARIATION: *Italian Lemon Nut Cheese*

YIELD: 1 ⅓ cups
TIME: 5 minutes

1 cup Lemon Nut Cheese
½ cup water
1 teaspoon chopped oregano
½ teaspoon granulated garlic
½ teaspoon salt

Mix together until evenly dispersed and serve.

SMOKED CREAM CHEESE

This recipe has a strong smoked flavor. If you want a lighter version, use half smoked and half unsmoked nuts. This cheese will soften to the texture of cream cheese and works well with a grilled cheese sandwich or with grilled or roasted vegetables of choice.

YIELD: 1¾ cup
TIME: 15 minutes prep and 24 hours incubation

¾ cup smoked whole cashews or pieces
¾ cup smoked whole almonds, blanched
⅞ cup vegan butter spread, warmed to melting point
¼ cup lemon juice
2 tablespoons water
1 teaspoon cracked black pepper
¼ teaspoon salt

1. Pour all ingredients into a blender and blend until smooth. To determine if the mixture is sufficiently blended, rub the cream between your fingers. If it is gritty, blending isn't complete. If smooth with no grit, the blending is complete.

2. Refrigerate for 24 hours to let flavor, osmosis, and curdling develop.

NUT CREAM CHEESE

YIELD: ¾ cup
TIME: 15 minutes prep and 24 hours incubation

1 cup raw whole cashews or pieces
½ cup water
1 ½ teaspoons nutritional yeast
⅛ teaspoon salt
2 ½ teaspoons lemon juice*

1. Pour all ingredients into blender and blend until smooth. The key factor in determining if it's sufficiently blended is rubbing the cream between your fingers. If it's gritty, blending isn't complete. If smooth with no grit, the blending is complete.

2. Refrigerate for 24 hours to let flavor, osmosis, and curdling develop.

NOTE: The yeast gives the recipe a cheesy note and the lemon causes curdling and neutralizes the cashew flavor. Water is necessary to turn the mixture into a cream, and the osmosis causes the mixture to become firm.

* For a neutral flavor cream cheese, use 2 ½ teaspoons cider or white vinegar instead of lemon juice.

CAULIFLOWER SOUR CREAM

This is an alternative macrobiotic version of sour cream and probably one of the healthiest sour creams one could eat.

YIELD: 2 cups
TIME: 15 minutes

2 cups chopped, cooked cauliflower
2 tablespoons tahini
2 tablespoons umeboshi paste
2 tablespoons brown rice vinegar
¼ cup water

Blend all ingredients until smooth.

Soy Yogurt

YIELD: 2 cups sauce
TIME: 15 minutes prep and cooking, and 24 hour incubation

1 cup plain, unsweetened soy milk

1 cup coconut milk

2 tablespoons unbleached white flour

¼ teaspoon salt

2 tablespoons lemon juice

1. Mix together milks, flour, and salt in a sauce pan. Bring to a simmer while constantly stirring.

2. When milk mixture thickens, add lemon juice, mix to incorporate, and remove from heat. Store in an airtight container and refrigerate for 24 hours, then serve.

Cashew Cream

Similar to traditional whipping cream, cashew cream serves as a great base for many sauces.

YIELD: About 1 ½ cups
TIME: 15 minutes

1 cup raw cashew pieces

Pinch of salt

1 cup water

1. Place the cashew pieces, salt, and water in a blender and blend for 3 minutes, or until the mixture is smooth.

2. Transfer to a covered container and store in the refrigerator, where it will last for about 1 week, or in the freezer, where it will keep up to six months.

Tofu Cashew Sour Cream

Tofu Cashew Sour Cream has a rich, creamy texture, with a slight hint of lemon. Use it as you would regular sour cream.

YIELD: 1 cup
TIME: 10 minutes prep and 24 hours incubation

1 tablespoon raw cashews

6 ounces silken tofu

¼ cup canola oil

2 tablespoons lemon juice

¼ teaspoon salt

1. Place the cashews in a blender, and blend into a fine meal.

2. Add the remaining ingredients, and blend until the mixture is smooth and creamy.

3. Transfer the mixture to a covered container. Refrigerate for 24 hours to incubate.

   Refrigerated, it will last about 2 months; frozen, it will keep for about 6 months. (After thawing the frozen sour cream, you will have to re-blend it before use to regain the texture.)

VARIATION: *Cashew Sour Cream*

YIELD: approximately 1 ⅛ cups

¾ cup water or soy milk

1 cup raw cashews

⅛ teaspoon salt

2 teaspoons lemon juice or cider vinegar

Place all ingredients in a blender and blend until smooth. Refrigerate for 24 hours before use.

Spreads & Condiments

This section describes several of my favorite butter spreads and condiments. Each spread starts with commercial vegan butter, then a special blend of oils and seasonings is added. The condiments add a rich flavor to any meal, their primary function as a spread on bread and crackers on a vegan canapé. All spreads and condiments must be refrigerated unless stated that refrigeration is not necessary.

ROSEMARY, THYME, & SAGE SQUASH BUTTER

YIELD: 1 cup
TIME: 15 minutes

½ cup butternut squash, peeled, seeded, and steamed
½ cup vegan butter spread, warmed if using a food processor or blender
¼ teaspoon dried thyme leaves
¼ teaspoon ground sage
⅛ teaspoon ground rosemary
⅛ teaspoon salt
1 tablespoon fresh chopped parsley

1. Place all ingredients in a food processor or blender and process until incorporated.

2. For a coarser blend, use a mixer on medium speed for about 3 to 5 minutes to break down the squash. Small squash particles will remain when finished. Those particles give the butter spread eye appeal.

SQUASH BUTTER

This is a recipe with many flavor options using different spices, herbs, caramelized onions, etc.

YIELD: 1 ¼ cups
TIME: 15 minutes prep and 20 minutes cooking

1 cup firmly packed butternut squash
⅝ cup vegan butter spread at room temperature
1 tablespoon coarsely chopped parsley (optional)
¼ teaspoon salt
⅛ teaspoon ground black pepper

1. Peel, dice into ½-inch pieces, and steam squash until soft (about 15 minutes). Prepare enough for 1 cup firmly packed squash.

2. Place all ingredients in a food processor or blender, mix for about 3 to 5 minutes to pulverize the mixture into a smooth, creamy texture. Refrigerate until firm.

3. Or use a mixer to blend on medium speed until incorporated. If there are squash particles in the butter, this will add to the eye appeal. Refrigerate until firm.

GREEK POTATO BUTTER

YIELD: 1 ¼ cups
TIME: 15 minutes prep and 20 minutes cooking

1 cup peeled diced red potatoes

¼ teaspoon salt

1 cup water

¾ cup vegan butter spread or extra virgin olive oil butter spread

¼ teaspoon ground rosemary

½ teaspoon chopped fresh oregano

1 teaspoon chopped fresh parsley

1. Cook potatoes in salted water in covered pot on medium heat until potatoes are soft (15 to 20 minutes). Drain and place in food processor.

2. Add remaining ingredients and process until a smooth mixture forms. Refrigerate until firm and serve.

Squash Butter

CRANBERRY APRICOT CHUTNEY WITH PORT WINE

YIELD: 5 cups (16 servings)
TIME: 15 minutes prep and 25 minutes cooking

24 ounces fresh cranberries, washed and picked through

Zest of large orange

1 cup orange juice

2 tablespoons balsamic vinegar

1 cup port wine

1 cup sugar

1 cup dried apricots, preferably Turkish, cut into strips

1 cup dried cherries

⅛ teaspoon salt

¼ teaspoon nutmeg

¼ teaspoon ground cloves

1 teaspoon cinnamon

1. In a large, heavy pot, combine the cranberries, orange zest, juice, balsamic vinegar, port, and sugar. Bring to low boil, then reduce heat to simmer. The mixture should simmer for about 10 minutes until cranberries "pop" or burst and collapse.

2. Add the apricots, cherries, and salt. Making sure the cranberries don't burn, continue cooking over medium-low heat, stirring occasionally, for about 10 minutes, until the cranberries start to pop.

3. Stir in the nutmeg, cloves, and cinnamon. Continue cooking on low until thick, another 5 to 7 minutes. Taste and adjust seasonings, if necessary. This will keep in the refrigerator at least 4 weeks.

MUSHROOM CONFIT

With excellent taste and texture, this is a perfect condiment to a plain, simple piece of protein such as a grilled piece of seitan or one of the grain loaves without a sauce. The confit can be served on or beside the protein. As a flavor enhancer, mushroom confit surpasses ketchup in taste and health.

YIELD: 1 ½ cups
TIME: 10 minutes prep and 50 minutes cooking

1 ½ cups chopped onions

2 cups sliced shiitake mushrooms

2 tablespoons fresh, chopped garlic

¼ cup canola oil

½ cup red wine

¼ cup balsamic vinegar

3 tablespoons reduced sodium "beef-style" broth powder or tamari

1. Sauté onions, mushrooms, and garlic in oil on medium-low heat for about 20 minutes to develop the sweetness and reduce moisture. Add red wine, vinegar, and broth powder.

2. Reduce heat to low. Simmer until confit is reduced to 1 ½ cups or until there is no steam rising from the mixture. Refrigerate to store. This confit will last about 1 month or longer depending on how much liquid has evaporated from the mix. The lower the moisture, the longer the shelf life.

GREMOLATA

A burst of flavor, gremolata is a combination of lemon zest, garlic, parsley, and olive oil. I add fresh red radish. Traditionally served on grilled meat and roasted potato dishes, gremolata is easy to make and best served fresh as it doesn't have a long shelf life (1 day maximum), but best if the flavors can meld an hour or so before serving. Fortunately it only takes about 5 minutes to make.

YIELD: approximately 6 servings
TIME: 5 minutes

2 teaspoons fresh minced garlic

2 tablespoons lemon zest

½ cup coarsely chopped fresh parsley

¼ cup coarsely shredded red radish

1 tablespoon extra-virgin olive oil

Pinch of salt or iodized salt

Toss garlic, lemon zest, parsley, and radish with oil and salt. Refrigerate if not using immediately.

Chapter Nine

GRAIN, STARCH, & VEGETABLE SIDES

Have you ever thought about the role played by grains, starches, and vegetables in giving entrées their flavor, culinary character, and eye appeal?

Seitan Swiss Steak

They add color, taste, texture, and, of course, nutrition. Side dishes abound in the culinary world. In foodservice there is an overreliance or emphasis on embellishing sides as entrées. While that may be a good way to cut back on excessive animal protein consumption, it isn't a balanced approach to vegetarianism nor does it usually offer sufficient protein to restaurant guests and family members.

Because many side dishes are vegetarian or vegan by default, good recipes can be found in most cookbooks. For that reason I have limited the sides to some of my favorites, such as Squash Polenta with Fennel and a few of my beloved classical sides like Peas Bonne Femme (beautiful woman) and Cauliflower "au Gratin." The sides were also chosen to complement the entrées presented in this book. For example, red cabbage and buckwheat pilaf are the right combination for vegan proteins, like smoked seitan, where the two strong flavor profiles stand up to each other.

I recommend that all sides be vegan. First, the industrialized nations are not protein deficient and don't need it in everything they consume. Second, vegan side dishes can be used with both vegan and meat entrées, simplifying the menu and cutting labor for those chefs who must serve both vegetarians and meat eaters.

SIDES AS ENTRÉES

The side grain, starch, or vegetable is a component of the entrée. In vegetarian cuisine the side can become the entrée so long as it has sufficient protein. The collective protein must provide a reasonable contribution to the RDA (Recommended Dietary Allowance), and it can come from the vegetables, grains, and sauce as well as the protein component. My position is that a side offered as an entrée should have a defined protein in it, such as nuts, seeds, beans, etc. This also adds perceived value.

Grains can easily be built as an entrée protein. Some vegetarian side dishes, like polenta, can be converted into an entrée by adding beans. The side dish becomes the main dish and needs only a sauce and side vegetable to make it a complete dinner menu. Polenta, oh polenta! Adding black beans with a side of vegetables and my spirit has reached culinary nirvana.

All sides (vegetable and grain) are designed to work off the center of the plate. In my kitchen the sides in this book are often combined as an entrée with a protein side dish. The protein and vegetables have an intimate culinary relationship in vegetarian cuisine. Unlike the side dishes with a meat entrée, the grain and vegetable are as central to the dinner as the protein. Quite often I make the protein the side because that is a balanced diet. Remember that a balanced diet is high complex carbohydrate, low fat, and low protein for adults. Sides are often high in complex carbohydrates. Why can't sides be a center of the plate combination of vegetables and grains with a protein side? I encourage you to consider this concept as you work with these recipes.

GRAIN & STARCH SIDES

Fried Cornmeal Mush

Buckwheat Pilaf

Sea Vegetable Polenta

Squash Polenta with Fennel

Basic Millet Quinoa Polenta

Herbed Mashed Potatoes

Whipped Squash Potatoes with Rosemary

Potato Pancakes

"Millet Style" Mashed Potatoes

White Basmati Rice

Home Fries with Caramelized Onions

Chestnut Pilaf with Black Rice

Brown Rice

Southern Black-Eyed Pilaf

Risotto Pesto

SIDE VEGETABLES

Braised Red Cabbage

Cauliflower with Coconut & Bok Choy

Tuscan Vegetable Sauté

Confit of Red Onions Merlot

Savoy Cabbage with Kale & Shiitake Mushrooms

   Variation: Savoy Cabbage & Kale with Coconut Cilantro Greens

Sautéed Arame with Leeks & Cranberries

Moroccan Ratatouille with Garbanzo Beans

Coconut "au Gratin" Topping

Breaded Vegetables

Peas Bonne Femme

   Variation 1: Italian Green Beans Bonne Femme

   Variation 2: Carrots Bonne Femme

   Variation 3: Butternut Squash Bonne Femme

Cauliflower "au Gratin"

Green Beans New Orleans

Carrots, Pecans,& Fennel

Brussels Sprouts with Walnut Oil

Tempura Side Vegetable

   Variation: Tempura Tofu, Tempeh, or Seitan

Grain & Starch Sides

FRIED CORNMEAL MUSH

Cornmeal mush is a popular Southern dish traditionally fried for breakfast and served with a syrup. But it works with entrées by adding color, taste, and texture.

YIELD: 4 to 6 portions
TIME: 30 minutes

1 cup yellow cornmeal
½ teaspoon salt
3 cups water
Flour for breading
Vegetable oil for frying
¾ cup maple syrup or syrup of choice to serve on fried cornmeal mush

1. Combine cornmeal, salt, and 1 cup cold water in a bowl and combine well.

2. Bring remaining 2 cups water to a boil.

3. Pour cold cornmeal and water mixture into the boiling water and whisk to smooth any lumps.

4. Reduce heat and cook on low heat for 20 minutes or until cornmeal becomes a thick smooth paste.

5. Pour hot cornmeal into a Pyrex loaf pan and refrigerate overnight. When ready to cook the next morning, invert pan onto a dish or cutting board and cut ¼-inch slices. Dredge in flour and fry in skillet with hot vegetable oil until golden brown on both sides. Serve with your favorite syrup.

BUCKWHEAT PILAF

I like this dish as a meal unto itself for a satiating low-protein meal. It is an excellent complement to any barbequed or smoked vegan protein and is especially complementary to smoked proteins.

YIELD: 6 cups
TIME: 15 minutes prep and 30 minutes cooking and resting

2 tablespoons high-heat oil (safflower or canola)
½ teaspoon salt
1 ½ teaspoons fresh, minced garlic
½ cup peeled and diced onions
1 cup shredded or finely diced carrots
2 cups water
½ cup sauerkraut
1 cup buckwheat, rinsed
½ cup fresh chopped parsley

1. Preheat a large sauté pot or pan on medium heat. Add oil, salt, garlic, onions, and carrots. Sauté until the onions are translucent.

2. Add the water, sauerkraut, and buckwheat. Stir to mix evenly, cover, and bring to a simmer.

3. Cook for 5 to 6 minutes covered and turn off heat. Let sit for 30 minutes. Add parsley and mix well.

Sea Vegetable Polenta

Sauce Renaissance (page 227) is a good match for this polenta.

YIELD: 8 servings (4 cups)
TIME: 10 minutes prep and 25 minutes cooking

½ cup finely diced onions
¼ cup finely diced red bell pepper
½ teaspoon minced garlic
2 tablespoons vegan butter spread or olive oil
2 ½ teaspoons Old Bay Seasoning
1 cup yellow corn grits
1 tablespoon chopped dried wakame
3 ¼ cups water

1. Sauté onions, red bell pepper, and garlic in butter spread or oil over medium heat until onions are translucent.

2. Add Old Bay Seasoning, grits, and wakame, and stir in water.

3. Cook for 15 minutes on medium heat, stirring every few minutes to prevent sticking.

4. Pour into an oiled mold of choice, cover, and let sit to become firm. Scoop and serve hot from the pan or refrigerate and serve cold or reheat as needed.

Squash Polenta with Fennel

YIELD: 3 cups
TIME: 10 minutes prep and 25 minutes cooking

1 cup peeled and shredded butternut squash
1 tablespoon olive oil
½ teaspoon salt
1 teaspoon fennel seed, ground
¼ cup dry sweetened cranberries, chopped
10 tablespoons yellow corn grits
2 cups water

1. Sauté squash in olive oil with the salt and fennel seed over medium heat for 7 to 10 minutes.

2. Add cranberries and grits and stir in water. Bring to a simmer.

3. Cook for 15 minutes on medium heat stirring every few minutes to prevent sticking. Spoon into an oiled mold of choice, cover, and let sit to become firm.

4. Scoop and serve hot from the pan or refrigerate and serve cold or reheat as needed.

Basic Millet Quinoa Polenta

YIELD: 4 cups (8 servings)
TIME: 10 minutes prep and 20 minutes cooking

4 cups water
½ cup millet, washed
½ cup quinoa, washed
½ cup whole kernel corn, fresh or frozen
1 cup peeled and medium-diced yam
½ teaspoon salt

Put all ingredients in a stock pot, bring to a simmer, and cover. Turn heat to low and cook for 20 minutes. Turn off heat and let mixture cool to set.

HERBED MASHED POTATOES

YIELD: 5 cups or 10 servings
TIME: 10 minutes prep and 30 minutes cooking and mixing

4 cups peeled and cubed russet potatoes

4 cups water

½ teaspoon salt

⅓ cup garlic cloves or confit of garlic

¾ cup soy milk

1 ½ teaspoons chopped fresh thyme

1 ½ teaspoons chopped fresh oregano

1 ½ teaspoons chopped fresh basil

½ teaspoon salt

⅛ teaspoon white pepper

¼ cup fresh chopped parsley to mix in or as a garnish

1. In a 3-quart saucepan combine potatoes, water, and salt, then simmer over medium heat until potatoes are soft.

2. Rub garlic cloves with olive oil and roast in oven for 20 to 30 minutes, then cool and mince. Or use confit of garlic as is.

3. Drain potatoes for 30 seconds and place into the bowl of an electric mixer. Using the paddle attachment, whip potatoes until they are creamy with few or no lumps.

4. Add soy milk, garlic, thyme, oregano, basil, salt, and pepper to the potatoes, and whip the mixture on high speed for 5 minutes until light and fluffy. Stir in parsley or sprinkle on top, and serve immediately.

WHIPPED SQUASH POTATOES WITH ROSEMARY

YIELD: 10 servings
TIME: 15 minutes prep and 30 minutes cooking and mixing

2 cups peeled and cubed russet potatoes

2 cups peeled and cubed butternut squash

4 cups water

½ teaspoon salt

¼ cup soy milk

⅛ teaspoon rosemary powder

¼ cup vegan butter spread

¼ cup chopped fresh parsley (optional)

1. In a 3-quart saucepan combine potatoes, squash, water, and salt, then simmer over medium heat until potatoes are soft, about 15 minutes. Drain the potato/squash mixture for 30 seconds.

2. Place potato/squash mixture in a mixing bowl. Using a whip attachment or paddle on an electric mixer, whip potato/squash mixture until it is creamy with few or no lumps.

3. Add soy milk, rosemary, salt, and butter spread to the potato mixture and whip on high speed for 5 minutes until light and fluffy. Stir in parsley or sprinkle on top, then serve immediately.

"MILLET STYLE" MASHED POTATOES

The cauliflower gives this grain a potato-like consistency.

YIELD: 10 to 12 servings
TIME: 15 minutes prep and 25 minutes cooking and mixing

2 cups millet

6 cups water

4 cups chopped cauliflower

¼ teaspoon black pepper

2 tablespoons vegan butter spread or unrefined corn oil

1 ½ teaspoons salt

⅛ teaspoon nutmeg

¼ teaspoon dill weed (optional)

1. Wash and drain the millet. Place all ingredients (except the dill weed) in a large pot and bring to a simmer over high heat.

2. Lower heat, cover, and continue cooking until the millet mixture is soft (about 25 minutes). Check periodically to make sure the mixture does not burn.

3. Mash the mixture using a potato masher, or blend for 30 seconds in a food processor. Add dill weed, if you wish, and serve hot.

POTATO PANCAKES

YIELD: 12 small or 6 large pancakes
TIME: 10 minutes prep time and 15 minutes cooking

4 cups unpeeled potatoes, grated & squeezed to remove moisture

½ cup finely diced leeks or onions,

¼ cup unbleached white flour or egg replacer

¼ cup finely chopped fresh parsley

¾ teaspoon salt

⅛ teaspoon black pepper

¼ cup canola oil

1. Mix potatoes with remaining ingredients (except oil) in a bowl.

2. Microwave shredded potatoes for one minute to swell the starch and hold water in the potatoes. This prevents the oil from saturating the potato or the potato pancake.

3. Form the mixture into pancakes about 4 inches in diameter. Heat the oil in a 10-inch frying pan over medium-low heat. Pan-fry the potato pancakes in the hot oil until they are golden brown on both sides and cooked through to the center. Place the pancakes on paper towels to drain off any excess oil and serve hot.

WHITE BASMATI RICE

YIELD: 2 cups (4 servings)
TIME: 5 minutes prep, 25 to 30 minutes cooking

1 ½ cups water

1 cup basmati rice

½ teaspoon salt

1. Into a 1-quart saucepan with a tight-fitting lid, pour water, rice, and salt and stir to combine.

2. Bring to a simmer. Stir once again, cover, and reduce heat to low. Simmer for 18 minutes without opening lid or stirring.

3. Remove from heat and let stand, covered, for 5 minutes; fluff with a fork and serve.

Home Fries with Caramelized Onions

Parboiling the potatoes in water with baking soda extracts some starch; too much can cause them to be pasty. The remaining starch allows the potato to brown when baked. Raw potatoes are hard and crunchy, like a raw carrot. As they cook the starch softens until the potato is like eating butter. This is a perfectly cooked potato. An overcooked potato becomes dry with a sawdust-like texture.

YIELD: 4 servings
TIME: 25 minutes prep and 20 minutes cooking

½ teaspoon baking soda

2 pounds russet potatoes, peeled and diced into ¾-inch cubes

Water to cover potatoes

1 teaspoon salt

¼ teaspoon ground black pepper (or more if preferred)

1 teaspoon Spanish paprika*

4 tablespoons high-heat safflower oil

Caramelized Onions

2 tablespoons oil

1 ½ cups peeled and diced onions

¼ teaspoon salt

1. Preheat oven to 450°F.

2. Using a one gallon pot, fill half full of water, bring to a boil, add baking soda, then potatoes. Bring potatoes to a boil, and simmer for about 1 minute. Drain into colander and let stand for 10 minutes to cool.

3. Mix together salt, pepper, and paprika.

4. Spray or lightly oil bottom of roasting pan or half sheet pan. Pour potatoes into a large bowl. Pour oil evenly over the potatoes, then spices, and toss to coat potatoes evenly. Bake on bottom rack in oven for 15 to 20 minutes until potato has soft buttery texture.

5. Heat 2 tablespoons oil on medium high heat and add onions and salt. Toss to coat with oil and salt. Sauté until onions begin to brown and stir every few minutes until at least half the onions are lightly caramelized.

*Spanish paprika has more bite than Hungarian paprika, which is sweeter but works.

Potato Pancakes

CHESTNUT PILAF WITH BLACK RICE

YIELD: 4 servings
TIME: 15 minutes prep and 40 minutes cooking

1 (6.5–ounce) package frozen chestnuts (or 1 cup by volume)
1 cup black rice or brown rice
2 ¼ cups water
1/16 teaspoon salt
1 tablespoon olive oil
½ cup finely diced onion
½ cup finely diced red bell pepper
½ cup finely diced fresh fennel or ½ cup finely diced fresh celery with 1 teaspoon ground fennel seed powder
2 teaspoons fresh, minced garlic
½ teaspoon salt
2 tablespoons fresh chopped parsley

1. Preheat oven to 375°F. Place the frozen chestnuts on a baking tray and roast in oven for 30 to 45 minutes. Remove the chestnuts from oven and set aside to cool. When cool, chop the chestnuts into quarters and set aside.

2. Wash the rice and place into a 2-quart pot with the water and pinch of salt. Cover and simmer 30 minutes or until the rice is soft and water is absorbed into the rice.

3. Preheat a skillet on medium heat for 1 minute, then add olive oil, onion, red pepper, fennel, garlic, and salt. Sauté for about 7 to 8 minutes, until onions are translucent.

4. When the rice is cooked, add the sautéed vegetables, roasted chestnuts, and chopped parsley, and mix. Serve immediately (to prevent discoloration of vegetables).

BROWN RICE

Brown rice is a staple and prominent side dish in natural foods cooking; however, many people don't know how to cook brown rice.

YIELD: 2 cups cooked rice
TIME: 5 minutes prep and 45 minutes cooking

1 cup short- or medium-grain brown rice
2 ¼ cups water
½ teaspoon salt

1. Measure out 1 cup short- or medium-grain brown rice and place in a sieve or strainer that is immersed in a bowl of water. Wash rice for one minute by moving sieve around in the water until it is cloudy. Remove sieve with rice from the water and rinse the rice with water under the faucet.

2. Combine rice with water and salt in a 1-quart pot and give it a quick stir.

3. Bring water to a simmer and cover the pot. Turn heat down to low and cook for 45 minutes; check after 30 minutes to be sure there is still water in the pot. Add a little if the rice is dry and not yet soft. As long as there is water in the pot, continue cooking until water has evaporated and rice is tender. Serve immediately or refrigerate.

SOUTHERN BLACK-EYED PILAF

YIELD: 8 servings
TIME: 15 minutes prep and 15 minutes cooking

2 tablespoons sunflower oil

1 ½ cups fennel, chopped fresh

1 cup sliced okra (⅛-inch thick)

3 tablespoons finely diced onions

1 tablespoon minced fresh garlic

8 sprigs fresh thyme

½ teaspoon salt

⅛ teaspoon white pepper

2 cups cooked short grain brown rice

2 cups cooked black-eyed peas

1 cup hominy, cooked or canned

½ cup each red, yellow, and green bell peppers, roasted, coarsely chopped (or raw, finely diced)

¼ cup pecans, chopped

2 tablespoons parsley, chopped, for garnish

1. Add oil to a 10-inch frying pan. Sauté the fennel, okra, onions, garlic, thyme, salt, and pepper over medium heat until the onions are translucent. Add the brown rice, black-eyed peas, and hominy, and throughly heat. Add the bell peppers, either raw or roasted.

2. Garnish with chopped pecans and parsley. Serve immediately.

RISOTTO PESTO

Risotto is a rice dish in which hot liquid is added gradually to grains of Arborio rice as they cook. The result is a heavenly blend of slightly chewy rice enveloped in a wonderful silky sauce.

YIELD: 6 servings
TIME: 10 minutes prep and 1hour cooking

1 ½ cups brown Arborio rice

4 cups water

3 tablespoons chicken-style broth powder or any vegan broth flavoring

2 tablespoons extra-virgin olive oil

1 tablespoon minced fresh garlic

2 cups finely chopped onion

6 tablespoons Sun-Dried Tomato Pesto (page 227)

1. Wash and rinse the rice.

2. Mix the water with the chicken-style broth powder to make vegan chicken-style broth.

3. Heat the oil in a 12-inch skillet over medium heat. Add the rice, and sauté, stirring often, for about 3 minutes, or until lightly brown.

4. Add the garlic and onion, and continue sautéing for 5 minutes, or until the onions begin to soften. Slowly stir 3 cups of the hot chicken broth into the rice mixture, and simmer for 30 minutes. While stirring slowly, add the remaining cup of broth to the rice. Continue to simmer another 20 to 30 minutes, or until most of the broth is absorbed and the rice is cooked, yet firm. Add the pesto and stir well to combine. Serve immediately.

Side Vegetables

It is the properly cooked vegetable that gives a special elegance to vegetarian cuisine. Even as omnivores we should build copious amounts of vegetables into every entrée. One of my favorite presentations is laying a protein on a bed of vegetables as an entrée. Serving a sautéed bok choy, kale, or spinach with a confit of red onions would make a colorful bed for chicken and vegan beef-style or chicken-style analogues, seitan, beans, tofu, or tempeh. And vegetables are easy to cook.

Note: Most fresh produce in the United States travels an average of 1,300 miles before it is eaten. These lengthy journeys result in lost nutritional value, especially for the more volatile vitamins such as vitamins C and A. Refrigerated broccoli, for example, loses nearly 20 percent of its vitamin C in one day and nearly 35 percent in two days. This is a good reason why farmers markets and Farm to Table programs deliver a fresher product. As you add vegetables to your menu, please only use the freshest that you can find. The freshest is always the best.

BRAISED RED CABBAGE

YIELD: 8 servings
TIME: 15 minutes prep and 20 to 30 minutes cooking

2 tablespoons canola oil
2 cups sliced onions
1 cup chopped unpeeled apple (optional)
1 cup grated carrots
2 cloves garlic, minced
1 ½ teaspoons ground caraway seeds
1 ½ salt
3 cups shredded red cabbage
3 cups shredded green cabbage
½ cup grated raw potatoes
1 ½ cups white wine
¾ teaspoon liquid smoke

1. In large skillet, heat oil over medium heat. Add onions, carrots, garlic, caraway seeds, and salt and cook, stirring often, about every 5 minutes.

2. Add cabbages and potatoes; cook, stirring often, about 10 minutes.

3. Add wine, cover and cook until cabbage and potatoes are tender, about 15 minutes.

4. Add liquid smoke, mix well, and cook 1 minute and serve.

OPTION: 1 cup chopped fresh unpeeled apple to sauté with the onions.

CAULIFLOWER WITH COCONUT & BOK CHOY

YIELD: 8 servings (8 cups)
TIME: 15 minutes prep and 15 minutes cooking

2 quarts cauliflower florets (approximately 1 large cauliflower)
½ cup finely diced red bell pepper
6 tablespoons coconut oil or cream*
½ teaspoon salt
½ cup water
2 cups bok choy, thin sliced
¼ cup cilantro, fresh, stemmed and coarsely chopped

1. Break cauliflower into small florets and heat oil on medium heat in large sauté pan.

2. Add peppers, cauliflower, and salt to heated oil and sauté for about 8 minutes. Cover the pan to bring out the flavor while stirring the vegetables occasionally to create an even sauté.

3. Add water and bok choy. Cover and cook for about 3 minutes. Turn off heat, stir cilantro into vegetable mixture. Let sit for about 3 minutes and serve.

*If using coconut cream, skim and use the fat at the top of the can.

TUSCAN VEGETABLE SAUTÉ

YIELD: 4 servings
TIME: 10 minutes prep and 10 minutes cooking

1 tablespoon extra-virgin olive oil
1 cup large-dice red bell pepper
1 cup large-dice green bell pepper or sliced baby fennel
1 cup zucchini, halved, diagonally sliced
1 cup yellow squash, halved, diagonally sliced
1 tablespoon fresh, chopped basil
¼ teaspoon salt

1. Heat the oil in a 12-inch sauté pan over medium heat. Add all of the ingredients except basil, and sauté for 5 to 7 minutes, or until the vegetables are cooked, but firm.

2. Add basil at end, mix into vegetables, and serve immediately.

CONFIT OF RED ONIONS IN MERLOT

YIELD: 4 servings
TIME: 10 minutes prep time and 15 to 20 minutes cooking

2 tablespoon sesame oil
4 cups peeled, thickly sliced red onions
1 tablespoon fresh, minced garlic
1 teaspoon dried thyme
¼ teaspoon salt
¾ cup merlot wine
1 tablespoon sugar

1. Heat oil in a sauté pan, then sauté the onions, garlic, thyme, and salt on medium heat 5 minutes.

2. Add the wine and sugar, then reduce liquid until liquid is evaporated. Serve immediately or store in refrigerator until ready to use.

SAVOY CABBAGE WITH KALE & SHIITAKE MUSHROOMS

Kale, the queen of the crucifers, is full of nutrients and a very popular vegetable in my kitchen. Hippocrates used it to counter drunkenness. It has eye appeal, taste, and nutrition.

YIELD: 2 cups
TIME: 10 minutes prep and 10 minutes cooking

2 tablespoons olive oil
½ cup onions, peeled, halved and sliced
¼ cup shiitake mushrooms, sliced
⅛ teaspoon salt
2 cups coarsely chopped red or green kale
2 cup coarsely chopped savoy cabbage
2 tablespoons water

1. Heat oil to medium heat in large sauté pan. Add onions, mushrooms, and salt. Sauté until onions are translucent and lightly browned.

2. Add kale, cabbage, and 2 tablespoons water. Cover and steam for about 4 to 5 minutes and serve.

VARIATION: *Savoy Cabbage with Kale & Coconut Cilantro Greens*

Use coconut oil in place of olive oil and add 2 tablespoons fresh chopped cilantro with the greens. Sauté on medium high heat for 5 to 7 minutes and serve.

SAUTÉED ARAME WITH LEEKS & CRANBERRIES

YIELD: 6 servings (3 ½ cups)
TIME: 20 minutes prep and 20 minutes cooking

⅔ cup dry arame, soaked, drained
2 cups water
1 tablespoon canola or oil of choice
2 cups peeled, julienned carrot
2 cups thinly sliced fresh fennel
2 cups thinly sliced fresh leeks (use lower third of stem only)
1 teaspoon ginger powder
1 teaspoon fennel powder
½ teaspoon salt
¼ cup dry sweetened cranberries
2 tablespoons mirin or sweet sherry

1. Cook the dry arame sea vegetable in water, uncovered, on medium heat for about 7 to 10 minutes. Remove from the heat, drain, and set aside.

2. Heat a 12-inch skillet on medium heat for 1 minute. Add the oil and carrots and sauté for 4 minutes.

3. Add the fresh fennel, leeks, ginger and fennel powders, and salt; sauté for 7 minutes.

4. Add the arame, cranberries, and mirin. Continue cooking another 1 to 2 minutes or until the whole mixture is hot. Serve immediately.

MOROCCAN RATATOUILLE WITH GARBANZO BEANS

Harissa is a hot and spicy North African sauce made from oil, chilies, garlic, cumin, coriander, and caraway seeds. There are many versions of this sauce, depending on the country of origin. Typically served with couscous, soups, and dried meat, it gives this ratatouille a unique flavor. The beans can be eliminated to make this a side dish to complement an entrée.

YIELD: 12 servings
TIME: 20 minutes prep and 25 to 30 minutes cooking

6 tablespoons extra-virgin olive oil
6 cups large-dice zucchini
6 cups large-dice eggplant
3 cups large-dice onions
3 cups large-dice yellow squash
3 cups large-dice red bell pepper
1 tablespoon salt
4 ½ cups Harissa Sauce (page 238)
1 ½ cups chopped parsley
3 cups cooked garbanzo beans or combination of cannelloni and garbanzo beans

1. Heat the oil in a deep 12-inch skillet over medium-high heat. Add the zucchini, eggplant, onions, squash, bell pepper, and salt, and sauté for 5 to 7 minutes, or until the vegetables are lightly browned.

2. Add the sauce and garbanzo beans. Cook another 7 to 10 minutes.

3. Sprinkle with parsley and serve immediately.

COCONUT "AU GRATIN" TOPPING

Au gratin is a French term referring to a dish that is topped with bread crumbs and butter and/or oil and perhaps a grated cheese, and then browned in an oven. This version uses coconut instead of cheese. This is an excellent topping on creamed vegetables such as Peas Bonne Femme (page 195), pastas, or casseroles.

YIELD: 2 cups
TIME: 15 to 20 minutes

⅓ cup vegan butter spread, softened, or palm shortening, or oil of choice
1 tablespoon fresh, minced garlic
1 cup unsweetened flaked coconut
½ cup sherry
½ cup whole wheat bread crumbs
3 tablespoons finely chopped fresh parsley
¾ teaspoon salt (use only ¼ teaspoon if using vegan butter spread)
¼ teaspoon ground paprika

1. Place the vegan butter spread in a sauté pan over medium heat. Add the garlic and coconut, and sauté for about 2 minutes, or until the garlic begins to soften and brown (be careful not to burn).

2. Add the sherry and continue to cook for about 10 minutes, or until the wine has evaporated.

3. Add the remaining ingredients to the pan, mix well, and remove from the heat.

4. Place the mixture in a sealed container and store in the refrigerator, where it will last up to 1 month. Frozen, it will keep for about 6 months.

BREADED VEGETABLES

YIELD: 4 servings
TIME: 10 to 15 minutes prep and 10 to 15 minutes cooking

Breading Mixture

¾ cup whole wheat bread flour

¼ cup gluten flour

4 teaspoons oregano

4 teaspoons basil

2 teaspoons granulated garlic

2 teaspoons salt

½ teaspoon white pepper

3 cups water

1 cup whole grain bread crumbs

Vegetables

4 slices eggplant

8 slices zucchini or yellow squash,
or a combination

2 medium portabella mushrooms

½ cup olive or untoasted sesame oil

1. Combine all of the breading mixture ingredients except water, bread crumbs, and oil in a bowl.

2. Pour the water into a separate bowl. Place the bread crumbs in a shallow bowl or on a large plate.

3. Dip each vegetable, one at a time, into the water. Drain for a few seconds, dredge it in the flour mixture, dip it quickly back into the water, and then into the bread crumbs. (The flour acts as the egg mixture to create the binder and the bread crumbs bind the coating to the vegetables.) Make sure each piece of vegetable is completely coated with bread crumbs on all sides. Set each aside till all vegetables are breaded.

4. Heat the oil in a 10-inch frying pan over medium heat until hot (if the oil is not hot enough, the vegetables will not fry properly and will be oily). Panfry the vegetables in the hot oil until golden on all sides. Drain them on paper towels. Serve hot.

Breaded Vegetables

PEAS BONNE FEMME

YIELD: 6 servings
TIME: 10 minutes prep and 20 minutes cooking

2 tablespoons vegan butter spread or corn oil

1 cup chopped onions (canned or fresh pearl onions optional)

1 teaspoon minced garlic (or ½ teaspoon garlic powder)

1 teaspoon salt

¼ teaspoon white pepper

¼ cup unbleached flour

3 drops liquid smoke

1 cup soy milk

2 cups fresh or frozen green peas

1 cup shredded lettuce

1. Heat the butter spread or oil in a medium saucepan. Sauté the onions and garlic with the salt and pepper until the onions are semi-translucent. Add the flour and liquid smoke, stirring constantly for 3 minutes or until the flour is cooked. Add the soy milk, pouring only half at a time and blending well after each addition.

2. Add the peas and cook for about 5 minutes. (The peas should become bright green and barely soft.) Add the shredded lettuce, mixing into the sauce; the lettuce need not be cooked. Serve hot.

OPTION: Add ¼ cup sliced seitan or tempeh when adding peas in step 2.

VARIATION 1: *Italian Green Beans Bonne Femme*

Substitute 2 cups green beans for the peas. You may need to cook the beans for more than 5 minutes, unless you use precooked beans.

VARIATION 2: *Carrots Bonne Femme*

Substitute 2 cups carrots for the peas. First, peel and slice the carrots into ¼ inch slices. Steam carrots *al dente* and add them to the sauce in place of peas.

VARIATION 3: *Butternut Squash Bonne Femme*

Peel and ½ inch dice 2 cups butternut squash to substitute for the peas. Steam it until soft. Add the squash to the sauce as you would add the peas.

CAULIFLOWER "AU GRATIN"

YIELD: 6 servings
TIME: 10 minutes prep and about 1 hour cooking

1 large cauliflower (about 6 cups)
1 cup diced onions
2 cups vegan Béchamel Sauce (page 204)
½ teaspoon salt
½ teaspoon black pepper
½ teaspoon garlic powder
1 teaspoon nutritional yeast
2 tablespoons whole wheat bread crumbs
½ teaspoon paprika (preferably Hungarian)

1. Cut the cauliflower into medium pieces and place in a bowl with the onions. Set aside.

2. Heat the sauce in a small saucepan. Add the salt, pepper, garlic powder, and yeast to the sauce. Pour the sauce over the vegetables and stir gently.

3. Oil a loaf or casserole pan. Pour the vegetables and sauce into the pan and press lightly. Sprinkle the bread crumbs and paprika over the vegetables. Cover and bake in a preheated 350°F oven for 45 to 55 minutes.

GREEN BEANS NEW ORLEANS

YIELD: 4 servings
TIME: 10 minutes and 15 minutes cooking

2 cups green beans, ends trimmed, cut diagonally
2 teaspoons sunflower oil
¼ cup finely diced red bell pepper
¼ cup finely diced Spanish onion
¼ cup finely diced celery
2 teaspoons fresh minced garlic
¼ teaspoon salt
¼ cup finely diced seitan, tempeh, or tofu (use just one protein)
6 drops liquid smoke (optional but recommended)

1. In a vegetable steamer, steam the beans for 5 minutes or until they turn bright green and tender-crisp. Remove beans and rinse under cold water, then drain and set aside.

2. In a 10-inch frying pan, heat the oil and sauté the bell pepper, onion, celery, garlic, salt, and protein of choice over medium heat for 5 minutes or until the onions are transparent.

3. Add beans and liquid smoke and cook another 5 minutes to thoroughly blend the seasonings. Serve hot.

CARROTS, PECANS, & FENNEL

YIELD: 4 servings
TIME: 10 minutes prep and 20 to 25 minutes cooking

2 cups peeled and Jardinière cut carrots

½ cup thinly sliced fennel (or 1 teaspoon ground fennel seeds)

1 tablespoon olive oil, oil of choice, or vegan butter spread

¼ cup maple syrup

¼ cup chopped roasted pecans

2 teaspoons cornstarch or arrowroot

1 tablespoon water

1 tablespoon chopped parsley

1. Steam the carrots in a small amount of water, for 10 to 15 minutes or until firm and cooked. Be sure not to overcook them. Set aside.

2. In a skillet, sauté the fennel (or seeds) in oil for 2 minutes.

3. Add the carrots, syrup, and pecans to the fennel, and simmer.

4. In a small bowl, mix together the cornstarch and water. Add this mixture to the carrot mixture. Stir in the chopped parsley and serve hot.

SAUTÉED BRUSSELS SPROUTS WITH WALNUT OIL

Brussels sprouts are among my favorite vegetables. In this dish, they are sautéed with flavorful walnut oil made from sautéing walnuts in canola oil.

YIELD: 3 servings
TIME: 10 minutes prep and 10 to 15 minutes cooking

3 tablespoons canola oil

¼ cup chopped walnuts

2 cups halved Brussels sprouts

⅛ teaspoon salt

¼ cup water

1. Heat the oil in a 12-inch sauté pan over medium heat. Add walnuts and sauté for 3 to 5 minutes or until walnuts are lightly browned. Leaving oil in pan, remove walnuts.

2. Add Brussels sprouts and salt and sauté for 3 minutes to lightly brown. Add water, cover pan and let cook until water has evaporated or Brussels sprouts are soft but firm and green (about 7 to 10 minutes). Add walnuts and mix into Brussels sprouts. Serve hot.

Tempura Side Vegetable (or Appetizer)

This can be served as a side dish to a sandwich in place of fries or a tasty and satisfying light meal. For an appetizer, serve with Balsamic Orange Marinade (page 231). With planning, this is a simple, last-minute appetizer. You can prepare the batter, vegetables, and sauce ahead of time; then assemble to serve.

YIELD: 10 servings as either a side or an appetizer
TIME: 30 minutes prep time and 15 to 20 minutes cooking

Tempura Batter (2 cups)

⅔ cup unbleached flour
⅔ cup arrowroot or cornstarch
2 teaspoons baking powder
1 tablespoon curry powder
1 ½ teaspoons salt
½ teaspoon black pepper
1 cup water

Mix together flour, cornstarch, baking powder, curry powder, salt, and pepper. Stir water into dry ingredients.

> **VARIATION:** *Tempura Tofu, Tempeh, or Seitan*
>
> Medium cubes (¾- to 1-inch pieces) of tofu, tempeh, and seitan may also be deep-fried in this light, spicy batter and served as an appetizer. Larger pieces of these vegetable proteins may be deep-fried and served as an entrée.

*The batter can be used immediately or refrigerated until needed. Leftover batter can be saved for up to a week.

Vegetable Preparation

15 cups vegetables (carrots, broccoli, cauliflower, red bell pepper, parsnips, etc.)
½ cup unbleached flour for dredging the vegetables
1 Tempura batter recipe (2 cups)
3 to 4 cups high-heat safflower cooking oil or high-heat oil of choice

1. Mix together flour, arrowroot, baking powder, curry powder, salt, and pepper. Add up to 1 cup water gradually until the mixture has the consistency of a light batter*. Add an extra ¼ teaspoon of baking powder to lighten the batter. Cut the vegetables into manageable pieces. For example, use florets of broccoli and cauliflower; cut carrots and parsnips into ⅜ inch slices; cut bell peppers into ½ inch wide strips, and so on. Drain the vegetables but not dry because moisture is needed to activate the flour. Dredge in flour and dust off the excess.

2. Pour about 2 inches of cooking oil into a deep frying pan and heat it to about 375°F. (The amount of oil is dependent on the size of the pan. If using a 1 quart pan, you will need about 2 cups, or about 4 cups for a 2-quart sauce pan.)

3. Dip the floured pieces of vegetable into the tempura batter to coat thoroughly. Deep-fry the vegetables until golden brown. Drain on paper towels and serve immediately, with a dipping sauce, such as the Grilled Vegetable Marinade & Citrus Dipping Sauce (page 236), Balsamic Glaze (page 226), or a sweet and sour sauce.

Chapter Ten

VEGAN SAUCES
& SOUPS

This chapter allows me to pay homage to both Antonin Carême and Auguste Escoffier.

It was Carême who set forth what he called the four mother sauces: Béchamel, Espagnole, Velouté, and Allemande. Escoffier later codified Allemande as a form of Velouté and added the sauces Hollandaise and Tomato, for a total of five mother sauces in his *Le Guide Culinaire*. While many traditional applications for these five sauces contain animal protein, I present vegan options for each sauce.

My vision for modern classical sauces is to create an extensive vegan/vegetarian line of recipe applications for each mother sauce. The final product would be a classical vegetarian sauce cuisine that could be paired with vegetarian or meat proteins. Vegetarianism should be able to stand on its merit as a cuisine and complement animal protein when required. What traditionally makes a great sauce are the vegetables, fruits, spices, herbs, wines, or oils it contains. While animal protein may offer the sauce a certain flavor profile, it doesn't give the sauce its character.

In the history of French cuisine, sauces were a flavored liquid originally used by the Franks and the Gauls before the Middle Ages to moisten their food. These early sauces, spiced and pungent, sweet and sour, do not qualify as what we know today as modern or classical French sauces. Sauces evolved into ethnic variations and the classical mother sauces and their derivatives.

As we move into the sauces, including a collection of my favorite vegetable-based sauces, think about how you can take what is presented here and continue to develop the recipe, remembering with ingredients that less is more. Study the sauce sections in the classical French cookbooks mentioned in the Reading Resources at the back of the book and develop your own ideas and applications for the *les grandes sauces*—vegan, of course!

Shiitake Black Bean Duxelle Rice Skin Rolls with Hollandaise and Savory Cabbage

BÉCHAMEL SAUCES

Béchamel Sauce #1 & #2

Mushroom Cream Sauce

Sardelon Sauce

Dill Sauce

Ecossaise Sauce

   Variation: Truffle Sauce

Sauce Soubise (Onion Sauce)

ESPAGNOLE SAUCES

Cajun Roux

Espagnole (French Brown) Sauce

Bigarade Sauce

Poivrade Sauce

Shiitake Mushroom Sauce

Sauce Lyonnaise

Sauce Robert

Sauce Romaine

Salisbury Steak-Style Sauce

Espagnole Maigre

VELOUTÉ SAUCES

Velouté Sauce

Supreme Sauce

Parsley Sauce

Aurora Sauce

Caper Sauce

Bretonne Sauce

French Curry Sauce

TOMATO SAUCES

Classical Tomato Sauce

Cream of Tomato Sauce

Spanish Tomato Sauce (Filling)

Sauce Concasse

Provençal Tomato Sauce

HOLLANDAISE, BEURRE BLANCS, & GLAZES

Basic Hollandaise Sauce

Yellow Pepper Hollandaise

   Variation: Red Pepper
   Hollandaise Sauce

   Variation: Yellow Pepper
   Coconut Hollandaise
   Sauce

Béarnaise Sauce

Coconut Lemon Beurre Blanc

Choron Sauce

Maltaise Sauce

Lemon Beurre Blanc

Thyme Garlic Beurre Blanc

Lemon Sauce Glaze

Lemon Olive Sauce Glaze

Red Wine Sauce Glaze

VEGETABLE-BASED SAUCES

Garlic Confit

Garlic Cream Sauce

   Variation: Italian Fennel
   Garlic Sauce

Gyros (Cucumber Yogurt)
Sauce

Balsamic Glaze

Sauce Renaissance

Sun-Dried Tomato Pesto

Puttanesca Sauce

Stout Caramelized Onion
Sauce

Wild Forager's au Jus

Sauce Niçoise

Balsamic Orange Marinade

Moo Goo Gai Pan Sauce

Spinach Basil Pesto

Sauce Dugléré

Mushroom Sauce

Classic Cuban-Style Picadillo
Sauce

Tikka Masala Sauce

Asian BBQ Sauce

Grilled Vegetable Marinade &
Citrus Dipping Sauce

Oriental Miso Sauce

   Variation: Oriental Orange
   Miso Sauce

Miso Mustard Onion Sauce

Piccata Sauce

Harissa Sauce

VEGAN SOUPS

Caramelized Vegetable
Consommé

New England Sea Vegetable
Chowder

Andalusian Vegetable Cream
Soup

Burgundy Soup

Cream of Chilled Pear Soup

Doukabar Vegetable Soup

Asian White Gazpacho

Vichyssoise (Cream of Leek
Soup)

Béchamel Sauces

Béchamel Sauce is a European white cream sauce traditionally made with cow's milk and a butter roux as the thickening agent. To this day, it remains a mystery as to who created the Béchamel Sauce. Some say Catherine de Medici in the 16th century or Philippe de Mornay in the 17th century, or Louis XIV's chief steward, Marquis Louis de Béchamel. Most likely it was created for Louis XIV by his personal chef, Pierre de la Varenne, a century before Carême.

We know it first appeared in aristocratic culinary cuisine during the reign of Louis XIV. I would suggest that Carême surely had a hand in its evolution in its categorization as one of the mother sauces. It is also the base for cheese sauces and fondue.

The primary difference in a vegan Béchamel Sauce is the use of a plant-based milk in place of cow's milk. My preference is unsweetened soy milk. A close second is the 50/50 soy/cashew milk combination. Cashew milk is easy to make by using 3 parts water to 1 part cashew cream and imparts a full, rich flavor.

The thickening agent for the Béchamel Sauce (as with Espagnole and Velouté Sauces) is the roux (usually equal parts of flour and oil), as discussed in the technique section ("Roux & Other Thickeners" on page 121). Use a plain roux of neutral flavor, not a browned roux, in Béchamel Sauce.

The soy milk must be room temperature to warm when making the sauce. A quarter of the milk should be added at a time to the measured roux to prevent the sauce from lumping. Neither the roux nor the milk should scorch or burn as that would ruin the flavor. Use white instead of black pepper. You can flavor the sauce by steeping a bundle of herbs called bouquet garni while warming the soy milk and remove before adding the milk to the roux. Or roux can be added to a room temperature soy milk, whisk into the milk until completely dissolved, and heat to thicken.

This section includes two vegan versions. The first can be made with straight soy milk. It does have a slight, but acceptable, back note of soy. When used in a recipe, the flavor is generally not noticed. It's important to use unsweetened soy milk or it could be too sweet, depending on the brand of soy milk.

The second version with an extra blending step is neutral in flavor. I developed this sauce in the early '80s before soy milk was readily available. When using the second version with blended cashew cream, the solids in the milk make the ratio of solids to liquid higher. The result is that less roux is needed to thicken the liquid. When preparing a sauce application, if the sauce becomes too thin from adding additional liquid, add more roux by whisking it into the sauce as it is being poured into the liquid. Always add small amounts of roux at a time to a sauce when adjusting its thickness to prevent the sauce from becoming too viscous.

BÉCHAMEL SAUCE #1

Béchamel Sauce is a cream sauce. My version is a little thicker than the traditional. If you prefer a thinner variety, add more soy milk. If you want a richer sauce, add about 1 tablespoon Cashew Cream (page 175). A lighter sauce gives the option of absorbing liquids and flavors from ingredients added for specific recipe applications.

YIELD: 2 cups
TIME: 10 minutes prep and 15 minutes cooking

2 ¼ cups unsweetened soy milk*
$^1/_{16}$ teaspoon ground nutmeg
⅛ teaspoon salt
¼ cup unbleached white flour
2 tablespoons canola oil

1. Combine the soy milk, nutmeg, and salt in a 1-quart saucepan, and place over medium heat.

2. Whisk together the flour and oil to make the roux. Add the roux to the milk mixture, and stir with a wire whisk until the sauce thickens.

3. Use immediately, or transfer to a covered container and store in the refrigerator, where it will keep for about two weeks.

* Use 2 cups soy milk and ¼ cup Cashew Cream (page 175) for a richer sauce and to neutralize the milk's soy flavor.

BÉCHAMEL SAUCE #2

YIELD: 4 ½ cups sauce
TIME: 10 minutes prep and 20 minutes cooking

2 cups soy milk
1 ½ cups water
¼ cup cashew nuts
1 teaspoon salt
⅛ teaspoon white pepper
Dash nutmeg
¼ cup oil (safflower, unrefined corn* oil, or a neutral flavored oil)
½ cup unbleached flour

1. Blend the soy milk, water, cashews, and seasonings in a blender until smooth (no nut grit in the liquid).

2. Heat the oil in a small saucepan. Whisk in the flour to make a roux. Then whisk 1 cup soy milk mixture into the roux to make a heavy, creamy sauce.

3. Whip thoroughly for even dispersion and add a second cup of the soy and whip until smooth. Finally, add the remaining soy milk. Whip into sauce to evenly disperse.

*"Unrefined" corn oil has a buttery flavor, which can also work, but is not necessary, in this sauce.

SARDELON SAUCE

Sardelon Sauce is a rich German cream sauce made with butter, cream, egg yolks, stock, capers, and roux. It is served with a German meatball called Königsberger Klopse. This is my interpretation via the Béchamel Sauce.

YIELD: 3 cups
TIME: 10 minutes

3 cups Béchamel Sauce #1 or #2 (page 204)
2 tablespoons vegan chicken-style broth powder
½ teaspoon salt (optional)
1 tablespoon capers, drained

1. Pour 3 cups Béchamel Sauce into a 2-quart saucepan.

2. Add broth powder, salt, and drained capers.

3. Whisk together while heating on medium heat until sauce is hot.

DILL SAUCE

YIELD: 2 ½ cups sauce
TIME: 10 minutes

2 ¼ cups Béchamel Sauce #1 (page 204)
1 ½ teaspoons paprika, preferably Hungarian which is sweeter
1 tablespoon dill weed
½ cup soy milk

1. In a 1-quart or larger saucepan, pour Béchamel Sauce and add paprika, dill weed, and soy milk.

2. Bring to a simmer on medium heat and simmer for 3 to 5 minutes and serve.

MUSHROOM CREAM SAUCE

YIELD: 4 cups sauce
TIME: 20 minutes

2 tablespoons safflower high-heat cooking oil
1 cup finely diced onions
1 ½ cups sliced button mushrooms
3 ½ cups Béchamel Sauce #1 or #2 (page 204)
⅛ teaspoon liquid smoke (or more if you prefer a stronger smoked profile)
¼ teaspoon salt (then adjust to taste)

1. Heat oil in saucepan on medium heat and add onions and mushrooms. Sauté until onions are translucent.

2. Add Béchamel Sauce, liquid smoke, and salt. If using liquid hickory smoke, dilute it in 2 tablespoons water before adding to the sauce to break it down, and add it to the sauce when sauce is hot.

3. Simmer for about 3 minutes and it's ready to serve.

ECOSSAISE SAUCE

In Escoffier's *Basic Elements of Fine Cookery*, this recipe is called Scotch Egg Sauce with chopped hard boiled eggs. I use chopped extra firm tofu in place of hard boiled eggs.

YIELD: 2 ¼ cups
TIME: 20 minutes

2 tablespoons finely chopped onions
2 tablespoons finely diced celery
2 tablespoons finely diced carrots
2 tablespoons finely diced green beans
2 tablespoons vegan butter spread or canola oil
2 cups Béchamel Sauce #1 or #2 (page 204)

Salt to taste

1. Sauté onions, celery, carrots, and green beans in oil on medium heat until the onions are translucent.
2. Add sauce, bring to a simmer, and cook for a few minutes. Salt and serve.

VARIATION: *Truffle Sauce*

Add ½ cup thinly sliced leeks and a teaspoon of minced truffle.

SAUCE SOUBISE (ONION SAUCE)

Sauce Soubise is the Béchamel version of the Espagnole version of the Sauce Lyonnaise (page 211).

YIELD: 1 ½ cups sauce
TIME: 20 minutes

2 cups finely chopped onions
½ cup water
1 tablespoon vegan butter spread or high-heat oil of choice
½ cup Béchamel Sauce #1 or #2 (page 204)

¼ teaspoon lemon juice
Salt and white pepper to taste

1. Scald or blanch onions in simmering water for 3 to 4 minutes until semi-translucent. Drain, discard water. Then sauté onions in butter spread until they are soft.
2. Add Béchamel Sauce. Stir and cook 2 to 3 minutes. Put through a sieve and return to the stovetop. Bring to a simmering point.
3. Add lemon juice and simmer for 1 minute. Season to taste with salt and pepper. Serve with seitan, tempeh, and tofu entrées.

Espagnole Sauces

There are a few theories on how Espagnole Sauce was invented. The more believable one in Kettner's 1877 *Book of the Table* states when the Spanish Bourbons ascended the French throne under Louis XV, they brought Spanish fashion back to France. French cooks learned of the Spanish pot au feu, which was made with bacon, sausage, and Estremadura sausage. French cooks used beef in their pot au feu. That is perhaps why the 19th century version of the sauce is made with beef, veal, and pork bones.

Carême helped develop the Espagnole Sauce as one of the mother sauces in French cuisine. And Escoffier codified the recipe, which has evolved over the last 150 years. When I was first taught to make the Espagnole Sauce, the recipe called for roasting beef and pork bones with a mirepoix, flour, and seasoning and cooking with water, wine, and tomato products for several hours. In Henri-Paul Pellaprat's *The Great Book of French Cuisine*, the recipe is quite simplified. It starts with a broth. There is no roasting of bones.

Espagnole has a strong taste and is rarely used directly on food. As a mother sauce it serves as the foundation for many sauce derivatives. The sauce and its variations work well with tempeh, tofu, beans, and meat analogues.

French sauces have complex flavors but are simple to make. Sauce Espagnole Maigre is a French brown sauce made with fish stock. (This Lenten dish is in *The Escoffier Cookbook*.) You can refer to *The Great Book of French Cuisine*, *The New Larousse Gastronomique*, or *The Escoffier Cookbook* for extensive classical sauce applications for Espagnole Sauce or any of the classical sauces.

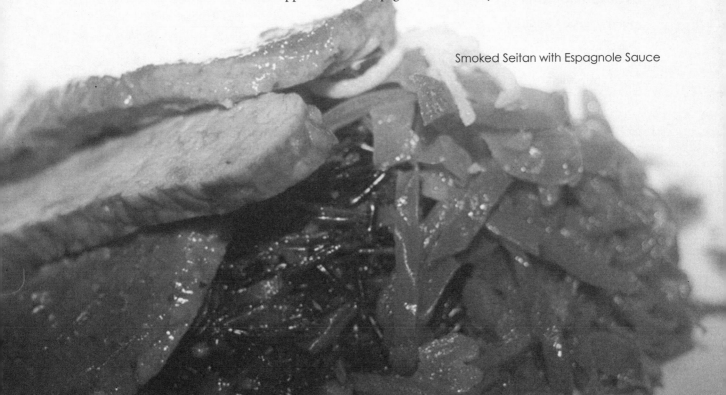

Smoked Seitan with Espagnole Sauce

CAJUN ROUX

Cajun Roux is the same as a brown roux. The roux is browned or roasted to give it a heartier flavor and darker color. Cajun cuisine is known for its brown roux, which is used in the Espagnole Sauce recipe. Béchamel Sauce calls for a mild flavored white roux to complement the delicate dairy flavors. Cajun cooks use clarified butter (butter that is warmed to separate the milk solids from the liquid; it makes the butter less likely to burn) but it isn't necessary and I don't recommend it. I like to use an oil such as canola that has a high heat tolerance when making a brown roux.

YIELD: 1 ¼ cups
TIME: 25 minutes

¾ cup high-heat canola oil or high-heat oil of choice
1 cup all-purpose white flour

1. Start by heating a saucepan or cast iron pot until hot. Add oil and heat for a few minutes. Add flour and mix until it is dissolved into the oil.

2. Continue to cook over medium-low heat, constantly stirring until the flour and oil blend have a light brown to dark copper color.

3. Cook slowly to control the brown color and let the roasted flavor develop. Remember that the longer you cook the roux, the darker it becomes. If the roux burns creating black particles, it will become bitter. Throw it out and start over.

NOTE: This amount will thicken about 2 quarts of sauce:

- ↻ 4 ounces of roux thickens 1 quart of liquid

- ↻ 1 pound of roux thickens about 1 gallon of liquid

Always add the water or stock to the roux slowly to prevent lumps from forming in the sauce. Unused roux can be stored at room temperature for as long as 2 months if using oil because it has no water in it to activate any microbial activity.

Bulgur Walnut Loaf Crepes with Roasted Vegetables and Bigarade Sauce

ESPAGNOLE (FRENCH BROWN) SAUCE

The traditional method of making Espagnole is to prepare a very dark brown roux, to which water, beef, or veal stock is added, along with browned bones, vegetables, various seasonings, tomato paste, and wine. This mixture is allowed to cook slowly and reduce and draw the flavor from the bones. Unlike the vegan version, it is a slow cooking process. The vegan sauce is significantly quicker to make. The vegetables are caramelized in oil with seasonings, flour is added and lightly browned, and then wine, water, and tomatoes are added. After cooking for an hour, I turn off the heat leaving the sauce covered for an extra 30 minutes before straining it.

YIELD: 3 cups
TIME: 15 minutes prep and 1 hour cooking

4 tablespoons canola oil

1 cup onions, coarsely diced

1 cup carrots, shredded or finely diced

1 cup celery, finely diced

2 tablespoons tamari or other soy sauce (optional to use reduced sodium)

1 teaspoon caramel coloring*

5 teaspoons vegan beef-style broth powder (option to replace with 5 teaspoons tamari—add more if necessary to desired taste)

1 tablespoons fresh minced garlic

2 tablespoons chopped fresh basil (or 2 teaspoons dried basil)

2 teaspoons dried thyme

½ cup unbleached white flour

4 ¼ cups water or vegetable stock

½ cup red wine

½ cup tomato paste

1. Heat the oil in a 2-quart saucepan over medium heat. Add the onions, carrots, celery, soy sauce, vegan beef-style broth powder, garlic, basil, and thyme, and sauté, stirring occasionally, for 15 minutes, or until the vegetables are beginning to soften and brown.

2. Mix in the flour and stir to combine. Continue to cook for 5 minutes, and then stir in half the stock. Add the wine, tomato paste, and remaining stock, and stir well. Cover and simmer for 30 minutes on low heat.

3. Strain the sauce before using. Serve immediately, or transfer to a covered container and store in the refrigerator, where it will keep 4 to 6 weeks. You can also freeze the sauce for up to 6 months.

* Instead of caramel coloring you can also use 2 tablespoons gills from the underside of portabella mushroom caps, which will add dark color and an earthy flavor to this sauce.

BIGARADE SAUCE

YIELD: 1 ½ cups
TIME: 20 minutes

1 ¼ cups Espagnole Sauce

¼ cup currant jelly

1 tablespoon orange juice concentrate

¼ cup red wine

Place all ingredients in a saucepan and cook on medium heat for about 5 minutes, stirring while it simmers.

POIVRADE SAUCE

YIELD: 8 servings (2 cups)
TIME: 15 minutes prep and 25 minutes cooking

2 tablespoons canola oil

¼ cup finely diced onions

¼ cup finely diced carrots

¼ cup finely diced mushrooms

¼ cup finely diced celery

1 tablespoon minced garlic

2 teaspoons savory

½ teaspoon thyme

2 ½ teaspoons coarsely cracked black peppercorns

3 tablespoons unbleached white flour

¼ cup brown sugar

1 ¼ cups water

1 cup red wine

3 tablespoons balsamic vinegar

3 tablespoons tamari

2 tablespoons tomato paste

½ teaspoon paprika

3 drops liquid smoke

This is a peppery French brown sauce similar to an Espagnole sauce and made in a similar fashion. You could make a similar sauce using the Espagnole with 2 ½ teaspoons coarse cracked black pepper per 2 cups sauce.

1. Heat oil in 2-quart saucepan on medium heat. Add onions, carrots, mushrooms, celery, garlic, savory, thyme, and black pepper, then sauté for 7 minutes.

2. Add flour to cook as a roux for 5 to 7 minutes.

3. Gradually add brown sugar and water, and cook until thickened. Add wine, vinegar, and tamari and whip to infuse.

4. Mix tomato paste and paprika into sauce. Cover saucepan, add liquid smoke, and cover and simmer 10 minutes. Remove from heat and let sit covered for 30 minutes.

5. Strain (optional) and serve. If straining, add ¼ cup water to strained pulp and restrain it. The 2 cup yield is strained yield.

SHIITAKE MUSHROOM SAUCE

YIELD: 1 ½ cups
TIME: 20 minutes

1 cup small diced onions

1 cup stemmed and sliced shiitake mushrooms*

2 tablespoons high heat canola or safflower oil

1 tablespoon chopped fresh garlic

¼ cup water

1 teaspoon tamari or vegan "beef style" broth powder

½ cup Espagnole Sauce

1. On medium heat sauté mushrooms and onions in oil until translucent to slightly caramelized. Add garlic and sauté for about 1 minute.

2. Add ¼ cup water, vegan beef style broth powder or broth of choice to deglaze pan.

3. When almost completely reduced, add Espagnole Sauce, stirring to infuse ingredients and let simmer on low heat for 5 minutes. If sauce is too dense, thin out with a little water.

*Or substitute button mushrooms.

SAUCE ROBERT

This sauce is traditionally served with pork. In vegan cuisine it is best served with strong savory proteins such as smoked tempeh, grain loaves, seitan, tofu loaves, and beans as a stew. As in classical French cuisine demi-glace can be used in place of Espagnole Sauce with its concentrated stock offering a more intense flavor.

YIELD: 1 ¼ cups
TIME: 20 minutes

⅓ cup finely chopped onions
1 tablespoon vegan butter spread or canola oil
½ cup dry white wine
1 cup Espagnole Sauce (page 209)
1 tablespoon prepared mustard
1 tablespoon chopped parsley
Salt and ground black pepper to taste

1. Sauté onions on medium heat until golden brown. Add wine and cook until reduced to three-fourths the original amount.

2. Add Espagnole Sauce and simmer for about 10 minutes. Add mustard and parsley and mix in until evenly incorporated. Season to taste with salt and pepper, serve warm.

SAUCE ROMAINE

This sweet and sour savory sauce needs a strong flavored protein that is smoked like seitan or a grain loaf.

YIELD: 1 cup
TIME: 20 minutes

2 tablespoons sugar
½ cup vinegar
1 cup Espagnole Sauce (page 209)
¼ cup dry white wine
1 tablespoon raisins
1 tablespoon currants (or 2 tablespoons raisins)

1. On medium heat, stir and cook 2 tablespoons sugar in a heavy saucepan until sugar has melted and is golden in color.

2. Add vinegar and cook until the liquid has reduced to a thick syrup. Stir in Espagnole Sauce. Heat to boiling point.

3. Add wine, raisins, and currants to sauce and cook 3 to 4 minutes or until fruits are plump. Use with seitan, tempeh, or vegan protein of your choice.

SAUCE LYONNAISE

YIELD: 1 cup
TIME: 25 minutes

⅓ cup peeled and chopped onion
2 tablespoons vegan butter spread or high-heat oil
½ cup dry white wine
1 cup Espagnole Sauce (page 209)
1 teaspoon chopped fresh parsley
Salt and ground black pepper to taste

1. Sauté onions on medium heat in oil or butter spread until golden brown.

2. Add wine and cook until quantity has been reduced by one-half.

3. Add Espagnole Sauce. Cook for 10 to 15 minutes, stirring occasionally.

4. Remove from heat and add parsley. Season to taste with salt and ground black pepper.

SALISBURY STEAK-STYLE SAUCE

This is a superb sauce for both vegan and meat proteins, especially vegan steaks and cutlets. Serve over Salisbury Steak (page 371), tempeh, or seitan or mix 1 cup of sauce with 1 cup cooked and drained beans as a Salisbury bean stew. Additional cooked vegetables such as carrots, bell peppers, etc., can be added to make a stew.

YIELD: 1 ¼ cups
TIME: 25 minutes

¼ teaspoon minced garlic
¼ cup chopped onions
¼ cup sliced button mushrooms or chanterelles (fresh or rehydrated)
1 tablespoon canola oil
2 teaspoons vegan beef-style broth powder or tamari
⅛ teaspoon thyme
1 cup Espagnole Sauce (page 209)
¼ cup red wine
2 teaspoons yellow prepared mustard

1. Sauté garlic, onions, and mushrooms in oil until onions are translucent.

2. Add the vegan beef-style broth powder, thyme, Espagnole Sauce, wine, and mustard and bring to a simmer in a covered saucepan. Simmer 8 to 10 minutes.

ESPAGNOLE MAIGRE

The traditional version of this sauce is a brown seafood sauce in the style of an Espagnole. Made with light fish stock and white wine, this sauce has been called Lenten Espagnole, reminding me of some German monks taking up a "liquid bread" diet of Doppelbock beer for Lenten fasting. This vegan version uses sea vegetables.

If making Espagnole exclusively for this sauce, use a vegetarian broth powder in place of the vegan beef-style broth powder and white wine in place of red wine. Follow the above directions adding wakame with Old Bay to complete the sauce.

YIELD: 1 cup sauce
TIME: 15 minutes

2 tablespoons hot water
1 tablespoon crushed wakame
1 cup Espagnole Sauce (page 209)
¼ teaspoon Old Bay Seasoning

1. Pour water and wakame into a bowl and let sit for 5 minutes.

2. Pour Espagnole Sauce, Old Bay Seasoning, and wakame into a saucepan, bring to a simmer, cover pan, and let sit for 15 minutes (the longer the better).

Velouté Sauces

Velouté means velvet. Originally it was a complex sauce created by Caréme and simplified by Escoffier. The three traditional variations of Velouté Sauce with a butter roux are veal, poultry, and fish. As the sauce cooks it becomes velvety and with the addition of a liaison (cream and egg yolks), making it a supreme sauce, it becomes more velvety with a rich flavor. I use the vegan chicken-style version to make a variety of sauces including Piccata Sauce (with capers) and Supreme Sauce. Chicken-style and fish-style (sea vegetable) versions are the two that I recommend in vegan cuisine. Different variations of the sauce can be paired with a variety of entrées and vegetables. In general the Velouté Sauce complements vegetable dishes, beans, tempeh, chicken analogues, sea vegetables, and tofu.

VELOUTÉ SAUCE

This white sauce is the basis for many classical French sauces. It is also one of my favorites.

YIELD: 3 cups
TIME: 15 minutes prep and 60 minutes cooking

1 tablespoon canola oil or any refined neutral-flavored oil like safflower oil

1 cup diced onions

1 cup diced celery

1 cup diced carrots

2 teaspoons minced fresh garlic

¼ teaspoon dried thyme

1 bay leaf

3 sprigs chopped parsley

⅛ teaspoon ground black pepper

3 tablespoon vegan chicken-style broth powder

6 cups water

½ cup roux (see "Roux & Other Thickeners" on page 121)

1. Add oil to a 3-quart saucepan over medium heat. Add the onions, celery, carrots, and garlic. Sauté for 5 minutes, or until the onion is transparent.

2. Add the thyme, bay leaf, parsley, black pepper, vegan chicken-style broth powder, and water. Mix well, reduce the heat to medium-low, and simmer for 45 minutes.

3. Strain the mixture and return it to the pan. Add the salt and the roux 1 tablespoon at a time, and stir with a wire whisk until the sauce thickens.

4. Use immediately, or transfer to a covered container and store in the refrigerator where it will keep for about 2 weeks.

NOTE: Approximately 6 tablespoons of roux are needed for 3 cups of sauce.

Supreme Sauce

Adding a nut cream to a sauce creates osmosis (the nut cream draws moisture from the sauce) and will cause the sauce to become more viscous (thicker). In a thin sauce it may give the perfect consistency, or it may cause the sauce to become too thick. Viscosity depends on the amount of cream added to the sauce. Cut back on cream or add very small amounts (1 to 2 tablespoons) of water to adjust if you think sauce is too thick to properly coat (drape) on a food item.

YIELD: 2 ½ cups
TIME: 10 minutes

2 cups Velouté Sauce (page 213)
¼ cup Cashew Cream (page 175)
Salt and ground pepper to taste

1. Heat sauce to simmering point and turn off heat.

2. Beat in cream, 2 tablespoons at a time, until sauce is desired consistency.

3. Add salt and pepper.

4. Thin out sauce with water or vegan chicken-style broth powder if sauce is too thick. If using water, adjust flavor with chicken-style broth powder and seasonings if necessary to create the desired flavor profile. Add more salt if necessary to enhance the flavor.

OPTION: Add about ½ teaspoon nutritional yeast to sauce for a bit of the dairy note.

Parsley Sauce

YIELD: 2 cups
TIME: 15 minutes

6 tablespoons coarsely chopped parsley
½ cup hot water
2 cups Velouté Sauce (page 213)
¼ cup Cashew Cream (page 175)
Salt and ground white pepper to taste

1. Blanch 5 tablespoons of parsley in the hot water (place parsley in a strainer and dip into simmering water then immediately remove). Drain, cool, and set aside on a clean towel to dry.

2. Add the 1 tablespoon remaining parsley to the Velouté Sauce. Bring to boiling point and simmer 3 to 4 minutes.

3. Add dry blanched parsley and cream to sauce. Heat for 30 seconds. Season to taste with salt and pepper. Thin with water if necessary and adjust flavor with salt.

Aurora Sauce

YIELD: 2 ¼ cups
TIME 10 minutes

2 cups Supreme Sauce (page 214)
3 tablespoons tomato sauce (preferred) or tomato puree
1 tablespoon vegan butter spread

Combine Supreme Sauce and tomato sauce in 1- or 2-quart saucepan and bring to a simmer. Add butter spread, mix, and serve.

CAPER SAUCE

YIELD: 2 cups
TIME: 10 minutes

2 cups Velouté Sauce (page 213)
2 tablespoons capers
¼ cup vegan butter spread
Salt and pepper to taste

1. In saucepan, bring the Velouté Sauce to a simmer.

2. Remove from heat and blend in capers and butter. Add salt and pepper to taste.

BRETONNE SAUCE

YIELD: 3 ¼ cups
TIME: 25 minutes

½ cup julienned celery
½ cup julienned fresh mushrooms
½ cup sliced leeks (use white portion only)
3 tablespoons vegan butter spread
½ cup vegetarian chicken-style broth/stock
2 cups Velouté Sauce (page 213)
Salt and ground white pepper to taste

1. Sauté vegetables in 2 tablespoons butter spread for 4 minutes on moderate heat. Add broth and cook until vegetables are tender.

2. Add to Velouté Sauce along with remaining butter.

3. Season to taste with salt and ground white pepper.

FRENCH CURRY SAUCE

Henri-Paul Pellaprat is writing from a French perspective in *The Great Book of French Cuisine* when he calls this a curry sauce because it is the French idea of a curry sauce. Yamuna Devi suggests in *The Art of Indian Vegetarian Cooking* that the French version dates back to the colonial period when servant cooks of expatriate merchants tried to create something similar to the Indian cuisine they enjoyed in their colonial kitchens. That is why I changed Pellaprat's title from "Curry Sauce" to "French Curry Sauce."

YIELD: 2 cups
TIME: 15 to 20 minutes

¼ cup finely diced onions
1 tablespoon vegan butter spread
1 tablespoon curry powder
¼ cup vegan chicken-style broth (¾ teaspoon of chicken broth powder added to ¼ cup of water)
1 ½ cups Velouté Sauce (page 213)
½ teaspoon dried thyme
$1/16$ teaspoon ground mace
¼ cup Cashew Cream (page 175)
Salt and pepper to taste

1. Sauté onions in butter spread on medium heat until the onion is translucent but not browned. Add curry powder and stir, cooking for 2 minutes.

2. Add broth and bring to a boil. Remove from heat and stir in Velouté Sauce, thyme, and mace.

3. Bring to a boil again stirring constantly. Stir Cashew Cream into sauce and serve.

Tomato Sauces

It is speculated that tomato sauce took the culinary stage in Naples, Italy. The city was known for its vegetarian leaf eaters who were considered impoverished. It was a tourist city and like most tourist cities, food cultures crossed borders and new dishes emerged. In Naples cooks started topping traditional dishes with tomatoes and tomato sauce.

Tournefort, a French botanist, gave the tomato, a New World plant, the Latin name *Lycopersicon esculentum.* The name translates to "wolfpeach"— round like a peach and poisonous (or dangerous) like a wolf.

Carême helped popularize the tomato in France and Escoffier added the *Sauce Tomate* to the five mother sauces. The classical tomato sauce calls for salt pork, veal, or chicken stock or a ham bone— loaded with meat flavor. I did not, in my classical version of this tomato sauce, add any meat-style flavors. This is a safe place to break from tradition with meats in sauces. Herbs, spices, oils, and wines are sufficient.

CLASSICAL TOMATO SAUCE

The original French tomato sauce uses a light stock, bacon, and flour. A *bouquet garni* (bundle of herbs) and bay leaves flavor sauce in cooking process and are removed at the end. I am using this vegan tomato sauce in place of the traditional French version to start developing the flavor of the sauce. I would leave the salt out and flavor sparingly with vegan bacon bits, which are high in salt. Then adjust the salt, if necessary.

Using sugar in a tomato sauce to give it sweetness is not a good cooking technique. I used to add a sweetener but truth be known, good technique will develop the natural sweetness of a sauce by bringing it out of the ingredients. That is why I sauté generous amounts of sweet vegetables (carrots and onions) in tomato sauce.

YIELD: 6 cups sauce
TIME: 30 minutes

1 ½ cups peeled and finely diced onions
1 ½ cups peeled and grated carrots
½ cup finely diced celery
3 tablespoons minced garlic
6 tablespoons extra-virgin olive oil
1 ½ teaspoons salt
4 teaspoons dried basil
4 teaspoons thyme
2 bay leaves
1 teaspoon black pepper
6 cups (2 [28-ounce] cans) crushed tomatoes

1. Sauté the onions, carrots, celery, and garlic in the oil for about 5 minutes on medium heat.

2. Add salt, basil, thyme, bay leaves, and pepper and continue to sauté for another 5 minutes.

3. Add the crushed tomatoes and simmer for 1 hour.

CREAM OF TOMATO SAUCE

YIELD: 2 ½ cups
TIME: 15 minutes

2 cups Classical Tomato Sauce (page 216)
½ cup Cashew Cream (page 175)
2 tablespoons vegan butter spread
Salt and pepper to taste

1. Pour sauce, cream, and butter spread into blender and blend until smooth.

2. Heat, adjust seasoning with the salt and pepper. Add water to thin sauce if too viscous (thick), which will not allow it to drape or evenly coat the food's surface.

SPANISH TOMATO SAUCE (FILLING)

Traditional Spanish tomato sauce is very thick and often used as an omelet filling. This version is a complement to chicken-style, seitan, tofu pâté, tempeh, and bean-stew type entrées. To make into a sauce, thin it with water and adjust seasoning, if necessary.

YIELD: About 5 cups as a filling and 6 cups (1 cup water added) as a sauce
TIME: 15 minutes prep and 30 minutes cooking

1 tablespoon extra-virgin olive oil
1 cup thinly sliced onions
½ cup grated or very thinly sliced celery
½ cup sliced button mushrooms
1 tablespoon minced fresh garlic
½ teaspoon dried thyme
1 bay leaf
3 cups tomato purée
1 cup diced tomatoes
¼ cup sliced green olives
½ teaspoon salt
1 cup diced green bell peppers

1. Heat the oil in a 2-quart saucepan over medium heat. Add the onions, celery, mushrooms, garlic, thyme, and bay leaf. Sauté the mixture for 5 minutes, or until the onions are soft and transparent.

2. Add the tomato purée, diced tomatoes, olives, and salt, and bring to a simmer. Cook on low heat for about 30 minutes.

3. Add the bell peppers, and cook another 3 minutes. Discard bay leaf.

4. Serve immediately, or transfer to a covered container and store in the refrigerator, where it will keep about 2 weeks.

Sauce Version

Add 1 cup water and ¼ teaspoon salt (optional) to finished Spanish Tomato Sauce Filling. Bring to a simmer and serve.

SAUCE CONCASSE

Concasse means to crush or grind. What makes this sauce incredibly delicious is using fresh tomatoes. This sauce goes especially well with either the New World (page 295) or Italian Shepherd's Pie (page 287), Pecan Nut Loaf (page 297), and Savory Greek Spinach Crepes (page 262), and many of the polenta entrées.

YIELD: 8 servings (2 cups sauce)
TIME: 20 minutes prep and 60 minutes cooking

1 cup finely diced onions
4 teaspoons minced fresh garlic
½ teaspoon salt, or more to taste
2 tablespoons extra-virgin olive oil
3 ½ cups fresh tomatoes, blanched, peeled, seeded, and chopped (about 5 medium tomatoes)
¼ cup dry sherry
2 tablespoons chopped fresh basil

1. In a 2-quart saucepan, sauté the onions, garlic, and salt in the oil over medium-low heat for 10 minutes.

2. Add the tomatoes, sherry, and fresh basil, and mix well. Cook the mixture, uncovered, until it reduces down to half the original amount, about 45 minutes to 1 hour. Use immediately or refrigerate in a covered container until needed.

PROVENÇAL TOMATO SAUCE

This sauce uses fresh tomatoes.

YIELD: 5 cups
TIME: 15 minutes prep and 45 minutes cooking

¼ cup olive oil
1 ¼ cups finely chopped onion
1 tablespoon chopped garlic
2 bay leaves
¼ teaspoon ground black pepper
½ teaspoon dried thyme
2 teaspoons dried marjoram
2 tablespoons pitted and chopped Kalamata olives.
6 cups fresh tomatoes, blanched, peeled and finely diced
2 tablespoons tomato paste
Salt to taste

1. Heat the oil in a saucepan. Add onions and sauté until onions turn translucent.

2. Add in the garlic, bay leaves, pepper, thyme, marjoram, and olives. Sauté about 5 minutes, stirring every minute or 2.

3. Stir in the tomatoes and tomato paste. Simmer for 30 minutes on low heat. Adjust salt and seasoning if needed and remove bay leaves.

Hollandaise, Beurre Blancs, & Glazes

Many factors drive the development of vegan classical sauces and none more important than health. Hollandaise is one sauce, with approximately 90 percent fat, that could use help. By using 50 percent silken tofu and 50 percent vegan butter spread with lemon juice and seasoning, a similar sauce can be created that doesn't need to be whipped periodically to remain emulsified and, unlike traditional Hollandaise, can be refrigerated and reheated. Removing almost 50 percent of the fat from a sauce that contained 90 percent fat will not ruin the flavor but it will significantly improve the nutritional profile.

The earliest record of Hollandaise was in 1758. No egg yolks were used in this early version. It was butter, flour, bouillon, and herbs. Without testing such a recipe, my sense of food chemistry leads me to believe that the flour and bouillon held the ingredients in suspension. Harold McGee explains that egg yolks are not needed to hold the butter in suspension. I agree, but something must do it, like a soy curd called silken tofu.

Like all mother sauces, many variations can be made from this one sauce base. Three of the most popular derivative sauces are Béarnaise, Choron (a variation of Béarnaise with tomato products), and Maltaise with its hint of citrus. Hollandaise is generally made with 2 tablespoons white wine vinegar or lemon juice as an acidifier, 3 egg yolks, 4 tablespoons water, ½ cup (4 ounces) unsalted butter, salt, and cayenne pepper (optional). Of course, there are variations of flavor for this sauce but the core traditional ingredients are egg yolks, butter, and lemon juice. For Béarnaise, tarragon and shallots are cooked in vinegar, strained, and added to the sauce.

The most important factor in creating the sauce derivatives from Hollandaise is the vegan mother sauce. You will notice in the Béarnaise recipe that I don't make the Hollandaise first. The two are merged together as one recipe. This is what is so unique about vegan classical sauces. Unique exceptions, such as blending vegan butter and tofu to make a Hollandaise to simplify the emulsion step, make vegan sauces easier to prepare.

Beurre Blancs are classical sauces but not mother sauces. Their closest relative to mother sauces is the Hollandaise Sauce. I use the same techniques but with a vegan butter spread. Vegan butter spreads function similarly to butter in the emulsification process. The exception is that butter spreads don't have the same heat tolerance of butter because the flavor systems used to create the vegan butter flavor don't hold up well under high heat. One cannot make a beurre noir (a darkened butter) with a vegan butter spread.

Glazes are traditionally understood to be meat, poultry, or seafood broths cooked into a concentrate. Unlike meat stocks that are loaded with collagen giving the concentrate body as it reduces, vegetable concentrates need body which is supplied by pureed cooked vegetables, especially starchy vegetables. There are exceptions like balsamic vinegar, which includes solids that reduce down to a concentrate, or glaze. Glazes can enhance sauce or protein as a flavor concentrate. What I call a glaze sauce is designed as a pseudo beurre blanc-style sauce using a starch as a stabilizer. The recipes in this book don't use a concentrated liquid. If a stronger flavor is desired, use a concentrated liquid in place of the wine or lemon juice called for in the recipe. With flavor paste and concentrates, the cook doesn't need to make concentrates. They can buy them. The main obstacle is salt, which is never used in making a glaze but is generally concentrated in most vegetarian or meat-based flavor pastes. I offer a few glaze sauces below, pseudo-beurre blancs with more liquid and beans to emulsify the sauce.

The Hollandaise-style sauces use a combination of silken tofu, roasted vegetables as the emulsifiers (for example, Roasted Red Pepper Hollandaise Sauce) with butter spreads and liquids. The resultant sauce has the texture of a Hollandaise that doesn't need to be whipped to maintain emulsification and can be cooled and reheated. These vegan sauces are user friendly.

These sauces don't have specific applications. They are generally served to complement a protein such as a seitan steak, veg loaf, tofu, tempeh, etc. The Hollandaise-style sauces can also be mixed with beans and vegetables to create a rich and luscious entrée.

BASIC HOLLANDAISE SAUCE

This vegan version is very forgiving. When making the traditional version with egg yolks, if the yolks are overheated the sauce will separate and yolks will curdle. When tofu overheats, it doesn't curdle because it was previously curdled. The vegan version can separate if too hot, but it can be blended back into shape. The sauce will re-emulsify and hold stable at 100 to 120°F. This recipe, unlike the dairy/egg version, does not need to be periodically whipped to maintain emulsification and can be refrigerated and reheated.

YIELD: 4 servings (1 cup)
TIME: 10 minutes

½ cup vegan butter spread
½ (12.3-ounce) package extra firm silken tofu
1 teaspoon lemon juice
¹⁄₁₆ teaspoon ground black pepper

1. Warm butter spread until liquid. Add tofu, lemon juice, and black pepper. If measuring out tofu by volume, crush it into a measuring cup to receive an accurate measurement. Blend the mixture until smooth and creamy.

2. Heat on stove top in saucepan on low heat while constantly stirring for 5 to 8 minutes or microwave for about 1 to 2 minutes until temperature reaches to 160°F. Let cool to 100 to 120°F.

3. Blend or vigorously whip until sauce emulsifies. I use a hand-held blender in a 1-pint (2-cup) measuring cup.

4. Blend and serve or refrigerate until ready to use.

YELLOW PEPPER HOLLANDAISE

This version of the sauce benefits from the wonderful sweet roasted flavor of yellow peppers while reducing the recipe's fat and increasing its nutritional density.

YIELD: 10 servings (2 ½ cups)
TIME: 10 minutes prep plus 30 minutes roasting

1 cup yellow bell pepper, cut in half and seeds removed
2 tablespoons chardonnay wine
½ cup vegan butter spread or olive oil butter spread
12 ounces extra firm silken tofu
2 tablespoons lemon juice
¼ teaspoon salt

1. Roast yellow bell peppers, sweat for 20 to 30 minutes in covered container, and peel off blackened skin.

2. Heat peppers and wine in saucepan on medium heat for 3 to 5 minutes. Warm butter spread.

3. Place all ingredients in blender and blend until completely smooth. Serve warm.

VARIATION: *Red Pepper Hollandaise Sauce*

Substitute 1 cup red bell peppers for yellow bell peppers.

VARIATION: *Yellow Pepper Coconut Hollandaise Sauce*

Replace butter spread with ½ cup coconut butter spread.

BÉARNAISE SAUCE

Béarnaise Sauce is generally served to complement a protein served as an entrée. It would go well with seitan steak, Salisbury steak, vegan chicken cutlets, bulgur walnut loaf, and seared tempeh.

YIELD: Approximately 1 cup
TIME: 10 minutes prep and 20 to 30 minutes cooking

¼ cup water (or 2 tablespoons each of water and red wine vinegar)
¼ cup white wine
1 tablespoon vegan beef-style broth powder (gluten) or 1 ½ tablespoons tamari (gluten free)
2 teaspoons dried tarragon leaf
⅛ teaspoon annatto (Turmeric is an alternative, but be careful—it has a strong flavor.)
1 tablespoon chopped shallots
6 ounces extra firm silken tofu
¼ cup vegan butter spread

1. Place water, white wine, broth powder, tarragon, annatto, and shallots into a 1-quart saucepan on medium-low heat and cook until reduced to about ¼ cup.

2. Place all ingredients (warm liquid reduction, tofu, and butter spread) into a blender and blend until smooth, about 30 to 60 seconds. (It is optional to use a hand blender, which will take longer to blend into a smooth cream.) Before serving, warm in a double boiler or microwave until approximately 160°F.

CHORON SAUCE

YIELD: Approximately 1 cup
TIME: 10 minutes prep and 20 to 30 minutes cooking

¼ cup water
¼ cup white wine
¼ teaspoon salt
2 teaspoons dried tarragon leaf
⅛ teaspoon annatto (Turmeric is an option but be careful—it has a strong flavor.)
1 tablespoon tomato paste
¼ teaspoon ground black pepper
6 ounces extra firm silken tofu
¼ cup vegan butter spread

1. Place water, wine, salt, tarragon, annatto, tomato paste, and black pepper into a 1-quart saucepan on medium-low heat and cook until reduced to about ¼ cup.

2. Put reduction, tofu, and butter spread into a blender and blend until smooth, about 30 to 60 seconds. A hand blender could also be used.

3. Warm in a double boiler until approximately 160°F then reduce temperature to 120°F. Let it sit, cool down, and serve.

MALTAISE SAUCE

This sauce is traditionally made with blood orange juice but any pure orange juice will work. Blood oranges are in peak season during the winter months, which limits their availability. I use orange juice concentrate in place of juice because it carries the same flavor and sweetness without the liquid that can break the sauce or make it more fragile. The juice and zest are added to the Hollandaise, heated, and served. This tangy semisweet sauce complements broccoli and asparagus but can be served with other green vegetables like spinach.

YIELD: 17 tablespoons sauce
TIME: 5 minutes prep and 5 minutes cooking

2 teaspoons orange juice concentrate
½ teaspoon orange zest
1 cup Hollandaise Sauce (page 220)

Mix orange juice concentrate and zest into Hollandaise, heat in saucepan on low for 1-3 minutes, constantly stirring until hot. Serve warm.

COCONUT LEMON BEURRE BLANC

YIELD: ½ cup
TIME: 15 minutes

½ cup coconut cream
2 tablespoons mirin or white wine
1 teaspoon lemon zest or 2 teaspoons lemon grass
⅛ teaspoon salt

1. Blend all ingredients together until smooth and creamy.

2. Pour into saucepan and bring to a low simmer and cook, stirring until the sauce emulsifies.

Lemon Beurre Blanc

YIELD: 7 tablespoons
TIME: 10 minutes

½ cup vegan butter spread or olive oil
1 tablespoon lemon juice
3 tablespoons white wine
1 teaspoon dry tarragon (optional)
¼ teaspoon salt
¼ teaspoon sugar

Place all ingredients in a saucepan and cook on low heat for about 10 minutes until moisture has evaporated. Serve with protein of your choice.

Lemon Sauce Glaze

Use this sauce as you would a traditional French butter sauce. The beans are the emulsifier.

YIELD: 10 tablespoons
TIME: 10 minutes

½ cup vegan butter spread or olive oil spread
2 tablespoons white navy beans, soft cooked/ canned, drained, pureed
1 tablespoon lemon juice
½ cup white wine
1 teaspoon dried tarragon (optional)
¼ teaspoon salt
¼ teaspoon sugar

1. Warm butter or olive oil spread.
2. Place all ingredients in blender and blend until smooth and creamy.
3. Serve warm with protein of your choice, or side vegetables.

Lemon Olive Sauce Glaze

YIELD: ¾ cup
TIME: 15 minutes

½ cup olive oil, extra-virgin
½ cup white wine
2 tablespoons white navy beans, soft cooked/ canned, drained, pureed
⅛ teaspoon salt
1 teaspoon of lemon juice

1. Blend all ingredients together until smooth and creamy.
2. Pour into saucepan and bring to a low simmer and cook, stirring until the sauce emulsifies. Serve with protein of your choice.

Red Wine Sauce Glaze

This glaze complements heartier entrées.

YIELD: ¾ cup
TIME: 5 minutes prep and 10 minutes cooking

¼ cup palm shortening or vegan butter spread
¼ cup red wine
¼ cup white navy beans, soft cooked/ canned, drained, pureed
1 tablespoon tamari

1. Warm shortening or vegan butter spread and wine in a saucepan.
2. Pour all ingredients into blender and blend together until smooth and creamy.
3. Return to saucepan and bring to a low simmer. Cook, stirring until the sauce emulsifies. Serve with protein of your choice.

THYME GARLIC BEURRE BLANC

YIELD: 6 to 8 tablespoons
TIME: 10 minutes

½ cup vegan butter spread or olive oil

¼ cup white wine

½ teaspoon dried thyme

½ teaspoon dried tarragon leaf (optional)

⅛ teaspoon salt

1. Place all ingredients in saucepan and cook on low heat for about 20 minutes until moisture has evaporated.

2. Serve with protein of your choice.

Vegetable-Based Sauces

Vegetable-based sauces often, but not always, use the vegetable's natural starch and pulp to give the sauce its body and ability to glaze the protein. These sauces are used in the same manner as a traditional sauce to complement the entrée.

Sauces, glazes, and *au jus* (French term for "juice") are what give proteins their flavor profile, and ingredients such as herbs, spices, vegetables, fruits, and wines give the sauces their flavor characteristics. Chefs and household cooks should use more of these healthy natural sauces across all spectrums of their cooking, to not only improve the flavor of vegan proteins but also to improve whatever they are cooking, since many industrial salt-laden sauces are sorely lacking in nutritional density and flavor character.

The following sauces include some new and innovative vegan sauces like the Balsamic Glaze, Sauce Renaissance, and vegan interpretations of sauces from different cuisines. Every cuisine has its popular sauces and vegan sauce innovation is an evolving process. I like these sauces because they bring a wonderful array of different flavors and cuisines to vegan proteins, offering more innovative vegan entrée options.

One of my favorites is the delicate Sauce Renaissance, which is made with roasted peppers, fennel, basil, and garlic.

Other vegetables sauces as components of other recipes are:

- ↻ Soy Milk Sauce (page 282)

- ↻ "Beef-style" Bolognese Sauce (page 373)

- ↻ Bolognese Sauce with Mostaccioli (page 373)

- ↻ Savory Red Wine Sauce (page 376)

1. Bulgur Walnut Loaf (page 298) with Béarnaise Sauce (page 221)

2. Tofu-Infused Polenta (page 304), sautéed Tofu Pâté (page 252), & Classic Cuban-Style Picadillo Sauce (page 234)

3. Black Bean Napoleon (page 294) with black beans substituting for pinto beans

4. Smoked Seitan Cutlet (page 276, with smoking instructions on page 314) with Red Cabbage, Potato Pancake (page 186), Smoked Non-Dairy Cheese, & Bigarade Sauce (page 209)

5. Dijon Potato Salad (page 163)

6. Seitan Swiss Steak (page 280) with Herbed Mashed Potatoes (page 185) & Green Beans New Orleans (page 196)

7. Thanksgiving Day Tofu (page 260) with Velouté (page 213) & Cranberry Sauce (page 353)

8. Southwestern Smoked Tofu Loaf (page 255) with Wild Forager's au Jus (page 230)

9. Speed Scratch Thanksgiving Day Vegan Chicken (page 378) with Velouté Sauce (page 213)

10. Speed Scratch "Chicken-Style" Piccata (pages 376 & 237)

11. Speed Scratch Chicken Le Coq au Vin (page 376)

12. Speed Scratch Surf (Sea Vegetable Cakes, page 258), & Turf (Seitan, page 276) with Hollandaise Sauce (page 220)

13. 1992 Culinary Olympics American Bounty—Silver Medal. Seitan Steak (page 276), American Barley Loaf (page 299), & Tofu-Infused Polenta (page 304)

14. Speed Scratch Army Gold Medal Burger (Salisbury Burger, page 371)—Gold Medal in Military Food Competition

15. 1992 Culinary Olympics European Bounty (Seitan, page 276; Tofu Pâté, page 252; & Tofu-Infused Polenta, page 304)— Silver Medal

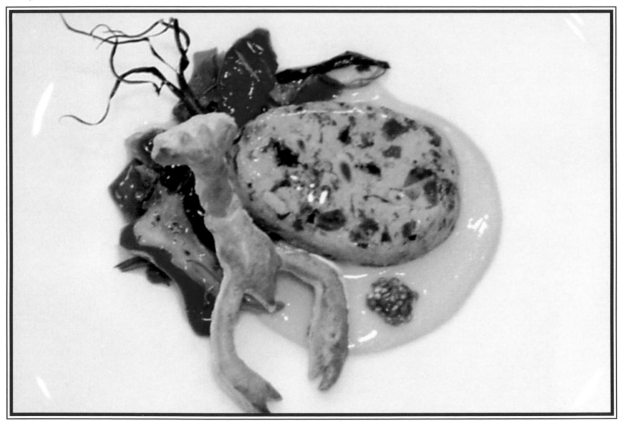

16. 1996 Culinary Olympics Sea Vegetable Cake (page 258) with Sauce Dugléré (page 233)—Bronze Medal

17. Thai Black Bean Shiitake Mushroom Duxelle Rolls (page 288) & Hollandaise Sauce (page 220)

18. Bulgur Walnut Loaf (page 298) with Vegan Crepes (page 337), Roasted Vegetables & Bigarade Sauce (page 209)

19. Almond-Crusted Tofu (page 267, pistachio version), Tofu-Infused Polenta (page 304) with Sauce Renaissance (page 227)

20. Tofu-Infused Polenta (page 304) with wrapped Quinoa Pinto Bean Loaf (page 300) & Spanish Tomato Sauce & Filling (page 217)

21. Lemon Cheesecake (page 361) with Gluten-Free Crust (page 336) & Raspberry Coulis (page 361)

22. Vertical Yellow Cake Torte (Yellow Cake, page 358) with Chocolate Ganache Icing (page 326), Chocolate Buttercream (page 327), & Raspberry Coulis (page 361)

23. Chocolate Chip Almond Biscottini di Prato (page 332), Florentine Cookies (page 329), Anko (Sweet Bean Paste) filled Ohagi (page 350), & Cupcake (use Chocolate, Carob, White, or Yellow Cake, page 356)

24. Poached Pear with Dessert Crepe (page 337) with Raspberry Sabayon Sauce (page 324)

25. Speed Scratch Chocolate Torte (Basic Brownie, page 382) & Almond Buttercream

26. Kanten Cake (page 357) with Raspberry Sabayon (page 324) & Hippen Masse (page 335)

27. Vegan Peanut Butter "Ice Cream" Cake (page 356)

28. Strawberry-Lemon Napoleon (page 323) with Lemon Crème Anglaise (page 326)

29. Speed Scratch Chocolate Brownie (page 382) with German Chocolate Cake Icing (page 328)

30. Jamaican Floating Isle (page 360)

31. 1996 Culinary Olympic Poached Pear with Pear Mousse (Poached Pears, page 346; Lemon Crème Anglaise, page 323; & Hippen Masse, page 335)—Gold Medal

32. Polynesian Crisp (page 354) with Coconut Whipped Cream Topping (page 345) or Ice Cream (page 342) & Raspberry Coulis (page 326)

GARLIC CONFIT

Confit (pronounced con-FEE) is a European cooking technique originally designed to preserve meats, specifically duck, but was also used to preserve goose and pork. It is addressed in the techniques section. For spoilage to occur, bacteria needs a host, the meat, plus moisture and warmth to incubate. Confit slowly cooks the moisture out of the meat, seals out air with fat, and was originally stored in cold European root cellars. Some chefs believe it is a term exclusive to cooking meats, but it is a more general cooking technique designed to preserve food. Meat probably drove its invention, but it is now being used with vegetables and fruits. Because this confit stores so well, you can make it in large quantities to always have on hand.

YIELD: 3 cups
TIME: 5 minutes prep and 1 ½ to 2 hours cooking

4 cups fresh, peeled garlic cloves
2 to 2 ½ cups canola or olive oil

1. Place the garlic in a 2-quart saucepan, and add enough oil to cover the cloves. Place over low heat, and slow-cook for about 1 ½ hours, or until the cloves no longer emit bubbles. (The bubbles are a sign that moisture is escaping from the garlic.)

2. Be sure to keep the heat low to prevent the cloves from browning.

3. Place the cooked garlic along with the oil in a covered container, and store in the refrigerator, where it will keep for up to 3 months.

GARLIC CREAM SAUCE

YIELD 1 ½ cups
TIME: 10 minutes

1 cup Garlic Confit (above)
1 cup soy milk
½ teaspoon salt
¼ cup white wine, preferably Chardonnay

1. Place all ingredients in a blender and blend until smooth (about 20 to 30 seconds).

2. Pour sauce into saucepan and heat on medium heat for about 3 to 5 minutes or until the sauce begins to simmer while occasionally stirring. Remove from heat and serve.

VARIATION: *Italian Fennel Garlic Sauce*

YIELD: 1 ½ cups
TIME: 10 minutes

Add 1 teaspoon Italian spice and ½ teaspoon ground fennel to the Garlic Cream Sauce after blending and before heating.

Gyros (Cucumber Yogurt) Sauce

YIELD: 1 ⅛ cups
TIME: 15 minutes prep and 1 hour salting cucumbers and making sauce

1 cup cucumbers
½ teaspoon salt
½ ounce white flour
½ ounce extra-virgin olive or canola oil
2 cups unsweetened soy milk
⅛ teaspoon salt
½ teaspoon dried dill weed
2 tablespoons lemon juice

1. Peel, seed, finely dice, and toss the cucumbers in ½ teaspoon salt and let sit for 45 minutes while making sauce.

2. Mix flour and oil together and heat until roux begins to simmer; immediately remove from the heat to prevent it from browning. Add soy milk slowly while whipping the sauce to prevent curdling.

3. When all soy milk is incorporated and sauce is smooth, add remaining salt, dill, and lemon juice. Lemon will cause the sauce to curd (thicken but remain smooth).

4. Drain, rinse, press, and add cucumbers to yogurt sauce.

NOTE: The sauce is rather viscous so you may be able to add the cucumbers directly to the sauce without salting to pull the water. If the sauce ends up too thin, cut back on the soy milk, making the sauce thicker and more viscous.

Balsamic Glaze

This glazing sauce is a perfect complement for the tofu pâté entrées, chicken-style proteins, and assorted appetizers. It could also be called a Sweet & Sour Balsamic Sauce.

YIELD: 3 ½ cups
TIME: 25 minutes

1 ½ cups brown sugar
1 ⅔ cups water
1 cup balsamic vinegar
¾ cup red wine
6 tablespoons tamari
¼ cup cornstarch or arrowroot powder

1. In a 1-quart saucepan on medium heat, add the brown sugar and stir constantly about 5 minutes, or until lightly caramelized.

2. Add ¾ cup water, vinegar, wine, and tamari, and bring to a simmer. The caramelized sugar will harden, but don't let it stick to the bottom of the pan or it will burn.

3. Cover and simmer for 5 to 10 minutes, stirring occasionally, until the caramelized sugar dissolves. Remove from the heat.

4. In a small mixing bowl, combine the cornstarch with 2 tablespoons water and mix well. Stir into sugar mixture.

5. Return the saucepan to medium heat, stirring constantly until the sauce thickens. Allow the sauce to cool before storing and refrigerate until ready to use. It will last for 2 months in the refrigerator but will need to be reheated and whipped to emulsify solids back into liquids.

Sauce Renaissance

This savory/sweet sauce won a Gold Medal in the 1996 International Culinary Olympics.

YIELD: 12 servings (3 cups)
TIME: 20 minutes prep and 40 minutes cooking

2 red bell peppers

1 yellow bell pepper

½ cup roasted pepper juice (or water)

½ cup diced onions

¼ cup diced fennel (or 1 teaspoon fennel powder and ¼ cup diced celery)

3 tablespoons chopped fresh basil

1 ½ tablespoons minced fresh garlic

1 ¼ teaspoons fresh marjoram leaves

1 teaspoon fresh oregano leaves

1 teaspoon fresh thyme leaves

¾ teaspoon salt

⅛ teaspoon saffron threads

1 tablespoon olive oil

OPTION: Substitute fresh herbs with 1 ¼ teaspoons dry Italian herb mix by mixing together 1 part each: dried basil, marjoram, oregano, and thyme.

1. Preheat the oven to 325°F. Wash, dry, halve, and seed the peppers. Rub the skins with olive oil. Place the pepper halves on a baking sheet and roast in the oven for 30 to 40 minutes or until soft and skins begin to shrivel. Remove peppers from oven and place in a covered container to steam for 10 minutes. When cool, remove the loosened skins. Dice the peppers to obtain ⅔ cup roasted red pepper and ⅓ cup roasted yellow pepper.

2. To collect the roasted pepper juice, take ½ cup of water and pour as much of it as possible onto the baking sheet while the sheet is still hot. Deglaze the pan and pour the liquid into a measuring cup to make ½ cup. Set aside.

3. In a 10-inch frying pan, sauté the remaining vegetables and the seasonings in the oil over medium-low heat for about 10 minutes, or until the onions are transparent.

4. Transfer the sauté mixture to a blender, add the roasted peppers and their juice, then blend until smooth. Serve heated or refrigerated until needed.

Sun-Dried Tomato Pesto

There are many ways to enjoy pesto; try spreading it on a sandwich, as a pasta sauce, or add to vegetables, beans, seitan, or tempeh.

YIELD: 4 servings (1 cup)
TIME: 10 minutes

¾ cup fresh basil

½ cup sun-dried tomatoes

¾ cup hot water

¼ cup olive oil, extra-virgin

¾ teaspoon salt

1. Wash, dry, and stem the basil. In a small mixing bowl, soak tomatoes in the water for 15 minutes. Drain and reserve the water.

2. In a blender, combine basil, tomatoes, water, oil, and salt and blend until smooth. Transfer to a container and refrigerate until ready to serve.

PUTTANESCA SAUCE

This sauce was inspired or created out of necessity from whatever foodstuffs or "any kind of garbage" were lying around in the kitchen after closing when a few hungry customers arrived looking for anything to eat. Puttanesca, the "worthless" sauce, is generally served with pasta but can be served with polenta, pasta, other carbohydrate, or any vegan protein.

Originally made with anchovies, the vegan version of this sauce is an example of how to replace anchovies. The rich, dark, salty miso gives the sauce the saltiness of anchovies and the sea vegetable provides the hint of seafood. Between the salt in the tomatoes, olives, capers, and miso, I would not recommend adding more salt. This so-called "low life," worthless sauce radiates with elegant flavors.

NOTE: It isn't recommended to cook any highly acidic food such as tomato in a seasoned cast iron pot. There are always exceptions to rules and the exception here is, if the pot is seasoned, you can cook an acidic food in it for a very short 5 or 10 minutes.

Yield: 4 cups
Time: 15 minutes prep and 30 minutes cooking

¼ cup olive oil

1 cup finely chopped onion

4 teaspoons minced garlic

2 (28-ounce) cans (52 ounces/6 cups) Roma plum tomatoes, broken into pieces, with juice

1 cup pitted, halved, tightly packed Kalamata olives

2 tablespoons tomato paste

2 tablespoons drained capers

2 tablespoons chopped wakame

½ teaspoon crushed dried basil

1 tablespoon dark miso or tamari (dissolved in 2 tablespoons water)

Salt to taste

1 pound penne pasta, cooked al dente

1. Heat the olive oil in a 2- to 3-quart saucepan over medium-high heat for about 1 to 2 minutes. Add the onion and garlic and sauté until lightly caramelized, about 6 minutes. Add the garlic and cook an additional 2 minutes.

2. Add the tomatoes, olives, tomato paste, capers, wakame, and basil and simmer until the sauce is thickened and slightly reduced, about 30 to 40 minutes.

3. Dissolve the miso in 2 tablespoons water and add to sauce.

4. Adjust seasoning, to taste, cover and set aside. Add cooked pasta to the pan and toss for 1 minute.

STOUT CARAMELIZED ONION SAUCE

The key to this sauce is using medium heat to slowly caramelize the onions, developing the sweetness along with the caramelization. Adding garlic toward the end of the caramelization process avoids burning it.

The traditional sauce calls for bacon. There are two options. One is to caramelize smoked tempeh bacon (see recipe for Hickory Smoked Tempeh in Smoked Proteins on page 314) or use a commercial tempeh bacon. The second option is to use vegan bacon bits.

In a restaurant environment this sauce works both ways on the vegan/conventional vegetarian and nonvegetarian menus. The tempeh bacon or bacon bits are added to the sauce after it is thickened.

YIELD: 8 servings (2 cups)
TIME: 30 minutes

4 cups sliced onions

3 tablespoons olive oil

¼ teaspoon salt

1 teaspoon fresh, minced garlic

¼ cup unbleached white flour or rice flour

2 tablespoons tamari or vegan beef-style broth powder

1 ½ cups dark stout beer

½ cup chopped smoked tempeh bacon (or 2 tablespoons vegan bacon bits)

¼ teaspoon liquid smoke (optional to emphasize the bacon flavor)

1. In a 10-inch frying pan, sauté the onions in medium heat with oil and salt until lightly caramelized. Add garlic and sauté another 3 minutes.

2. Add the flour and continue to cook 3 to 4 minutes longer. Add tamari and ¾ cup of the stout, then cook until thick and smooth.

3. Add the remaining stout, tempeh bacon, and liquid smoke. If using the smoke flavor, then simmer slowly over low heat for about 10 minutes on low to medium heat. Thin with water if too thick (no more than 2 tablespoons of water, adding one tablespoon at a time).

Puttanesca Sauce with Penne Pasta

WILD FORAGER'S AU JUS

Jus is the natural juices given off by food. In traditional cooking, this includes meats such as beef, veal, and lamb. The mirepoix, seasonings, and meat caramelization in the roasting pan are deglazed and the flavor adjusted. In American cuisine, tamari or soy sauce, garlic, onion, vegan Worcestershire sauce, salt, pepper, and a very little brown sugar (if the sweetness of the vegetables wasn't developed) is used to make a vegan au jus.

As a by-product from roasting meat, fat in the pan needs to be skimmed off. Vegan jus eliminates that step. There are two different techniques for making a vegan American jus. First is the traditional way of caramelizing the vegetables and pot roasting the protein or just caramelizing the vegetables to make the jus. The second is to cook down a beef-style vegan vegetable stock to a concentrate (about ¼ the original volume of the stock). In French this is called *glace de viande*.

Mushrooms are used in this sauce. I call this a wild sauce because it works well with wild game. On the vegetarian side Wild Forager's au Jus goes especially well with seitan and hearty proteins like smoked tofu pâté-type entrées and tempeh. This fresh-tasting sauce will keep for up to 2 months in the refrigerator (see step 4).

YIELD: 3 cups
TIME: 15 minutes prep and 20 minutes cooking

¼ cup canola oil
1 cup finely diced mushrooms (shiitake or portabella, or any single or combination of mushrooms)
½ cup finely diced onions
½ cup finely diced red bell pepper
1 tablespoon fresh, minced garlic
½ teaspoon chopped dried rosemary
½ teaspoon chopped dried basil
¼ teaspoon whole dried thyme
1 cup finely diced fresh tomatoes
1 cup red wine
¼ cup tamari soy sauce (or 1 tablespoon vegan beef-style broth powder in ¼ cup water)

1. Heat the oil in a 2-quart saucepan over medium heat.

2. Add the mushrooms, onions, bell pepper, garlic, rosemary, basil, and thyme, and sauté about 10 minutes, or until the vegetables begin to soften and lightly caramelize.

3. Add the tomatoes, wine, and tamari to the pan, and simmer about 20 minutes. Remove from the heat.

4. Use immediately, or allow the sauce to cool, then store in a covered container in the refrigerator. Properly cooked, it will keep up to 2 months.

Sauce Niçoise

Anchovies or sardines are often used with Sauce Niçoise along with pitted Kalamata olives. I switch to green pimento-stuffed olives and, for a little seafood flavor, use 2 tablespoons crushed dried wakame.

YIELD: 5 ¼ cups
TIME: 15 minutes prep and 20 minutes cooking

2 tablespoons extra-virgin olive oil
1 ½ cups finely diced onions
3 tablespoons chopped garlic
1 cup chopped green pimento-stuffed olives
3 cups diced or chopped canned tomatoes
¾ cup whole capers
¼ cup lemon juice
½ teaspoon ground black pepper
2 tablespoons dried wakame, pressed to break into smaller pieces
¼ cup water

1. Heat the oil in a 2-quart saucepan over medium-low heat. Add onions and garlic and sauté about 10 minutes, or until the onions begin to soften.

2. Add olives, tomatoes, capers, lemon juice, pepper, wakame, and water to the pan, and simmer about 20 minutes, stirring occasionally.

3. Use immediately, or store in a covered container in the refrigerator, where it will last up to 6 months.

Balsamic Orange Marinade

This recipe is superb for grilling vegetable and proteins. If using a dry protein mix, the marinade can be added as part of the water/oil ratio creating an instant marinade that will permeate the protein's flavor. Note: If using dry protein, eliminate the salt from this recipe.

YIELD: 1 ¼ cups
TIME: 20 minutes

½ cup balsamic vinegar
¼ cup olive oil
¼ cup tamari (soy sauce is an alternative.)
¼ cup orange juice
¾ teaspoon salt
½ teaspoon ground ginger
¼ teaspoon granulated garlic

Combine all ingredients in a mixing bowl and stir well. Set aside until ready to use or store the marinade in a covered container in the refrigerator, where it will keep about 6 months.

Sauce Niçoise with Chicken Analogue

MOO GOO GAI PAN SAUCE

Garlic and ginger define this sauce in Chinese cuisine. It is traditionally used in stir fry with a variety of vegan proteins (seitan, tofu, tempeh, chicken-style proteins, etc.) and perhaps a second protein. If you are using it with a chicken-style stir-fry, add 1 teaspoon vegetarian chicken-style broth powder (optional) to the sauce to intensify the flavor.

YIELD: 2 cups
TIME: 20 minutes

¼ cup sesame oil

4 ½ teaspoons fresh minced ginger

4 ½ teaspoons fresh minced garlic

2 cups plus 2 tablespoons water

1 ½ teaspoons salt

⅛ teaspoon white pepper

¼ cup sherry wine

3 tablespoons arrowroot

1. Heat oil in a 1-quart saucepan over medium heat. Add ginger and garlic, and sauté about 3 minutes, or until they are soft, but not browned.

2. Add 2 cups water, salt, pepper, and wine, and stir well. Bring to a simmer, then turn off the heat.

3. Mix arrowroot with 2 tablespoons water and stir in, turn the heat to medium, and continue to stir for 3 to 5 minutes, or until the sauce has thickened.

4. Use immediately, or transfer to a covered container and store in the refrigerator, where it will keep for about 1 week.

SPINACH BASIL PESTO

Pesto is traditionally used in pastas but has many diverse uses beyond pasta. It is used in meatballs, pesto creams, in and on burgers, on pizzas and Italian sandwiches. It is a sauce with many recipe and menu applications.

YIELD: 14 (2 tablespoon) servings, 1¾ cups
TIME: 25 minutes

24 fresh, peeled cloves garlic

1 tablespoon extra-virgin olive oil

½ cup pine nuts

4 cups fresh spinach, firmly packed

1 cup fresh basil, firmly packed

¼ cup sun-dried tomatoes (optional)

¼ cup water

3 tablespoons extra-virgin olive oil

¾ teaspoon salt

2 tablespoons soy parmesan cheese (optional)

1. Preheat oven to 325°F. Rub garlic cloves with first measure of oil. Place cloves on a baking sheet and roast 15 to 20 minutes or until lightly browned. Remove from oven and transfer to a container to cool.

2. Spread pine nuts on a baking sheet and roast about 5 to 10 minutes or until lightly browned. Remove from oven and transfer to another container to cool.

3. Wash, dry, and stem the spinach and basil.

4. In a blender, combine garlic, pine nuts, spinach, basil, tomatoes, water, second measure of oil, salt, and cheese and blend until smooth. Transfer to a container and refrigerate until ready to use.

SAUCE DUGLÉRÉ

Chef to the Rothschild family, Adolphe Dugléré developed this pink sauce with a delicately balanced flavor that I use with sea vegetables and other delicately flavored proteins.

YIELD: 2 cups
TIME: 15 minutes

¼ cup raw cashew pieces
1 cup water*
½ cup soy milk
½ cup canned tomatoes, crushed in puree
½ teaspoon chopped dried sweet basil
1 teaspoon nutritional yeast
¼ teaspoon salt
¼ teaspoon fresh minced garlic

1. Blend the cashews in ½ cup water until the mixture is smooth with no grit when rubbed between your fingers (about 3 to 5 minutes). Add the remaining ½ cup water and soy milk and blend to mix.

2. Pour the milk solution into a 1-quart saucepan and add remaining ingredients. Mix well and cook on medium heat about 5 minutes after it comes to a simmer to develop the flavors and reduce the moisture.

3. Strain the sauce through a fine wire mesh strainer or china cap, pressing the pulp to remove all the sauce. Serve hot or store and refrigerate until needed. This sauce can be frozen up to 3 months.

*OPTION: Replace ½ the water with white wine. Sauce thickens with little or no reduction.

MUSHROOM SAUCE

This version of a mushroom sauce shows how to make this sauce without needing to create either the Béchamel or Espagnole mother sauces.

YIELD: 4 ½ cups
TIME: 15 minutes prep and 20 minutes cooking

2 cups sliced onions
2 cups chopped mushrooms, mixed varieties
1 cup grated carrots
2 tablespoons extra-virgin olive oil
2 tablespoons fresh, minced garlic
2 cups water
½ cup white wine (Chardonnay preferred)
6 tablespoons vegan chicken-style broth powder
4 tablespoons roux

Sauté onions, mushrooms, and carrots in oil on medium heat until onions are translucent. Add garlic and sauté for another few minutes. Combine water, wine, broth powder, and roux, then add to vegetables. Whisk vigorously to ensure that the roux evenly disperses. Bring to a simmer and let cook for about 10 minutes. Remove from heat, cover, and let cool.

CLASSIC CUBAN-STYLE PICADILLO SAUCE

Picadillo with smoked seitan is a superb combination. The two complex flavors stand up to each other. Other ideas include Cuban black bean picadillo, grilled tempeh picadillo, and vegan chicken picadillo.

YIELD: 8 servings (2 cups sauce; serving ¼ cup sauce per 3 to 4 ounces of protein)
TIME: 20 minutes prep and 30 minutes cooking

1 tablespoon olive oil

2 teaspoons minced garlic or more to taste

¾ cup chopped onion

½ cup chopped green bell pepper

1 pound seitan or cooked black beans or rehydrated vegan ground-beef analogue

¼ cup quartered pitted green olives

½ cup raisins

1 tablespoon capers (optional)

1 cup tomato sauce

1 tablespoon sazon seasoning (purchase commercially or make your own; see directions)

2 teaspoons ground cumin

1 teaspoon white sugar

Salt to taste

1. Heat olive oil in a skillet over medium heat; stir garlic, onion, and green bell pepper into the hot oil and cook until softened, 5 to 7 minutes.

2. Add cooked protein to the skillet; cook and stir until browned completely, 7 to 10 minutes.

3. Add olives, raisins, capers, tomato sauce, sazon seasoning, cumin, sugar, and salt to the hydrated ground beef, beans, or prepared seitan.*

4. Cover the skillet, reduce heat to low, and cook until the mixture is heated through, 5 to 10 minutes.

* Optional seasonings to add in step 3:

-   ⅛ teaspoon cinnamon
-   ⅛ teaspoon nutmeg

Sazon (The Dry Mix)

1 ½ teaspoons of this mix equals one packet of commercial sazon.

YIELD: 5 tablespoons

1 tablespoon ground coriander

1 tablespoon ground cumin

1 tablespoon ground annatto seeds or paprika

1 tablespoon granulated garlic

1 tablespoon salt

1. Combine all ingredients and mix well

2. Store in an airtight container. Will stay fresh for 2 to 3 months.

Tikka Masala Sauce

The tasty Tikka Masala Sauce includes the yogurt sauce to balance the flavors. This sauce is especially good with the suggested vegan chicken analogue.

YIELD: 3 cups sauce
TIME: 20 minutes prep and 15 minutes cooking

Yogurt Sauce

1 cup Soy Yogurt (page 175)
2 teaspoons ground cumin
2 teaspoons paprika
1 teaspoon ground cinnamon
1 teaspoon ground ginger
½ teaspoon salt
½ teaspoon ground black pepper
⅛ teaspoon ground cayenne pepper

To Soy Yogurt add cumin, paprika, cinnamon, ginger, salt, and pepper and mix well.

Tikka Masala Sauce

1 tablespoon canola oil
½ teaspoon garlic, fresh, minced
6 tablespoons banana pepper or green bell pepper, finely diced
1 ½ cups tomato sauce, canned or plain
¼ cup fresh cilantro, coarsely chopped

1. In a saucepan on medium heat add oil, garlic and pepper. Sauté for 4 to 5 minutes.

2. Add tomato sauce to sauté mixture and blend well. Add Yogurt Sauce to tomato sauce and stir to incorporate.

SERVING OPTIONS: For vegan chicken cutlets, heat and sauce separately and serve sauce on plate and protein on sauce. Or add sauce to cooked chicken and serve chicken coated in sauce. Vegan chicken can also be cubed and cooked in sauce. Cubed chicken can also be served as shish kabob.

Asian BBQ Sauce

This is an excellent sauce with a balanced, yet complex mix of flavors (spicy, savory, and sweet) and a delicate tang from the rice vinegar. As it sounds, this sauce has many applications in Asian vegan cuisine.

YIELD: ¾ cup
TIME: 10 minutes

6 tablespoons hoisin sauce
2 tablespoons rice vinegar
1 tablespoon bean paste or bean sauce
2 teaspoons fresh, minced garlic
½ teaspoon ground ginger
½ teaspoon Chinese five-spice powder
¼ cup brown sugar
⅓ cup minced scallions

Mix all ingredients together. Store and refrigerate until ready to use.

GRILLED VEGETABLE MARINADE & CITRUS DIPPING SAUCE

This marinade works well as a dipping sauce or for grilled vegetables.

YIELD: 8 servings (1 cup)
TIME: 10 minutes

½ cup balsamic vinegar
¼ cup olive oil (or 10 teaspoons canola oil and 2 teaspoons roasted sesame oil)
¼ cup tamari
¼ cup orange juice or pineapple juice (fresh or from concentrate)
¾ teaspoon salt
½ teaspoon ground ginger
½ teaspoon granulated garlic

In a bowl, mix all ingredients together. Set aside until ready to use. (This marinade doesn't have to be refrigerated until vegetables are added.)

Recommended Vegetables

- Zucchini, yellow squash, eggplant: cut off ends and slice lengthwise about ¼ to ⅜ inch thick.
- Carrots: slice ⅛ inch thick lengthwise.
- Portabella mushrooms: remove gills before marinating.

ORIENTAL MISO SAUCE

I love this sauce on grilled tofu, seitan, and tempeh entrées coupled with a vegetable. It is good on side vegetables, pasta salads, kasha (buckwheat), porridge, and stir-fry (added at the end of the cooking process).

YIELD: 8 servings (2 cups)
TIME: 10 minutes prep and 15 minutes cooking

1 cup peeled and medium-diced onions
½ cup chopped oyster mushrooms or mushroom of choice*
1 tablespoon chopped garlic
¾ cup peanut oil or canola oil
¼ cup white miso
4 ounces (½ cup) crushed firm tofu
1 teaspoon ground ginger
2 tablespoons water
1 tablespoon apple cider vinegar

1. Sauté onions, mushrooms, and garlic in oil on medium-low heat until onions are translucent. Remove from heat. Add crushed tofu, ginger, water, miso and cider vinegar. Mix.

2. Place mixture in blender and blend until smooth. If the sauce seems to separate, add more tofu.

3. Pour the sauce into a saucepan, bring to a simmer, and cook gently for a few minutes.

*Using different mushrooms will give the sauce the flavor of the mushroom being used (see Sauce Coloring Techniques on page 124).

Variation: *Oriental Orange Miso Sauce*

Add 3 tablespoons frozen orange juice concentrate to 2 cups Oriental Miso Sauce for a light orange flavor. This sauce can be used in the same above recipe applications.

MISO MUSTARD ONION SAUCE

YIELD: 3 cups
TIME: 5 minutes prep and 25 minutes cooking

2 tablespoons canola or safflower oil

2 cups sliced onions

½ cup shredded carrots

1 tablespoon fresh minced garlic

2 tablespoons miso, mellow sweet white

2 cups water

1 tablespoon Dijon mustard

¼ teaspoon salt

2 tablespoons cornstarch or arrowroot powder

2 tablespoons water

1. Heat a saucepan over medium heat. Add the oil, onions, carrots, and garlic. Sauté until the onions are translucent.

2. Mix and dissolve miso in ¼ cup water. Add remaining 1 ¾ cup of water to the sautéed onions with the mustard and salt. Bring to a simmer. Add miso mixture and bring to a simmer.

3. Mix the 2 tablespoons cornstarch into the 2 tablespoons of water and blend well. Add to the liquid mixture and bring to a simmer. The sauce is ready for service.

OPTION: Add ¼ cup finely diced parsley to the sauce when finished cooking.

PICCATA SAUCE

YIELD: approximately 4 cups
TIME: 5 minutes prep and 20 minutes cooking

3 tablespoons extra-virgin olive oil

1 cup chopped onions

½ cup shredded carrots

1 ½ tablespoon fresh minced garlic

5 tablespoons white flour

1 ½ cups vegetarian chicken stock (add 2 tablespoons chicken-style broth powder to 1 ½ cups water)

1 ¼ cup plus 2 tablespoons white wine

¼ cup lemon juice

¾ teaspoon salt, optional (check flavor before adding at end of cooking)

6 tablespoons capers

¼ cup finely chopped parsley

1. Heat oil in a saucepan over medium heat. Add the onions, carrots, and garlic; sauté for 5 to 7 minutes, or until the onions are soft and transparent.

2. Gradually add the flour, stirring constantly until it is totally dissolved.

3. Add the stock, continuing to stir until the mixture becomes thick. Stir in the wine, capers, and lemon juice. Continue cooking on low heat.

4. Add salt to adjust flavor, if necessary, and heat over medium-low heat. Serve with your favorite recipe.

HARISSA SAUCE

YIELD: 10 servings (5 cups)
TIME: 15 minutes prep and 35 to 40 minutes cooking

2 ½ teaspoons ground cumin

2 ½ teaspoons ground coriander

¾ teaspoon ground cloves

¾ teaspoon ground cardamom

¼ cup olive oil

3 cups chopped carrots

2 cups diced onions

2 cups chopped red bell peppers

3 cups fresh cloves garlic

1 teaspoon ground ginger

1 teaspoon salt

1 cup water

1. In a small mixing bowl, combine the cumin, coriander, cloves, and cardamom for spice blend. Mix well and set aside.

2. Heat the oil in a 2-quart saucepan over medium heat. Add the carrots, onions, bell peppers, garlic, ginger, and salt. Sauté the mixture for 15 minutes, or until the vegetables are cooked. Add water, cover, and continue to cook another 10 minutes. Remove the pan from the heat and set aside.

3. In a blender, add the sautéed vegetables along with spice blend. If you don't like spicy dishes, cut spice in half and add more, if needed, to the finished dish. Gently pulse the mixture in a blender 3 to 5 times about 1 second each, then blend on low speed until the mixture is smooth.

4. Use immediately, or transfer to a covered container and store in the refrigerator, where it will keep for about two weeks. In the freezer, it will last about six months.

Vegan Soups

Vegan soups are popular and relatively easy to prepare so I am only listing a few favorites. This selection includes classical and traditional recipes with some unique ingredients for new and fresh ideas. The techniques are standard cooking methods except the consommé that is prepared without a traditional "float."

CARAMELIZED VEGETABLE CONSOMMÉ

Consommé is made the traditional way by adding egg whites to a combination of cold, raw ground meat, a mirepoix of vegetables, and stock. As the mixture is heated, a purification of the stock is achieved. Consommé is prepared by stirring together all of the ingredients and then simmering without further stirring. As it simmers, the ingredients in the mixture fall to the bottom of the stock pot and congeal and form a float, which rises to the surface purifying the soup in the process. These solids form a "raft." Once the raft forms, the heat is reduced, and the consommé simmers until it reaches the desired flavor in about an hour.

This vegan version was a gold medal-winning recipe at the 1996 International Culinary Olympics. The vegetables are caramelized, and the seasonings and water added to the mixture. There is no "raft." The liquid is cooked on a low heat for 90 minutes to 2 hours. A high heat would cloud the stock in the same manner as it would the meat-egg version. Slow cooking is the key to making a clear vegan or meat consommé.

YIELD: 6 servings
TIME: 30 minutes prep and 2 hours cooking

2 tablespoons high heat sunflower oil
2 unpeeled onions, quartered
2 coarsely chopped carrots
2 coarsely chopped celery stalks
1 coarsely chopped parsnip
¼ coarsely chopped cup leeks
5 cloves garlic
5 quarts water
½ cup tamari or shoyu
¼ cup dried, sliced shiitake mushrooms
2 ½ cups chopped fresh button mushrooms
1 ½ teaspoons green peppercorns
6 sprigs fresh tarragon
3 bay leaves

1. In 6-quart stockpot, heat oil and add onions, carrots, celery, parsnip, leek, and garlic and sauté for 15 minutes on medium high heat to caramelize, stirring occasionally.

2. Add the water, tamari, mushrooms, peppercorns, tarragon, and bay leaves, and simmer for about 2 hours.

3. Remove pot from heat and allow to cool. It should yield about 8 ½ cups of consommé. If not, continue to reduce it until it yields the desired amount. Strain out the vegetables and serve hot.

4. For the classical cook, if there is oil on the soup surface, place paper towel on top of soup to absorb oil.

New England Sea Vegetable Chowder

YIELD: 7 cups
TIME: 20 minutes prep and 35 minutes cooking

1 tablespoon olive oil

1 cup finely diced onions

¾ cup peeled, diced potatoes

½ cup diced celery

¼ cup diced red bell pepper

1 cup fresh or canned oyster mushrooms

¼ cup chopped, rehydrated wakame

1 tablespoon vegan chicken-style broth powder

1 bay leaf

½ teaspoon dried thyme

¾ teaspoon salt

3 tablespoons unbleached white flour

5 cups unsweetened soy milk

2 tablespoons chopped parsley

1. Add oil to a 3-quart saucepan on medium heat. When oil is warm, add onions, potatoes, celery, red pepper, oyster mushroom, wakame, broth powder, bay leaf, thyme, and salt and cook over medium heat for 10 to 12 minutes, stirring to prevent them from burning (add a little water if necessary).

2. Add flour and stir until well blended, about 3 minutes. Add 1 cup soy milk and continue to cook, stirring constantly until thickened. Add another cup of soy milk and continue stirring until thickened.

3. Add the remaining 3 cups soy milk and bring the soup to a simmer. Remove from heat, cover, and let sit 15 minutes or longer for the flavor to develop. Remove bay leaf. Serve hot. Optional to garnish with chopped parsley and a piece of sautéed oyster mushroom.

Andalusian Vegetable Cream Soup

YIELD: 4 servings
TIME: 15 minutes prep and 35 minutes cooking

2 cups peeled and finely diced potatoes

1 cup peeled and finely diced onions

2 cups diced canned tomatoes, drained, juice reserved

1 teaspoon minced garlic

2 tablespoons canola oil

½ teaspoon salt

⅛ teaspoon ground white pepper

4 tablespoons unbleached flour

¼ cup vegan beef-style broth powder or dark miso

3 cups soy milk

½ cup cooked brown rice

1 diagonally sliced scallion for garnish

1. Sauté the potatoes, onions, tomatoes, and garlic in the oil, with the salt and pepper, for about 5 minutes, stirring occasionally. If using miso, add it at this step. (The miso enzymes may break down the starch in the flour if added to soup after the flour.)

2. Stir in the flour, and cook until the mixture has thickened and the flour is cooked (about 5 minutes).

3. Dissolve the vegan beef-style broth powder in the reserved tomato juice and add it to the vegetable mixture. Add the soy milk and cook, stirring constantly to prevent the vegetables from burning, until the soup thickens. Stir in the rice. Serve the soup hot with a garnish of scallions.

BURGUNDY SOUP

YIELD: 4 servings
TIME: 15 minutes prep and 30 minutes cooking

1 ½ cups diced onions

¼ cup diagonally sliced celery

¾ cup sliced mushrooms

2 tablespoons canola oil

1 teaspoon minced garlic

1 ½ teaspoons chopped basil (or ½ teaspoon dried basil)

¼ teaspoon + ⅛ teaspoon ground black pepper

½ cup dry red wine

¾ cup tomato puree

1 cup flaked seitan (thinly sliced)

1 ½ cups water

2 tablespoons vegan beef broth powder or tamari

½ teaspoon salt (optional)

1 shredded red radish or 1 tablespoon chopped parsley for garnish

1. Sauté the onions, celery, and mushrooms in the oil, together with the garlic, basil, and pepper, until the onion becomes translucent. Add the wine and simmer for 2 minutes.

2. Add the tomato puree, seitan, and water. Continue to simmer, covered, over low heat for 30 minutes.

3. Dissolve the broth powder in 3 tablespoons water and add to the soup.

4. Simmer over very low heat for 5 minutes more and serve. Garnish with shredded red radish or chopped parsley.

CREAM OF CHILLED PEAR SOUP

YIELD: 4 servings
TIME: 15 minutes

8 peeled, cored and diced pears

2 cups unsweetened soy milk

¼ teaspoon salt

4 tablespoons brown rice syrup

½ teaspoon peeled, finely minced ginger (or ¼ teaspoon ground ginger)

¼ teaspoon anise extract (optional)

4 sprigs fresh mint and/or 4 small fresh strawberries, stems removed, sliced thin and fanned, all for garnish

1. Bring pears, soy milk, and salt to a simmer in a large saucepan.

2. Add rice syrup and ginger (and anise extract for a delicate licorice flavor to this cold fruit soup). Simmer for 3 more minutes. Allow the mixture to cool.

3. Puree the mixture and chill. Serve garnished with mint leaves and/or thinly sliced strawberries.

DOUKABAR VEGETABLE SOUP

This soup was created originally by Russian emigrants who settled in Canada. They wanted a soup similar to a warm, hearty borscht. Normally, this soup includes dairy sour cream; my version is vegan. Unlike the original borscht, this very hearty winter soup is served hot. There are hot and cold versions of Russian Borscht Soup. The cold version is made with vegan sour cream but without cabbage.

YIELD: 4 servings
TIME: 20 minutes prep and 35 minutes cooking

1 peeled medium-sized raw beet (2 cups whole beets or 1 [16-ounce] can, juice reserved)

1 ¼ cups (1 large) peeled, julienned potato

1 peeled, diced medium carrot

½ large onion, diced

1 small wedge (½-inch) green cabbage, shredded

⅓ cup seeded and diced green bell pepper

2 tablespoons canola oil

⅓ cup tomato paste mixed with ⅓ cup water

2 ½ cups water (or juice from canned beets plus water)

1 teaspoon dried dill weed

1 ½ teaspoons fresh, minced garlic

1 teaspoon salt

¾ teaspoon ground caraway seeds

½ cup Cashew Sour Cream (page 175)

2 teaspoons chopped fresh dill for garnish

1. Cut the peeled beet into julienned pieces. (If you are using canned beets, drain, reserve the liquid, and set aside three beets for another use. Cut the remaining beets into julienned pieces. Measure the juice, and add water to make 2 ½ cups, and set aside for the soup.)

2. Sauté the julienned beets, potato, carrots, onion, cabbage, and bell pepper in the oil for about 5 minutes over medium heat. Add the tomato paste mixture and the water (or beet juice and water mixture). Stir in the dill, garlic, salt, and ground caraway seed. Cover and simmer for about 30 minutes.

3. Serve the soup hot. Add a small dollop of Cashew Sour Cream (page 175) to each small bowl. Garnish with fresh dill.

OPTION: Stir 4 tablespoons sour cream into the soup before serving.

White Gazpacho Soup

ASIAN WHITE GAZPACHO

This Spanish soup with coconut milk could as easily be Caribbean or Asian. Using coconut milk takes this soup into fusion cuisine while soy milk would return the soup to its origin as a Spanish Ajo Blanco soup. Ajo Blanco soup is a cold soup common in Extremadura, Spain and often called White Gazpacho. It is traditionally made with white bread, milk, crushed almonds, olive oil, salt, white grapes, and vinegar. The cuisine of this region is simple as reflected in this recipe. The Asian White Gazpacho takes the recipe concept to another culture. This soup's flavor comes from a handful of ingredients and doesn't need many spices or herbs. The original soup calls for crustless bread, probably old bread past its time. White rice replaces bread. Roasted almonds also add a sparkling flavor.

YIELD: 4 servings
TIME: 10 minutes prep and 30 minutes cooking

¼ cup coarsely ground roasted almonds

2 teaspoons fresh, chopped garlic

½ cup cooked white rice

2 cups coconut milk (or soy milk for conventional recipe)

1 ½ cups water

2 tablespoons dried wakame

½ teaspoon salt

¼ cup rice vinegar

½ cup fresh, chopped cilantro (save 4 teaspoons for optional garnish)

4 teaspoons silvered almonds for garnish (optional)

Candied ginger (optional)

1. Preheat oven to 350°F. Spread the almonds on a rimmed baking sheet and toast, tossing occasionally, until golden, about 7 to 10 minutes. Let cool and divide in half. Use 2 tablespoons in the soup and grind 2 tablespoons into a coarse nut meal and set it aside as a garnish.

2. Place garlic, rice, coconut milk, water, wakame, salt, rice vinegar, and 2 tablespoons almonds into a blender and blend until smooth and creamy. In the original recipe the ingredients are soaked for 6 or more hours before blending. Not necessary. Blend until smooth and creamy. (You should not have to put the soup through a fine-mesh screen.)

3. Add cilantro and blend about 3 to 5 seconds at maximum speed to chop the cilantro into the soup. Cover and chill until very cold, about 2 hours. Soup can be made 1 day ahead. Keep chilled. Optional to garnish with fresh cilantro, and/or toasted silvered almonds or candied ginger.

VICHYSSOISE (CREAM OF LEEK SOUP)

Vichyssoise is a cold cream of leek soup, not a potato soup. The potato is used primarily as the thickening agent, not as the main ingredient. The key to successful vichyssoise is to cook the leeks slowly. The vegetables make this soup aromatic, not the seasonings. Traditionally, a light chicken stock is used; here I used a chicken style-broth powder to approximate that flavor. The finished soup should have a mild taste of leeks and not of potatoes.

YIELD: 6 (1cup) servings
TIME: 30 minutes prep and 60 minutes cooking

12 medium leeks (enough to yield 6 cups, white part only)

1 ½ cups thinly sliced onions

1 cup peeled potatoes (½-inch cubes)

3 tablespoons olive oil

1 bay leaf

1 teaspoon salt

⅛ teaspoon white pepper

2 cups water

1 tablespoon vegan reduced-sodium vegetable or chicken-style broth powder

1 cup soy milk

2 tablespoons chopped fresh chives or parsley for garnish

6 tablespoons Cashew Sour Cream (page page 175) (optional)

1. Using the white part only, remove the roots from the leeks, quarter, wash well, and slice thinly to yield 6 cups.

2. In a 2-quart saucepan, stir the leeks, onions, and potatoes in the oil to coat. Add the bay leaf, salt, and pepper, then stir well again. Place the pan over medium-low heat, cover, and cook gently for about 45 minutes, stirring occasionally. (Important: This "sweating" of the vegetables must be done slowly so they will release their flavor without burning). Add water and vegan broth powder to the vegetables and cook for another 5 to 10 minutes. Remove the bay leaf, then puree the soup in a blender until smooth.

3. Stir in the soy milk and remove the saucepan from the heat. Chill thoroughly.

4. Serve cold, garnished with the dollop of Cashew Sour Cream and chives or parsley.

Chapter Eleven

VEGAN ENTRÉES, SANDWICHES, & SMOKED PROTEINS

As I was working on this book I had an epiphany that continues to create a question related to the proteins and entrées in this section.

We now know that plant proteins can provide all our protein needs. At the same time, complex carbohydrates are the primary macro nutrient we need to fuel our bodies when we physically mature at about age 27. Why can't complex carbohydrates share the center of the plate with protein as an entrée since it is a macro nutrient in a human's diet?

I don't have all the answers but would suggest that the center of the plate can be a carbohydrate complemented by a protein as a side dish to balance the dinner being served. The protein would be nutritionally sufficient but put into perspective by the plate presentation.

Many of the recipes in this section (such as grain loaves) are designed as a complex carbohydrate/protein entrées for a balanced diet. The grain loaves are an excellent example of an entrée that can easily become or take center stage as a high-protein complex carbohydrate entrée. Only a sauce and side vegetable are needed to complete the dinner plating.

In this chapter we explore the diverse recipe applications of an array of plant-based proteins used in ethnic and classical recipes. I have heard it stated that all cuisines east of France are French cuisines. Italian Tuscan cuisine is the encapsulation of foods the Romans adopted in their conquest of the known world, and the Medici family brought Tuscan cuisine to France. Perhaps there is some truth to this belief and why I have addressed many European cuisines in this section with different proteins.

One of the unique elements of vegetarian cooking is the infinite possibilities that exist within each recipe. Every vegan entrée recipe has unlimited protein options that should be considered in choosing a recipe. Each vegan protein will have a different look, eating quality, and flavor. Tofu, tempeh, seitan, beans, grains, and the analogues are all interactive. You have to choose what works for your family or your customer and find a protein option that will hold its integrity in the recipe (it won't break down in the cooking process or it will hold up on the hot line). If you don't want to use a chicken analogue in the cacciatore, you can caramelize tofu or tempeh and add it in place of the analogue. Or you can serve the Tofu Cacciatore (page 266) with a different protein over a grain loaf or add beans to make a cannelloni beans cacciatore.

The mother sauces work in the same versatile manner in combination with any of the proteins. Any mother sauce can be modified to work with any of the vegan proteins. I run a classical kitchen in my home. I always have a few of the mother sauces in my refrigerator and a few protein options.

Beans seem to be undervalued as center plate protein entrées in Western cultures, relegated to Southwestern cuisine and side dishes. They belong in vegan entrées. While they don't have much texture, they contribute a rich flavor and fatty mouthfeel from the starch. With the exception of the soybean, they generally work best as a component of an entrée, not as a stand-alone entrée. For example, mix them into a tofu pâté or a grain loaf or add them to a meat-style analogue. Tofu, tempeh, and textured soy protein are the exception as stand-alone proteins.

Seitan is my favorite as it has a meat-like texture. Once smoked it looks, feels, and tastes like an authentic protein, raising the bar on vegetar-

ian cuisine and adding some incredible recipes to your vegetarian repertoire.

Another unique feature about vegan proteins is that they work best when combined. Wheat protein strengthens soy protein while creating a complete protein with all of the amino acids. A good example are the meat analogues that use both soy and wheat proteins. Tofu pâté is used with infused corn polenta or whole beans are added to classical grain dishes. Nuts and seeds are used in my vegan protein recipes to give flavor, texture, and nutritional diversity. Many entrées are from classical cuisines with some being authentic original vegan recipes, part of the effort to define vegan food as a cuisine. While vegetarianism is a cuisine within cuisines as exemplified by the diverse ethnic vegan recipes in this section, it is a freestanding cuisine attempting to find its voice. The grain loaves (entrées) exemplify vegetarianism as an emerging authentic cuisine and my effort to help find its voice.

This section concludes with another innovation: smoked proteins. Smoked vegan proteins resonate with traditional European and classical cuisines. Smoking brings the traditional flavor used with meat to vegetarian proteins. Where a smoked protein is traditionally used, a smoked vegetarian protein is an easy substitute. It is my favorite food preparation technique for proteins, giving vegetarian proteins a rustic flavor that simulates meat in color and taste.

Be creative with the recipes, viewing them as having infinite possibilities. I recommend following the recipe instructions to the letter for an honest critique and become comfortable with the techniques. Then spread your wings and give the recipes your own creative twist.

TOFU ENTRÉES

Basic Tofu Pâté
  Variation: Smoked Tofu Pâté
Spinach Tofu Pâté
Tarragon Tofu Pâté
Carrot Tofu Pâté
Pâté Français
Tofu Vegetable Loaf
Southwestern Smoked Tofu Loaf
Wakame Tofu Croquettes

Barley Croquettes
Almond Tofu Croquettes
Sea Vegetable Cakes
Alsatian Onion Pie
Thanksgiving Day Tofu
Tofu Spinach Quiche
  Variation: Savory Greek Spinach Crepes
Vegetarian Frittata
  Variation: Mushroom Quiche

Scrambled Breakfast Tofu
Smoked Tofu Schnitzel with Braised Red Cabbage
Vegetarian Frittata
  Variation: Mushroom Quiche
Southern Batter-Fried Tofu
Tofu Cacciatore
Sea Vegetable Tofu
Almond-Crusted Tofu
Tofu Fricassee
Almond-Crusted Portabellas with Tofu Forcemeat

TEMPEH ENTRÉES

Macrobiotic Lyonnaise Tempeh
Tomato-Apricot-Ginger Coulis
Southern Blackened Tempeh with Tomato Apricot Ginger Coulis

Bacon-Style Tempeh
BBQ Tempeh
Tempeh Piccata

Moo Goo Gai Pan Tempeh
Tempeh à la Bigarade
Tempeh Provençal

SEITAN ENTRÉES

Seitan Method I & II
Swiss-Style Shredded Seitan
Seitan Swiss Steak
  Variation: Tofu Swiss Steak

Broccoli Seitan Delmonico
  Variation: Broccoli Delmonico with Cannellini Beans
Szekely Goulash
  Variation: Bean-Style Szekely Goulash

Hot Seitan Sandwich
Hearty Seitan Pepper Steak
Seitan à la Normandie
New England Boiled Dinner

BEAN ENTRÉES

Italian Shepherd's Pie
Thai Black Bean Shiitake Mushroom Duxelle
  Variation: Thai Spring Rolls
Mediterranean Humma-Nusha
Peruvian Pot au Feu

Cajun Gumbo
Italian Cannellini Beans with Fennel Garlic Sauce
Potage-Purée Soissonnaise (White Bean Puree)

Lentil Pâté
Pinto Bean Napoleon
  Variations: Seitan, Tofu, Tempeh, or Chicken-Style Napoleon
New World Shepherd's Pie

GRAIN, NUT, & SEED PROTEIN ENTRÉES

Basic Butter Paste

    Variation: Gluten-Free
    Butter Paste

Pecan Nut Loaf

Italian Pistachio Pilaf

Bulgur Walnut Loaf

American Barley Loaf

    Variation: American
    Spinach Barley Loaf

Quinoa Pinto Bean Loaf

Millet Loaf

Open-Face Kalamata Olive
Date Ravioli with Sauce
Renaissance

Pistachio Polenta

Cannellini Bean Polenta Loaf

Tofu-Infused Polenta

Quinoa Duxelle

    Variation: Quinoa Duxelle
    with Pine Nuts & Black
    Beans

SANDWICHES (LUNCH ENTRÉES)

Grilled Vegetable Masala
Sandwich

    Variation: Grilled Vegetable
    Sandwich with Smoked
    Black Bean Pâté

Tempeh Masala Sandwich with
Roasted Peppers

Seitan Pesto Sandwich

Tempeh Reuben Sandwich

Garbanzo Bean Burger

    Variation: Open-faced
    Garbanzo Bean Sandwich

Smoked Seitan, Lettuce, &
Tomato Sandwich

    Variation: Smoked Tempeh,
    Lettuce, & Tomato
    Sandwich

BBQ Seitan with Caramelized
Onions on a Bun

Cuban Pressed Sandwich

SMOKED PROTEINS & PRODUCE ENTRÉES

Smoked Black Bean Date Pâté

Mesquite Smoked Seitan
Ragoût à la Bigarade

Smoked Black Bean Pâté

Smoked Black Beans

Smoked Proteins (Tempeh,
Tofu. Seitan), Potatoes,
Tomatoes, or Nuts (Cashews or
Almonds)

Tofu Entrées

Tofu is one of the ancient proteins with great unrecognized culinary potential. It is unrecognized because professional chefs haven't fully engaged in finding ways to develop that potential and integrate this important vegetarian protein into classical and modern cuisines. Its importance rests in four areas. First, it is high in protein with the potential to be a stand-alone entrée. Second, it is a neutral flavored protein with no definitive flavor aside from the soy flavor that can be masked. Tofu can take on any ethnic flavor or meat style (poultry, pork, or seafood) the cook desires. Third, it can be used in both desserts and savory foods from entrées to sauces. The tofu pâté is a superb substitute for forcemeat, which is used in classical cuisine to make, as an example, galantines. Fourth, tofu is a multifunctional ingredient within a recipe.

The different types of tofu with unique characteristics allow it to be applied to almost every type of recipe from cheeses and desserts to entrées and sauces. One example of tofu's versatility in classical French cuisine is the tofu pâté.

As a high-protein and very bland soy curd, tofu will absorb copious amounts of seasoning before it develops any flavor. As with the tofu pâté, the ideal means of infusing flavor is to pulverize the tofu by adding cornstarch or arrowroot or unbleached white flour to reset the structure when heating. By pulverizing or crumbling it, depending on the texture sought, you can integrate spices, herbs, and/or classical or ethnic seasonings into the tofu, intensifying the flavor. Tofu also lacks any textural mouthfeel so important in entrées. Chopped nuts, seeds, and grains are a few options that can provide texture to tofu.

If using solid pieces of tofu, it is best to cut thin (¼-inch or 2-ounce) slices for breading and sautéing. Do not bread thick slices since the surface flavor will be lost in the thick, bland tofu. Only use extra firm tofu and refer to the "Vegan Breading Technique" on page 116 for additional insight and instructions. Substituting Basic Tofu Pâté (page 252) as a cutlet also works well; you can make thicker cutlets because the Basic Tofu Pâté will be infused with flavor through the preparation technique.

The Basic Tofu Pâté mixture can be substituted into any loaves and quiches as long as the flavor systems (ingredients) from the recipe are transferred to the pâté. Simply replace the separate tofu, starch, and agar ingredients with the Basic Tofu Pâté mixture.

THE "MOTHER PROTEIN RECIPE" APPLICATION FOR TOFU

One of the many innovations of *The Classical Vegetarian Cookbook* is the development of the versatile Basic Tofu Pâté. This is a unique culinary creation I developed in the late 1980s to give tofu versatility in recipe development. The process allows the cook to instantly flavor-infuse the protein and add grains, beans, and vegetable items into the tofu pâté to give it additional texture, color, flavor, and nutritional density. The pâté is a combination of pulverized tofu, starch, agar, oil, and seasonings in a paste form. It is similar to what French cuisine calls a forcemeat, which is meat pulverized into a paste.

The tofu pâté acts like an egg in that it binds ingredients together and becomes a deliciously flavored protein. Tofu pâté is used to make quiches, grain loaves, sea vegetable cakes, burgers, and croquettes. That is why I call it the "Mother Protein" of tofu. (It could be called the basic recipe of tofu.) Like a mother sauce, a creative cook can take this item in many directions. The pâté recipe is the foundation of creative tofu cooking and developing classical and modern entrées. Where tofu, not the pâté, is built into the recipe, you can calculate the amount of tofu called for in the recipe and increase it by 10 percent to determine the amount of tofu pâté need to replace it. Do not change the seasonings.

The croquette (from the French *croquer*, "to crunch") is a traditional French fast food delicacy. It is generally made of mashed potatoes and/or ground meat or seafood, bound with eggs, and mixed with a thick sauce such as Béchamel or a brown sauce and soaked bread crumbs. Wine or beer is often used in croquettes. They are sometimes stuffed with a filling before breading and deep frying, with shapes varying from cylindrical to oval.

Whether in a foodservice operation or a home kitchen, if you are using fresh tofu, steam or microwave it to 160°F, cool it, and make a pâté with it. The mix will keep for a minimum of a week, properly stored. I get about 10 days refrigerated shelf life with proper handling in a covered and sterile food-grade container.

BASIC TOFU PÂTÉ MIXTURES

These pâté recipes were developed for the 1984 Culinary Olympics and won a bronze medal. Simple and elegant, these pâtés are also versatile. They may be served as appetizers; as a salad, on a bed of Boston or other loose-leaf lettuce and garnished with julienned carrots, tomato wedges, and pickled peppers; or as a dinner entrée, for which you might make a combination pâté, using 1¼ cups of the mixture for each of the different pâtés (spinach, tarragon, and carrot), layering them in a pan in that order, baking them according to the directions for carrot pâté, and serving two slices arranged on a pool of Sauce Renaissance (page 227) or Sauce Concasse (page 218) accompanied by a complementary vegetable and quinoa or couscous with chopped parsley.

The vegetable purées used in these pâtés are delicate. At an internal temperature of 220°F, the steam in the mixture begins to rise, the starch in the cornstarch or arrowroot is cooked, and the agar is activated and gels. Therefore, it is important to use only enough heat to make the formula set and not so much that it becomes rubbery. The pâté is cooked when it has risen up in the pan; it should rise, like custard, and then drop when it cools.

BASIC TOFU PÂTÉ

It is the combination of the agar powder and cornstarch that create the egg-like gelling effect in the pâté mixture.

YIELD: 4 cups
TIME: 15 minutes prep and 1 ½ to 2 hours baking depending on recipe

2 pounds extra firm tofu
¼ cup olive oil (or canola oil)
1 teaspoon minced fresh garlic (or ¼ teaspoon granulated garlic)
2 tablespoons nutritional yeast (optional)
4 teaspoons cornstarch or arrowroot
½ teaspoon salt
½ teaspoon agar powder
Pinch of white pepper
2 tablespoons white wine (optional)

Place all ingredients in a food processor and blend until smooth. The base mix is now ready.

VARIATION: *Smoked Tofu Pâté*

In place of plain tofu, use Smoked Tofu (see "Smoked Proteins" page 314). Smoking tofu gives it a rustic meat-like flavor. It makes easier the task of replicating smoked meats in classical meals. In a smoked pâté the cook has a cooking medium that can be used as a cutlet for a vegan entrée with a complementary sauce, as a sandwich, or as a complement to a salad or Swiss butcher's platter. The options and flavors are endless.

SPINACH TOFU PÂTÉ

YIELD: 10 servings (almost two pounds)
TIME: 20 minutes prep and 1 to 2 hours baking

4 cups Basic Tofu Pâté
1 (10-ounce) package frozen spinach, thawed and squeezed dry
½ teaspoon nutmeg, ground
1 tablespoon chopped fresh basil (or 1 teaspoon dried basil)
1 teaspoon salt
1 tablespoon cornstarch or arrowroot
2 teaspoons fresh, minced garlic

1. Place all ingredients in a food processor and blend well.

2. Oil a loaf pan, line it with plastic wrap, and spread the pâté mixture evenly in the pan. Cover the top of the pâté with plastic wrap. Place the loaf pan in a larger pan, with about 1 inch of water, and cover the water pan with aluminum foil.

3. Bake in a preheated oven at 325°F for 1 to 2 hours. Check the pâté after 1 hour. The pâté will be done when a toothpick, inserted into the middle of the pâté, comes out clean. You can also tell that it has baked sufficiently when it rises or by checking the temperature with a thermometer. It should be about 170°F. If the pâté is not done, check again in another 30 minutes and cook till done.

TARRAGON TOFU PÂTÉ

YIELD: 10 servings
TIME: 20 minutes prep and 1 to 2 hours baking

4 cups Basic Tofu Pâté
1 teaspoon chopped dried tarragon (or 2 teaspoons fresh)
½ teaspoon salt
¼ teaspoon white pepper
1 teaspoon savory

1. Place all ingredients in a food processor and blend well.

2. Oil a loaf pan, line it with plastic wrap, and spread the pâté mixture evenly in the pan. Cover the top of the pâté with plastic wrap. Place the loaf pan in a larger pan, with about 1 inch of water, and cover the water pan with aluminum foil.

3. Bake in a preheated oven at 325°F for 1 to 2 hours. Check the pâté after 1 hour. The pâté will be done when a toothpick, inserted into the middle of the pâté, comes out clean. You can also tell that it has baked sufficiently when it rises or by checking the temperature with a thermometer. It should be about 170°F. If the pâté is not done check again in another 30 minutes and cook till done.

CARROT TOFU PÂTÉ

YIELD: 12 servings
TIME: 20 minutes prep and 1 to 2 hours baking

3 cups peeled, chopped carrots
4 cups Basic Tofu Pâté
½ teaspoon salt
1 tablespoon arrowroot or cornstarch
1 tablespoon dill weed

1. Steam the carrots until they are soft. Drain and pat them dry. Place the Basic Tofu Pâté in food processor followed by carrots, salt, arrowroot, and dill weed and blend well.

2. Oil a loaf pan, line it with plastic wrap, and spread the pâté mixture evenly in the pan. Cover the top of the pâté with plastic wrap. Place the loaf pan in a larger pan, with about 1 inch of water, and cover the water pan with aluminum foil.

3. Bake in a preheated oven at 325°F for 1 to 2 hours. Check the pâté after 1 hour. The pâté will be done when a toothpick, inserted into the middle of the pate, comes out clean. You can also tell that it has baked sufficiently when it rises or by checking the temperature with a thermometer. It should be about 170°F. If the pâté is not done check again in another 30 minutes and cook till done.

PÂTÉ FRANÇAIS

This pâté won a Culinary Olympic medal in the 1996 competition. The classical charcutière seasoning blend is used in making pâtés, terrines, galantines, sausages, and crepinettes.

YIELD: About 12 servings (3 cups)
TIME: 20 minutes prep with subcomponents prepared and 30 minutes cooking

Classic Charcutière Seasoning Blend

YIELD: ⅔ cup
TIME: 5 minutes

1 tablespoon ground white pepper

1 tablespoon ground black pepper

1 tablespoon paprika (Hungarian preferred)

1 tablespoon nutmeg

1 tablespoon ginger powder

1 tablespoon dried basil

1 tablespoon whole dried thyme

1 tablespoon marjoram

1 tablespoon allspice

1 tablespoon garlic powder

½ tablespoon ground cloves

Blend all ingredients until evenly dispersed. Store in a tightly sealed container for up to 1 year. (Also use in breading, Smoked Bean Pâté and Smoked Tofu Pâté applications.)

Pâté

2 cups cooked or canned navy or pinto beans, drained

½ cup chopped walnuts

1 cup Basic Tofu Pâté

2 tablespoons Classic Charcutière Seasoning Blend

2 ½ tablespoons finely chopped parsley

½ tablespoon paprika (Hungarian preferred)

¼ teaspoon salt

1. Place the walnuts on a baking sheet and roast in 350°F preheated oven for 10 minutes.

2. In a mixing bowl, combine Basic Tofu Pâté, seasoning blend, parsley, paprika, and salt, then mix with large spoon until thoroughly blended. Add the beans and walnuts and mix well.

3. Form the pâté into a roll and wrap in plastic. Seal the plastic, then wrap the roll with a second piece of plastic and a piece of aluminum foil.

4. Steam in preheated 350°F oven. Place rack in a pot roast pan with boiling hot water up to the rack. Place pâté roll on the rack, cover and bake about 30 minutes or until the roll reaches 160°F.

5. Remove the roll and place in refrigerator until cold (about 4 hours). Remove the aluminum foil from the roll and slice about ¼ inch thick with the plastic on it, then remove the plastic wrap from each slice before serving.

NOTE: 1 ½ cups of the pâté mixture will form one 8 x 5 ½ x ½-inch piece for rolling.

Plating Pâté

1 ½ cups Cranberry Port Vinaigrette

12 cups field greens (or 1 cup per serving)

12 slices toasted French bread or 48 small diced croûtons

½ cup dried sweetened cranberries

To assemble salad, place field greens on plate. Place two slices pâté on the greens, drizzle with dressing, and garnish with croûtons and dried cranberries.

TOFU VEGETABLE LOAF

YIELD: 6 servings (5 cups)
TIME: 25 minutes prep and 40 to 50 minutes baking

2 tablespoons olive oil or garlic-infused oil
(optional)
1 ½ cups shredded carrots
½ cup chopped raw or roasted shallots
1 cup coarsely chopped confit of garlic or 6
tablespoons chopped fresh garlic
½ cup diced red bell pepper
3 cups Basic Tofu Pâté (page 252)
¼ cup vegan chicken-style or vegetable broth
or Italian or southwestern seasoning

1. Sauté carrots in oil on medium heat for 5
    minutes. Add shallots, garlic, and red bell
    pepper to the carrots and sauté for 10 min-
    utes or more on medium heat.

2. Mix vegetables, pâté, and broth powder
    together until evenly distributed. Place the
    mixture into an oiled loaf pan with a mini-
    mum 6 cup volume.

3. Bake in 375°F preheated oven for 40 to 50
    minutes or until the center of the loaf is
    165°F. Remove from oven and let rest for
    20 minutes to allow loaf to set.

OPTIONS: Use Smoked Tofu Pâté (see
"Smoked Proteins" page 314) in place of
Basic Tofu Pâté to make a European smoked
meat-style entrée. You can also add 1 cup of
any cooked bean to the loaf. Drain beans, toss
in flour unless going gluten free, and add to
tofu pâté with vegetables and broth powder.
Roasted seeds or nuts are another option.

SOUTHWESTERN SMOKED TOFU LOAF

YIELD: 8 servings (4 ½ cups)
TIME: 30 minutes prep and 40 to 50 minutes baking

1 ¼ cups cooked pinto or black beans*,
drained
6 tablespoons frozen whole kernel corn
1 ½ tablespoons white flour, unbleached
1 cup shredded carrots
½ cup chopped onions
1 tablespoon oil
6 tablespoons chopped red bell pepper
1 tablespoon fresh, minced garlic
6 tablespoons chopped sundried tomatoes
1 ½ teaspoons cumin powder
¾ teaspoon salt
6 tablespoons chopped fresh cilantro
3 cups Smoked Tofu Pâté (see "Smoked
Proteins" page 314) or Basic Tofu Pâté (page
252)

1. Mix beans, corn and flour. Set aside.

2. Sauté carrots, onions, and peppers in oil on
    medium heat for 5 minutes. Add garlic and
    sauté another 2 minutes. Add sundried to-
    matoes, cumin, and salt to the sauté mix.
    Stir and mix well.

3. In a mixing bowl or the sauté pan, combine
    the bean mixture, vegetable mixture, cilan-
    tro, and pâté. Pour the mix into an oiled 8
    x 4 x 2 ½-inch loaf pan. Bake in preheated
    375°F oven for 40-50 minutes or until the
    center of the loaf is 165°F. Remove from
    oven and let rest for 20 minutes to allow
    loaf to set.

*Roasted seeds or nuts can replace the beans.

Wakame Tofu Croquettes

Basic Tofu Pâté makes a perfect and simple substitute for a traditional croquette. This recipe produces a Wakame Croquette, but you may add different grains, nuts, or seeds to the mixture to create a wide variety of croquettes.

The basic ratio is ¼ cup of any grain, seed, or nut, etc., per cup of the Basic Tofu Pâté. I have used up to equal amounts of a cooked grain to the tofu pâté. You can even go with a little more. If the mixture doesn't hold together in the cooking process, you have exceeded the pâté's binding threshold.

If you choose to use a high sodium seasoning (such as Old Bay), do not exceed 2 teaspoons. If using a low sodium seasoning or herbs and spices, you set the flavor limitation.

This recipe lays out a basic croquette that allows you to be creative. It is also a protein that could easily be served as an entrée with wilted lettuce or wilted spinach salad tossed in a warm French vinaigrette. A good complement is the Puttanesca Sauce (page 228).

YIELD: 6 appetizer servings of 3 croquettes each or about 2 cups
TIME: 30 minutes prep and 10 to 15 minutes cooking

1 tablespoon dry wakame
1 ½ cups Basic Tofu Pâté (page 252)
½ cup medium mesh bread crumbs
2 teaspoons Old Bay Seasoning or vegan seafood-style seasoning of choice
1 teaspoon Dijon mustard (optional)
High heat canola or safflower oil to fry
½ cup white bleached or plain white flour
½ cup fine meshed bread crumbs put into food processor and processed into a fine mesh bread crumb for breading

*OPTION: On the Wakame and Almond Tofu Croquettes recipes you may choose to dip croquettes in oil, place on baking sheet, and broil until lightly browned. Finish in preheated 350°F oven.

1. Place wakame on a cutting board, fold a towel over it, and crush hard with a rolling pin.

2. Mix wakame with a spoon into the Basic Tofu Pâté and let sit for 10 minutes to rehydrate. (Note: If you do not give the sea vegetable time to hydrate—to draw moisture from the tofu—before adding the bread crumbs, the bread crumbs may steal the moisture from the sea vegetables. The end result is semi-hard wakame creating an unpleasant dining experience.) Mix in medium mesh bread crumbs, seafood seasoning, and mustard.

3. Form croquettes. To bread them, spritz the croquettes with water, roll them in fine mesh bread crumbs, and spritz them again, then roll them again in fine mesh bread crumbs and press breadcrumbs gently into the croquette. Or you can use the "Vegan Breading Technique" on page 116.

4. Fry in preheated high-heat oil to 350°F for about 3 to 5 minutes or until the croquettes are browned and cooked to the center (160°F). Finish cooking 15 to 30 seconds in the microwave or 5 to 10 minutes in a preheated 350°F oven.*

ALMOND TOFU CROQUETTES

YIELD: 6 appetizer servings of 3 croquettes each or about 2 cups
TIME: 10 to 15 minutes prep and 10 to 15 minutes cooking

4 to 5 tablespoons almonds
1 ½ cups Basic Tofu Pâté (page 252)
2 tablespoons finely chopped parsley
½ teaspoon salt
6 tablespoons medium mesh bread crumbs
½ cup white bleached or plain white flour

1. Preheat oven to 350°F. Roast almonds for 5 to 10 minutes or until heat develops the roasted almond aroma. Coarsely grind the almonds in a spice or coffee grinder.

2. Add parsley and salt to the Basic Tofu Pâté in the food processor, and pulse until all ingredients are evenly blended. Place mixture into bowl. Add ground almonds and mix with large spoon until evenly dispersed.

3. Using 2 tablespoons of mixture, form croquettes, roll them in bread crumbs, and either deep fry or bake according to the instructions below.

4. To bread them, I spritz the croquettes with water, roll them in flour, spritz them again, and then roll them in bread crumbs, which I press gently into the croquette. Or you can use the "Vegan Breading Technique" on page 116.

5. Fry in preheated high-heat oil at 350°F for about 3 to 5 minutes or until the croquettes are browned and cooked to the center (160°F). Finish cooking 15 to 30 seconds in the microwave or 5 to 10 minutes in a preheated 350°F oven. (*see note on opposite page below the Wakame Tofu Croquettes recipe)

OPTION: Add additional seasonings such as ground fennel or a basic herbs de Provence.

BARLEY CROQUETTES

The Classical Tomato Sauce (page 216) or Caper Sauce (page 215) is a superb complement.

YIELD: 6 servings of 3 croquettes each (about 2 ¼ cups or 2 tablespoons per croquette)
TIME: 30 minutes prep and 10 to 15 minutes cooking

1 ½ cups cooked barley
2 tablespoons white flour
2 tablespoons Fried Chicken-style Spice Blend (page 265)
1 ½ cups Basic Tofu Pâté (page 252)
¼ cup panko or white bread crumbs
½ cup high-heat canola or safflower oil

1. Mix together with a spoon cooked barley, flour, broth, and spice blend into Basic Tofu Pâté and let sit for 5 minutes.

2. Use 2 tablespoons of mixture to form each croquette. To bread, spritz croquette mixture with water, roll it in panko or bread crumbs, gently pressing the breading into the croquette.

3. Dip the croquettes into oil and set on a baking sheet pan. Broil until golden brown (about 3 to 5 minutes) and then bake for 15 minutes in a preheated 375°F. oven for 15 minutes.

Sea Vegetable Cakes

YIELD: 4 servings (16 sea vegetable cakes of 2 tablespoons each)
TIME: 15 minutes prep and 20 to 25 minutes cooking

¼ cup panko or white bread crumbs

2 tablespoons dry wakame

2 tablespoons water

1 tablespoon olive oil and more for frying the cakes

¼ cup finely diced red bell pepper

½ teaspoon fresh, minced garlic

¼ cup cooked barley or coarsely chopped cashews

1 teaspoon Old Bay Seasoning

1 tablespoon chopped parsley

2 teaspoons Dijon mustard

¼ teaspoon salt

¼ cup finely diced oyster mushrooms

1 ½ cups Basic Tofu Pâté (page 252)

¼ cup cornstarch or arrowroot

1. Put panko or bread crumbs in a plastic bag, place on table top, and roll over them with rolling pin to crush them.

2. Soak the wakame in water for 5 minutes, then drain and coarsely chop.

3. In a 10-inch frying pan, heat the oil, then sauté the pepper and garlic for several minutes on medium.

4. In a large mixing bowl, combine the barley or nuts with Old Bay seasoning, parsley, mustard, and salt and mix well. Combine the barley or nut mixture, wakame, sautéed vegetables, and mushrooms with the pâté. Mix well. Finally, add the bread crumbs and mix well until everything is evenly coated.

5. Use approximately ¼ cup of the mix to form each cake into a round shape, then flatten to about ½- to ¾-inch thickness. Dust the cakes with cornstarch. Heat the oil in a sauté pan and brown the seafood cakes evenly on each side. Serve hot with Sauce Renaissance (page 227) or Dugléré Sauce (page 233).

SEA VEGETABLE CAKE WITH DUGLÉRÉ SAUCE

ALSATIAN ONION PIE

Onions were grown by farmers in the Middle East as much as 5,000 years ago. Because the layers of the onion form a sphere within a sphere, the Egyptians revered the onion as a symbol of eternity. Our word "onion" actually comes from the Latin word *unis,* meaning "unity of many things in one."

Jean-Marie Martz, a French professional ballet dancer from Los Angeles who is a serious French cook, came to South Florida to apprentice with me for three months. He was raised in Alsace, in the northeast of France, and it was Jean-Marie who brought the dairy version of this recipe to my attention. This nondairy version is splendid, too. Because it is so delicate, it actually resembles a dairy vegetable pie. It has been a success in every place I have served it, and it is very easy to prepare.

Using the soy milk and butter spread gives the pie a dairy-like flavor. Unrefined corn oil is an option to the butter spread. The original pie recipe calls for bacon, so add 2 tablespoons vegan "bacon" bits and cut the salt in half. (Vegan bacon bits can be high in sodium.) I prefer using a maximum of ¼ teaspoon smoked flavor blended into the protein for a semblance of bacon. The pie stands on its own and is excellent without any smoked flavor. I focus on slow sautéing the onions to bring up the sweetness and using the butter spread for a dairy note. Vegetarian dishes can stand on their own without an animal protein flavor profile.

YIELD: 6 servings (one 10-inch pie)
TIME: 30 minutes prep and 30 minutes baking

3 large, finely diced onions (about 6 cups)
2 tablespoons oil (preferably unrefined corn oil), butter spread, or canola oil
1 cup soy milk
⅓ cup extra firm tofu, crushed by hand
1 ½ teaspoons salt
¼ teaspoon ground black pepper
⅛ teaspoon ground nutmeg
¼ cup white flour
1 tablespoon dry couscous
1 (10–inch) whole wheat or white flour pie shell

1. Sauté the onions in oil until translucent, stirring occasionally.

2. Mix with a spoon the soy milk, tofu, salt, pepper, nutmeg, and flour until smooth.

3. Combine the onions, soy milk mixture, and couscous. Pour into the prepared 10-inch pie shell. Bake in a preheated oven at 350°F for about 30 minutes.

THANKSGIVING DAY TOFU

This is a superb substitute for the traditional Thanksgiving turkey or an anytime meal. The dressing carries this dish. The corn oil gives it that wonderful buttery taste that poultry dressing usually has. A vegan butter spread will have the same effect, and the Velouté Sauce (page 213) or Mushroom Sauce (page 233) would be a good choice to drape over your Thanksgiving Day Tofu.

YIELD: 8 servings (1 medium loaf)
TIME: 35 minutes prep and 60 minutes baking

Sage Dressing

YIELD: 2 cups
TIME: 20 to 25 minutes

½ cup finely diced onions

½ cup finely diced celery

½ cup finely diced carrots

1 ½ teaspoons fresh, minced garlic

2 tablespoons unrefined corn oil or butter spread

½ teaspoon ground sage

¼ teaspoon chopped basil

¾ teaspoon salt

⅛ teaspoon ground black pepper

3 tablespoons vegan chicken-style or vegetarian broth powder

1 cup water

2 cups whole wheat or white bread crumbs

¼ cup coarsely chopped dry sweetened cranberries

¼ cup coarsely chopped roasted pecans

Sauté the onions, celery, carrots, and garlic in oil for 5 minutes. Add the sage, basil, salt, pepper, and broth powder and continue cooking 5 minutes longer. Add the water and bring to a simmer. Stir in the bread crumbs, cranberries, and pecans and mix. Cook briefly until mixture is firm then remove from heat.

THANKSGIVING DAY TOFU

Thanksgiving Day Tofu Pâté Mixture

1 ½ pounds extra firm tofu

2 tablespoons arrowroot or cornstarch

3 tablespoons vegan chicken-style or vegetarian broth powder

¾ teaspoon salt (optional)

¼ teaspoon ground white pepper

1 ½ teaspoons agar flakes (or 1 teaspoon agar powder)

2 tablespoons barley malt syrup, dissolved with 2 tablespoons water

1. Wash the tofu, pat it dry, and cut it into small pieces. Put the tofu, arrowroot, broth powder, salt, pepper, and agar flakes (or powder) in a food processor and blend to a smooth paste.

2. Oil and flour an 8 ½ x 4 x 2 ¾-inch loaf pan (or oil then line it with baking liner paper). Spread a layer of tofu paste inside the pan, lining the bottom and all four sides. (Spread only a thin layer approximately ½-inch thick on the ends.) Use all but about 1 cup of the paste to use for topping on loaf. Firmly but gently press the dressing into the pan, inside the tofu paste "liner." Try to avoid displacing the tofu. Cover the dressing with the remaining tofu, carefully sealing the edges. Cover the pan with foil, making certain the foil doesn't come in contact with the tofu. (The tofu will eat into the foil.)

3. Bake in a preheated oven at 350°F for 30 to 40 minutes. Remove the foil cover, glaze the top of the loaf with the dissolved barley malt syrup, turn the oven up to 450°F, and continue baking for 10 minutes. Remove from oven and allow the loaf to cool for about 20 to 25 minutes. Unmold, slice, and serve hot with a sauce of your choice.

OPTIONS: You can place half the tofu mixture into an oiled loaf pan, cover with the dressing, and top with the remaining half of the tofu. Or, for the easiest option, place all of the tofu mixture in the bottom of an oiled loaf pan and layer dressing on top. Bake either as described in step 3 above.

TOFU SPINACH QUICHE

To make this recipe gluten free, use Gluten-Free Crust (page 336) and eliminate barley malt glaze.

YIELD: 6 servings (10-inch quiche)
TIME: 30 minutes prep and 40 minutes baking

1 recipe Basic Pie Crust (page 336)

Tofu Spinach Quiche Filling

6 cups fresh, chopped spinach (or 10-ounce package frozen spinach, thawed, and squeezed dry)
¼ cup olive or high-heat oil
3 cups peeled and diced onions
1 tablespoon fresh, minced garlic
1 cup sliced mushrooms
2 tablespoons chopped parsley
(or 1 tablespoon dried parsley)
2 ½ teaspoons dill weed
2 tablespoons fresh, chopped basil
 (or 2 to 3 teaspoons dried basil)
1 ½ teaspoons salt
4 cups (2 pounds) extra firm tofu
2 tablespoons arrowroot dissolved
in 1 tablespoon cool water

Glaze

¼ cup barley malt syrup mixed with
2 tablespoons water (optional)

1. Roll out half of the pie dough and line the bottom of a 10-inch pie pan. Then roll out the top crust. Set aside.

2. If you are using fresh spinach, steam or sauté it for about 2 to 3 minutes and squeeze out water.

3. Heat the oil in a large saucepan. Sauté the onions, garlic, mushrooms, parsley, dill, basil, and salt until the onions are semitransparent. Add the spinach and allow it to cook down for 2 to 3 minutes.

4. Rinse the tofu and mash it. Use a spoon to mix it into the vegetables, then add the dissolved arrowroot, mixing thoroughly.

5. Pour the filling into the pie shell. Place the top crust over the filling and seal the edges. Bake in a preheated oven at 350°F for 35 minutes.

OPTIONS: When the pie has baked for about 20 minutes, lightly glaze the top crust with the barley malt syrup mixed with water then return pie to oven. The glaze will make the crust shiny and brown. Serve the pie hot.

You can also prepare this pie open-faced, with only a single crust. Cover quiche with aluminum foil when baking. In this case, after baking brush the cooked filling with a little oil; this will give the top a fresh glossy look.

VARIATION: *Savory Greek Spinach Crepes*

YIELD: 6 servings (2 crepes each) ¼ cup per crepe
TIME: 25 minutes prep and 20 minutes cooking (not includes making crepes)

½ recipe Tofu Spinach Quiche filling (above)
1 recipe Crepe batter for 12 crepes (page 337)

Prepare Tofu Spinach Quiche Filling and cook al dente. Cook crepes and place ¼ cup filling in each crepe in each crepe. Place the crepes in an oven in a covered pan to keep warm until ready to serve.

NOTE: Also see "Crepes" on page 146.

SCRAMBLED BREAKFAST TOFU

Scrambled for breakfast, in a wrap, as a cold egg-like salad with scallions, as an appetizer—this recipe has diverse menu applications.

YIELD: 4 servings (2 cups)
TIME: 15 minutes prep and 15 minutes cooking

14 ounces (2 cups) extra firm tofu
1 tablespoon canola oil
½ cup chopped onions
¼ cup finely diced red bell pepper
½ teaspoon minced garlic
1 ¼ teaspoon salt
⅛ teaspoon ground black pepper
Dash of annatto or turmeric (very small amount needed to create a light yellow color)
½ cup Soy Mayonnaise (page 154) or commercial vegan mayonnaise
¾ teaspoon yellow mustard
2 tablespoons chopped parsley

1. Rinse and drain tofu (wrap in towel and press to remove excess water). Crumble.

2. Sauté onion, bell pepper, and garlic in oil.

3. Add crumbled tofu, salt, pepper, and turmeric. Sauté until onions are translucent.

4. Remove from heat. Add mayonnaise and yellow mustard. Stir to coat. Finish with parsley.

NOTE: It is important to add the mayonnaise at the end of the cooking process to prevent it from separating. Mayonnaise, vegan or traditional, will break down under intense heat.

SMOKED TOFU SCHNITZEL WITH BRAISED RED CABBAGE

YIELD: 8 servings
TIME: 20 minutes prep and 15 minutes cooking

2 pounds extra-firm tofu* (must be extra-firm)
½ cup white flour
1 ½ teaspoons ground caraway seeds
½ teaspoon salt
1 cup water, cold
1 teaspoon liquid smoke
1 cup dry bread crumbs
3 tablespoons sunflower or canola oil
4 cups cooked Braised Red Cabbage (page 190)

1. Drain tofu and let stand 5 minutes. Slice each 1-pound block of tofu horizontally into 8 (2-ounce) slices. In shallow bowl, mix flour, caraway, and salt. In another shallow bowl, mix water and liquid smoke.

2. Spread bread crumbs on a sheet pan or sheet of waxed paper. Carefully and quickly dip tofu into water mixture, then into flour mixture to evenly coat. Quickly dip coated tofu into water mixture again (about 1 second), then into bread crumbs to evenly coat. Place coated tofu cutlets on plate.

3. In large skillet, heat 2 tablespoons oil over medium heat. Sauté the tofu cutlets in batches until lightly browned, 2 to 3 minutes per side. Transfer to baking sheet and keep warm in preheated 200°F oven until ready to serve. Sauté the remaining tofu cutlets in the same manner, adding additional tablespoon of oil to skillet if necessary.

4. To serve, spoon cabbage mixture onto plate and top with tofu cutlets.

VEGETARIAN FRITTATA

YIELD: 3 servings (3 ½ cups)
TIME: 20 minutes prep and 60 minutes baking

1 pound tofu, extra firm

¼ cup water

1 tablespoon arrowroot powder

2 teaspoons nutritional yeast

1 ½ teaspoons agar flakes (or ¼
teaspoon agar powder)

⅛ teaspoon turmeric

1 cup peeled, cubed potatoes

2 teaspoons olive oil

½ cup diced onions

½ cup seeded, cubed zucchini

¾ cup diced red bell pepper

2 teaspoons fresh minced garlic

1 teaspoon salt

½ teaspoon fennel seed powder

½ teaspoon rosemary powder

⅛ teaspoon ground white pepper

1. Place the tofu, water, arrowroot powder, nutritional yeast, agar flakes, and turmeric into a food processor, process until smooth.

2. Boil or steam cubed potatoes approximately 20 minutes in a vegetable steamer or until they are cooked through but are still firm enough to retain their shape. Remove the potatoes from the steamer and set aside.

3. In a 10-inch frying pan, sauté the onions, zucchini, red bell pepper, garlic, and salt in the oil for 2 minutes. Add the fennel seed, rosemary, and white pepper; stir to well combine.

4. Pour the mixture into a very lightly oiled 8 x 8 x 2-inch baking dish and cover the dish securely with aluminum foil. Place the baking dish into a larger pan filled with ½- to 1-inch of water.

5. Bake the frittata in a 350°F preheated oven for 45 minutes, or until it is starting to puff up (internal temperature over 160°F). Remove the pan from the oven. Serve hot, cold, or at room temperature.

Variation: *Mushroom Quiche*

1. Replace potatoes and zucchini with sliced mushrooms.

2. Prepare and pre-bake one 9 or 10 inch Basic Pie Crust* (page 336) for 7 minutes in a preheated 350°F oven.

3. Add filling and bake about 45 minutes, or until done, which is firm to the touch.

*Save or freeze additional dough.

SOUTHERN BATTER-FRIED TOFU

YIELD: 4 servings
TIME: 20 minutes prep and 25 minutes cooking

Fried Chicken-Style Spice Blend

2 teaspoons whole thyme

2 teaspoons curry powder

2 teaspoons onion powder

2 tablespoons vegan chicken-style broth powder

4 teaspoons dried parsley

2 teaspoons whole savory

2 teaspoons salt

2 teaspoons garlic powder

2 teaspoons dried basil

Mix the spices and herbs together; set aside.

Southern Country Gravy

1 cup diced onions

¾ teaspoon fresh minced garlic

3 tablespoons oil (use the oil from frying the tofu)

¼ cup leftover breading mixture (from the main recipe) or unbleached flour

5 teaspoons chicken-style or vegetable broth powder

½ teaspoon salt (optional)

⅛ teaspoon ground black pepper

1 cup water

Sauté onions and garlic in the oil for 4 to 5 minutes. Stir in breading mixture, yeast, soup base, salt, and pepper; cook 3 to 4 minutes longer. Add half the water, whisking it into the onion and flour mixture. When thickened, add the remaining water, whisking to a light consistency.

Tofu

1 pound extra firm tofu*

1 ¼ cups unbleached flour

3 tablespoons vegan chicken-style or vegetable broth powder

2 tablespoons gluten flour

1 teaspoon salt (optional)

4 tablespoons Fried Chicken-Style Spice Blend

1 tablespoon high-heat canola oil (or safflower oil)

1 cup water

2 cups high-heat oil (sunflower or commercial frying oil)

1. Drain and rinse tofu. Slice it horizontally into 4 (4-ounce) pieces. Place tofu on a plate and add 1 tablespoon broth powder; coat and set aside.

2. Stir together ½ cup of the unbleached flour and the remaining 2 tablespoons of broth powder. Set breading mixture aside.

3. Mix remaining ¾ cup of unbleached flour, gluten flour, salt, and spice blend. Blend to remove lumps. Stir in the water and 1 tablespoon canola oil. If lumps form, blend batter in blender.

4. Heat the oil in a deep skillet. Dip a piece of tofu into the breading mixture, coat it completely, and dip it into the batter, using tongs. Place battered tofu into hot oil and completely submerge. Deep-fry tofu to a light brown, about 1 to 2 minutes. Remove with a slotted spoon and drain on paper towels for 30 seconds. (Note: You can place the tofu in the oven at 250°F for up to 15 minutes to retain crispness.)

5. Pour equal portions of Southern Country Gravy on each plate and set hot fried tofu atop gravy.

*Substitute tofu with 4 (4-ounce) pieces of chicken-style protein analogue.

TOFU CACCIATORE

YIELD: 4 servings
TIME: 20 minutes prep and 25 minutes cooking

2 tablespoons white flour

8 teaspoons vegan chicken-style broth powder or seasoning of choice

1 pound extra firm tofu*

2 tablespoons olive oil

2 teaspoons minced fresh garlic

1 cup diced onions

2 cups fresh quartered mushrooms

½ cup of ½-inch diced green bell pepper

1 tablespoon Italian spice blend

1 teaspoon whole rosemary

½ teaspoon salt**

⅛ teaspoon black pepper

½ cup burgundy wine

2 cups Classical Tomato Sauce (page 216) or canned tomato sauce

1. Mix flour and broth powder together. Rinse and slice the 1-pound brick of tofu into 8 slices by cutting in half, each half in half, and each resultant piece in half again (2-ounce pieces). In a bowl, toss the tofu with the seasoned flour until all pieces are evenly coated.

2. In a 10-inch frying pan, heat the oil over medium heat. Sauté the tofu pieces until a light golden brown on both sides. Remove the tofu pieces from the oil and set on plate. Leave the remaining oil in the frying pan.

3. Sauté the garlic, onions, mushrooms, pepper, Italian spice, rosemary, salt and pepper, and broth powder in the leftover oil over medium heat for 5 minutes, stirring occasionally. Add the tomato sauce and wine to the sautéed vegetables.

4. Continue to cook the cacciatore over medium-low heat for 10 minutes. Serve hot over brown rice or pasta of your choice.

*Tempeh, seitan, or chicken analogue can be used in place of tofu.

**I recommend holding the salt and adjusting the flavor when the sauce is complete. You may not need the additional sodium, depending on the tomato sauce selected.

OPTION: In the traditional entrée, the chicken is cooked in the sauce, but the tofu and the chicken analogue may be cooked either in the sauce or not. For a more classical presentation, place sauce on pasta or polenta and lay tofu atop sauce.

SEA VEGETABLE TOFU

This recipe uses the basic ratio (1 ½ cups Basic Tofu Pâté to 1 tablespoon dried sea vegetable) for any sea vegetable tofu dish. Because the sea vegetable simulates seafood, any complementary vegan seafood-style seasoning can be used. Do not salt the protein until spice blends have been chosen because many contain salt and the blend may be sufficient.

YIELD: 1 ⅔ cups mixture
TIME: 15 minutes prep and 15 to 20 minutes cooking

1 tablespoon (plus) canola oil for sautéing
¼ cup finely diced carrots*
1 tablespoon dried wakame
1 ½ cups Basic Tofu Pâté (page 252)
2 teaspoons Old Bay Seasoning

1. Heat small sauté pan on medium heat. Pour in oil and carrots. Sauté for 2 to 3 minutes. Remove from heat.

2. Place wakame on cutting board, fold a towel over it, and crush hard with a rolling pin. Or pulse in a clean coffee grinder or food processor.

3. Add crushed dry wakame to Basic Tofu Pâté with Old Bay seasoning and mix until evenly blended. If using a salt-free seasoning, add ¼ teaspoon salt.

4. Add carrot mixture and oil to food processor and pulse about 15 seconds to evenly disperse the carrots into the mixture.

5. Make cakes using 2 tablespoons mixture per cake, dredge in bread crumbs, and sauté in canola oil on medium high heat until golden brown on each side.

*OPTION: Use pine nuts (roasted or raw) or a cooked whole grain (such as barley, kamut, or quinoa) in place of carrots.

ALMOND-CRUSTED TOFU

YIELD: 4 servings
TIME: 20 minutes prep and 15 minutes cooking

½ cup white flour (for stronger bind use ¼ cup white flour and ¼ cup vital gluten flour)
½ teaspoon ground fennel
1-pound block extra-firm tofu, rinsed and drained
¼ teaspoon salt
1 cup ground almonds (or pistachios)
1 tablespoon extra-virgin olive oil
¾ cup Balsamic Glaze (page 226)
Chopped tomatoes for garnish
Chopped parsley for garnish

1. In a mixing bowl, combine the flour, fennel, and salt. Using a knife, slice tofu in half and subdivide into 4 pieces and subdivide again into 8 pieces (2 ounces each). Dredge the tofu in the flour mixture to coat well. Move coated tofu to separate plate. Lightly brush or spritz top of each piece of floured tofu with water, making sure it is moist. Cover the tofu with the ground almonds; press to coat well, flip tofu and repeat. Set aside.

2. Heat oil in a 12-inch skillet on medium-low heat. Add the tofu and cook each side 30 to 60 seconds, or until lightly browned.

3. To serve, mound equal amounts of pasta in the center of four dinner plates; drizzle 2 tablespoons of the balsamic glaze over each portion. Lean 2 pieces of tofu on either side of each mound. Drizzle with more balsamic glaze; garnish with tomatoes and parsley.

Tofu Fricassee

The difference between *fricassee* and *à la king* is that fricassee is made with a Velouté Sauce and *à* la king is made with a cream sauce. This was one of my favorite post-Thanksgiving dinners when we needed to use leftover turkey in creative ways. This recipe is so close to the original that all you need to do is simply substitute tofu for turkey. You also can use tempeh or chicken-style analogue in place of the tofu.

YIELD: 3 servings (3 ½ cups)
TIME: 25 minutes prep and 30 minutes cooking

1 tablespoon corn oil, unrefined (or oil of choice)

½ cup diced onions

1 cup carrots, peeled, cut in half lengthwise, and thinly sliced in half moons

½ cup diced red bell pepper

½ pound firm tofu cut into ½-inch cubes

½ cup celery, cut diagonally into ¼-inch pieces (flaked)

½ cup diced green bell pepper

2 tablespoons sherry

2 tablespoons chicken-style or vegetable powder*

½ teaspoon salt (optional depending on sodium content of broth powder)

⅛ teaspoon white pepper

½ cup peas, fresh or frozen

2 cups Supreme Sauce (page 214)

2 slices tomato held together by 1 scallion (optional garnish)

1. In oil in a 10-inch frying pan, sauté the onions, carrots, and red bell peppers over medium heat for 5 minutes, stirring occasionally.

2. Add the tofu, celery, green pepper, sherry, broth powder, salt, and pepper; continue to sauté for another 5 to 6 minutes, or until the vegetables are hot but still tender-crisp. (The vegetables should retain their bright color when being served.)

3. Add the peas and the Supreme Sauce to the sautéed ingredients; mix them in well. Cook for about 2 minutes. Garnish with tomato and serve hot.

*Veggie base that is similar to chicken-style broth powder

NOTE: The celery and green bell peppers can be divided in half, using the first half of each for the sauté and the second half for the sauce. The half reserved for the sauce will retain a bright color, while the sautéed half will impart a richer flavor to the sauce.

OPTIONS: Tofu Fricassee can also be served over pasta, rice, couscous, whole grains, or baked potato. Broccoli florets are a good option for a vegetable side dish. For a unique serving idea, hollow out small (4- to 6-ounce) round loaves of whole grain bread and serve the fricassee in each as an individual portion.

Almond-Crusted Portabellas with Tofu Forcemeat

This superbly decked-out mushroom won a silver medal in the International Culinary Olympics using hazelnuts in place of almonds. I call the filling a forcemeat, which was used as a flavored filling in traditional cooking. A vegan tofu forcemeat can be used similarly.

YIELD: 3 servings
TIME: 30 minutes prep and 15 to 20 minutes cooking

3 portabella mushroom caps (about 4 inches each)

2 tablespoons canola or extra-virgin olive oil

1 cup finely diced or grated carrots

1 pound, 2 ounces extra-firm tofu

4 ½ teaspoons arrowroot or cornstarch

1 tablespoon sunflower or canola oil

1 teaspoon agar powder

¼ teaspoon salt

¼ teaspoon liquid smoke (optional, or use smoked tofu [see "Smoked Proteins" page 314])

¼ cup chopped parsley

½ cup unbleached white flour

½ cup finely ground almonds

1. Using a teaspoon, carefully remove the gills from the underside of mushrooms. Lightly salt the mushroom bottoms and set aside.

2. Heat 1 tablespoon of the oil in a 12-inch sauté pan over medium heat. Place the mushrooms in the pan salted side down. Sauté for 5 minutes, gently pressing the mushrooms with a spatula to extract moisture. Remove from pan and press with paper towels to extract additional moisture.

3. In the same pan, add the remaining oil and carrots. Sauté for about 3 minutes; remove from the heat.

4. Place the tofu, arrowroot, oil, agar powder, salt, and liquid smoke (if using) in a food processor; process until smooth. Transfer the mixture to a large mixing bowl along with the sautéed carrots and chopped parsley. Mix well and set aside.

5. Flour the bottoms of the mushroom caps and fill each with the tofu-carrot mixture. Brush water on the top of the caps; coat with flour and sprinkle with more water so the flour is wet and pasty. Press the caps into the almond meal, shake gently to remove any excess meal, and set aside. Heat the remaining oil in the sauté pan over medium heat. Add the caps nut-side up and cook for 3 minutes, or until the bottom of the tofu-carrot mixture is lightly browned.

6. Transfer to a baking sheet, and bake in preheated 350°F over for 10 to 15 minutes, or until the caps are heated through and the nuts are lightly browned. Remove from the oven. Cool the mushrooms for 5 minutes, or until they are cool enough to handle but still warm.

7. Using a very sharp or serrated knife, slice the mushrooms on a 45-degree angle into ½-inch-thick slices. Fan each mushroom on a plate or over a grain side dish, with each person getting a complete mushroom cap. Serve with your favorite sauce. My recommendations are Sauce Robert (page 211), Bigarade Sauce (page 209), Béarnaise Sauce (page 221), or Wild Forager's au Jus (page 230).

Tempeh Entrées

Tempeh, like all vegan proteins, is very versatile and can be used as a replacement protein in many of the entrée and sandwich recipes in this book and elsewhere. Tempeh is similar to tofu—it doesn't have a strong, defined flavor. Without seasoning and other ingredients, it tastes like cooked soybeans with a little fermented flavor. If over-fermented, it will have large black spots and smell like ammonia. Commercial tempeh is pasteurized to kill the culture. In my 30-plus years of cooking with branded commercial tempeh, I have never experienced poor quality tempeh.

Tempeh differs from tofu in the way the soybeans are processed. Tempeh is a whole soybean, cooked, skins removed, and incubated for about 12 hours with a culture that creates a white mold binding the beans together. Tofu is made by grinding soybeans, cooking them, separating the "milk," and adding a curdling agent. The water is pressed out of the curd, leaving a solid mass.

In a few variations of tempeh, sea vegetables and/or whole grains or flaxseed are added. The tempeh flavor is modestly changed with the additional ingredients, but basic cooking techniques do not change. The major changes are texture and eye appeal.

This is the basic technique I use: Split 4-ounce pieces of tempeh horizontally into 2 even 2-ounce pieces. Pour a thin layer of reduced-sodium tamari or soy sauce on a large plate with a ridge; lay slices in sauce and flip to coat both sides. Preheat a large sauté pan over medium heat with a light coat of raw, not roasted, sesame oil. Brown tempeh on one side; flip and brown the second side. Remove each piece from pan and continue sautéing until all the tempeh is browned. Place all the cooked tempeh back in the pan with about ¼ inch of water; cover and let cook over medium heat until all the water has evaporated. This helps develop flavor while masking the tempeh's original flavor if that's not desirable in the specific recipe. The tempeh is ready to serve with a sauce or refrigerate until ready to use.

The recipe options for tempeh exemplify the versatility of this ancient protein. In general, I recommend sautéing tempeh for caramelization following the instructions for Macrobiotic Lyonnaise Tempeh (opposite page). Unlike seitan, tempeh doesn't hold up well when sliced thin and added to a stir-fry, stroganoff, or pepper steak-style entrée like a fricassee, where it is continually stirred in the cooking process. I recommend precooking the tempeh to give it flavor before integrating it into the recipe.

In addition to the list below, other tempeh recipe applications are found throughout the book, including variations such as the Smoked Tempeh, Lettuce, & Tomato Sandwich (page 310). Tempeh also works well marinated, grilled, or broiled (see "Vegan Protein Grilling" on page 112) and served as an entrée with appropriate sauce such as Supreme Sauce (page 214) or Mushroom Sauce (page 233).

MACROBIOTIC LYONNAISE TEMPEH

This is one of my favorite macrobiotic tempeh dishes. This easy entrée can be made in advance and heated as needed. You can double the amount of tempeh you prepare and have it ready for additional tempeh recipes. To make this entrée gluten-free, use gluten-free tamari and miso. Since this entrée is macrobiotic, it is traditionally served with brown rice, but can be served with polenta or mixed whole-grain pilaf. Traditionally, steamed kale or collards and a sea vegetable side dish, such as arame and carrots, are served with it.

YIELD: 4 servings
TIME: 15 minutes prep and 20 to 25 minutes cooking

1 pound tempeh, cut into 4-ounce pieces and then cut horizontally into 2-ounce pieces.
4 tablespoons high-heat canola or safflower oil
2 tablespoons tamari (gluten-free)
½ cup water
1 cup Miso Mustard Onion Sauce (page 237)

1. Pour tamari onto a plate; lay each piece of sliced and cut tempeh in tamari and flip to coat both sides.

2. Heat oil over medium heat and lay tempeh in oil, sautéing about 3 to 5 minutes, or until lightly browned. Flip and brown the opposite side for the same amount of time. Add the ½ cup water to the tempeh, cover pan, and cook tempeh for 3 minutes. Check; continue to cook until all water has evaporated. Serve with Miso Mustard Onion Sauce on plate or place tempeh on sauce.

TOMATO-APRICOT-GINGER COULIS

YIELD: 4 servings
TIME: 10 minutes prep and 20 minutes cooking

3 tomatoes, medium
5 apricots, fresh, medium
2 tablespoons minced onions or shallots
2 tablespoons brown or white sugar
2 tablespoons white wine
2 tablespoons olive oil
1 tablespoon lemon juice
⅓ teaspoon ground ginger

1. Blanch, peel, seed, and chop the tomatoes. (You should end up with 1 cup.)

2. Cut the apricots into small pieces. Place them in a saucepan with the tomatoes and other ingredients and simmer until the liquid is reduced by one-half (about 20 minutes). Serve this sauce hot or cold.

NOTE: If you are using canned apricots instead of fresh apricots, you will need about 10 small apricot halves. Choose fruit that is canned in a fruit-juice concentrate rather than sugar syrup, and use only 1 tablespoon of brown sugar. Drain the fruit well.

SOUTHERN BLACKENED TEMPEH WITH TOMATO-APRICOT-GINGER-COULIS

This dish won a silver medal at the 1988 Culinary Olympics. Serve the blackened tempeh with any complementary sauce. I like the Tomato-Apricot-Ginger Coulis because it seems to have a cooling effect on the spicy tempeh.

YIELD: 4 servings
TIME: 15 minutes prep and 10 to 15 minutes cooking

Black Bean Filling

Yield: 1 cup
TIME: 15 minutes prep and 25 minutes cooking

1 cup cooked black beans, crushed to a paste with a fork

⅛ teaspoon salt

¼ teaspoon cumin

1 teaspoon Cajun spice

Mash all ingredients together and set aside.

2 (8-ounce) pieces tempeh

2 tablespoons Cajun spice

2 tablespoons water

2 tablespoons tamari (gluten-free)

1 tablespoon Sucanat, brown, or white sugar

2 tablespoons raw sesame or canola cooking oil

1. Slice each piece of tempeh vertically in half for a total of 4 pieces. Make a cut along the length of each piece of tempeh, on the cut (flat) side, keeping the edges intact.

2. Gently open and fill the tempeh, using ¼ cup of the bean mixture for each piece. Press the tempeh closed; set aside.

3. In a small bowl, mix the Cajun spices with 2 tablespoons of water, the tamari, and the Sucanat. Brush the mixture onto both sides of each piece of tempeh.

4. Heat the oil in a skillet and sauté the tempeh on both sides until brown (about 1 minute on each side). Place the browned tempeh in a baking dish. Cover baking pan with lid or aluminum foil. Bake, covered, in a preheated oven at 350°F for about 10 to 15 minutes. Serve immediately with the Tomato-Apricot-Ginger Coulis or Asian BBQ Sauce (page 235).

NOTE: Stuffing the tempeh is optional. But if you want to, you can use a commercial instant black bean filling to stuff the tempeh. If using the mix, place the contents of the mix in a bowl. Add hot water and stir until well blended. Set aside for about 5 minutes.

BACON-STYLE TEMPEH

This is a good basic recipe for tempeh bacon. You can slice and smoke the tempeh for a more authentic smoked flavor. Bacon-style tempeh is exceptional on sandwiches, as a breakfast protein, in salads, and as an appetizer.

YIELD: 4 servings (3 slices each portion)
TIME: 10 minutes prep and 10 to 15 minutes cooking

8 ounces tempeh (preferably smoked)
¼ cup water
½ teaspoon salt
2 teaspoons liquid smoke (if using smoked tempeh, liquid smoke unnecessary)
2 tablespoons raw sesame oil
½ teaspoon smoked or plain paprika

1. Slice tempeh at 45-degree angle into 8 equal pieces.

2. Pour water, salt, and liquid smoke (if using) in large 12-inch sauté pan. Lay tempeh slices in liquid and sprinkle evenly with paprika. Cover and cook over medium heat until liquid is dissolved (about 5 to 8 minutes).

3. Heat sauté pan over medium heat with a little oil. Lightly brown tempeh and serve.

OPTION: For smoked tempeh bacon, smoke the tempeh and slice according to above directions. Mix salt and paprika together and rub on tempeh. Sauté in 2 tablespoons oil and serve immediately or refrigerate until ready to use.

BBQ TEMPEH

YIELD: 4 servings
TIME: 10 minutes prep and 15 to 20 minutes cooking

1 teaspoon liquid hickory smoke (optional)
1 ½ cups traditional BBQ sauce or Asian BBQ Sauce (page 235)
1 pound tempeh
½ cup water
2 tablespoons tamari (gluten-free)
1 tablespoon sugar
3 tablespoons canola oil, or oil of choice

1. Stir the liquid smoke into the BBQ sauce.

2. Cut tempeh (rectangle) in half. Take two pieces and cut diagonally to create even triangles. Slice each triangle in half horizontally to make a thinner triangle, until you have a total of 8 triangles. Pour tamari on plate and coat each piece of tempeh in tamari.

3. In a sauté pan on medium heat, pour oil and place tempeh in pan. Brown on both sides. Add water and BBQ sauce stirring to evenly coat. Cook until sauce becomes viscous (thickens to sauce consistency), about 4 to 8 minutes.

4. Serve on a bun as a sandwich or with corn mush and collard greens.

Tempeh Piccata

YIELD: 6 servings (4 ounces each of protein)
TIME: 20 minutes prep and 25 minutes cooking

3 (8-ounce) pieces tempeh (1 ½ pounds total)
¼ cup canola oil
¼ teaspoon salt
1 ½ cup Piccata Sauce (page 237)

1. Slice each 8-ounce piece of tempeh into 2 (4-ounce) pieces; slice each 4-ounce piece horizontally in half.

2. Heat the oil in a large sauté pan over medium heat.

3. Add cutlets; sprinkle with salt and sauté about 2 to 4 minutes, or until brown. Turn and sauté for another 2 to 4 minutes, or until the second side is browned. Transfer the browned tempeh to a plate. Serve the tempeh cutlets hot with at least ¼ cup of sauce per person. Garnish with parsley.

Moo Goo Gai Pan Tempeh

YIELD: 4 servings
TIME: 10 minutes prep and 20 minutes cooking

2 (8-ounce) pieces tempeh (1 pound total)
1 tablespoon tamari
1 tablespoon water
3 tablespoons sesame oil
1 cup snow peas
1 cup red bell pepper, medium diced
2 cups Moo Goo Gai Pan Sauce (page 232)

1. Cut the tempeh into 4 equal 4 ounce pieces. Then dice each quarter into 6 cubes (slice in half and then thirds). Pour tamari and water into a bowl and toss the tempeh in tamari to coat.

2. Heat 2 tablespoons sesame oil over medium heat and place tempeh in oil, sautéing about 3 to 5 minutes, until lightly browned.

3. Heat third tablespoon sesame oil in large sauté pan over medium-high heat. Add snow peas and pepper and sauté for 3 to 5 minutes. Add sauce and tempeh and cook for about 4 minutes. Serve over rice, pasta, or grain of choice.

BLACKENED TEMPEH

TEMPEH À LA BIGARADE

YIELD: 4 servings
TIME: 10 minutes prep and 20 minutes cooking

2 (8-ounce) pieces tempeh (1 pound total)

1 tablespoon tamari

1 tablespoon water

2 tablespoons canola oil

2 cups Bigarade Sauce (page 209)

2 tablespoons chopped parsley

1. Cut the tempeh into 4 equal 4 ounce pieces and then slice each piece horizontally. Pour tamari onto a plate; lay each piece of tempeh in tamari and flip to coat both sides.

2. Heat oil over medium heat; lay tempeh in oil, sautéing about 3 to 5 minutes, until lightly browned. Flip and brown the opposite side for the same amount of time. Add the ½ cup water to the tempeh, cover pan, and cook for 3 minutes. Check and continue cooking until all water has evaporated.

3. Add sauce and let simmer for about 5 minutes. Add a little water to thin out sauce if it becomes too thick. Garnish with chopped parsley.

TEMPEH PROVENÇAL

YIELD: 4 servings
TIME: 10 minutes prep and 20 minutes cooking

2 (8-ounce) pieces tempeh

1 tablespoon tamari

1 tablespoon water

2 tablespoons canola oil

½ cup water

2 cups Classical Tomato Sauce (page 216)

2 tablespoons chopped parsley

2 tablespoons vegan Parmesan cheese (optional)

1. Cut the tempeh into 4 equal 4-ounce pieces and then slice each piece horizontally. Pour tamari onto a plate; lay each piece of tempeh in tamari and flip to coat both sides.

2. Heat oil over medium heat and lay tempeh in oil, sautéing about 3 to 5 minutes, until lightly browned. Flip and brown the opposite side for the same amount of time.

3. Add the ½ cup water to the tempeh, cover pan, and let cook for 3 minutes. Check and continue cooking until all water has evaporated. Add tomato sauce and continue cooking for another 5 minutes. Cover and let rest for 5 minutes before serving. Serve with polenta or angel hair pasta. Garnish with parsley and vegan Parmesan.

Seitan Entrées

This section covers a number of seitan recipes that lean toward European cuisine and show how a classical meat-based entrée can be converted to vegetarian or vegan. Seitan preparation techniques are addressed in Method 1 and Method 2, the first two recipes in this section. In Appendix A there is a seitan quick mix product. You have the option of making seitan from scratch or from a speed scratch mix. Making a pound of seitan from scratch would take about two and a half hours. With a speed scratch seitan mix, it would take about 30 minutes. Eco-Cuisine has produced two seitan cooking technique videos, which are available on YouTube or at eco-cuisine.com for reference. In general, seitan substitutes well for chicken analogue and some tempeh recipes and where extra-firm tofu is used as a cutlet. Other unique seitan variations and recipes listed in other sections include Mesquite Smoked Seitan Ragoût à la Bigarade (page 313).

SEITAN METHOD I

This is the most basic, straightforward method of making seitan. The recipe may seem long, but that is only because the steps are carefully explained. Once you understand the procedure and the practice, the production of seitan will seem less formidable.

YIELD: 14 ounces uncooked; 16 ounces cooked
TIME: 1 hour prep and 2 hours cooking

6 cups stone-ground whole wheat bread flour or high-gluten unbleached white flour
6 cups water (or more, depending on the amount of gluten in the flour)
½ cup tamari
12 slices fresh ginger, each ⅛ inch thick
1 piece kombu, about 3-inches long

1. Mix the flour and water by hand or in a machine to make a medium-stiff but not sticky dough.

2. Knead the dough by hand on a breadboard or tabletop, until it has the consistency of an earlobe or by machine until the dough forms a ball that follows the path of the hook around the bowl. You may need to add a little extra water or flour to achieve the desired consistency. Kneading will take about 10 to 12 minutes by hand or about 6 to 8 minutes by machine.

3. Allow the dough to rest in a cold water for about 10 minutes. While the dough is resting, prepare the stock. In a large pot, bring to a boil 3 quarts of water. Add the tamari, ginger, and kombu, and cook for 15 minutes. Remove from heat and allow to cool. This stock must be cold before it is used. (The cold liquid causes the gluten to contract and prevents the seitan from acquiring a bready texture.) You will be using this stock to cook the seitan later.

4. To wash out the starch, use warm water to begin with. Warm water loosens the dough and makes the task easier. Knead the dough, immersed in water, in the bowl.

5. When the water turns milky, drain it off and refill the bowl with fresh water. In the final rinses, use cold water to tighten the gluten. If you wish, save the bran by straining the water through a fine sieve; the bran will be left behind. Save the starch by allowing the milky water to settle in the bottom of the bowl; slowly pour off the water and collect the starch, which you can use for thickening soups, sauces, and stews.

6. When kneading, remember to work towards the center of the dough so that it does not break into pieces.

7. After about eight changes of water, you will begin to feel the dough become firmer and more elastic. The water will no longer become cloudy as you knead it.

8. To make sure you have kneaded and rinsed it enough, lift the dough out of the water and squeeze it. The liquid oozing out should be clear, not milky.

9. To shape the seitan, lightly oil a 1-pound loaf pan. Place the rinsed seitan in the pan and let it rest until the dough relaxes. (After the dough has been rinsed for the last time in cold water, the gluten will have tightened and the dough will be tense, tough, and resistant to taking on any other shape.) After it has rested for 10 minutes, it will be much more flexible.

10. Seitan is cooked in two steps. In the first step, the dough is put into a large pot with about 3 quarts of plain, boiling water. Boil the seitan for about 30 to 45 minutes, or until it floats to the surface. Drain the seitan and cut it into usable pieces (steaks, cutlets, 1-inch chunks, or whatever) or leave whole. Return the seitan to the cold tamari stock. Bring the stock to a boil, lower the temperature, and simmer in the stock for 1 ½ to 2 hours (45 minutes if the seitan is cut into small pieces). This second cooking step may also be done in a pressure cooker, in which case it would take between 15 and 30 minutes.

11. To store seitan, keep it refrigerated, immersed in the tamari stock. Seitan will keep indefinitely if it is brought to a boil in the tamari stock and boiled for 10 minutes once a week. Otherwise, use it in eight or nine days.

SEITAN METHOD II

This recipe yields considerably more seitan, and the flavor of the stock is slightly different. This recipe is enough for about three different seitan dishes.

YIELD: 1¾ pounds uncooked; 2 ½ pounds cooked
Time: 40 to 50 minutes prep and 3 to 4 hours cooking

16 cups (5 pounds) white bread flour
6 to 8 cups water, or more
¾ cup tamari
1 onion, peeled and sliced
1 piece kombu, about 4 inches long
¼ cup ginger, slices (or 2 teaspoons ginger powder)

1. Mix the four and water together to make a medium-stiff dough. Knead it until it is elastic when pulled (about 8 to 10 minutes). Allow the dough to rest for about 5 minutes in a bowl of cold water.

2. Wash out the starch by filling a large bowl (1 ½ to 2 gallons) with warm water and kneading the dough in it, under water. When the water turns white (after 1 to 2 minutes), drain it through a strainer, adding the floury residue back to the ball of dough. Keep kneading, washing, and changing the water, until no more starch is given off. This may take as many as eight rinses, about 20 to 25 minutes.

3. Pour 6 pints of water into a large pot. Add the tamari, onion, kombu, ginger and dough, and simmer for about 3 hours. (To speed up the cooking, you could cut the dough into small pieces, each about 1 ½ inches, the pieces would cook in about one hour). The seitan is properly cooked when it is firm to the touch and when it is firm in the center. You can check by cutting into the seitan. If it is not done, it will feel like raw dough in the center.

SEITAN VARIATIONS

Instead of boiling the seitan in plain water and then stock, let the seitan drain for a while after it has been rinsed. Slice it and either deep-fry or sauté the slices until both sides are brown. Then cook it in the tamari stock according to the recipe.

Seitan also may be cooked (at the second step) in a broth flavored with carrots, onion, celery, garlic, tamari, and black pepper, which will give it a flavor similar to that of pot roast. Shiitake mushrooms may also be added to the steak.

Swiss-Style Shredded Seitan

This entrée is traditionally prepared using veal. Seitan is the perfect substitute, and eliminating the tamari from the seitan will give it a more veal-like look. I am presenting this traditional Swiss dish as a refreshing change to the traditional vegan Stroganoff.

YIELD: 8 servings
TIME: 15 minutes prep and 20 minutes cooking

4 tablespoons sunflower or canola oil

1 cup sliced scallions

2 cups sliced mushrooms

4 cups cooked seitan sliced into thin strips

4 teaspoons demi-glace*

8 tablespoons sherry or dry white wine

4 teaspoons tamari

½ teaspoon ground black pepper

½ teaspoon minced garlic

4 tablespoons arrowroot powder

3 cups plain soy milk

8 cups cooked artichoke spaghetti or udon, or pasta of choice

2 tablespoons chopped parsley

*Demi-Glace

1 tablespoon water

1 tablespoon barley miso

1 tablespoon barley malt or rice syrup

1. Make a vegan demi-glace by combining miso, syrup, and water.

2. Heat oil and sauté scallions for 1 minute.

3. Add mushrooms and seitan and sauté for 3 minutes.

4. Add demi-glace, sherry, tamari, pepper, and garlic; bring the mixture to a simmer. Dissolve arrowroot in soy milk. Add to seitan mixture. Stir constantly until thickened. Pour over cooked noodles and garnish with parsley. Serve while hot.

Seitan Swiss Steak

In this recipe seitan can be replaced by tempeh, tofu (infused pâté, plain cutlets), or chicken analogue. This variety gives the cook numerous protein options with the same recipe. They all work well in this recipe, with seitan being the lead protein option. The beef version was the Monday-evening special when I was a child.

YIELD: 6 servings (6 steaks & 5 cups sauce)
TIME: 25 minutes prep and 30 minutes cooking

6 (3-ounce) seitan steaks*

¼ cup white flour

2 tablespoons tamari

4 tablespoons canola oil (1 to 2 tablespoons more if needed)

1 ½ cups fresh sliced mushrooms

1 cup onions, halved and sliced

1 cup diced green bell peppers

2 tablespoons minced garlic

1 tablespoon chopped basil

¼ cup dark barley miso or red miso, dissolved in ¼ cup water

3 cups (28-ounce can) diced tomatoes in juice

¼ cup tomato paste

1 cup water

½ teaspoon black pepper

1. Pour 1 teaspoon of tamari on each seitan steak and let set for a minute. Pour any excess tamari into sauce.

2. Dredge seitan steaks in flour. Heat 6 tablespoons oil in a large sauté pan over medium heat and brown the seitan steaks on both sides until golden brown. Place in an 8-quart roasting pan or baking dish.

3. In the remaining oil, sauté the mushrooms, onions, bell peppers, and garlic with the basil for 5 to 8 minutes. Stir in the dissolved miso. Add diced tomatoes, tomato paste, water, and pepper. Simmer for 5 minutes.

4. Place a little sauce in a 2-quart roasting pan or baking dish. Place the seitan steaks on the sauce and cover with the remaining sauce. Cover the dish and bake at 350°F for 25 minutes. (If the seitan is baked too long, the sauce will evaporate and may not look appetizing; adding more water should solve the problem.)

5. Serve hot with mashed potatoes or cooked white or brown rice and vegetable of your choice.

*Use seitan cutlets in place of seitan steaks.

VARIATION: *Tofu Swiss Steak*

Use tofu cut into steak-size pieces in place of seitan. Follow the directions in the same manner.

BROCCOLI SEITAN DELMONICO

Tempeh, beans, and chicken-style analogues are additional protein options.

YIELD: 5 servings
TIME: 25 minutes prep and 30 minutes cooking

3 tablespoons corn oil

1 cup finely chopped onions

½ cup sliced mushrooms

¼ teaspoon salt

¼ teaspoon nutmeg

6 tablespoons white flour

2 tablespoons nutritional yeast

½ cup chopped pimiento-stuffed green olives

¼ cup cashew nuts

2 cups soy milk

2 ½ cups broccoli florets

1 ½ cups cooked and diced seitan

6 cups cooked pasta (spaghetti, linguine, soba, or other pasta)

1. Heat the oil in a medium saucepan. Sauté the onions and mushrooms with the salt and nutmeg until the onions are translucent (about 5 to 7 minutes).

2. Stir in the flour and yeast and cook 3 to 5 minutes longer. Add the chopped olives; set aside.

3. Blend the cashews with 1 cup soy milk to a smooth paste in a blender. (You should be able to feel only a slight gritty texture if you rub the mixture between your fingers.) Add the remaining 1 cup soy milk and blend for a few seconds.

4. Pour the cashew milk over the sautéed onion mixture and stir until well blended. Cook over medium heat, stirring occasionally, until the sauce thickens. (This would be a good time to begin cooking the pasta.)

5. Steam the broccoli for about 5 minutes, or until tender but crisp. Add it to the sauce mixture. Stir in the diced seitan. Spoon the broccoli-seitan sauce over pasta. Serve hot.

VARIATION: *Broccoli Delmonico with Cannellini Beans*

Use 1 ½ cups beans in place of seitan, or use ¾ cup seitan and ¾ cup cannellini beans.

SZEKELY GOULASH

This is the Hungarian version of the Russian Stroganoff. The main difference is that the Szekely Goulash has sauerkraut and paprika in the sauce and is generally made with pork, not beef. This vegan dish has a superb taste and a delicate texture. It contains no cholesterol while maintaining the rich creamy flavor of Hungarian cuisine. While I have a decent Russian Stroganoff, it is a common entrée in vegan cuisine; I thought I would show another version.

YIELD: 4 servings
TIME: 20 minutes prep and 30 minutes cooking

1 cup diced onions

1 ½ cups flaked seitan

1 tablespoon oil

1 tablespoon vegan chicken-style or vegetable broth powder or concentrate

1 teaspoon salt

1 tablespoon paprika, preferably sweet Hungarian

1 cup sauerkraut, measured after being rinsed and pressed relatively dry

¼ cup Tofu Cashew Sour Cream (page 175)

2 cups Soy Milk Sauce (below)

1. Sauté the onions and seitan in the oil along with the soup base, salt, and paprika over medium heat, stirring for about 5 minutes.

2. Add the sauerkraut, sour cream, and Béchamel Sauce; mix in well. Continue to stir the mixture over medium heat. If the mixture becomes too thick, add just enough water to thin it to a sauce consistency (one that will coat the back of a spoon to ¹⁄₁₆ of an inch or so). Serve hot, over noodles, with a vegetable side dish.

OPTION 1: Substitute ¼ cup Cauliflower Sour Cream (page 174) for Tofu Cashew Sour Cream or commercial vegan sour cream.

OPTION 2: Substitute Béchamel Sauce (page 205) for Soy Milk Sauce.

Soy Milk Sauce

YIELD: 4 servings (2 cups)
TIME: 15 minutes

3 tablespoons canola oil (or other cooking oil)

¼ cup unbleached flour

2 cups soy milk

1. Heat the oil in a small saucepan until it is hot but not smoking. Add the flour and stir constantly to prevent it from burning. Cook this roux for 3 to 5 minutes.

2. In a separate pan, heat the soy milk. Add the hot milk slowly to the roux and whip in vigorously to make a smooth sauce. When all the milk is added and the sauce thickens, cook for a few more minutes.

VARIATION: *Bean-Style Szekely Goulash*

Replace the seitan with 1 ½ cups cooked and drained kidney beans, or try ¾ cup seitan and ¾ cup kidney beans.

HOT SEITAN SANDWICH

YIELD: 1 sandwich
TIME: 15 minutes

3 slices seitan, cut ⅛-inch thick

2 slices whole grain bread

½ cup Espagnole Sauce (page 209) or any other brown sauce, such as Mushroom Sauce (page 233)

¾ cup mashed potatoes

½ cup steamed broccoli, green beans, or asparagus; or coleslaw

¼ cup medium chopped tomatoes and scallions mixed together (optional garnish)

1. Heat the seitan in some of the cooking broth it is stored in or in ¼ inch water in pan with 2 teaspoons tamari; or steam it. Remove from heat; drain the seitan slices and pat them dry. (Make sure the seitan is dry, or it will cause the sandwich to become soggy.) Place all the seitan pieces on top of one slice of bread.

2. Place ¼ cup of sauce over the seitan. Place the other slice of bread on top. Cut the sandwich in two and place on a dinner plate.

3. Mound the potatoes next to the sandwich and the cooked vegetables beside the potatoes. Make a hollow in the center of the potatoes and pour the remaining ¼ cup sauce over the potatoes and over the vegetables, if you wish.

4. Garnish with tomato/scallion mixture. Serve warm. This sandwich is meant to be eaten with knife and fork.

HEARTY SEITAN PEPPER STEAK

To make this recipe at its best, use the Espagnole Sauce (page 209). A quick basic brown sauce works, but I recommend taking the time to make the slow-cooking sauce.

YIELD: 6 servings
TIME: 25 minutes prep and 20 minutes cooking

3 cups sliced mushrooms

2 cups diced onions

2 cloves minced garlic

¼ cup sunflower or canola oil

1 ½ teaspoons salt

4 cups flaked seitan

1 cup diced bell pepper, red or yellow

½ cup red wine

3 cups Espagnole Sauce (page 209) or other basic brown sauce

1 cup tomato puree

1 cup diced green bell peppers

1 cup flaked celery

1. Over medium heat in a skillet or saucepan that holds at least 2 ½ quarts, sauté the mushrooms, onions, and garlic in the oil. Add the salt, seitan, red bell peppers, and wine. Reduce the wine to almost nothing.

2. Add the Espagnole Sauce and tomato puree. Simmer for 15 minutes, being careful not to burn the mixture. Add the green bell peppers and celery at the very end to prevent their overcooking. Cook these vegetables for just 5 minutes. Their color will bloom and make the entrée very attractive.

3. Serve this hearty dish over rice, noodles, or mashed potatoes with a mixed-vegetable side dish.

SEITAN À LA NORMANDIE

Apples add taste and texture to seitan as they do to meat. For this dish, which is suitable for lunch or dinner, use golden apples. Red apples will work. I have served this dish many times for Thanksgiving.

YIELD: 4 servings
TIME: 20 minutes prep and 70 minutes cooking

4 (2-ounce) pieces uncooked seitan*

2 tablespoons sunflower oil or oil of choice

1 ¼ cups ice water

4 cups sliced onions

2 tablespoons minced garlic

6 tablespoons tamari

4 tablespoons apple juice concentrate

½ cup roasted pecans, ground (optional: the dish is more delicate without it)

3 medium apples, peeled, cored, and thinly sliced

2 tablespoons calvados or apple brandy of choice (or additional tablespoon apple juice concentrate)

1. About 30 minutes before baking, fry the seitan in hot oil in a sauté pan until lightly browned on both sides. Add ¼ cup of ice water to shock the seitan and cook (without lid) until water has evaporated. (Note: If you don't simmer the seitan first, you may need to add more liquid to the recipe.) Set aside.

2. In a separate smaller skillet sauté the onions and garlic in the oil until the onions are soft and translucent but not fully cooked.

3. Place the seitan in an ovenproof 2-quart baking dish and cover it with tamari, apple juice concentrate, and 1 cup water. Cover with the sautéed onion mixture.

4. Fan the apples over the onions and pour the calvados on top. Optional to sprinkle the ground pecans over it, if you wish. Cover the dish with a tight-fitting lid or aluminum foil and bake in a preheated 300°F oven for 1 hour. Serve hot.

*NOTE: This recipe requires uncooked seitan. Cut the seitan into four thin pieces (⅛ to ¼ inch thick), each about 2 ounces. The thinner the better.

New England Boiled Dinner

An example of country-style cooking, this is the New England version of the French pot-au-feu, or "pot on the fire." The key to this recipe is proper timing in cooking the vegetables. A practical way is to start by cooking those that take the longest time and adding the other vegetables in order. As each vegetable is cooked, remove it from the pot and keep it warm until needed. The time of 1 hour to prepare this meal is only if the seitan is already prepared.

YIELD: 4 servings
TIME: 25 minutes prep and 35 minutes cooking

1 cup peeled and coarsely grated carrots

2 cups thickly sliced onions

2 potatoes, halved (peeled or unpeeled)

2 cups sliced parsnips (optional)

8 slices of seitan ⅛ inch thick (or 1 pound extra-firm tofu)

8 cups water (or 4 cups seitan water and 4 cups plain water)

¼ cup minced basil (or 4 teaspoons dried basil)

½ teaspoon black pepper

2 tablespoons minced garlic

1 cup butternut squash, peeled and cut into ½-inch thick slices

1 ½ cups thinly sliced celery

4 wedges cabbage, each 2 inches wide

3 to 6 tablespoons dark barley miso (if using seitan water, use less and add to taste)

1. Cook the carrots, onions, potatoes, parsnips, and seitan in the water with the basil, pepper, and garlic. Note: If using tofu, it can be small (¼-inch dice) and added at the end of the cooking process to heat it through.

2. When the first vegetables are almost cooked, add the squash, celery, and cabbage and cook until tender-crisp. (As an alternative, stir the squash into the stew and place the cabbage and celery on top of the other ingredients.)

3. Cover the pot and let the vegetables steam briefly. Check the vegetables frequently, and remove them promptly when done.

4. Dissolve the miso into some of the stock, return to the pot, and let simmer for about 5 minutes. To thicken the stock, drain the vegetables and seitan from the stock and set aside. Put the stock over a low heat and add the dissolved arrowroot, stirring constantly to make a smooth sauce.

5. Divide seitan and vegetables evenly onto four dinner plates. Pour the sauce evenly over each serving.

Bean Entrées

In the introduction to this chapter, I suggested that perhaps carbohydrates could share the center of the plate, as they are the center of our diets when we mature. It reminded me of why I like beans. They are my favorite food aside from vegetables. Beans are like a balanced diet of protein, complex carbohydrates, dietary fiber, and fat in a capsule. If I had to choose one food to survive on for a prolonged period of time, it would be beans.

I've already mentioned that five hundred billion tons of beans are grown annually worldwide—70 pounds for each person on Earth—but I seldom, outside of soy, see them used in classical cuisine. They are a major source of protein and, soy beans aside, should have a prominent presence in vegan cuisine.

Beans were cooked into stews or porridges and often served over rice. Ethnic bean cuisine developed around this simplistic style. When Escoffier appeared on the culinary scene in the late 1800s, he moved beans from porridges to purees such as *Soissonnaise* (puree of white beans with butter and milk) and *Purée Musard*, a kidney bean-consommé purée particularly suitable for garnishing mutton. But beans still have not taken a center-plate entrée position in the classical sense to replace animal protein.

Globalization, coupled with a lack of innovative culinary applications, have contributed to beans' struggle for culinary prominence. Now, with nutrition science validating the bean, all that's needed to increase consumption is the culinary applications. Consumers would increase their consumption of beans if the dishes were innovative and relevant to twenty-first-century tastes.

Infinite best describes the potential culinary applications for beans. They are used in vegetarian soups, salads, condiments, pâtés, sauces, burgers, entrées, pastas, appetizers, and bakery and dessert products. Applications are limited only by the cook's creative imagination. Beans can stand alone as the protein. There are three options: vegetarian (simply beans), as in beans with rice or as a hummus. The second is as an inclusion with another protein (such as in a tofu pâté or meat analogue). Using beans with vegetarian meat analogues or tofu is an innovative way to build beans into entrées. Grain loaves with bean inclusions are the third option.

In addition to the following list, check out other entrées that include beans, such as Quinoa Pinto Bean Loaf (page 300), Bean-style Szekely Goulash (page 282), and Smoked Black Beans (page 313). All are tasty and nutritious.

Italian Shepherd's Pie

Shepherd's pie in any ethnic form is a traditional comfort food. Any bean/nut combination such as cannellini beans and almonds or vegan protein can be substituted for the beans in this recipe. If using rice flour in place of wheat flour, this recipe is gluten free.

YIELD: 6 to 8 servings
TIME: 30 minutes prep and 40 minutes cooking

Potato Topping

3 cups peeled and cubed potatoes

¼ cup soy milk

1 tablespoon Spinach Basil Pesto (page 232)

½ teaspoon salt

1. In a 2-quart pot, boil the potatoes in salted water to cover until soft enough to mash.

2. Drain the potatoes; place into a mixer with the soy milk, Spinach Basil Pesto, and salt. On medium speed with a paddle, blend well. Set aside until ready to use.

Italian Protein Filling

¾ cup pistachios, roasted (or almonds or cashews)

2 tablespoons olive oil

1 cup medium-diced onions

1 cup peeled, medium-diced carrots

1 cup medium-diced red bell pepper

1 cup medium-diced green bell pepper

1 cup flaked (thin-sliced) celery

2 tablespoons chopped fresh garlic

3 cups cooked garbanzo beans (or two 15.5-ounce cans, drained)

¼ cup chopped fresh basil

2 tablespoons fresh marjoram leaves

2 tablespoons fresh thyme leaves

2 teaspoons fennel powder

2 teaspoons salt

¼ cup unbleached white flour (use 6 tablespoons rice flour for gluten-free recipe)

Cilantro leaves and ground pistachios for garnish

1. Spread the pistachios on a baking sheet and roast them in a preheated 325°F oven for about 15 minutes, or until very lightly browned and fragrant. Remove the nuts immediately from the baking sheet and transfer them to a container to cool.

2. In a 3-quart pot, sauté the onions, carrots, red and green peppers, and celery in the oil over low heat for about 15 minutes. Add the garbanzo beans, garlic, basil, marjoram, thyme, fennel powder, salt, and pistachios; sauté for 2 minutes longer. Add the flour and stir until thickened. Transfer the filling to a lightly-oiled 2-quart baking dish (9 ½ x 7 ½ x 3 inches).

3. Cover mixture with the potatoes and smooth them with a rubber spatula until flat and even. Cover with foil and bake at 325°F for 30 minutes. Remove from the oven and serve hot, garnished with cilantro leaves and ground pistachios.

THAI BLACK BEAN SHIITAKE MUSHROOM DUXELLE

Duxelle (dook-SEHL) is a French stuffing mixture made from chopped mushrooms, onions or shallots, and butter. Duxelles are generally used in appetizers as a filling for items like mushrooms or for a Beef Wellington (vegan: Seitan Wellington). I believe they can be served as an entrée or center-of-the-plate protein in vegetarian cuisine or integrated into a protein like tofu as a filling. By tightening the texture, duxelles can be served in the form of a patty, loaf, or filling for acorn squash or bell peppers. Mushrooms belong in all duxelles. Beans, along with seeds or chopped nuts for texture, are the primary protein when serving a duxelle as an entrée, but an entrée version can have additional protein, unless your intent is a complex-carbohydrate entrée.

I served a 4-ounce duxelle portion with a ½-inch-thick slice of peeled and steamed butternut squash, julienned carrots sautéed in coconut oil, and baby bok choy. The complementary sauce was Basic Hollandaise Sauce (page 220).

YIELD: 4 servings (2 cups)
TIME: 20 minutes prep and 20 minutes cooking time

4 tablespoons coconut butter*

¾ cup finely diced onions or green onions

2 teaspoons fresh minced garlic

1 ½ cups finely diced fresh shiitake or button mushrooms (or 1 ½ cups rehydrated dried mushrooms for improved texture)

½ teaspoon salt

½ teaspoon ground ginger

2 tablespoons brown or white rice flour**

2 tablespoons rice vinegar

¼ cup sun-dried tomatoes in oil, drained & chopped (or plain sun-dried tomatoes)

6 tablespoons chopped fresh cilantro

½ cup chopped unsalted, dry-roasted peanuts

4 tablespoons creamy peanut butter

1 ¼ cups cooked black beans (or 15-ounce can), drained, and rinsed***

¾ cup Coconut Lemon Beurre Blanc (page 222)

1. In coconut butter sauté onions, garlic, mushrooms, salt, and ginger over medium heat for 5 to 10 minutes, or until onions are transparent.

2. Add rice flour, rice vinegar, and sun-dried tomatoes and mix together. Stir and cook for a few minutes until ingredients are well combined; remove from heat.

3. Add cilantro, peanuts, peanut butter, and black beans. Gently fold into cooked mixture with rubber spatula to keep the beans intact. Mix until blended.

4. To form the duxelles, spritz oil into a ½-cup measuring cup or line it with plastic wrap. Press the mixture to fill the measuring cup, remove onto prepared plate, and top each serving with 3 tablespoons of Coconut Lemon Beurre Blanc.

NOTE: It is best to form the duxelle while the mixture is hot. If the mixture is cold, microwave for about 1 ½ minutes. Or place on an oiled steam pan; cover with plastic wrap, aluminum foil, or an airtight lid to prevent water from diluting the duxelle; and steam for about 7 minutes.

*Coconut butter contains coconut fiber that will burn at high heat, so low to medium heat must be used. Pure coconut oil and coconut butter spread are options.

**Use 1 tablespoon each of unbleached white and gluten flour mixed together instead of the rice flour for a firmer gluten duxelle.

***Rinse to prevent discoloring the duxelle with black bean juice.

VARIATION: *Thai Spring Rolls*

The spring roll wrap technique is a simple, innovative way to upscale a duxelle presentation. Until you're used to them, spring roll skins might seem delicate to handle when either dry or wet.

YIELD: 3 servings (6 rolls)
TIME: 15 minutes to make spring rolls

6 spring roll wrappers* (8 ¼ inch diameter)
2 cups Thai Black Bean Shiitake Mushroom Duxelle

1. For each spring roll dip spring roll wrapper in water; immediately pull out and place on a wetted plate.

2. Portion ⅓ cup duxelle and form into roll about 4 inches long.

3. Place duxelle roll on edge of a wetted wrapper and wrap, folding in the ends after the first wrap around the duxelle.

4. Repeat until all spring rolls are formed.

5. In a preheated sauté or frying pan on medium heat with ½-inch oil in pan, place the spring rolls and fry until golden brown, rolling until all sides are browned.

NOTE: If not frying immediately, tightly wrap each spring roll in plastic wrap or the wrapper will dry out and begin peeling off the duxelle.

*Spring roll wrappers are available at most Asian grocery stores.

MEDITERRANEAN HUMMA-NUSHA

This unique dish is a cross between a hummus and baba ganoush. It is fusion Mediterranean, offering a refreshing new flavor combination with a textured mouthfeel.

YIELD: 3 ½ cups
TIME: 35 minutes if beans are cooked

2 cups cooked garbanzo beans
½ cup chopped roasted red bell pepper
½ cup chopped roasted or grilled eggplant
½ cup chopped fresh cilantro
¼ cup tahini
1 teaspoon minced garlic
1 tablespoon tamari (gluten-free)
¼ cup lemon juice

1. Place all ingredients in a blender or food processor and process until mixture is nearly smooth.

2. Serve as a dip, or use ¼ cup per sandwich.

PERUVIAN POT AU FEU

YIELD: 5 servings (10 ½ cups)
TIME: 35 minutes prep and 40 minutes cooking

2 tablespoons sunflower oil
1 ½ cups medium-diced onions
1 cup medium-diced red potatoes, washed, skin-on
1 cup thinly sliced leeks
1 cup flaked celery
¾ cup carrots, cut into ¼-inch-thick rounds
½ cup diced red bell peppers
1 tablespoon chopped fresh garlic
2 cups diced green cabbage
5 cups water
½ cup quinoa, rinsed and drained
2 teaspoons salt (or 2 tablespoons vegan chicken-style powder)
1 teaspoon ground cumin
1 ½ cups diced butternut squash
1 (15-ounce) can black beans, drained and rinsed
½ cup chopped parsley
½ cup chopped fresh cilantro

1. Heat the oil in a 2-gallon stockpot over medium heat. Add the onions, potatoes, leeks, celery, carrots, bell peppers, and garlic. Sauté for about 10 minutes, or until the vegetables begin to soften.

2. Add the cabbage, water, quinoa, squash, salt or broth powder, and cumin. Cook for 10 minutes, or until the squash is soft.

3. Add the black beans to the pot along with the parsley and cilantro; stir well. Heat thoroughly.

4. Ladle the hot stew into bowls and enjoy.

PERUVIAN POT AU FEU

CAJUN GUMBO

The trinity of vegetables in Cajun cuisine is onions, celery, and green peppers. This traditional southern Louisiana dish has been converted to a vegan recipe. It is delicious and decadently nutritious—the *gumbo of gumbos*. Its main ingredient is a vegan chicken-style protein. For those who love chicken, this dish will be a delightful dining experience. This Cajun Gumbo recipe has been made so many times and is so perfectly refined that there is no tweaking or modifying needed. Just follow the recipe precisely for a flawless dish.

Unlike flesh protein, which gives off moisture in the cooking process, vegan protein analogues absorb water and may need additional water to maintain a sauce consistency in the gumbo. And since the proteins are completely cooked before being added to the sauce, the cooking time is significantly less. Covering and letting the gumbo sit for 30 minutes after removing from the stovetop will allow the flavors to develop.

YIELD: 4 servings (4 cups sauce & protein)
TIME: 20 minutes prep (doesn't include protein prep time) and 35 minutes cooking

½ cup white flour

6 tablespoons canola or unrefined corn oil

1 cup medium-diced onions

1 cup medium-diced green bell pepper

½ cup flaked or finely diced celery

1 teaspoon minced garlic

1 bay leaf

¼ teaspoon salt

.5 teaspoons Cajun spice

¾ teaspoon Tabasco, optional

3 cups water

3 tablespoons vegan chicken-style broth powder

¼ cup thinly sliced green onions

2 tablespoons chopped parsley

4 ounces smoked tempeh, diced, or navy beans

4 ounces seitan, thick sliced (smoked optional), or 1 cup kidney beans

4 ounces vegetarian chicken protein analogue, diagonally diced, or smoked tofu

1. Put oil and flour in a large heavy pot. Brown flour to make a dark roux about the color of milk chocolate.

2. When roux is browned, add onions, green pepper, celery, and garlic. Keep heat on low and sauté until vegetables are soft, about 10 minutes. Stir often so that nothing sticks to the bottom of the pot. The roux will darken as the vegetables cook.

3. Add water 1 cup at a time, mixing until evenly dispersed.

4. Add proteins and all other ingredients except for green onions and parsley. Stir well. Bring to a simmer; reduce heat to low and simmer for about 30 minutes, stirring occasionally. Remove from heat; cover and let sit for 30 minutes.

5. Stir in the green onions and parsley; salt to taste and serve.

6. Serve in bowls with cooked white or brown rice in proportions of ⅓ cup rice to ⅔ cup gumbo. Don't forget to include toasted French bread with vegan garlic butter.

ITALIAN CANNELLINI BEANS WITH FENNEL GARLIC SAUCE

Any bean or appropriate vegan protein can be used in this recipe. The sauce can also be changed to Sauce Renaissance or any of the classical sauces. Different seasonal vegetables, such as an Asian mix of bok choy, snow peas, and enoki mushrooms or a mix of celery root, winter squash, and Napa cabbage, can also be used. Vegetable and bean combinations are almost endless.

YIELD: 2 servings (2 cups)
TIME: 20 minutes if sauce and beans are ready

¼ cup thinly sliced fresh fennel
¼ cup thinly sliced red bell pepper
2 teaspoons olive oil
⅛ teaspoon salt
1 cup cooked cannellini beans, drained
½ cup Italian Fennel Garlic Sauce (page 225)

Optional garnish:
¼ cup roasted pine nuts, preferred (pistachios second choice)
2 tablespoons chopped fresh parsley

1. Sauté fennel and red bell pepper over medium heat in oil with salt for about 5 minutes.

2. Add beans and sauce. Bring to a simmer.

3. Serve partially draped over polenta, pasta, or grain; garnish with nuts or parsley.

POTAGE-PURÉE SOISSONNAISE (WHITE BEAN PUREE)

The original recipe calls for salt pork. I've used liquid smoke to take the potage in the direction of a cured meat.

YIELD: 2 servings (2 cups)
TIME: 15 minutes prep and 15 minutes cooking

2 tablespoons vegan butter spread
¼ cup finely diced celery
¼ cup finely diced onions
¼ cup finely diced or shredded carrots
¼ cup thinly sliced leeks
1 bay leaf
1 ½ cups cooked & drained cannellini or white navy beans
4 teaspoons vegan chicken-style broth powder
¼ teaspoon ground black pepper
1 cup unsweetened soy milk
¼ teaspoon liquid smoke
1 tablespoon chopped parsley

1. In a 1 quart or larger saucepan, combine butter spread and celery, onions, carrots, leeks, and bay leaf. Sauté for about 10 minutes over medium heat.

2. Add beans, broth powder, black pepper, soy milk, and liquid smoke. Bring to a simmer; cover and let cook for about 10 minutes.

3. Pour mixture into blender and blend until smooth. Mix in parsley and serve.

LENTIL PÂTÉ

YIELD: Approximately 16 servings (4 cups)
TIME: 15 minutes prep and 40 minutes cooking

2 cups green lentils, dry

5 cups water

1 (4 inch) kombu strip (optional)

¼ cup finely diced celery

½ cup finely diced carrots

4 cloves garlic

½ cup finely diced onion

1 bay leaf

3 tablespoons arrowroot or cornstarch

4 tablespoons water

2 tablespoons smoked yeast (or 6 drops natural liquid hickory smoke)

1 teaspoon salt

¼ cup barley miso

¼ teaspoon ground black pepper

¼ cup vegan butter spread

1. Wash the lentils and put in a medium saucepan with the water. Add kombu, celery, garlic, carrot, onion, and bay leaf.

2. Boil, reduce heat then simmer for 30 to 35 minutes. Remove the bay leaf.

3. Pour mixture into a blender (in two batches if using a small blender); blend until smooth. Return mixture to the pan.

4. In a small bowl, mix the arrowroot, water, yeast, and salt, along with the barley miso and black pepper.

5. Add seasonings to the lentil purée; stir until well-blended. Simmer until the mixture reaches the right consistency. When the pâté detaches from the sides of the pan, remove from heat.

6. Add vegan butter spread and mix until dissolved. If the pâté seems too liquid, just add another tablespoon of arrowroot, dissolved in a tablespoon of water, to make the mixture firmer, and heat to cook starch. Turn the pâté mixture out into a lightly oiled mold or serving dish and refrigerate. You can leave pâté in the mold or unmold it onto a plate and garnish.

LENTIL PÂTÉ

PINTO BEAN NAPOLEON

This recipe is a template for many possibilities. Any of the mother sauces or different beans work in this entrée. Black beans with Béchamel Sauce is also a striking presentation with a delicate flavor profile. Note: The bean mixture must be on the viscous (thicker sauce) side so that the mixture will stack.

YIELD: 6 servings
TIME: 20 minutes prep and 40 minutes cooking (includes making Short Dough Skins)

¼ cup pine nuts or cashew pieces
18 (3 ½-inch squares) Short Dough Skins (page 339) or phyllo pastry squares, baked*
1 ½ cups cooked pinto beans, black Beluga lentils, or other bean of choice
2 tablespoons sunflower or canola oil
2 cups sliced onions
1 ½ cups peeled carrot strips
1 cup diced red bell pepper
1 cup frozen whole kernel corn
1 tablespoon minced fresh garlic
2 teaspoons dry whole savory
1 teaspoon dry whole thyme
¾ teaspoon salt
1 tablespoon unbleached white flour (optional)
1 cup Garlic Cream Sauce (page 225), Béchamel Sauce (page 204), or other sauce of choice

*Make extra Short Dough Skins or phyllo dough if recipe is made frequently. The pastry keeps for at least a month.

1. Preheat the oven to 350°F. Spread the pine nuts on a baking sheet and roast for about 5 minutes, or until light brown. Be careful not to burn. Remove the roasted nuts from the baking sheet; set aside to cool.

2. Prepare short dough skins or phyllo dough. Lay a sheet of phyllo on an oiled baking sheet. Lightly brush the top with oil, and cover with another phyllo sheet. Repeat with the process with all four sheets. Cut the phyllo into 12 pieces (3 x 4-inch-square) and bake at 350°F for about 5 minutes, or until light brown. Immediately remove from oven and transfer the phyllo squares to paper towels. (Leaving them on the hot baking sheet will cause them to burn.)

3. Heat the oil in a 12-inch sauté pan over medium heat. Add the onions, carrots, bell peppers, corn, garlic, savory, thyme, and salt. Cover and sauté, stirring occasionally, for 10 minutes, or until the vegetables are soft.

4. Add the flour toward the end of the sauté process and let it cook for about 2 to 3 minutes. This will give the bean mixture structure for stacking on the phyllo and will allow the phyllo to hold its structure.

5. Add the beans, pine nuts, and sauce to the pan; stir well. Simmer on low for 5 minutes, or until thoroughly heated.

6. To serve, lay a phyllo square on plate. Spoon ½ cup of the bean mixture onto the phyllo square and top with second phyllo square. Repeat the process, topping the stack with a third square of phyllo. Serve immediately, while the filling is hot and the pastry is crisp. Optional to garnish with parsley sprigs and chopped tomatoes.

VARIATIONS: *Seitan, Tofu, Tempeh, or Chicken-Style Napoleon*

In place of beans, substitute strips of seitan, tofu, tempeh, or chicken-style analogue.

NEW WORLD SHEPHERD'S PIE

YIELD: 8 servings
TIME: 15 minutes prep and 30 minutes cooking

Whipped Sweet Potatoes

YIELD: 4 cups

5 cups (1¾ pounds) sweet potatoes, washed and cubed (peeling optional)

¼ cup vegan butter spread or canola oil

½ cup chopped fresh parsley

1 teaspoon salt

½ cup soy milk

1. Place the sweet potatoes in a 3-quart saucepan; cover with water and add ¼ teaspoon salt. Bring to a boil and simmer over medium heat. Cook until soft, approximately 30 minutes.

2. Drain and place the cooked potatoes, oil, salt, soy milk, and parsley in a mixing bowl. Whip with electric mixer, using a paddle (preferably) on low speed for 1 minute to blend ingredients. Scrape potatoes from the sides of the bowl and mix at medium speed for another minute, or until potatoes are smooth.

New World Protein Filling

1 ½ cups quinoa

3 cups water

½ teaspoon salt

¼ tablespoons coconut or olive oil

1 cup finely diced fennel (or 1 cup celery with 1 teaspoon ground fennel)

1 cup finely diced onions

¾ cup finely diced red bell pepper

4 teaspoons minced fresh garlic

2 teaspoons dried marjoram

1 teaspoon salt

½ teaspoon cardamom

2 cups cooked black beans

¼ cup tahini (sesame butter)

½ cup pumpkin or sunflower seeds, preferably roasted

4 tablespoons white flour

4 tablespoons gluten flour

1. Place the quinoa in a medium saucepan along with the water and ½ teaspoon salt. Bring to a simmer and cook, covered, until all the water has evaporated (about 15 minutes). Set aside.

2. Heat the oil in a medium saucepan. Sauté the fennel, onions, garlic, and bell pepper, along with the salt, marjoram, and cardamom, for about 5 minutes. Stir occasionally to prevent burning.

3. Add the cooked quinoa and the pumpkin seeds, black beans, and tahini to the sautéed vegetables. Blend the ingredients. Mix the two flours together and blend into the vegetable and quinoa mixture.

4. Oil a half steam pan (11 ½ x 9 ¼ x 2 ½ inches). Press the loaf mixture evenly in pan and spread potatoes evenly over loaf mixture. Lightly oil potatoes.

5. Cover pan with lid or foil and place in preheated 350°F oven; bake for approximately 35 minutes. (The loaf should reach an internal temperature of 160°F-170°F.) Let the loaf cool for 10 minutes before serving in slices.

NOTE: The binding protein in this recipe is the combination of gluten and whole wheat flour. The nuts and seeds add texture. Notice that no water was added to the mix. Moisture in the ingredients is activating the binders. If there isn't enough moisture, the gluten cannot be activated to bind. Too much moisture and the mixture becomes stringy and mushy.

Grain, Nut, & Seed Protein Entrées

Grains can be taken to entrée status if they are combined with nuts, seeds, and beans to create a complete protein. Combined and presented as a center-plate entrée, they can deliver a satisfying culinary experience.

Nuts are higher in fat (up to 50 percent) than grains and a lighter source of protein but are also essential to the human diet. Nutrition research confirms that nuts help prevent certain chronic diseases and contribute to human longevity. When used appropriately, nuts are a game changer in both the flavor and nutritional value of a vegan entrée.

All grain loaves contain protein. The cook can build in additional protein by using beans, tofu, nuts, and seeds. The latter two add more texture and fat than protein. Does the entrée have to be protein concentrated? Or can the protein be a side dish? It can be what you want it to be. The following recipes are culinary platforms for grain entrées.

BASIC BUTTER PASTE

This was developed as a vegan egg replacement in grain loaves. It gives structure to the loaf, making it firm while hot. I use it specifically in polenta.

YIELD: 8 tablespoons
TIME: 10 minutes

2 tablespoons white flour
2 tablespoons vital gluten flour
2 tablespoons cashew butter
2 tablespoons canola oil or oil of choice

Combine the two flours. Add oil to nut butter and mix until evenly blended. Add flour to oil mixture; mix until evenly combined.

VARIATION: *Gluten-Free Butter Paste*

Ground flax meal is the best as a gluten-free option because it has strong binding qualities and is osmotic (draws moisture, which tightens loaf mixture).

2 tablespoons cashew butter or pure creamy nut butter of choice
2 tablespoons canola oil or oil of choice
4 tablespoons flax meal
1 tablespoon rice flour (white or brown), cornstarch, arrowroot, or kudzu root

Mix ingredients together until evenly dispersed.

NOTE: The gluten-free factor is significantly strengthened with flax meal, but flax meal is not as strong as vital wheat gluten flour to strengthen a grain loaf.

PECAN NUT LOAF

YIELD: 8 servings (1 loaf)
TIME: 30 minutes prep and 60 minutes cooking

2 (6 inch) pieces kombu, cooked and chopped into ½-inch pieces

2 ½ pounds tofu, extra firm, pressed dry then crumbled

1 ½ cups finely diced onions

¾ cup finely chopped parsley (or ¼ cup dry parsley)

6 tablespoons dark barley miso

½ cup whole wheat all purpose or bread flour, mixed with 3 tablespoons gluten flour

½ cup pecan meal

2 tablespoons Dijon mustard

1 tablespoon garlic powder

1 teaspoon dry whole thyme

¼ teaspoon ground black pepper

1. In a 2-quart saucepan, cook the kombu in 4 cups of water over medium heat for 20 minutes. Drain and chop the kombu. Mix all the ingredients together until blended.

2. Oil a 1-pound loaf pan and line it with parchment paper. Firmly press the tofu mixture into the pan.

3. Bake in preheated 375°F for 1 hour, or until thoroughly cooked (160°F+). Remove pan from the oven and let the loaf stand for about 10 minutes to cool slightly. Remove loaf from the pan. Slice and serve it hot.

ITALIAN PISTACHIO PILAF

YIELD: 6 servings (6 ½ cups)
TIME: 30 minutes

1 ¾ cups water

1 cup white basmati rice

½ teaspoon salt

2 tablespoons olive oil

1 cup diced onions

2 tablespoons chopped fresh garlic

2 cups seitan, thinly sliced at a 45-degree angle

1 cup diced red bell pepper

2 tablespoons fennel seed powder

1 teaspoon salt

¼ teaspoon ground black pepper (optional)

1 cup sliced scallions

½ cup chopped pistachios (optional to roast nuts)

1. In a 2-quart saucepan, bring water to a simmer over medium heat. Add the salt and rice; cover and simmer for 10 to 15 minutes, or until all water has been absorbed. Turn heat off, fluff rice with a fork, then set aside.

2. In a 10-inch frying pan, sauté onions and garlic in olive oil over medium heat until the onions are translucent. Add the seitan*, pepper, fennel seed powder, salt, and pepper; sauté for about 3 minutes.

3. Add the rice, scallions, and pistachios; mix well and serve. For a light meal, serve ½ cup of pilaf per person along with a vegetable side dish or salad. As an entrée, increase the portion to 1 cup or more, as desired.

OPTION: Substitute beans, tempeh, or tofu for the seitan to create a gluten-free meal.

BULGUR WALNUT LOAF

The binding protein is the combination of gluten and whole wheat flour. The nuts and seeds add texture. Notice that no water was added to the mix (water is only used to cook the bulgur). Moisture in the ingredients is activating the binders. If there isn't enough moisture, the gluten cannot be activated to bind. Too much moisture and the mixture becomes stringy and mushy. Serve slices of this loaf with the complementary Espagnole Sauce (page 209).

YIELD: 8 servings (1 loaf)
TIME: 30 minutes prep and 60 minutes cooking

3 cups water

1 ½ cups bulgur

1 ½ cups finely diced onions

3 cloves minced garlic

1 ½ cups peeled and shredded carrots

1 tablespoon unrefined corn oil or canola oil*

6 tablespoons barley miso

1 ¼ teaspoons powdered thyme

1 cup roasted, coarsely chopped walnuts

¼ cup roasted sunflower seeds

½ cup vital gluten flour

½ cup whole wheat or white flour

*NOTE: Unrefined corn oil will give this loaf a pleasant buttery note.

1. Bring water to boil in a medium (2-quart) saucepan. Add bulgur and let it simmer for 5 minutes, or just long enough to absorb the water in the pot. The bulgur must be cooked and dry.

2. Sauté onions, garlic, and carrots in oil until onions are translucent. Add miso and thyme and mix until miso paste is dissolved into vegetables.

3. Add walnuts and sunflower seeds; mix until evenly dispersed through vegetable mixture.

4. Mix gluten and whole wheat or white flours together until evenly dispersed.

5. Add cooked bulgur to sautéed vegetable mixture and mix into vegetables.

6. Sprinkle flour mixture over bulgur mixture; blend evenly.

7. Oil a 2-pound (approximately 1 quart) loaf pan. Press mixture into the pan. Cover and bake in preheated 350°F for 50 to 60 minutes. Cool loaf in pan for about 5 minutes. Then remove loaf from pan and cool for 30 minutes.

American Barley Loaf

Job's tears and pearl barley are interchangeable in this recipe. Job's tears is a form of barley, and I prefer it to pearl barley for taste. I only purchase Job's tears when it has multiple recipe applications on the menu.

This loaf seems time-consuming, but it's much easier to make the second time. The cilantro gives this loaf a wonderful flavor. My favorite sauce with this entrée is Espagnole (page 209) or Bigarade (page 209)

YIELD: 8 servings (1 loaf)
TIME: 45 minutes prep and 60 minutes baking

1 ¼ cups Job's tears or pearl barley

2 ¾ cups water

1 ¼ teaspoons salt

2 tablespoons corn or olive oil

1 cup whole-kernel corn

¾ cup diced onions

2 teaspoons minced garlic

¾ cup peeled, small diced carrots

5 teaspoons chopped fresh cilantro

1 teaspoon chopped fresh basil (or ½ teaspoon dried basil)

1 ¼ teaspoons salt

¼ teaspoon ground black pepper

¾ pound silken tofu, extra firm

¼ cup cornstarch or arrowroot powder

3 tablespoons agar flakes

¼ cup water

1. Mix barley, water, and ¼ teaspoon salt. Cook in a covered pot over medium heat about 30 minutes, or until barley is soft.

2. Heat the oil in a saucepan. Sauté the corn, onions, garlic, and carrots with the seasonings and the remaining 1 teaspoon salt for about 6 minutes. Remove from heat and allow the vegetables to cool slightly.

3. Add the cooked barley to the vegetable mixture and let stand. Put the tofu, arrowroot, agar flakes, and ¼ cup of water in a food processor and process until the mixture is smooth. Add tofu mixture to the vegetables and Job's tears or barley.

4. Line a large loaf pan with a baking sheet liner; oil liner. Press loaf mixture into loaf pan. Cover with aluminum foil. Bake in preheated oven (375°F) for about 50 to 60 minutes, or until internal temperature reaches 160°F.

5. Allow the loaf to cool slightly. Remove loaf from the pan, unwrap it, and cut it into 1-inch slices. Serve with a sauce of your choice.

VARIATION: *American Spinach Barley Loaf*

For a more complex, gourmet version of this recipe, one recipe of Spinach Tofu Pâté (page 252) can be lined in the pan, with barley loaf in the center, and topped with remaining pâté, covered, and baked. If using the pâté, add 2 tablespoons arrowroot to the pâté for additional firmness.

Quinoa Pinto Bean Loaf

Serve slices of this loaf with a vegetable side dish and perhaps a leafy green salad. You may also wish to serve it with a sauce, such as Classic Cuban-Style Picadillo Sauce (page 234), Classical Tomato Sauce (page 216), Velouté Sauce (page 213), or Sauce Renaissance (page 227).

YIELD: 8 servings (1 loaf)
TIME: 30 minutes prep and 45 minutes baking

1 ½ cups quinoa

3 cups water

¼ teaspoon salt

2 tablespoons olive oil

2 cups finely diced celery

½ cup finely diced fennel

1 cup finely diced onions

4 teaspoons minced fresh garlic

½ cup finely diced red bell pepper

1 teaspoon salt

2 teaspoons dried marjoram

½ teaspoon cardamom

4 tablespoons sesame seeds

1 ½ cups pinto beans, cooked

4 tablespoons tahini or almond butter

4 tablespoons whole wheat flour

4 tablespoons vital gluten flour

1. Bring quinoa, water, and salt to a simmer; cook, covered, until all the water has evaporated (about 15 minutes). Set aside.

2. Heat the oil in a medium saucepan. Sauté the celery, fennel, onions, garlic, and bell pepper along with the salt, marjoram, and cardamom for about 5 minutes. Stir occasionally to prevent burning.

3. Add the cooked quinoa and the sesame seeds, pinto beans, and tahini to the sautéed vegetables. Blend the ingredients. Mix the two flours together and blend into the vegetable and quinoa mixture.

4. Line a large loaf pan with a baking sheet liner and lightly oil the liner. (Note: In place of the baking sheet liner, you can oil and flour the pan.) Press the mixture into the pan. Bake at 375°F for about 45 minutes. (The loaf should reach an internal temperature of 180°F to 200°F.) Let the loaf cool, inverted, for 10 minutes before removing it from the pan. Serve the loaf in slices.

MILLET LOAF

You can also serve this versatile loaf for lunch or as an appetizer. Place slices on a bed of Bibb lettuce with vegetable garnishes and a light, creamy salad dressing.

YIELD: 8 servings (1 loaf)
TIME: 30 minutes prep and 1 hour baking

1 ½ cups millet

3 ¾ cups water

2 teaspoons salt (1 teaspoon for reduced sodium)

1 ½ cups peeled and finely diced carrots

1 cup finely diced celery

1 cup finely diced onions

1 clove garlic, minced

2 tablespoons extra-virgin olive or canola oil

1 ½ teaspoons dill weed

1 teaspoon dried thyme

1 cup pistachio nuts or roasted sunflower seeds (optional)

3 tablespoons white flour

3 tablespoons gluten flour

1. Rinse the millet and place in a medium saucepan with the water and ½ teaspoon salt. Cook the millet, covered, over medium heat for about 30 minutes, or until soft and all the water is absorbed. (If the grains are too moist, the loaf will not bind properly.)

2. Sauté the carrots, celery, onions, and garlic in oil for 6 minutes, or until the onions are translucent.

3. Add dill weed, thyme, and remaining 1 ½ teaspoons salt to the sautéed vegetables. Mix to evenly disperse. Add vegetables to millet; mix.

4. Mix the two flours together and add them to the millet mixture, blending well so the loaf will hold together.

5. Lightly oil and flour a large loaf pan. Press the millet mixture into the pan and bake in preheated oven at 375°F for about 1 hour. (If the millet mixture is warm when placed in the pan, reduce the baking time to about 45 minutes.)

6. Allow the loaf to cool for 30 minutes before removing it carefully from pan. To avoid breaking the loaf, you may wish to slice it in the pan.

OPEN-FACE KALAMATA OLIVE DATE RAVIOLI WITH SAUCE RENAISSANCE

This recipe won a silver medal in the 1996 International Culinary Olympics. There are many interesting options for fillings and sauces, as demonstrated by this simple but elegant recipe. The delicate sweet dates play off the salty olives and roasted nuts, giving the filling an enriched roasted lubricity. This recipe is a modern interpretation of a traditional food. Lasagna noodles are cut in half and filled with a splendid filling. Although you can use any sauce to top these "ravioli," I recommend the Sauce Renaissance (page 227). I also suggest serving them on a bed of braised fresh spinach or Napa cabbage. A thin slice of polenta complements the entrée but must be no more than a half serving.

YIELD: 2 servings
TIME: 15 to 20 minutes for filling

4 wide lasagna noodles
¼ cup pine nuts, roasted (optional to roast the nuts) or cashew pieces
½ cup whole pitted Kalamata olives
½ cup whole pitted dates
½ cup Sauce Renaissance (page 227) or sauce of choice
4 teaspoons vegan Parmesan cheese (optional)

Pinwheel Presentation

Spread filling on each half-slice portion of cooked lasagna noodle. Tightly roll into a pinwheel. Cover with plastic wrap and steam for 15 minutes. Serve with Sauce Renaissance.

1. Bring a 4-quart pot of water to a rolling boil. Add the lasagna noodles and cook according to package directions.

2. While the water is heating, roast the pine nuts in preheated 375° F oven for 5 minutes and check. If they are slightly brown they are finished. If not brown in 5 minutes, check every minute and remove when browned and pour nuts into a cold tray to stop cooking process or they could burn sitting on hot pan.

3. Place the roasted pine nuts along with the olives and dates in a food processor and process for 1 to 2 minutes, or until finely pulverized into a paste.

4. Drain the cooked lasagna noodles; blot excess water with a paper towel. Cut the noodles in half crosswise. Place 2 tablespoons of the filling mixture on the center of each, then fold the top half of the noodle over the bottom half. Fold the noodle off center to show a little of the dark filling.

5. Carefully place the ravioli on a lightly oiled steamer tray that is set over boiling water; heat for 1 or 2 minutes. (You can also heat the ravioli in a lightly oiled sauté pan over medium heat or cover them with plastic wrap and microwave for 20 to 30 seconds, or until hot.)

6. Top ravioli with sauce and serve with a sprinkling of vegan Parmesan.

Polenta Menu Options

The options or variations of the following polentas using different grain combinations (such as 75 percent corn and 25 percent quinoa), inclusions, beans, and flavors such as a Caribbean coconut polenta, are infinite. In my approach to vegetarian cuisine, I use polenta in three different styles:

Traditional Inclusion Polenta style is used as grain or side dish. Vegetable inclusions (such as confit of vegetables and/or olives) can be added to it for character and flavor. Consisting of plain cooked polenta with sautéed vegetables, it can be as exciting or plain as desired. Recipe examples in the grain side dish section are Squash Polenta with Fennel (page 184) and Sea Vegetable Polenta (page 184).

Entrée (Inclusion) Polenta is when the added bean or a plant-based protein complements the grain, making it a complete plant-based protein. The next two recipes, the Pistachio Polenta and Cannellini Bean Polenta Loaf, are examples of entrée polentas.

Tofu Infused Polenta (also the recipe title) is the third version. The tofu also makes this dish a complete protein. Additional beans and inclusions can be added to an infused tofu. It can be wrapped around another medium, like the tofu around the dressing in the Thanksgiving Day Tofu (page 260). Different nuts, seeds, or beans are added along with additional seasonings to intensify the polenta flavor and protein. You have infinite flavor options to build into the polenta, or you can use one of the sauces in the sauce section to serve the polenta as a free-standing entrée.

Pistachio Polenta

YIELD: 8 entrée servings or 16 side dish servings (8 cups)
TIME: 30 minutes prep and 30 minutes cooking

1 cup pistachio nuts, roasted
1 tablespoon extra-virgin olive oil
1 cup finely diced onions
1 cup finely diced red bell pepper
1 cup finely diced celery
1 tablespoon minced fresh garlic
1 tablespoon minced fresh basil
1 tablespoon ground fennel seed
1¼ teaspoons salt
4 cups water
2 cups yellow corn meal

1. Preheat oven to 300°F. Roast the pistachio nuts on a baking sheet in the oven for 25 minutes, or until they give off a roasted-nut scent. Remove nuts from the oven and transfer to another dish to cool.

2. Heat a 3-quart saucepan over medium heat. Pour in the oil, followed immediately by the onions, red bell peppers, celery, garlic, basil, fennel, and salt.

3. Sauté over medium heat for 8 minutes; add the water and corn meal. Cover saucepan and bring to a simmer; cook for 20 minutes, or until soft.

4. Stir in the pistachio nuts. Serve hot; or let the polenta cool until set, slice, and serve. Grilled vegetables make a good complementary side dish.

CANNELLINI BEAN POLENTA LOAF

Cannellini Polenta is a complete protein with the bean grain combination. It is an entrée that needs only a sauce and vegetable.

YIELD: 7 entrée servings or 14 side dish servings (7 cups)
TIME: 30 minutes prep and 30 minutes cooking time

2 tablespoons extra-virgin olive oil
1 cup finely diced onions
1 cup finely diced red bell pepper
1 tablespoon minced fresh garlic
¼ cup chopped fresh cilantro
1 tablespoon ground fennel seed
1 ¼ teaspoons salt
4 cups water
2 cups yellow corn meal or corn grits*
1 ½ cups cannellini beans (or dark red kidney beans for color)
½ cup pitted and chopped Kalamata olives

1. Place the oil in a 3-quart saucepan; add the onions, red bell peppers, garlic, cilantro, fennel, and salt.

2. Sauté over medium heat for 8 minutes, or until onions are transparent. Add the water and corn meal. Bring to a simmer and cook for 20 minutes, or until mixture is soft and thick.

3. Stir in the beans and olives. Transfer mixture to an oiled 2-quart loaf pan; cover and let set for 30 minutes. Slice in ½-inch or thicker slices and serve.

TOFU-INFUSED POLENTA

The following recipe is a "basic" recipe to which you add approximately ¾ cup of any combination of plant proteins (beans recommended) or sautéed vegetables. The Sauce Renaissance (page 227) would be the perfect complement to this entrée.

YIELD: 4 servings (2 ½ cups)
TIME: 30 minutes prep and 30 minutes cooking time

1 cup water
1 teaspoon agar powder
1 teaspoon salt
½ teaspoon saffron
¾ cup yellow corn meal
1 (12.3 ounces) package ounces extra firm silken tofu
2 tablespoons arrowroot powder
1 teaspoon minced fresh garlic
1 teaspoon chopped cilantro

1. For the corn polenta wrap, in a 2-quart saucepan add the water, agar, salt, and saffron. Bring the water to a boil; stir in the corn meal. Cover, reduce heat to medium, and simmer until the mixture is soft, about 10 minutes.

2. Place the tofu, arrowroot, garlic, and cilantro into a food processor; blend until smooth.

3. Add the tofu mixture to the warm polenta and mix to evenly disperse. Form into patties and fry, or loaves and steam. Serve as a vegan protein.

Quinoa Duxelle

The following recipe is a basic vegetarian entrée duxelle. It has a whole grain mouthfeel but is not significantly textured. About ¼ cup of chopped nuts or whole seeds can be added to this recipe. One-fourth cup beans can be added to boost the protein content but will not enhance the texture. Duxelle can be integrated into menus as a vegetable or crepe filling; formed into the desired shape, covered, and steamed; or shaped into a burger or steak and lightly browned in a sauté pan or under a broiler. I served this recipe with 3 tablespoons Yellow Pepper Hollandaise Sauce (page 221) per serving and Savoy Cabbage with Kale and Shiitake Mushrooms (page 192). (Napa cabbage is an option for the Savoy.)

YIELD: 3 servings (1 ½ cups)
TIME: 15 minutes prep and 20 minutes cooking time

¼ cup millet

2 tablespoons red quinoa

2 tablespoons black quinoa

2 cups water

⅛ teaspoon salt

2 tablespoons olive oil (or extra oil from sun-dried tomatoes if oil packed)

½ cup medium-dice onions

¼ cup chopped sun-dried tomatoes

1 teaspoon minced fresh garlic

1 teaspoon dried whole thyme

½ teaspoon salt

3 teaspoons rice flour*

¼ cup chopped fresh cilantro

1. Rinse millet and red and black quinoa; pour into a 1-quart saucepan with water and salt. Bring to a simmer over medium heat; cover and let simmer until grains are completely cooked (soft) and all water has evaporated, about 20 minutes. Note: The grain mixture must be dry when finished cooking.

2. In a sauté pan over medium to high heat, sauté onions, tomatoes, garlic, thyme, and salt until the onions are translucent and slightly caramelized. Add rice flour and mix into vegetables until evenly blended. Mix sautéed vegetable mixture and fresh cilantro into cooked grains until evenly dispersed.

*Use 1 ½ teaspoons each unbleached white flour and gluten flour mixed together for firmer gluten duxelles.

NOTE: An additional 1 to 2 tablespoons rice flour can be added to duxelle if mixture is too wet. You will know if it is too wet if the grains are soggy versus dry. The test is that the duxelle can be pressed into a ball if it is dry.

VARIATION: *Quinoa Duxelle with Pine Nuts & Black Beans*

YIELD: 4 servings (2 cups)
TIME: 20 minutes

¼ cup pine nuts, roasted (optional to roast)
¼ cup rehydrated, drained, and finely diced shiitake mushrooms*
1 ½ cups Quinoa Duxelle
½ cup rinsed and drained black beans
2 tablespoons rice flour**
⅛ teaspoon salt

1. Roast pine nuts (if roasting); rehydrate mushrooms.

2. Add all ingredients in any order to the duxelle. Mix sufficiently to blend evenly.

*Fresh shiitake mushrooms can be used, but they will not have the texture of rehydrated dry mushrooms.

**For a non-gluten-free option, mix together 1 tablespoon each unbleached white flour and gluten flour for firmer texture.

NUT OPTIONS: ¼ cup walnuts or pecans, chopped to about ⅛-inch pieces. Nuts can be roasted (preferred) or raw.

SEED OPTIONS: ¼ cup pumpkin, sunflower, or sesame seeds, roasted (preferred) or raw.

BEAN OPTIONS: ½ cup of any cooked bean, drained and fairly dry so as to not wet (loosen) duxelle texture.

Sandwiches (Lunch Entrées)

The sandwich, like every recipe, has a history. Named for John Montagu, Earl of Sandwich, the exact circumstances of its origin are intertwined with myth in Pierre Jean Grosley's travel book *Tour to London*. As the tale goes, Lord Sandwich, a gambler, asked his servants to bring him meat between two pieces of bread so that he would not have to leave the gaming table, allowing him to gamble through the night. Others then would order "the same as Sandwich!" N. A. M. Rodger, John Montagu's biographer, offers a less-colorful version: Lord Sandwich's commitment to the arts, politics, and navy probably left him little time to eat, causing him to order fast food (meat between two slices of bread).

This section presents a few protein sandwich options for you to build on. Using traditional sandwiches as a platform, the stage is set for you to become creative with the proteins, sauces, and condiments presented in this book.

In my opinion, burgers and wraps are sandwiches. The burger is between the halves of a bun, a form of bread. The wrap serves the same function by wrapping the protein with vegetables and condiments instead of sandwiching them. Many of the sandwiches presented below can be converted to a wrap. For other sandwiches in this book, check out the Hot Seitan Sandwich (page 283), the Tofu "Egg" Salad (page 162), and remember that any of the vegan entrée loafs (tofu, grain, or analogue) work as sandwiches.

GRILLED VEGETABLE MASALA SANDWICH

Grilled vegetables can be sandwiched between two slices of bread just as easily as meat. This is one of my favorites.

YIELD: 1 serving
TIME: 10 minutes prep time (if sauce is pre-prepared) and 15 to 20 minutes grilling

2 slices whole wheat bread, toasted
4 tablespoons Tikka Masala Sauce (page 235)
3 zucchini in ¼-inch-thick slices, grilled or sautéed
1 eggplant in ¼-inch-thick slices, grilled or sautéed
½ red bell pepper, grilled or sautéed
1 tablespoon sunflower oil for vegetables
⅛ teaspoon salt for vegetables

1. Oil and salt vegetables.

2. Use high heat to grill or sauté vegetables to quickly caramelize the outside and semi-cook the inside, giving the vegetables texture.

3. Toast bread and spread 1 tablespoon of Tikka Masala Sauce on each slice.

4. Place vegetables on bread; cover with second slice of bread or make into a wrap.

VARIATION: *Grilled Vegetable Sandwich with Smoked Black Bean Pâté*

Replace vegetables with 2 ounces of thinly sliced grilled tempeh, seitan, or chicken-style analogue. Top with Smoked Black Bean Pâté (page 313) in place of Tikka Masala Sauce.

TEMPEH MASALA SANDWICH WITH ROASTED PEPPERS

YIELD: 1 serving
TIME: 10 minutes if all cooked ingredients are already prepared

2 ounces tempeh, sliced (approximately 4 to 5 slices)
2 slices whole wheat bread, toasted
2 tablespoons Tikka Masala Sauce (page 235)
1 slice eggplant, ¼-inch thick, grilled or sautéed over medium heat
½ red bell pepper, roasted or sautéed
1 tablespoon sunflower oil for vegetables
⅛ teaspoon salt for vegetables
Oil and salt to grill the sandwich

1. Oil and salt a sauté pan and heat to medium. Brown sliced tempeh in pan and set aside.

2. Oil and salt vegetables. Use high heat to grill or sauté vegetables to quickly caramelize the outside and keep the inside semi-cooked to raw to maintain the vegetables' texture.

3. Toast bread and spread 1 tablespoon of Tikka Masala Sauce on each slice.

4. Place tempeh on bread, followed by eggplant and pepper. Cover with second slice of bread. Can be served hot or at room temperature.

PROTEIN OPTIONS: Replace vegetables with sautéed tofu or seitan.

OPTION: Smoked Black Bean Pâté (page 313) to replace Tikka Masala Sauce.

Seitan Pesto Sandwich

YIELD: 1 serving
TIME: 15 minutes

2 slices whole grain bread
3 ounces seitan in thin-sliced strips or large slices
2 tablespoons Sun-Dried Tomato Pesto (page 227)
6 arugula leaves or mâche (corn salad)
1 slice tomato

1. Press the seitan dry. Spread the pesto on one slice of the bread.

2. Lay the slices of seitan on the plain slice of bread. Lay the arugula leaves on the seitan, the tomato on the arugula, and top with the slice of bread with pesto.

3. Slice sandwich diagonally and serve with the side dish of your choice. (Note: This sandwich is best if eaten right away. The bread tends to get soggy if packed to go.)

OPTIONS: Substitute sautéed tempeh or tofu for the seitan.

Tempeh Reuben Sandwich

YIELD: 4 servings
TIME: 15 minutes prep and 10 minutes cooking

4 slices (2 ounces each) tempeh
2 tablespoons tamari
6 tablespoons canola or safflower oil
8 slices pumpernickel bread
1 cup drained sauerkraut
½ cup Thousand Island Dressing (page 154) or commercial option
4 ounces sliced vegan mozzarella cheese
¼ cup Cashew Cream (page 175)

1. Coat each piece of tempeh on both sides with tamari.

2. Heat sauté pan to medium; add 2 tablespoons oil and then the tempeh. Sauté until lightly brown; turn over. Add ¼ cup water; cover sauté pan and cook until water has evaporated (about 10 minutes).

3. Lay out 4 slices of bread. Place 2 ounces of tempeh on each slice; top with ¼ cup sauerkraut, 2 tablespoons dressing, 1 ounce cheese (or spread 1 tablespoon cashew cream or lemon cream cheese on inside of each slice bread), and second slice of bread. Gently press to compact the sandwich.

4. Using the same pan over medium heat, add remaining 2 tablespoons of oil and the 4 sandwiches. Sauté until lightly toasted. Flip the sandwiches, pouring the remaining 2 tablespoons oil in center of pan. Lightly toast the second side. Remove sandwiches from pan and cut each into triangles. Serve with salad, soup, and/or garnish.

GARBANZO BEAN BURGER

The seasoning can be modified to any ethnic flavor profile. The bean and nut/seed can also be modified to keep your menus interesting.

YIELD: 4 servings
TIME: 20 minutes prep and 15 minutes cooking

1 tablespoon olive oil

½ cup diced onions

½ cup peeled and grated carrots

1 ½ teaspoons chopped fresh garlic

1 ½ teaspoons dried cilantro

1 teaspoon cumin powder

1 teaspoon celery seed

½ teaspoon salt

½ cup walnuts (or ¾ cup chopped sunflower seeds)

1 ½ cups cooked garbanzo beans (or 1 [15 ½-ounce] can, drained)

5 tablespoons gluten flour

2 tablespoons arrowroot powder (or unbleached white flour)

4 whole grain burger buns

Canola or olive oil for sautéing burgers

1. In a 10-inch frying pan, sauté the onions, carrots, garlic, cilantro, cumin, celery seed, and salt in the oil over medium heat until the onions are transparent. Remove pan from heat; set aside.

2. Place the nuts or seeds in a food processor; process until half are broken down into a coarse meal, with the other half cracked or whole. Remove the nuts or seeds from the processor and place in a large mixing bowl.

3. Place the cooked garbanzo beans in the food processor; process the same way.

4. Add the processed beans and sautéed vegetables to the mixing bowl and mix well. Combine the gluten and arrowroot flours and add to the mixing bowl. Mix everything together well until the mixture has enough body to form a patty. If too dry or crumbly, add a small amount of water to help bind the mixture.

5. Shape the mixture into 4 burgers. Lightly oil the frying pan and pan-fry the burgers over medium heat for 3 to 4 minutes on each side until lightly browned. Remove the burgers from the pan and serve immediately on a whole grain bun with the condiments of your choice. Mushroom Confit (page 178); Rosemary, Thyme, and Sage Squash Butter (page 176); and Tikka Masala Sauce (page 235) are superb complements to this burger.

VARIATION: *Open-faced Garbanzo Bean Sandwich*

For something different, serve this sandwich open-faced by placing two bun halves or bread slices on a plate. Cut each burger in half and place each half on the bun half or bread slice. Top the burger halves with Red Wine Sauce Glaze (page 223) or the Grilled Vegetable Marinade & Citrus Dipping Sauce (page 236).

SMOKED SEITAN, LETTUCE, & TOMATO SANDWICH

YIELD: 1 serving
TIME: 10 minutes prep and 10 minutes cooking

2 tablespoons tamari
2 tablespoons water
1 teaspoon granulated garlic
3 slices smoked seitan (about 1 ounce each),
(See "Smoked Proteins" page 314)
2 tablespoons high-heat safflower oil
2 slices whole wheat bread
2 tablespoons Soy Mayonnaise (page 154) or
commercial vegan mayonnaise
2 slices tomato
2 pieces leaf lettuce

1. Mix the tamari, water, garlic, and liquid smoke together. Marinate the seitan in this mixture for a few minutes.

2. Heat the oil in a small skillet. Sauté the seitan until golden brown; drain.

3. Toast the bread and spread the soy mayonnaise on both pieces.

4. Place the seitan on one piece of bread. Add the tomato slices and lettuce leaves; top with the other slice of bread.

Variation: _Smoked Tempeh, Lettuce, & Tomato Sandwich_

Replace the seitan with an equal amount of sliced tempeh (sliced horizontally and into 2-ounce pieces). Prepare the sandwich according to the recipe.

BBQ SEITAN WITH CARAMELIZED ONIONS ON A BUN

YIELD: 6 servings (5½ cups)
TIME: 10 minutes prep and 30 minutes cooking

¼ cup canola oil
2 cups medium-diced yellow onions
1 tablespoon finely chopped or minced fresh garlic
½ teaspoon salt
1 pound, 6 ounces seitan, cooked and sliced ⅛-inch thick
2 ½ cups natural commercial smoked flavor BBQ sauce or Asian BBQ Sauce (page 235)
½ cup water

1. In a preheated sauté pan over medium-high heat, add the oil, onions, garlic, and salt.

2. Sauté, stirring occasionally, until onions are caramelized (lightly brown). Remove from heat.

3. Immediately add seitan, BBQ sauce, and water to the sauté mixture, stirring ingredients together. Return to heat, reduce heat to medium-low, and let cook for 10 minutes, or until simmering.

4. Remove from heat. Cover and let cook in ambient heat for 10 to 15 minutes. Remove from pan and serve.

NOTE: The thin-sliced seitan will immediately absorb the barbecue flavor. Because the seitan is sliced thin, it is best to minimize stirring to give it a pulled-pork effect.

CUBAN PRESSED SANDWICH

YIELD: 4 servings
TIME: 10 minutes prep and 10 minutes cooking

4 large sandwich rolls or burger buns, or
8 slices of bread
8 teaspoons Dijon mustard (or mustard
to taste)
8 tablespoons vegan cream cheese or
Coconut Lemon Cream Cheese (page
174)
16 (½-ounce) slices Bacon-Style Tempeh
(page 273), thinly sliced
16 (½-ounce) slices seitan or chicken-style
analogue
8 horizontally sliced bread & butter
pickles or dill pickle slices
4 tablespoons vegan butter spread or oil
of choice

1. Heat grill to medium heat.

2. Spread 4 slices of bread (or bun halves) with mustard and 4 with the cream cheese option. Lay strips of grilled tempeh bacon vertically and chicken or seitan horizontally on the mustard-coated bread slices. Top with two horizontally thin sliced pickles. Top with second slice of bread. Repeat for each sandwich.

3. Oil a grill or skillet and grill sandwiches top side down for 1 minute, pressing with spatula or a sanitized bacon press. Turn sandwiches over and continue pressing until golden brown. Press sandwiches with spatula several times during grilling to compact proteins. Cut in half and serve hot.

OPTION: The Smoked Black Bean Pâté (page 313) would work exceptionally well on this sandwich in place of the cream cheese for lubricity and flavor. Commercial vegan cream cheese or sliced vegan mozzarella are additional options.

Smoked Proteins & Produce Entrées

Smoking is an ancient cooking technique that both flavors and preserves food. It can also be a cooking method. There are both cold and hot smoking techniques. The technique exposes the food to smoke from burning or smoldering wood chips. Different wood chips impart different flavors. In traditional cuisine, meats, fish, poultry, and cheeses are the most common smoked foods. Vegetables are also smoked; so is beer.

Smoking is a natural preservative for vegetarian proteins. When hot smoking tofu, I can get up to a month of refrigerated shelf life as opposed to only about 10 days with an opened package of unsmoked tofu.

In vegetarian cuisine, smoking is a superb means of enhancing the flavor of bland foods like tofu and bringing vegetarian ingredients into the flavor realm of meat dishes. This section contains directions on how to smoke beans, tofu, tempeh, seitan, meat analogues, and nuts. Any wood chip, such as hickory or mesquite, can be used in the smoking process and each will create a slightly different flavor. I use a Camerons smoker, which works in both commercial and home kitchens. See the resource section in Appendix B for more information on smoking equipment and wood chips. Just about any food ingredient can be smoked at home.

SMOKED BLACK BEAN DATE PÂTÉ

Dates add a delicate sweetness to this robust-flavored pâté.

YIELD: 5 servings (1 ¼ cups)
TIME: 20 minutes

1 cup Smoked Black Beans (page 313)
¼ cup pitted and chopped dates
¼ cup roasted almond butter
1 tablespoon tamari
¼ teaspoon granulated garlic
¼ cup water

Place all ingredients in a food processor and blend until smooth.

OPTION 1: For a firmer pâté that could be cut with a knife, put beans, dates, tamari, garlic, and 2 tablespoons water in food processor. Blend until smooth and creamy. Add nut butter and process until pâté is evenly blended.

OPTION 2: For a softer pâté more like hummus, add an extra 2 tablespoons water and 2 teaspoons tamari.

MESQUITE SMOKED SEITAN RAGOÛT À LA BIGARADE

This is an excellent recipe with a subtle and delicately balanced flavor combination of sauce, vegetables, and meat. The smoke flavor is a defined back note rather than an overpowering flavor.

YIELD: 2 servings
TIME: 20 minutes prep and 25 minutes cooking

½ pound smoked seitan cutlets cut into ½-inch-thick strips
¾ cup Bigarade Sauce (page 209)
1 medium yellow beet, cooked, peeled, and diced (about ½ cup)
1 cup diced onions
¾ cup jardinière carrots (about 1 medium carrot)
¼ cup medium-diced red bell pepper
½ cup Brussels sprouts (8 sprouts, peeled and cut in half)
2 cups whipped potatoes
2 tablespoons canola oil

1. Prepare seitan, the sauce, the beet, onions, carrots, peppers, Brussels sprouts, and whipped potatoes. Set all aside.

2. In a 10-inch skillet, heat the oil over medium heat.

3. Add the onions, carrots, and bell peppers. Sauté for 7 minutes, stirring occasionally to ensure even cooking. Add the seitan, Brussels sprouts, and diced beet. Continue sautéing for another 5 minutes. Add the sauce and bring to a simmer. Serve over whipped potatoes.

SERVING SUGGESTIONS: Lightly steam collard or kale greens and chiffonade, or lightly sauté 1 ½ cups julienne of leeks. Place a bed of the cooked greens around the entrée and serve. To achieve height in the presentation, insert 5 to 10 strands or pieces of lightly sautéed (browned) raw spaghetti vertically into the potatoes at serving time.

OPTION: Add ½ cup quartered mushrooms with seitan in the second stage of sautéing.

Smoked Black Bean Pâté

Hummus is one of my favorite foods. This recipe is an example of how an ethnic recipe can be taken in another direction.

YIELD: 12 servings (3 cups)
TIME: 15 minutes prep and 15 minutes cooking/blending time (add 1 hour for smoking if beans not pre-smoked)

2 ½ cups canned black beans (or prepare and cook 1 ¼ cups dry black beans)

¼ cup hickory chips

¼ cup warm water for smoker

1 tablespoon oil

1 cup chopped onions

⅔ cup chopped mushrooms

3 cloves garlic (2 teaspoons minced)

1 teaspoon thyme

½ teaspoon salt

¼ teaspoon cumin

⅔ cup tahini (sesame butter)

⅓ cup juice from cooked beans

2 tablespoons tamari

1. Drain and rinse beans. Soak hickory chips in the smoker for 10 minutes.

2. Preheat large burner to high heat. Transfer drained beans to metal pan; place pan on rack inside smoker and close lid. Place smoker on burner and let smoke over high heat for 8 minutes; turn off heat.

3. Let smoker sit, covered, on the burner for an additional 5 minutes. Remove smoker from burner and let beans smoke, covered, for an additional 30 minutes.

4. In a 10-inch frying pan, heat oil and sauté onions, mushrooms, garlic, thyme, salt, and cumin over medium heat for 5 minutes.

5. In a food processor, combine smoked beans, sautéed vegetables, tahini, bean juice, and tamari; process until smooth. Transfer mixture to a container or mold; refrigerate until chilled. Serve pâté with bread or crackers.

Smoked Black Beans

YIELD: 6 servings (3 cups)
TIME: 15 minutes prep and 25 minutes smoking time

3 cups or 2 (15.5-ounce) cans black beans, drained and rinsed

½ cup mesquite chips

¼ cup water

1. Spread chips in bottom of smoker and spritz with ¼ cup water.

2. Spread beans on a food-grade wire (called a cross-wired cooling rack in the foodservice industry) grate, laying it on top of the smoker's grate.

3. Slide lid on the smoker and turn heat on high for about 3 to 5 minutes maximum, or until smoke seeps around lid.

4. Turn heat down to low and smoke for 30 minutes. Turn heat off and leave beans in smoker for another 30 minutes. Remove beans and store until ready to use.

SMOKED PROTEINS (TEMPEH, TOFU, SEITAN), POTATOES, TOMATOES, OR NUTS (CASHEWS OR ALMONDS)

¼ cup hickory or chips of choice

¼ cup warm water

(Choose one of the following options)

Ingredient	Instruction
1 ½ pounds tempeh (3 [8-ounce] pieces)*	**TEMPEH:** Quarter each 8-ounce piece of tempeh and place on rack in smoker. * **OPTION**: Rub 1 ½ pounds tempeh with 2 tablespoon maple syrup and sprinkle with salt.
2 pounds extra-firm tofu cut into 16 (2-ounce) pieces (8 per pound)	**TOFU:** Cut each 1-pound block into 8 pieces (1 ½ to 2 ounces each) and place on rack in smoker.
2 pounds seitan	**SEITAN:** Can be smoked in any form, but 2- to 3-ounce cutlets are preferred.
2 to 3 pounds potatoes	**MAPLE SMOKED NEW POTATOES:** Use 2 to 3 pounds small new potatoes, boiled and ¼ cup maple chips.
12 tomatoes	**OAK SMOKED TOMATOES:** Use 12 medium large plum tomatoes and ¼ cup oak chips.
2 cups whole cashews (266 grams) *or* 2 cups whole almonds, blanched or skin on (288 grams)	**NUTS:** Place a wire rack on the smoking rack. Spread nuts evenly on the rack.

1. Soak chips in smoker for 10 minutes. Preheat one large or two small electric burners to high heat.

2. Place tempeh, tofu, seitan, potatoes, or tomatoes on a rack in smoker. Close lid and place smoker on burner to smoke for 8 minutes over medium-high heat. (Note: When smoking nuts, you will need a fine wire mesh or perforated piece of aluminum laid on the rack. Pour the nuts onto the aluminum foil.)

3. Turn heat off and let covered smoker sit on the burner for an additional 30 minutes.

4. Remove smoker from burner and let food smoke, covered, for an additional 30 minutes.

NOTE: A 10-minute smoke on high heat plus 30 minutes smoking off the heat is a "soft smoke." A "hard smoke" is a 20- to 30-minute smoke on medium heat plus 45 minutes smoking off the heat.

Chapter Twelve

VEGAN PASTRIES &
DESSERTS

Pastries and desserts are an integral part of every menu, dating back to prehistoric times when early humans made sweet foods using maple or birch syrup, honey, fruits, and seeds.

Making pancakes is believed to have started in the Neolithic Age with the idea of cooking a cereal paste on a stone in the sun. Greek pastries have records dating back to the fourth and fifth century BCE. The ancient Mediterranean paper thin multi-layered Baklava made with filo dough was embraced by the crusaders. Medieval Europe quickly adopted it. French and Italian Renaissance chefs went on to perfect puff pastry and *pâté à choux*. In the seventeenth and eighteenth centuries, chefs introduced brioche, Napoleons, and cream puffs. Antonin Carême was a leader in the renaissance of French pastry. Sweet yeast breads and cakes shared a parallel evolution in this evolution of pastries.

Often when I would dine out in upscale or fine dining, the general dessert of choice was a variety of fruit sorbets, fresh fruit, or after-dinner liqueurs. Vegan desserts don't have to be baked or complicated, calling for a number of specialty ingredients as found in some of the following recipes. Vegan recipes can be as simple or complicated as you wish. I like working with whole grains in desserts and prefer modestly sweetened desserts.

Bakery speed scratch pre-blended mixes combined with advanced pastry and bakery equipment have improved the ease of preparing pastry in both the professional pastry shop and domestic kitchen. And vegan desserts, which are generally perceived as hard to produce, requiring numerous specialty ingredients and techniques, can actually be easier to produce. Two examples are crème patisserie (pastry cream) and ice cream. For the traditional crème patisserie, the milk and sugar have to be heated in a steam kettle. The eggs and starch have to be blended with milk. The mixture is gradually whipped into the hot milk mixture. In the vegan version, all of the ingredients are blended in a blender until smooth and heated in a sauce pan while the mixture is gently whipped until it thickens.

Making vegan ice cream is as easy as blending all ingredients until smooth and creamy, freeze and serve. And I have achieved a twenty percent overrun in the ice cream's yield. The blender is whipping air into the ice cream mixture. Overrun is the amount of air whipped into ice cream. Example: with four cups of solid ice cream mixture, when whipped in a blender or put into an ice cream machine, at 20-percent overrun, you would have five cups of ice cream.

Vegan pastries are made with the same core ingredients used in conventional pastries but without eggs and dairy. If vegan pastries have too many ingredients and techniques, I suggest that they were made by a passionate and wild artist who doesn't understand the disciplines of culinary art. On the vegan ingredient side, make sure the sugar is bone char free. From the health side, avoid trans fats and artificial ingredients.

There are many vegan fruit desserts, sorbets, and fruit pies made with vegan crusts (substituting a vegan butter spread or trans fat-free shortening). The focus here is on preparing vegan desserts from classical and modern desserts that traditionally use dairy and eggs. That is the challenge in mastering vegan pastries. It is the pastry creams, tortes, and cakes that are challenging to convert to vegan.

An essential component of vegan desserts should be fruit desserts. Some are listed here. They should be abundant in pastry offerings as they are nutrient-dense whole, and naturally sweet, foods. Combined with the modest use of sugar and abundant use of whole grains, your pastries will be equal in health and decadency. The consumer wants to enjoy a decadent dessert but they also want it to be healthy. Decadent health is popular amongst healthy dining consumers and the following pastries, subjectively speaking, offer both.

Desserts help us relax. "Stressed" spelled backward (or reversed) is "Desserts." Desserts do leave fond memories on the human psyche.

Strawberry Kanten Cake
with Raspberry Sabayon Sauce

PASTRY CREAM

Vanilla Pastry Cream

   Variation: Diabetic Pastry Cream

   Variation: Nut Milk Pastry Cream

Diabetic Coconut Custard

Vanilla Pudding

Chocolate Pudding

Amaretto Rice Pudding

Peanut Butter Mousse

Lemon Crème Anglaise

   Variation: Lemon Crepe Filling #1

   Variation: Diabetic Lemon Crème Anglaise

DESSERT SAUCES

Raspberry Sabayon Sauce

Lemon Cream Sauce

Lemon Crepe Filling #2 and #3

Stout Sabayon Sauce

Raspberry Coulis

ICINGS

Basic Vanilla Buttercream Icing

   Variation: Lemon Buttercream Icing

   Variation: Chocolate Buttercream Icing

   Variation: Peanut Buttercream Icing

German Chocolate Cake Icing

Chocolate Ganache Icing

COOKIES

Florentine Cookies

   Variation: Chocolate Filling

   Variation: Sandwich Cookies

   Variation: Chocolate Decoration

Golden Macaroons

Whole Wheat Gingersnap Cookies

Almond Crisp Cookies

Chocolate Chip Almond Biscottini di Prato

Chocolate Chip Cookies

   Variation: Coconut Chocolate Chip Cookies

   Variation: Walnut Chocolate Chip Cookies

Sugar Dough

Fig Bars

   Variation: Sweet Fig Bars

   Variation: Dried Fruit Options

Dream Bars

Hippen Masse

CRUSTS, CREPES, & SHORT DOUGH SKINS

Gluten-Free Crust

Basic Pie Crust

Vegan Crepes

   Variation: Dessert Crepes

Crepes Suzette

   Variation: Tropical Crepes

Short Dough Skins

   Variation: Cannoleon

ICE CREAM, SORBETS, & REFRIGERATED DESSERTS

Chocolate Coconut Ice Cream

Vanilla Coconut Ice Cream

Vanilla Soy Ice Cream

Avocado Lemon Ice Cream

Variation: Avocado Lime Ice Cream

Variation: Avocado Mint Ice Cream

Banana Ice Cream

Mango Sorbet

Peanut Butter Ice Cream

Cranberry Sorbet

Variation: Elderberry Sorbet

Variation: Blueberry Sorbet

Dutch Apple Custard

Coconut Whipped Cream Topping

Dutch Honey

Poached Peaches in Simple Syrup

Poached Pears with Raspberry Sabayon Sauce

CONFECTIONS (OHAGI)

Sweet White Rice Balls

Cinnamon Raisin Ohagi

Coconut Date Ohagi

Variation: Chocolate Coated Coconut Date Ohagi

Candied Ginger-Cranberry Sweet Rice Balls

Anko (Sweet Bean Paste) filled Ohagi

TORTES, CAKES, BROWNIES, PIES, & SPECIAL OCCASION DESSERTS

Swiss Burnt-Pecan Torte

Variation: Almond Coconut Torte

Lime Torte

Pear Torte

Polynesian Crisp

Dry Cooked Apple Pear Winter Compote

Nancy's Peach Pie

Variation: Peach Rhubarb Pie

Variation: Peach Blueberry Pie

Chocolate Cake

Variation: Carob Cake

Variation: Cupcakes

Variation: "Ice Cream" Cake"

Apple Kanten Cake

White Cake

Variation: Yellow Cake

Chocolate Fudge Brownie

Mince "Wheat Meat" Pie

Jamaican Floating Isle

Lemon Cheesecake with Raspberry Coulis

Variation: Vanilla Cheesecake

Chocolate Cheesecake

Variation: Chocolate Fudge Cream Filling

Strawberry-Lemon Napoleon

Streusel Topped Fresh Mango Pie

Pastry Cream

Traditional pastry cream, or crème patisserie, is a thick custard made with milk, eggs, sugar, cornstarch (or a mixture of flour and cornstarch), and flavoring. Thickening a mixture of milk and eggs with heat is an integral part of French cuisine. Egg custards baked in pastry (custard tarts) were very popular in the Middle Ages, and from whence came the English term "custard." These "basic" custards became the ingredient platform for developing a number of recipes. Pastry cream is the foundation to create a variety of desserts or recipe applications. Whether cooking in a professional kitchen or at home, cooking efficiently is essential. Time is a precious commodity.

Pastry cream is every pastry chef's staple, used to make mousses, pie fillings, cream sauces, and any number of cakes, tarts or pastries. Vanilla is the most popular flavor for pastry cream but any dessert-type flavor or liqueur, chocolate, or fruit puree can be used.

Traditionally made by bringing the milk almost to a boil, then tempering a mixture of eggs, sugar, and cornstarch with the hot milk, the vegan version is easier since no eggs need tempering. After blending, the mixture is cooked on the stovetop, stirred constantly, over a low heat until thickened. Agar is used along with cornstarch or arrowroot starch in place of eggs to create a custard texture; the tempering isn't necessary.

Pastry cream is the dessert equivalent of the mother sauces. It can be made in advance and used in a variety of dessert applications. Because it is so simple to prepare, it can also be produced as needed. It is the building block or foundation to making pudding, mousses, dessert cream sauces, and pie fillings in classical French cuisine.

To make a pudding from pastry cream requires two things. One is the thinning out of the pastry cream to the texture of a pudding by adding more soy milk or nut milk of choice. Second is the addition of a flavor. Pudding options are infinite and included are recipes for vanilla, chocolate, and amaretto rice puddings.

When I became a vegan in 1976, honey wasn't a vegan issue on my radar. If it was, I wasn't aware of it. Since then, I have pulled it from my recipes. A better replacement is agave syrup which has a better glycemic index reading and simple syrup which you can make in your kitchen. I resist using brown sugar, Sucanat or maple syrup in a recipe unless the flavor profile is an essential part of the recipe. My experience is that too often an alternative sweetener's flavor runs interference with the dessert's delicate flavor, especially with fruits.

When working with vegan cream-type desserts, the challenge lies in not having any "off" flavors. For example, the cashew milk created in the blending process will neutralize the soy milk. Pastry cream is essentially an equivalent of a very thick pudding, giving it a wide variety of recipe application from pie fillings and puddings to mousses and dessert sauces.

VANILLA PASTRY CREAM

This is an exceptional pastry cream for vegans in terms of color, texture, and delicate flavor. It does not have the Parisian cuisine flair of butter, eggs and cream but it has a flavor which is the perfect building block for some incredible desserts.

YIELD: 3 cups
TIME: 10 minutes prep and 10 to 15 minutes cooking

2 cups unsweetened soy milk

¾ cup water

¼ cup cashews whole or large pieces

6 tablespoons white sugar

¼ teaspoon agar powder

¹⁄₁₆ teaspoon annatto powder

6 tablespoons cornstarch

1 teaspoon vanilla extract

¼ teaspoon salt

1. Starting with the liquids, pour the soy milk, water, cashews, sugar, agar powder, annatto powder, cornstarch, vanilla, and salt into the blender on high speed until the cashews are dissolved into the liquid. When the mixture is sufficiently blended, rub the liquid between your thumb and index finger; it will be smooth (no grit).

2. Pour into a 2-quart sauce pan and place on medium heat and constantly stir about 6 to 7 minutes or until pastry cream thickens. Store in a covered container and refrigerate until ready to use.

VARIATION: *Diabetic Pastry Cream*

Replace 6 tablespoons sugar with ½ teaspoon powdered stevia.

VARIATION: *Nut Milk Pastry Cream*

This is both gluten free and soy free if using soy-free butter spread.

YIELD: 2 ¼ cups
TIME: 10 minutes prep and 10 to 15 minutes cooking

2 cups water

¼ cup almonds, blanched

¼ cup cashews, whole or large pieces

6 tablespoons white sugar

¼ teaspoon agar powder

¹⁄₁₆ teaspoon annatto powder

¼ cup cornstarch

1 teaspoon vanilla extract

⅛ teaspoon salt

2 tablespoons vegan butter spread

1. Place water, almonds, cashews, sugar, agar powder, annatto powder, cornstarch, vanilla extract, and salt in blender and blend until smooth on high speed until there is no grit when nut milk is rubbed between your thumb and index finger.

2. Transfer to a 1- to 2-quart sauce pan and bring to a simmer while constantly stirring with a whip.

3. Bring to a simmer, remove from heat and mix in cold butter spread. The butter spread moves the pastry cream closer to a dairy flavor and smooths out the nut flavor. Using two different nuts helps neutralize a specific nut flavor. As a basic mix, it is the final application that determines the flavor.

DIABETIC COCONUT CUSTARD

For this recipe, I have coated fresh pineapple slices with coconut flour and lightly browned them in coconut oil. This custard has been served with fresh strawberries tossed with a dash of lemon juice and diabetic sugar (such as stevia).

YIELD: 8 servings (2 cups pudding)
TIME: 10 minutes

2 cups Diabetic Pastry Cream (page 321)
¼ cup coconut, minced, toasted
½ teaspoon coconut extract
½ teaspoon vanilla extract
⅛ teaspoon agar powder

1. Mix all ingredients together and heat in a double boiler until about 120°F.

2. Portion into ¼ cup lightly oiled molds (ramekins), cover, and refrigerate.

VANILLA PUDDING

YIELD: 1 ½ cups (3 half cup servings)
TIME: 10 minutes

1 cup Vanilla Pastry Cream (page 321)
½ cup soy milk (unsweetened)
1 teaspoon vanilla extract or flavor of choice

Pour all ingredients into a mixing bowl and mix until smooth.

CHOCOLATE PUDDING

YIELD: 1 ½ cups (3 half cup servings)
TIME: 10 minutes

1 ½ cup Vanilla Pastry Cream (page 321)
½ cup soy milk (unsweetened)
¼ cup cocoa powder
¼ cup powdered sugar
2 tablespoons water
2 teaspoons vanilla extract or flavor of choice

Pour all ingredients into a mixing bowl starting with wet ingredients and mix until smooth.

AMARETTO RICE PUDDING

YIELD: 2 cups (4 half cup servings)
TIME: 10 minutes

1 ½ cups soft cooked white rice
1 cup Vanilla Pastry Cream (page 321)
4 teaspoons vegan butter spread
¼ cup sugar
1 teaspoon vanilla extract
¼ cup almonds, roasted, chopped
4 teaspoons amaretto

1. Cook rice and set aside.

2. Measure all ingredients into a mixing bowl with a paddle, or heavy whip by hand. Mix all ingredients until evenly dispersed.

Peanut Butter Mousse

YIELD: 6 servings (3 cups)
TIME: 15 minutes

1 cup Rich's Whip Topping*
¼ cup cold water
¼ cup sugar
¼ cup peanut butter, creamy, salted
½ cup Vanilla Pastry Cream (page 321)
1 teaspoon vanilla extract

1. In a cold mixing bowl whip topping until it forms stiff peaks.

2. In a separate bowl mix water, sugar, peanut butter, pastry cream and vanilla together until evenly combined (creamy and smooth).

3. Gently fold whipping cream into peanut butter mixture. Refrigerate until ready to serve.

* This commercial topping is available in both vegan and nonvegan varieties. See resource section (page 390) for more information on commercial vegan whipped toppings in both retail and foodservice.

Lemon Crème Anglaise

The primary traditional ingredients in this dessert sauce are sugar, egg yolks, and wine which are whipped together and heated to create a rich sauce. In the vegan version I use the pastry cream thinned to consistency of heavy cream. It has the equivalent of the egg yolks in the starch and agar, a delicate lemon flavored cream sauce with the perfect drape and hue.

YIELD: 3 servings (¾ cup)
TIME: 10 minutes

½ cup Vanilla Pastry Cream
2 teaspoons lemon flavor extract
¼ cup soy milk (plain or vanilla)
2 tablespoons sugar

Place all ingredients into a bowl and whip with a wire whip until smooth and creamy.

VARIATION: *Lemon Crepe Filling #1*

Eliminate soy milk and proceed with recipe. Prepare Crepes (page 337) and serve.

VARIATION: *Diabetic Lemon Cream Anglaise*

Use Diabetic Pastry Cream (page 321). Follow instructions for Lemon Crème Anglaise and leave out the sugar.

Dessert Sauces

Silken tofu replaces vanilla pastry cream in several dessert sauces, an easier option when making a small amount of a recipe, while my favorite fruit sauce, Raspberry Coulis, is useful for many vegan dessert applications.

RASPBERRY SABAYON SAUCE

YIELD: 1 ¼ cups sauce
TIME: 15 minutes

½ cup firm silken tofu
½ cup fresh raspberries, pureed
3 tablespoons agave syrup or 3 tablespoons sugar
¼ teaspoon lemon juice
3 tablespoons rum

1. Blend the tofu with the raspberries until smooth.

2. Transfer to a small saucepan and place over a low heat.

3. Whip the agave syrup, lemon juice, and rum into the tofu mixture and keep warm until ready to use.

LEMON CREAM SAUCE

This sauce is closer to the traditional *Crème Anglaise* with tofu similar to the cooked egg yolk that emulsifies the sauce. Any flavor can be used in place of lemon. Tofu absorbs a great deal of flavor. Don't hesitate to use liberal amounts of flavor to reach the desired flavor profile.

YIELD: 7 servings, ¼ cup each (1¾ cups sauce)
TIME: 10 minutes

12.3 ounce package extra firm silken tofu
½ cup sugar
¼ cup canola oil
¹⁄₁₆ teaspoon annatto
¼ cup water (add ⅛ to ¼ cup additional water for thinner sauce)
1 tablespoon lemon extract (or less depending on strength of flavor) or ¼ cup lemon zest

Place tofu, sugar, oil, annatto, water, and lemon extract into blender and blend until smooth and creamy.

LEMON CREPE FILLING #2

YIELD: 3 servings (1 ½ cups filling)
TIME: 10 minutes

12.3 ounce package extra firm silken tofu

½ cup sugar

2 tablespoons oil (canola oil or warm butter spread)

1/16 teaspoon annatto

1 tablespoon lemon flavor or ¼ cup lemon zest

2 tablespoons cashew, macadamia, or pine nuts (optional for a firmer filling)

Pour all ingredients into blender and blend until smooth and creamy.

Poached Pear with Crepe
and Raspberry Sabayon Sauce

LEMON CREPE FILLING #3

With agar, cornstarch, and squash, this silken tofu lemon filling has more substance.

YIELD: 4 servings (1¾ cup filling) for 8 crepes with 3.5 tablespoons filling per crepe
TIME: 10 minutes prep and 10 minutes cooking

1 teaspoon agar powder

¾ cup water

2 tablespoons cooked butternut squash, pureed (optional)

6 ounces (half package) extra firm silken tofu

6 tablespoons sugar

2 tablespoons cornstarch

1 teaspoon lemon extract

8 drops of yellow food color (optional for presentation)

8 Vegan Crepes (page 337)

1. Mix the agar and water together.

2. Peel and steam the butternut squash (if using it).

3. Place agar-water mixture, squash, tofu, sugar, cornstarch, lemon extract, and yellow food coloring into a blender. Blend on medium speed until the mixture is smooth.

4. Place the mixture in a one quart sauce pan on medium heat and stir while cooking for a smooth and even cooking of the filling. When it begins to simmer, remove from the heat, cover, and let cool.

NOTE: This filling will have a firm set when cool, so place it in the desired mold while warm to develop the desired shape or roll it into crepes.

STOUT SABAYON SAUCE

Zabaione (also called *sabayon* in French) is an Italian dessert sauce made with egg yolks, sugar, and a Marsala wine beaten together over heat until thick; served either hot or cold. The sauce is similar to a sweet Hollandaise Sauce only with more sugar and significantly less fat. It is usually served with strawberry, blueberry, or peach crepes, and could be used in the modern interpretation of the Napoleon. I use sabayon as a dessert version of a Hollandaise Sauce. In this recipe I use a beer and brown sugar reduction with silken tofu which takes the place of cooked egg yolks in a sauce.

YIELD: 8 servings (2 cups sauce)
TIME: 5 minutes

1 cup brown sugar

1 cup stout beer

12 ounces extra firm silken tofu

¼ cup oil

2 teaspoons vanilla extract

Mix brown sugar and stout beer. Cook down to 1 cup and measure for accuracy. Pour all ingredients into blender and blend until smooth. Serve or refrigerate for future use.

RASPBERRY COULIS

YIELD: 6 servings (1 ½ cups)
TIME: 15 minutes

3 cups raspberries, fresh or frozen

1 cup sugar

2 teaspoon lemon juice

¼ cup water

1. Crush the raspberries in sugar in a one quart sauce pan. If frozen, thaw in bowl with sugar.

2. Add lemon juice and bring to a simmer. Cook for about 5 minutes to reduce the mixture to 75 percent of its original volume.

3. Strain while hot and immediately place the remaining pulp back in same cooking pot, adding ¼ cup water. Mix and strain into the existing strained coulis, with ratio of ¼ cup water to 2 cups fruit pulp. (There is no exact ratio of water to pulp. The water is added to extract additional flavor from the pulp.)

4. Add lemon juice, bring to a simmer, store and refrigerate until ready.

OPTION: to use Kirschwasser, a sour cherry brandy, in place of lemon juice or to add 2 teaspoons of lemon juice at the end of the cooking to bring out the fruit flavor. I prefer lemon juice because it brings out the berry flavor.

Icings

A wide variety of different icings are used for specific recipe pastry applications. Dairy is more predominant in icing than eggs, used in specific icings like French buttercream consisting of egg whites, simple syrup, and butter. Icings include traditional buttercreams, ganaches, fondants, and topping icings such as German Chocolate Cake Icing, similar to a butter cream icing with pastry cream, coconut and pecans. The key to working with vegan icings is to refrain from excessive sugar, trans fats, and artificial colors as much as possible. Vegetarian cuisine is driven by many values of which one is health.

BASIC VANILLA BUTTERCREAM ICING

This adjustable recipe (sweetness and texture) is the perfect consistency for spreading and decorating.

YIELD: 2 ¾ cups
TIME: 15 minutes

½ cup palm or solid vegetable shortening
½ cup vegan butter spread
2 teaspoons vanilla extract
4 cups sifted confectioner's sugar
(approximately 1 pound)
2 tablespoons soy milk or water

1. In large bowl with a paddle, cream shortening and butter spread on medium speed until blended (about 1 minute).

2. On low speed add vanilla and one cup of sugar. Mix to integrate, add another cup of sugar, and mix continuing until all sugar is evenly dispersed into the shortening. Scrape sides and bottom of bowl.

3. Add milk and beat at medium speed until light and fluffy. Keep bowl covered with a damp cloth until ready to use.

VARIATIONS

Lemon Buttercream Icing

1 tablespoon lemon extract*
2 ¾ cups Basic Vanilla Buttercream Icing

Add together and whip with paddle until evenly dispersed.

*Lemon extract varies in intensity and one tablespoon is a medium from which you can reduce or add more flavor.

Chocolate Buttercream Icing

½ cup cocoa powder
2 tablespoons soy milk
Up to ⅓ cup sugar
2 teaspoons vanilla extract
2 ¾ cups Basic Vanilla Buttercream Icing

Add together and whip with paddle until evenly dispersed.

Peanut Buttercream Icing

¼ cup creamy peanut butter
1 tablespoon vanilla extract
2 ¾ cups Basic Vanilla Buttercream Icing

Add together and whip with paddle until evenly dispersed.

German Chocolate Cake Icing

YIELD: 2 ½ cups
TIME: 15 to 20 minutes

¾ cup pecans, chopped, (roasted optional to enhance flavor)

¾ cup sweetened coconut, shredded, (toasted optional)

1 ½ cups Vanilla Pastry Cream (page 321)

½ cup sugar

1 tablespoon vanilla extract

½ cup palm shortening, or vegan butter spread

1. Roast pecans and toast coconut first, if desired. This option gives the icing a traditional intense flavor.

2. Pour pastry cream, sugar, and vanilla in mixing bowl with paddle. Mix on slow speed for about two minutes to evenly mix the ingredients.

3. Add shortening and mix until the shortening is completely integrated with the other ingredients.

4. Finally, add pecans and shredded coconut. Mix until ingredients are evenly dispersed in a mixing bowl or mixer with a paddle on medium speed. Use immediately or refrigerate.

Chocolate Ganache Icing

This vegan version is just as rich as a heavy cream ganache but without the dairy flavor (See Vegan Pastry Techniques, page 138).

YIELD: 1 ½ cups icing
TIME: 10 minutes

1 tablespoon palm shortening or vegan butter spread (optional for a richer flavor)

½ cup soy milk

1 ½ cups bittersweet chocolate chips

1 teaspoon vanilla extract

1. Place the vegan butter and soy milk in a 2-quart saucepan over medium heat, or in a double boiler set over boiling water.

2. Heat thoroughly, and add the chocolate chips. Stir gently or until the chips have melted and the sauce is well-blended with the consistency of thick cream.

3. To use as a cake glaze, pour the warm ganache over a cake that is placed on a wire rack and set over a baking sheet. Spread the ganache with a spatula. It will run down the sides of the cake and onto the baking sheet.

4. If not using immediately, transfer the ganache to a covered container and refrigerate, where it will keep for about 3 weeks. Reheat in a double boiler before using.

Cookies

Cookies have a rich history, and their variety is just as rich. This book taps into that history ever so briefly in both classical cookies like Florentine, Biscottini, Hippen Masse, and Sugar Dough. It also addresses traditional American cookies like the chocolate chip cookies and cookie and fig bars. Finally, it contains a few natural foods cookie recipes such as the Almond Crisp. One of my favorite cookies in the natural foods category is the Golden Macaroon, which has a heavy texture lightened up by coconut. It has a wonderful combination of coconut, almond, and orange flavors with a mild sweetener. The cookie looks like a macaroon when baked but is denser with a rich flavor and nutritional value.

FLORENTINE COOKIES

YIELD: 24 wafers (2 ¾ inch), 1 tablespoon cookie dough (1 ½ cups)
TIME: 20 minutes prep time and 13 minutes baking

1 ⅛ cups almond meal (whole almonds ground in spice or coffee grinder), about 2 ½ ounces
3 tablespoons all-purpose flour
1 tablespoon grated orange zest (½ medium orange)
⅛ teaspoon salt
6 tablespoons sugar
1 tablespoon Cashew Cream (page 175)
1 tablespoons light corn syrup or rice syrup
2 tablespoons vegan butter spread
¼ teaspoon pure vanilla extract
Chocolate topping (optional)
2 ounces semisweet dairy-free chocolate, chopped (2 ounces more if using as filling)

1. Position a rack in the center of the oven and preheat to 350°F. Line a baking sheet with a silicone baking mat or parchment paper.

2. Pulse the almonds in a food processor or coffee grinder until it has a mealy texture but not pasty. Stir together the nuts, flour, zest and salt in a large bowl.

3. Put the sugar, cream, corn syrup and butter spread in a small sauce pan. Cook over medium heat (1 to 2 minutes), stirring occasionally, until mixture is warm and butter spread has melted.

4. Remove from heat and stir in the vanilla, then pour mixture into almond mixture and stir just to combine. Set aside until cool enough to handle (15 minutes).

5. Scoop rounded tablespoons (for 3-inch cookies) or 2 tablespoons (for 6-inch cookies) of batter and roll into balls. Place on prepared baking sheet, leaving about 3 to 4 inches between each cookie since they spread.

6. Bake 1 pan of cookies at a time. Rotate the pan halfway through baking time. These cookies should be thin and an even golden brown color throughout when done.

7. Cool on baking sheet for 5 minutes, then transfer cookies to racks to cool. Serve when cool.

FLORENTINE COOKIE VARIATIONS

VARIATION: *Chocolate Filling*

1. Put the chocolate in a medium microwave-safe bowl. Heat for 30 seconds and check.

2. Continue in 10-second intervals until chocolate melts. Melting temperature is 88°F. Go light on heat. Stir, and continue heat until completely melted, about 1 to 2 minutes more.

3. Alternative is bain-marie or putting chocolate in a small heatproof bowl. Pour water in sauce pan that a bowl will sit on (bowl must not touch water).

4. Bring water to a low simmer, but not touching, the water. Stir the chocolate occasionally until melted and smooth.

VARIATION: *Sandwich Cookies*

Drop about ½ teaspoon melted Chocolate Filling onto on the flat side of half of the cookies and press together with remaining halves. Return to rack and let chocolate set.

VARIATION: *Chocolate Decoration*

Drizzle melted chocolate over Florentines to gives this plain but elegant cookie a little more eye appeal.

STORAGE: These cookies will stick over time if not stored properly in an airtight container with parchment, wax paper, or plastic wrap between them.

GOLDEN MACAROONS

YIELD: 48 cookies (24 servings)
TIME: 25 minutes prep and 15 to 20 minutes baking

2 cups sweetened coconut, grated, lightly toasted

2 cups carrots, finely grated

½ cup sunflower seeds, toasted

½ cup brown rice flour

1 ¼ cups brown rice syrup

¼ cup oil, unrefined corn or warm butter spread

½ orange rind, grated

½ orange, juiced

1 teaspoon almond extract

Glaze

2 tablespoons barley malt syrup

1 tablespoon water

1. Preheat the oven to 325°F.

2. Mix coconut, carrots, sunflower seed, and brown rice flour ingredients together in a bowl and set them aside.

3. Combine rice syrup, oil, orange rind, orange juice, and almond extract. Add to the first mixture and blend well.

4. Measure in 2 tablespoon units, form the dough into mounds, and place them on a lightly-oiled baking sheet. Bake the cookies in the preheated oven for 15 to 20 minutes.

5. Prepare the glaze by mixing the barley malt syrup with the water in a small bowl.

6. After 10 to 15 minutes in oven, the macaroons can be brushed with the glaze to give them a light golden brown color and shine (do not glaze the cookies at the beginning of the baking period or they will burn). When the macaroons are done, remove them from the oven and transfer them to a cookie rack to cool. Serve or store until ready to serve.

Whole Wheat Gingersnap Cookies

YIELD: 2 dozen cookies
TIME: 15 minutes prep and 12 to 15 minutes baking

¾ cup sugar

½ cup canola oil

1 cup all-purpose flour

¾ cup whole wheat pastry flour

3 teaspoons ginger powder

¼ teaspoon nutmeg

½ teaspoon baking soda

½ teaspoon salt

¼ cup blackstrap molasses (or regular molasses)

3 tablespoons water

½ teaspoon vanilla extract

1. Preheat oven to 350°F. Line with parchment paper or lightly grease two baking sheets.

2. In a large bowl, evenly mix sugar with oil. Add the two flours, ginger, nutmeg, baking soda, and salt, then mix. Add molasses, water, and vanilla extract and mix well.

3. Scoop dough with 2-ounce scoop (about 2 tablespoons), onto oiled baking sheet about 3 inches apart on baking sheets. Press with wet hand to about ¼ inch thick. Sprinkle lightly with about 2 teaspoons sugar (optional) for all cookies. Bake for 12 minutes until edges start to brown. Let the cookies rest on the baking sheet for 5 minutes, then transfer to a wire rack to complete cooling.

OPTION: For a softer cookie

Use only ¼ cup oil.
Add ¼ teaspoon baking powder.

Almond Crisp Cookies

YIELD: About 16 cookies
TIME: 15 to 20 minutes prep and 20 minutes baking

2 cups whole wheat pastry flour

¼ teaspoon salt

2 cups almonds, raw

1 cup corn syrup or rice syrup

¾ cup palm shortening

½ teaspoon vanilla extract

⅛ teaspoon almond extract

16 whole almonds for garnish

1. Preheat the oven to 325°F. Combine the flour and salt in a mixing bowl, and set aside. Lightly oil a baking or cookie sheet.

2. Spread the almonds on a baking sheet. Place in the oven and roast the nuts for 7 to 10 minutes, or until roasted almond scent is detected. Remove from the oven and let cool for about 5 minutes.

3. Place the almonds in a food processor, along with the rice syrup, palm shortening, vanilla extract, and almond extract. Blend until smooth. Add the flour/salt mixture and continue to mix about 30 seconds, or until a dough forms.

4. Roll 2-tablespoon portions of dough into balls and place them about 2 inches apart on the cookie sheet. Gently flatten each ball into a ¼ inch thickness, and press a whole almond into the center of each.

5. Bake for 15 to 20 minutes, or until lightly browned. Remove from the oven, and cool the cookies on the tray for 1 minute. Transfer the cookies to a wire rack and cool completely.

CHOCOLATE CHIP ALMOND BISCOTTINI DI PRATO

YIELD: 13 servings (26 Biscottini)
TIME: 20 minutes prep and 20 to 25 minutes baking

¼ cup almonds, roasted and medium coarsely chopped*

¼ cup butter spread or palm shortening

⅝ cup or 10 tablespoons sugar

1 tablespoon vanilla extract

⅞ cup or 14 tablespoons unbleached white flour

¾ cup whole wheat flour

2 tablespoons golden flax meal

1 teaspoon baking powder

⅛ teaspoon salt

¼ cup petite chocolate chips (2000-3000 count)

½ cup water

Chocolate Chip Almond Biscottini di Prato

1. Preheat oven to 350°F. Spread the almonds on a baking sheet and roast them in the oven for about 15 minutes or until they are lightly browned. Remove the sheet from the oven and immediately transfer the almonds to a separate container to prevent further roasting and to cool them slightly.

2. Place the almonds in a food processor and grind them into a medium-coarse meal. Measure out ¼ cup and store the rest for future use.

3. Increase the oven temperature to 375°F.

4. In mixing bowl with paddle, pour butter spread, sugar, and vanilla until ingredients are evenly dispersed.

5. In a separate bowl, mix two flours, flax meal, baking powder, salt, almonds, and chocolate chips together.

6. Add the dry ingredients to the butter mixture and mix until the two are well-blended and with a coarse sandy texture. Add water and mix until a soft cookie dough develops.

7. On an oiled baking pan, form a long roll of dough about 14 inches long and press until about 3 inches wide for the length of the roll.

8. Bake 20 to 25 minutes or until the top springs back when lightly touched, or when a toothpick inserted in the center comes out clean. Remove the pan from the oven and let cool for 15 minutes. Measure and slice half-inch thick slices. Lay flat on same baking sheet. Reduce heat to 250°F and place biscuits in the oven for 15 to 20 minutes. When done, remove the biscuits from the oven and cool them completely. Store in a dry, air tight container until ready to use, then cut into smaller pieces and serve.

*For a stronger almond flavor, use ⅛ to ¼ teaspoon almond extract.

CHOCOLATE CHIP COOKIES

YIELD: 12 servings (24 cookies/2 per serving)
TIME: 20 minutes prep and 15 to 20 minutes baking

1 ¼ cups all-purpose flour

1 cup whole wheat flour

1 teaspoon baking powder

2 tablespoons golden flax meal

⅞ cup or 14 tablespoons
vegan butter spread (or palm
shortening*), room temperature

1 ¼ cups sugar (or ¼ cup brown
sugar and 1 cup white sugar)

¼ cup water

2 teaspoons vanilla extract

1 cup semi-sweet non-dairy
chocolate chips

*If using palm shortening, use add
¼ teaspoon salt.

1. Preheat your oven to 375 °F. Line two cookie sheets with parchment paper.

2. Mix flours, baking powder, and golden flax together. Cream the shortening or butter with sugar. Add water and vanilla and mix until evenly dispersed (about 1 minute). Add the flour mixture and chocolate chips and mix until a cookie dough forms (about 1 minute). Do not over mix. The dough will be firmer than traditional cookie dough because it has no eggs.

3. Use a #40 scoop (little over 2 tablespoons of dough). Form the dough into 1 ½ inch balls. Place them on the cookie sheet and space about 2 to 3 inches apart. Flatten to about ¼-inch thick.

4. Bake for 15 minutes. Cookies will store in an air tight container at room temperature for about one week or in a freezer bag in the freezer for up to 6 months.

VARIATION: *Coconut Chocolate Chip Cookies*

When adding chocolate chips, also add ½ cup sweetened shredded coconut.

VARIATION: *Walnut Chocolate Chip Cookies*

When adding chocolate chips, add ½ cup chopped walnuts.

SUGAR DOUGH

YIELD: 1 ½ pounds of dough (24 ounces),
12 cookies, 2 ounces each
TIME: 30 minutes

¾ cup palm shortening or coconut butter

6 tablespoons sugar

2 tablespoons liquid lecithin

6 tablespoons water, cold (or 1 more
tablespoon if dough too dry)

1 tablespoon vanilla extract

1 ½ cups whole wheat bread flour

1 cup white flour

1. In a mixing bowl, combine the coconut butter, sugar, and liquid lecithin, then cream using an electric mixer.

2. Mix in the water and vanilla. Add the flours and mix to blend all ingredients thoroughly. Freeze dough for 30 to 40 minutes to make dough firmer and easier to handle. Use as needed for torte bases and to line pans that will hold creamy fillings.

3. To make cookies roll out dough on floured surface ¼ inch thick. Cut into shapes with any cookie cutter. Place cookies 1 inch apart on an oiled cookie sheet. Bake 6 to 8 minutes in 375°F or until fully baked (firm to gentle touch).

FIG BARS

YIELD: 12 servings (3 ½ cups fig filling)
TIME: 20 minutes prep time and 40 minutes baking

2 cups water

4 cups figs, whole, dry, finely chopped

2 tablespoons arrowroot dissolved in 2 tablespoons cool water

2 tablespoons vanilla extract

1 teaspoon cinnamon, ground

1 ½ pounds sugar dough, chilled

Mango Sorbet with Hippen Masse

1. Preheat oven to 350°F.

2. In a 2-quart saucepan, bring the water to a simmer over medium heat. Add the chopped figs and cook them until they are almost a thick paste, about 5 to 10 minutes, stirring constantly to prevent burning.

3. Add the dissolved arrowroot and cook until thickened.

4. Remove the saucepan from the heat and add the vanilla, and cinnamon. Set the filling aside. Lightly oil 2 loaf pans, each 4 ½ x 9 x 2 ¾ inches.

5. Divide the sugar dough into 4 pieces. Roll each piece out on a lightly-floured surface. Lay 1 piece in each pan. Divide the filling in half and spread it evenly over the dough in each pan.

6. Lay the remaining 2 pieces of rolled dough over the top of the filling in each pan, and lightly press it into the filling. Place the pans in the preheated oven and bake them for 30 to 40 minutes (if you are using a gas oven, first place a baking sheet on the shelf, then place the loaf pans on the baking sheet to prevent the bottoms from burning).

7. When baking is done, remove the pans from the oven and set them aside to cool completely. With a knife, cut around the sides of each loaf pan, hugging the sides with the knife. With one hand covering the top of the pan, gently flip it upside down to release the loaf. Repeat this procedure with the second loaf pan. Place both loaves on a tray and slice them into ½- inch to 1-inch pieces. Serve as desired.

VARIATION: *Sweet Fig Bars*

To increase the sweetness of these otherwise delicately-flavored bars, add ¼ cup or more (to taste) of sugar. Be sure to keep the figs as the predominant sweetener.

VARIATION: *Dried Fruit Options*

Pitted dates, raisins, or dried fruit of choice in place of figs offer infinite choices.

Dream Bars

YIELD: 8 to 10 servings
TIME: 20 minutes prep and 30 minutes baking

1 ¼ cups whole wheat flour

1 ¼ cup unbleached white flour

¾ cup oil

1 ¾ cups agave syrup

5 teaspoons Ener-G Egg Replacer

½ cup water

1 teaspoon baking soda

½ teaspoon salt

2 teaspoons vanilla

1 ½ cups chopped walnuts

1 cup unsweetened coconut

1 tablespoon lemon juice

½ lemon zest (rind only)

1. Preheat oven to 350°F.

2. In a mixing bowl, blend the two flours together and set aside.

3. In a separate bowl, mix the oil with 6 tablespoons of agave syrup and 2 cups of flour mixture to form a batter. Spread the batter evenly on the bottom of a lightly oiled 9 x 12 pan.

4. Mix remaining agave syrup and flour mixture with the egg replacer, water, baking soda, vanilla, walnuts, coconut, lemon juice, and zest. Stir to combine thoroughly. Spread this mixture evenly over the batter in the pan.

5. Be careful that you don't cut through the batter; that would cause the topping to run beneath the batter and possibly stick to the pan. Bake in a preheated oven at 350°F for 25 to 30 minutes.

Hippen Masse

This unique recipe can be used to make cones. It is also suitable for diabetics because it has no added sugar.

YIELD: 8 servings (1 cup)
TIME: 10 minutes prep time and 5 to 10 minutes cooking

¼ cup water

2 tablespoons creamy almond butter or almond paste (preferred)

½ cup soy milk powder

½ cup white flour

2 tablespoons Ener-G Egg Replacer

1. Preheat oven to 325°F. In a mixing bowl, place water and almond butter, then blend with hand or standup mixer until smooth. Add soy milk powder, flour, and egg replacer, then mix on low speed to mix until smooth and creamy.

2. Transfer mixture from bowl to a container. Spread on a lightly oiled and floured half size sheet pan in a thin layer with a spatula.

3. Bake for about 5 to 8 minutes or until very lightly browned yet still pliable. Remove from the pan and immediately form into whatever shape is desired and let it cool. The cookie will become crisp and at that point is ready to serve.

Crusts, Crepes, & Short Dough Skins

Gluten-Free Crust

YIELD: 1 10-inch crust
TIME: 15 minutes prep and 30 to 35 minutes baking

1 cup white rice flour
¼ cup almond meal, medium to fine ground
(or roasted walnut meal)
¼ cup golden flax meal (dark flax meal will
also work)
2 tablespoons sugar
¼ teaspoon salt
6 tablespoons palm shortening or coconut
butter (or other non-hydrogenated
shortening)
6 tablespoons water

1. Using a paddle, mix rice flour, almond meal, flax meal, sugar, and salt together for one minute or until evenly blended.

2. Add shortening and mix about 2 minutes on medium speed to integrate all ingredients.

3. Add water and mix to bind. (You cannot over mix gluten-free dough.)

4. Use rice flour to flour the bench where the dough will be rolled out. Roll out crust to about ⅜ to ¼ inch thick, wrap onto rolling pin, place in pie pan, and press in evenly and up sides. Optional to use a spring form torte pan.

5. Bake in a pre-heated 375°F oven for 35 minutes or until baked (160°F in center of torte). Remove and cool.

Basic Pie Crust

YIELD: Two 9-inch crusts
TIME: 15 minutes

¾ cup whole wheat pastry flour
¾ cup unbleached flour
6 tablespoons palm shortening
2 teaspoons sugar
Pinch salt
½ cup ice water

1. In a large mixing bowl, combine the flours. Using a pastry blender or two knives, cut the shortening into the flour until the mixture becomes a crumbly meal.

2. Stir the salt and sugar into the ice water and pour it over the flour mixture. Using a fork, mix the water with the flour mixture until the dough binds together. (If the dough appears too wet, add a little whole wheat flour.) Form the dough into two balls, and let rest a few minutes to relax the gluten in the dough making it easier to roll out.

3. Turn one ball of dough onto a floured surface, and flatten it into a ½-inch-thick circle. With a floured rolling pin, roll out the dough (from the center outward) to a 10-inch circle that is $1/16$ to ⅛ inch thick. Transfer the dough to a 9-inch pie pan.

4. If using a single crust, crimp or flute the edge, and press it firmly against the sides of the pan. Add the filling and bake according to the specific recipe.

Vegan Crepes

Vegan crepes are a little more delicate to make and "may" be slightly thicker or denser than an egg-based crepe. Holding up a vegan crepe with your hand, you should be able to see the shadow of your hand through the crepe. The recipe is easy but does take a little practice to get the technique down. The most efficient way to produce these crepes is using 2 or 3 pans at a time for mass production. The crepes are freeze thaw stable. You can make them in advance, freeze them, and thaw as needed.

YIELD: 6 servings of 2 crepes each (1 ½ cups batter for 12 crepes, using 2 tablespoons batter for each crepe)
TIME: 10 minutes prep and 20 to 30 minutes cooking

¼ cup whole wheat bread flour
¼ cup unbleached white flour
2 tablespoons golden or dark flax meal (golden preferred)
¼ teaspoon salt
1 tablespoon Ener-G Egg Replacer
1 ¼ cups water
1 tablespoon canola oil*

1. Mix the two flours, the flax meal, salt, and egg replacer together and add the water and oil to dry mixture.

2. Mix until the all dry ingredients are dissolved in water, a liquid pourable batter is formed, and ingredients are evenly dispersed.

*Or oil of your choice depending on the filling.

Technique for Making Crepes

1. After batter is mixed it must set for 10 to 15 minutes to allow the batter to fully hydrate, becoming the consistency of a light cream. At that point it should be pourable.

2. Heat an oiled non-stick 8-inch skillet or crepe pan on medium low heat. Measure two tablespoons crepe batter into pan and swirl pan to spread batter out into a crepe while using the bottom of a spoon to help spread batter evenly. If pan is too hot the batter will coagulate (cook too quickly) and you will not be able to spread the batter. Let cook for 1 to 1 ½ minutes, until top looks cooked. Gently flip with spatula and cook second side for about 1 to 1 ½ minutes. Remove and cool. If going to stack for a period of time, place plastic wrap between the crepes to prevent sticking and place in sealable plastic bag.

VARIATION: *Dessert Crepes*

The above crepe recipe can be used as is for desserts. The dessert filling will carry the crepe. To enhance the sweetness and flavor of the crepe, which essentially has little flavor (traditional or vegan), one can add sugar and fruit zests. (Adding sugar to this recipe does weaken the structure making the crepes a little more delicate to handle.) Another dessert crepe option is to use spiced sugar (¼ teaspoon ground cinnamon, ginger, or nutmeg to 1 tablespoon sugar) and sprinkle on crepes. Dessert or fruit flavors or vanilla can be added to the crepe recipe to give the crepes a dessert profile. To convert the above recipe to a dessert crepe, add 3 tablespoons sugar and 1 tablespoon orange or zest.

CREPES SUZETTE

YIELD: 8 crepes (4 servings)
TIME: 20 minutes prep and 15 minutes cooking

½ cup orange juice concentrate, frozen

¼ cup cashew butter

2 tablespoons barley malt syrup, agave or corn syrup

1 tablespoon Grand Marnier

1 teaspoon vanilla extract

⅛ teaspoon salt

1 cup bananas, diced

1 teaspoon orange zest (optional)

8 dessert or basic crepes (previous page)

2 tablespoons cognac

1. Blend the cashew butter with the orange juice concentrate, barley malt syrup, Grand Marnier, vanilla extract, and salt.

2. Mix the diced bananas into ¼ cup of the orange juice mixture until they are well coated.

3. Divide the banana mixture between the 8 crepes. Place a small amount in the center of each crepe, fold the crepe in half, then again into quarters. Pour the sauce into a 10-inch frying pan and heat it over medium heat. Lay the folded crepes in the pan and heat them for 1 minute, then turn them to the other side and heat them for another minute.

4. Pour the cognac into the sauce, stir it, and ignite it with a match. Serve the crepes while they are still flaming, 2 crepes per person.

NOTE: Do not use more than amount of cognac called for in recipe because when flambéing crepes, it could create more flame than desired. Measure the amount needed for the flambé presentation and remove the bottle from the serving area. And don't use the flambé presentation unless you know how to or have practiced the technique several times before serving.

VARIATION: *Tropical Crepes*

½ cup coconut, toasted

½ cup pineapple, fresh, diced

½ cup bananas, diced

½ cup pineapple juice concentrate, frozen

¼ cup coconut cream

2 tablespoons rum

¼ teaspoon ginger powder (optional)

1. Mix coconut, diced pineapple, bananas, and frozen pineapple juice concentrate to make the filling mixture.

2. Divide filling evenly between eight crepes folding them in half and then into quarters.

3. Pour rum and coconut cream into sauté pan (and ginger if using). Lay crepes in cream mixture, heat to a simmer, flip and heat for another minute, and serve while hot.

SHORT DOUGH SKINS

**YIELD: 8 ounces Short Dough (12 to 14 skins,
3 ½-inch squares)**
TIME: 30 to 45 minutes

¾ cup white flour

¼ cup cornstarch

⅛ teaspoon salt

1 teaspoon sugar

2 tablespoons shortening

1/16 teaspoon annatto, or yellow food color of
choice (optional)

5 tablespoons water

1. In mixing bowl, mix flour, cornstarch, salt
    and sugar together. Cut shortening into
    flour until coarse texture develops. Dissolve
    annatto into water and add to flour mixture.

2. Mix to create dough. Flour bench and roll
    out paper thin (less than 1/16 inch). Cut to
    recipe specification or desired size.

3. Heat the oil in a 12-inch skillet over medi-
    um heat. Place the short dough skins in oil
    and lightly brown about 20 to 30 seconds
    on each side. Transfer the skins to a paper
    towel-lined plate. Lightly sprinkle with some
    of the sugar.

VARIATION: Cannoleon

An author-created term to reflect fusion cuisine,
the cannoleon combines the napoleon and the
cannoli, a fusion of French and Italian cuisine
in this vegan presentation.

YIELD: 6 to 8 portions
TIME: 30 minutes prep time and 30 minutes cooking

Skins

Add ¼ teaspoon cinnamon to flour in Short
Dough Skins recipe. (To cut 2 ½-inch square
skins which will total about 24 skins.)

Cannoli Filling

4 cups Lemon Cheesecake Filling (page 361)

½ cup confectioner's sugar

½ cup chopped candied citron

4 ounces semisweet chocolate, chopped

½ cup pistachio nuts, roasted and finely chopped

1. Make short dough skins by adding cinna-
    mon to flour mixture before adding shorten-
    ing and water (see above).

2. Mix cannoli filling and set aside.

3. Roll out short dough skins and cut into 2 ½
    inch squares.

Sauce to Garnish Plate

1 cup Raspberry Coulis (page 326)
8 mint leaves

Assembly

1. Drizzle plate with raspberry coulis.

2. Place one skin on plate, ¼ cup cannoli filling
    on skin, second skin on filling, second por-
    tion of filling on skin and top with third skin.

3. Put a teaspoon of filling on top layer (take
    from top portion of cannoli filling) and
    place a mint leaf in the filling.

NOTE: This same short dough skin can be used
to make savory napoleons such as Pinto Bean
(page 294) and other variations with different
beans, seitan, tempeh, or chicken analogue.

Ice Cream, Sorbets, & Refrigerated Desserts

I created the following vegan ice cream and sorbet recipes for chefs who don't have access to vegan ice cream and sorbets in foodservice packs and for everyday cooks who want to almost effortlessly make their desserts. Making vegan ice cream can be as easy as blending all ingredients until smooth and creamy, freeze and serve. Sorbets are just as easy.

The recipes and cooking techniques used are an exceptional foundation to build an understanding of classical vegan cuisine and food chemistry. The chemistry is simple and taken to the most basic level of food science. Too much sugar and the ice cream will not freeze. Not enough sugar and it will freeze as hard as ice. The blender whips air into and emulsifies the ice cream.

Creating an easy-to-produce ice cream requiring no heating or ice cream machine was a formidable culinary challenge. I took a recipe online that called for heating the coconut milk with sugar, refrigerating until cold, and running through an ice cream machine. There had to be a better formula.

My approach was to use raw cashews and water in the ice cream to emulsify the ingredients and slightly neutralize the coconut flavor. More sugar was added to increase the Brix, the term used to quantify the amount of sugar in a liquid. The sugar has to be a certain level in different frozen desserts to allow for proper freezing. The Brix in ice cream should be between 25 and 35 percent depending on the recipe. If sugar is too low, ice cream will freeze hard as a rock and if too much sugar, it will not freeze.

I used a powerful blender to pulverize the nuts into a cream. At the same time, the blender was aerating the mixture to lighten the texture. In food science it is called "overrun" which is the percent increase in volume of ice cream greater than the amount of mix used to produce that ice cream. Simply stated, if 1 gallon of ice cream mix run through a soft serve machine set at 50 produced 1.5 gallons of frozen product, the overrun would be 50. That translates to a light ice cream with 33 percent air in it. The blender may produce an overrun of 10 which is sufficient.

Making ice cream without an ice cream machine that creates the overrun means the technique has to create the overrun. Blending will whip air into the emulsion, but to hold that aeration the emulsion has to have a degree of viscosity (body) to hold it or the air will surface from the liquid in the same manner bubbles surface in water. The solution is to add more nuts to the mixture to develop a stronger viscosity. When using an ice cream machine, it aerates the solution as it is freezing so there is no need to be concerned about viscosity. The fat has to be sufficient or the ice cream will have the texture of a sorbet, not an ice cream.

I did not use gages to calculate the formulas. They are intuitive estimations. How the product performed when frozen would tell if corrections were necessary.

CHOCOLATE COCONUT ICE CREAM

The emulsifier replacing the egg yolk in this recipe is the nut. When pulverized it creates a hydroscopic mass of carbs and oil that is receptive to drawing moisture (osmotic). It is a simple matter of getting the correct ratio of pureed nuts, oil, water, and sugar. The ratio has to be correct to create a successful recipe.

When the following mixture is blended and frozen, it has about a 20 percent overrun and is firmer. If placed in a frozen mixer bowl and beat until soft, the ice cream will shrink by about 20 percent losing its overrun but the texture will be much softer.

YIELD: 5 servings (2 ½ cups)
TIME: 15 minutes prep time and 12 hours in freezer

1 can coconut cream (13 ½-ounce)
¼ cup water
1 teaspoon vanilla extract
1 cup sugar
¼ cup unsweetened cocoa powder
2 tablespoons cashews (whole or coarse pieces)
⅛ teaspoon salt

1. Pour all ingredients into a 1- to 2-quart blender and blend for about a minute on high speed. The mixture must be smooth and creamy with no grit when rubbed between one's fingers.

2. Pour into a container and freeze.

VANILLA COCONUT ICE CREAM

This is a very rich vegan ice cream for very special occasions with a mild coconut back note. The vegan butter spread off sets the coconut milk's flavor but is higher in fat. It is possible to cut the butter spread to a half cup and add ¼ cup water to lower the richness.

YIELD: 5 servings (2¾ cups)
TIME: 15 minutes prep and 12 hours in freezer

¾ cup (7 ounce) butter spread
15 tablespoons full fat coconut milk
¼ cup water
1 teaspoon vanilla extract
¾ cup sugar
2 tablespoons cashews (whole or coarse pieces)

1. Warm the butter spread.

2. Pour all ingredients into a 1- to 2-quart blender and blend for about a minute on high speed. The mixture must be smooth and creamy with no grit when rubbed between one's fingers.

3. Pour into a container and freeze.

VANILLA SOY ICE CREAM

This version uses soy milk and butter spread for the dairy components and is an exceptional ice cream. The percentage of nuts was significantly increased to give the additional emulsification and richness. The increased percentage of nuts allows the pastry chef to make additional nut versions of the ice cream, such as roasting the cashews or substituting roasted almonds or pecans.

YIELD: 5 servings (2¾ cups)
TIME: 15 minutes prep and 12 hours in freezer

½ cup butter spread

1 ¼ cups soy milk

2 teaspoons vanilla extract

¾ cup sugar

½ cup cashews* (whole or coarse pieces)

Warm the butter spread. Pour all ingredients into a 1 to 2-quart blender and blend for about a minute on high speed. The mixture must be smooth and creamy with no grit when rubbed between ones fingers. Pour into a container and freeze.

*OPTION: Roast cashews or substitute roasted almonds or roasted pecans. For roasting nuts, preheat oven to 350° F. Spread nuts on tray. Roast for 7 to 10 minutes until aroma is detected. Remove immediately from tray.

AVOCADO LEMON ICE CREAM

For very special occasions this is a very rich avocado ice cream with a complementary lemon note and a mild coconut back note. The avacado offsets the coconut milk's flavor but is higher in fat. Flavors can be adjusted to your satisfaction. It will not affect the texture of the ice cream.

YIELD: 5 servings (2 cups)
TIME: 15 minutes prep and 12 hours freezer time

1 cup sugar

¾ cup ripe avocado (about 1 ½ avocados)

¾ cup coconut milk

2 tablespoons lemon juice or ¼ teaspoon lemon extract

Pour all ingredients into a 1- to 2-quart blender and blend for about a minute on high speed. Pour into a container and freeze.

VARIATION: *Avocado Lime Ice Cream*

Replace lemon juice with lime juice and blend two tablespoons lime zest into avocado mixture.

VARIATION: *Avocado Mint Ice Cream*

Remove lemon flavor and replace it with ¼ to ½ teaspoon mint extract or 2 tablespoons fresh mint leaves pressed into measuring spoon. Blend the leaves into the avocado mixture.

Banana Ice Cream

YIELD: 6 servings (3 cups)
TIME: 15 minutes prep and 12 hours in freezer

1 cup bananas, fresh, room temperature, packed into cup
1 ¼ cups sugar
½ cup room temperature coconut cream*
2 tablespoons almonds, raw, blanched
2 teaspoons vanilla extract

1. Measure by pressing ripe bananas into a one cup measure. Place banana puree into a commercial blender.

2. Add coconut cream, sugar and vanilla. Blend until smooth.

3. Containerize and freeze until frozen. Freezing time depends on the freezer and temperature of the solution.

*Coconut cream must be blended into room temperature banana puree to evenly disperse fat into the ice cream. Otherwise the coconut fat will congeal.

Mango Sorbet

YIELD: 2 ½ cups
TIME: 20 minutes prep and 12 hours in freezer

2 cups peeled and pitted ripe mangoes (2 medium mangos)
½ cup agave nectar
⅛ teaspoon stevia extract powder (or an additional ½ cup of agave nectar if you don't have stevia)
¼ cup Cashew Cream (page 175) or coconut cream (optional)
1 teaspoon lemon juice

1. Slice up the mangoes and put in a blender/ food processor with agave nectar or stevia and blend for 1 minute at high-speed.

2. Add the coconut cream and lemon juice and blend for 15 seconds to thoroughly mix all ingredients together.

3. Pour your entire mixture into a freezer friendly container and freeze for at least 6 hours. Make sure you take it out of the freezer for 15 minutes before you serve to allow it to soften, making it easier to serve.

Peanut Butter Ice Cream

YIELD: 6 servings (half cup per serving)
TIME: 15 minutes prep time and 12 hours in freezer

1 ½ cups (14 fluid ounces/1 can) coconut cream
2 teaspoons vanilla extract
1 cup sugar
½ cup peanut butter
¼ cup water

1. Starting with cream, pour all ingredients into a blender and blend until smooth and creamy.

2. Pour into a container and freeze until frozen (about 12 hours). Or pour into an ice cream machine and run until ice cream sets.

CRANBERRY SORBET

YIELD: 12 servings (6 cups)
TIME: 10 minutes prep, 15 minutes cooking, and 12 hours in freezer

2 cups whole cranberries

2 cups sugar

¼ teaspoon salt

4 cups orange juice

1. Place the cranberries, sugar, salt, and 2 cups of the orange juice in a blender, and blend until smooth.

2. Transfer the mixture to a 2-quart saucepan over medium heat, and bring to a boil. Remove from the heat, add the remaining 2 cups of orange juice, and mix well.

3. Pour the mixture into a flat plastic 2-quart container, and place in the freezer.

4. When the mixture is completely frozen, cut it with a sharp, sturdy knife into 1 ½-inch cubes. Place the cubes in a food processor, and process until completely pulverized.

5. Serve immediately, or place in a plastic container and return to the freezer until ready to use.

VARIATION: *Elderberry Sorbet*

2 cups fresh or frozen elderberries in place of cranberries

VARIATION: *Blueberry Sorbet*

2 cups fresh or frozen blueberries in place of cranberries

2 teaspoons lemon juice

DUTCH APPLE CUSTARD

YIELD: 4 servings
TIME: 10 minutes prep and 15 minutes cooking

24 ounces unsweetened applesauce

2 tablespoons agar flakes

½ cup Dutch Honey (page 346)

¼ teaspoon cinnamon

1 cup soy milk

1 teaspoon vanilla extract

1. Combine the applesauce with the agar flakes, Dutch Honey, and cinnamon in a medium saucepan.

2. Bring the mixture to a simmer over a medium heat and cook until the agar is dissolved (10 to 12 minutes).

3. Add the soy milk and vanilla, stir until well-blended, and cook for a few more minutes.

4. Pour the mixture into a lightly oiled 4-cup mold. Refrigerate until set (2 hours). Unmold and serve.

COCONUT WHIPPED CREAM TOPPING

This is a superb stable whipped cream that functions similarly to a regular whipped cream but does not whip up as light as dairy-based whipped cream and has a pleasant coconut flavor. The psyllium husk powder is often used in cleansing diets as a cleanser. It is available in pharmacy stores, should be inexpensive, and has an infinite shelf life. It is the stabilizer in the whipped cream holding the moisture in suspension. Here is osmosis at work again using a medicinal ingredient in a decadent dessert. The whipped cream holds for a week in the refrigerator and can be frozen. If frozen, it must be rewhipped. The one advantage of this whipping cream over traditional whipping cream is that it cannot be over-whipped, which causes separation.

NOTE: One 13.66 ounce can of coconut cream = 1 ½ cups coconut cream

YIELD: 4 servings (1 cup)
TIME: 15 minutes

1 (13.66 ounce can) or 1 ½ cups unsweetened coconut cream (refrigerated)

2 tablespoons palm shortening

1 teaspoon vanilla extract

½ cup powdered sugar or to taste*

½ teaspoon psyllium husk powder

*OPTION: To use regular sugar. Add 1 to 2 teaspoons water or drained coconut water to dissolve the sugar. Add only enough water to make sugar moist enough to hold together when compressed.

NOTE: For flavoring the whipped cream, any liquid flavor extract or ground spice option works. If using coffee or cocoa powder, you will need to increase sugar to neutralize the bitterness. Liqueurs are an excellent flavoring option.

1. Refrigerate coconut cream for about 3 hours or until cream solidifies.

2. Pour refrigerated coconut cream into mixing bowl with whip.

3. Add palm shortening and vanilla and whip for about 30 seconds on medium speed.

4. Mix powdered sugar and psyllium husk powder together and add to coconut cream.

5. Using a whip on the mixer, start on slow speed to integrate dry ingredients into coconut cream (about 20 seconds). Turn up to high speed and whip the thick coconut cream in the chilled bowl until firm, light, and fluffy.

6. Using a rubber spatula, transfer the whipped cream topping to a covered storage container, and keep refrigerated until ready to use. Serve chilled.

DUTCH HONEY

Pioneers of the American West used Dutch Honey when genuine honey was scarce. Use immediately or store refrigerated.

YIELD: 6 servings (1 ½ cups)
TIME: 30 to 45 minutes cooking time

1 cup brown rice syrup
1 cup soy milk
1 cup Sucanat or brown sugar
½ teaspoon vanilla extract

Combine all ingredients, except the vanilla, in a medium saucepan. Bring to a simmer and cook until it is reduced by one half (about 30 to 45 minutes). Stir in the vanilla. Cool.

POACHED PEACHES IN SIMPLE SYRUP

YIELD: 6 servings (3 cups)

TIME: 20 minutes prep and 5 minutes cook time

3 cups peaches, fresh, blanched, and cut into ½-inch thick slices
1 cup sugar
1 cup water
1 tablespoon lemon juice

1. Blanch, peel, and slice peaches.

2. Bring sugar and water to a boil. Turn down to medium heat. Let simmer for 5 minutes.

3. Add lemon juice and peaches and let simmer for 1 minute and remove from heat. Immediately containerize and refrigerate until ready to use if not immediately using them.

POACHED PEARS WITH RASPBERRY SABAYON SAUCE

YIELD: 4 servings
TIME: 10 minutes prep and about 15 minutes cooking

4 pears Bartlett or Anjou on the green side, peeled
2 cup red wine
2 cups water
2 cups sugar
Raspberry Sabayon Sauce (page 324)

1. Peel the pears. Mix the wine, water, and sugar together.

2. Place the pears in the poaching liquid and bring the mixture to a simmer. Let simmer for 5 minutes if the pears are on the green side or turn off the fire immediately if it is ripe.

3. Let the pears continue to cook in the poaching liquid until the liquid cools to room temperature.

4. Cut each pear in half from top to bottom, and remove the seeds. Quarter the pear and slice one for each plate. Serve with Raspberry Sabayon Sauce.

OPTION: Use a chardonnay wine in place of red wine.

Confections (Ohagi)

One of my favorite confections is *ohagi,* an ancient Japanese dessert traditionally prepared using a cooked sweet rice and a sugar sweetened adzuki bean paste. *Botamochi* is the same as ohagi except a different size adzuki bean is used in making the filling. I think of ohagi as a whole food, sugar-free, and gluten-free dessert (sweet rice is "glutinous," meaning sticky and contains no gluten) that can be served as dessert or a healthy snack. The Japanese use sugar in the adzuki bean paste. I use half-cooked black beans and half-pitted dates pulverized into a paste in place of adzuki beans and sugar.

Traditional ohagi consists of a ball of sweet rice wrapped in adzuki bean paste. The paste can be inside the ball. Using either option, ohagi is generally rolled in soy flour or sesame seeds for easier handling. I prefer to roll ohagi in roasted almond meal.

I learned about ohagi while studying macrobiotic cooking at the Kushi Institute in Brookline, Massachusetts, outside Boston. It was an appealing dessert because their version was a simple sweet brown rice with raisins and cinnamon and rolled in roasted almond meal. It is a very simple dessert with diverse menu applications in both casual and fine dining. Not only is it vegan, this macrobiotic version is gluten free and sugar free.

A very simple complex carbohydrate dessert to make, it keeps refrigerated for several days and is very nutritious. The cost is pennies. The perceived value is in the nuts and dried fruits. The ohagi can be chocolate-coated and rolled in roasted ground nuts. Sweet white rice is a better option than sweet brown rice unless the ohagi are immediately consumed. If sweet brown rice ohagi is refrigerated, it can become chewy to the point one may feel as though they are eating half-cooked rice. If consumed on the same day, the rice does not have to be refrigerated and will taste delicious. It is ideal to mix the fruits into the rice while warm and form into balls.

One exception for using sweet brown rice is placing cooked brown rice in a food processor with dried fruits (chopped dates) and pulse several times to pulverize the rice into a paste and integrate it into the mix. If you don't use this process and don't consume the ohagi the same day, it will become chewy like semi-cooked rice. The Japanese would use a suribachi to pulverize the rice and while traditional, it takes significantly more time. White rice breaks down easier because it contains no bran.

Ohagi can be whole grain, sugar-free and gluten-free or the opposite (white rice and sugar). They can be served at breakfast, lunch, dinner or as a snack.

SWEET WHITE RICE BALLS

Sweet rice is also called sticky rice and is more glutinous (sticky). It will hold ingredients together in ohagi and cause nut meal to stick when finished.

YIELD: 32 servings (4 cups - 2 tablespoon portions rice balls)
TIME: 5 minutes prep and 40 minutes cooking and cooling

1 ½ cups sweet white rice
2 ½ cups water
¹⁄₁₆ teaspoon salt

1. Pour rice, water, and salt into a 2-quart sauce pan with lid.

2. Stir and bring rice to a simmer on medium heat, turn down to low heat, and cook for about 20 minutes or until cooked with a lid on the pot.

3. When finished cooking, remove from fire, and stir with a fork. Let cool for 20 minutes or until cool enough to handle and ready for making ohagi by mixing spices and dried fruits into the rice, forming into balls, and rolling in ground nuts.

CINNAMON RAISIN OHAGI

YIELD: 26 servings (3 ¾ cups or 2 tablespoons per rice balls)
TIME: 5 minutes prep and 30 minutes cooking and finishing recipe

1 cup roasted walnuts or pecans, ground into a meal
2 cups cooked sweet white rice
1 ¾ cup whole dark raisins
2 teaspoons cinnamon powder
1 tablespoon vanilla

1. Pour rice, raisins, cinnamon, and vanilla together in a food processor and run until the mixture develops into a coarse polenta-type texture or paste.

2. Roast the nuts in a 350°F oven for 5 to 10 minutes until lightly roasted. Cool, put in food processor to form a coarse grind or chop the nuts.

3. Make the ohagi using two tablespoons of mixture and spoon (#40 scoop) to portion the ohagi. Roll the dumplings in the nuts until well coated. Serve immediately or cover and refrigerate until ready to serve.

OPTION: Add ¼ cup powdered sugar for sweeter version.

COCONUT DATE OHAGI

YIELD: 28 servings (3 ½ cups or 2 tablespoon per rice ball)
TIME: 5 minutes prep and 30 minutes cooking and finishing recipe

2 cups cooked sweet white rice
¾ cup flaked sweetened coconut, chopped (best flavor comes from toasting the coconut)
¾ cup dates, pitted and chopped
1 tablespoon vanilla extract
1 ¼ cup unsweetened coconut meal or finely chopped

1. Place rice in a mixer, add flaked coconut, dates, and vanilla and mix with paddle on medium speed until it becomes a polenta-type paste. Option to put in a food processor and pulse until mixture forms a coarse paste.

2. Press into a 2 tablespoon #40 scoop. Form and roll in coconut meal. Containerize in a sealed container until ready to use.

VARIATION: *Chocolate Coated Coconut Date Ohagi*

These balls can be coated in chocolate or Chocolate Ganache Icing (page 328). If coating in chocolate ganache, do so immediately after making the ohagi using a very warm ganache. If the ganache is too thick, the icing will not evenly coat the ohagi. After coating, immediately roll in ground nuts.

1 ½ cups ganache, warmed

1. Place rice in a mixer, add flaked coconut, dates, and vanilla and mix with paddle on medium speed until it becomes a polenta-type paste. Option to put in a food processor and pulse until mixture forms a coarse paste.

2. Measure 2 tablespoons mixture and form into a ball with wet hands and use a #70 scoop. Roll in coconut. Store in a sealed container until ready to use.

3. Warm ganache in the microwave or double boiler. If microwaving, place icing in microwave-safe container for 15 seconds and mix. If too stiff, microwave in 10 seconds and 5 second intervals until warm. If using double boiler, heat till warm stirring occasionally.

4. Dip ohagi in ganache with prongs, remove from ganache and hold over it for 10 seconds to let excess drip off.

5. Then roll in coconut meal to evenly coat and refrigerate until ready to serve.

Ohagi with an Assortment of Desserts

CANDIED GINGER-CRANBERRY SWEET RICE BALLS (OHAGI)

YIELD: 28 servings (3 ½ cups or 2 tablespoon portions rice balls)
TIME: 10 minutes prep and 25 minutes cooking and finishing recipe

2 cups cooked sweet white rice
¾ cup candied ginger, finely diced or minced
¾ cup dry sweetened cranberries, chopped
1 ¼ cup roasted pecan or walnut meal

1. Pour rice, ginger, and cranberries into food processor and pulse until mixture forms a coarse paste like polenta.

2. Remove from processor and mix candied ginger and cranberries into the warm rice.

3. With #40 scoop, portion 2 tablespoons of mixture and roll with wet hands into balls. Roll in roasted nut meal. Containerize in a sealed container until ready to use.

ANKO (SWEET BEAN PASTE) FILLED OHAGI

Anko is traditionally made with the popular Asian adzuki bean. Other bean options will work. I use black beans and to avoid sugar, use dates. Nut meal gives the filling a little oil.

Yield: 48 portions (1 cup anko and 6 cups cooked white rice)
TIME: 35 minutes prep and about 30 minutes assembling

¾ cup cooked black beans, rinsed after cooking
¾ cup pitted dates, chopped
¼ cup roasted pecan or walnut meal
¼ cup water
½ teaspoon cinnamon
6 cups cooked sweet white rice
1 cup roasted pecan or walnut meal

1. Place beans, dates, pecans, water, and cinnamon in a food processor and process into a paste.

2. On benchtop or counter top, lay a piece of plastic about 6 inches long and the width of plastic wrap.

3. Scoop 2 tablespoons cooked rice using a #40 scoop which is about 2 tablespoons or measure 2 tablespoons. Flatten to about a 3-inch round. Place 1 teaspoon of Anko in center of rice. Place plastic with rice in palm of hand and pull clenched palm closing rice around filling. Pull plastic together and twist until the rice tightens into a solid ball.

4. Remove from plastic and roll in nuts to coat surface. Cover and refrigerate until ready to serve.

Tortes, Cakes, Brownies, Pies, & Special Occasion Desserts

In the food world a culinary term may carry many different meanings. The torte is one good example. The Hungarian Dobos Torte is several layers of pastry with thin layers of buttercream. Kirschwasser Torte is a layered German chocolate cake soaked with Kirschwasser, a cherry brandy, and sprinkled with dark cherries iced with whipping cream. The Swiss have their Pecan Torte which is nut filling in a crust, not layered, and baked. Each is totally different and yet all are called tortes. Whether we call it a torte, a cake, a pie, or a floating isle, these special occasion desserts offer a rich and often decadent end to any meal. Health concerns make these special occasion only. However, celebrations are always a joyful part of life.

SWISS BURNT-PECAN TORTE

This torte is one of my signature pastries and has always been a four-star dessert. The original recipe calls for caramelized sugar, whipping cream, and butter. Not only is my version more healthful, since it eliminates these ingredients, but the flavor and texture of this dessert are more delicate than the original. The barley malt syrup in this recipe gives the torte a subtle caramel flavor. After tasting it, you will know why it is a delicately sweet, special dessert.

YIELD: 8 servings (one 11-inch torte)
TIME: 35 minutes prep and 40 minutes cooking (excludes 40 minutes to roast nuts)

4 cups pecans
¾ cup barley malt syrup
½ cup brown rice syrup or agave syrup for a sweeter dessert
1 heaping tablespoon arrowroot
1 teaspoon vanilla extract
1 recipe Basic Pie Crust (page 336)

Glaze

2 teaspoons barley malt syrup, dissolved in 2 teaspoons water

1. Roast the pecans at 275°F for about 40 minutes or until roasted. (Slow roasting is essential to this dessert, because it allows for a delicate roasted pecan flavor to develop.)

2. Using a food processor, grind the pecans to the consistency of coarse flour. Mix the finely ground pecans with the syrups, arrowroot, and vanilla. Set aside while you make the pie dough, if you haven't made it already.

3. Roll out half of the pie dough and place it in an 11-inch fluted torte pan, trimming the edges. Add the pecan mixture on top of this bottom crust. Then roll out the remainder of the pie dough, place it over the filling, and trim the edges. Seal the edges of the top and bottom crust together. Cut a few holes in the top crust to let the steam escape.

4. Bake in a preheated oven at 350°F for 35 minutes. Then brush the top crust with the dissolved barley malt syrup and bake until lightly browned (5 to 10 minutes). Cool and serve.

(Swiss Burnt-Pecan) VARIATION: *Almond Coconut Torte (One 11-inch torte)*

4 cups almonds

½ cup coconut, unsweetened

3 tablespoons cornstarch or arrowroot

¼ cup agave syrup

1¾ cups brown rice syrup

1 teaspoon vanilla extract

1 recipe Basic Pie Crust (page 336)

Roast the almonds at 325°F until lightly browned (15 to 20 minutes). Remove from the oven and spread the almonds on another pan to cool. Grind the almonds to a fine meal but be careful not to over-process them (or you will end up with almond butter). Add the coconut, cornstarch, agave syrup, brown rice syrup, and vanilla to the ground almonds. Roll out the pie crust, fill the torte, and bake as directed in step 4 for Swiss Burnt-Pecan Torte.

NOTE: Osmosis is the migration of moisture from a higher concentration to a lower concentration and causes the filling to set. If the nuts are too coarse the filling will not set up. The arrowroot will draw any excess moisture, tightening the filling. The arrowroot will cook out in the event that there is no moisture to draw on.

LIME TORTE

YIELD: Serves 6 (one 9-inch cake)

TIME: 35 minutes (excludes baking cake)

1 prepared Chocolate or Carob Cake (page 356)

2 (10.5 ounce) packages firm or extra firm silken tofu

¾ cup brown rice syrup

½ cup agave syrup

¾ cup lime juice (preferably key lime)

1 tablespoon agar powder

4 tablespoons arrowroot powder

2 tablespoons canola oil

2 to 3 kiwi fruits (optional)

Natural green food color, 1 to 2 drops as desired (optional)

Glaze

1 teaspoon agar powder

½ cup water

½ cup brown rice syrup

1 to 2 drops mint extract

1. Blend the tofu, brown rice syrup, agave syrup, lime juice, agar, arrowroot, corn oil, and natural green color, if using color, until smooth. Transfer to a double boiler and heat until the mixture thickens. It should reach the consistency of heavy cream. Set aside to cool.

2. Split the cake into two layers. (For this recipe, you will need only one layer. Freeze second layer for later use.) Line a 9-inch cake pan with a sheet of plastic wrap. Place one layer of cake in the bottom of the pan and refrigerate while the tofu filling is cooling. When the filling is cool, pour it onto the cake and refrigerate until the filling sets completely (about 2 hours). For added color and flavor, add the kiwi fruit: peel the fruit, cut into thin slices, and fan out the slices over the entire torte.

3. Glaze the cake by lightly pouring a thin layer of the still warm glaze over the cool cake. (Use ½ to ¾ of the recipe for a light glaze.) Refrigerate cake again for 10 minutes before cutting. To serve, lift plastic wrap to remove the cake from the pan.

Glaze: In a small saucepan, dissolve the agar in the water. Add the brown rice syrup and mint extract. Bring to a simmer and remove from heat. Allow to cool slightly.

PEAR TORTE

YIELD: 8 to 10 portions (one 10-inch torte)
TIME: 35 minutes prep and 40 minutes cooking, baking and assembling

One recipe Gluten-Free Crust (page 336)

Cranberry Sauce

Yield: 2 cups

12 ounces cranberries, fresh or frozen

1 cup water

¾ cup sugar

Mix ingredients together and bring to a simmer on medium heat and let simmer for 10 minutes. Remove from heat leaving pot open to set until cool. Place in container until ready to use.

Pear Filling

2 cups warm Vanilla Pastry Cream (page 321)

½ teaspoon ground ginger

1 ½ cups room temperature water

2 tablespoons warm non-hydrogenated shortening

2 large ripe pears

½ cup Cranberry Sauce (above)

¼ teaspoon agar powder

2 large ripe pears, peeled and sliced

4 ounces almond meal

1. Prepare Vanilla Pastry Cream, measure out 2 cups, and add ginger to evenly disperse. If using cold pastry cream, warm enough to allow it to spread evenly on torte crust.

2. Mix Cranberry Sauce and agar powder together and heat to a simmer when ready to use.

Assembly

1. Sprinkle almond meal on crust.

2. Evenly spread filling on torte.

3. Optional to sprinkle filling with another 4 ounces of nut meal.

4. Fan sliced pears around torte at the peripheral (edge).

5. Warm and place cranberry filling in the center of the torte.

OPTION: Glaze pears with about ¼ cup or less apricot glaze which is a commercial apricot jelly warmed to about 140°F to melt the pectin, heat and brush on pears.

Polynesian Crisp

YIELD: 6 servings (1 pan, 10 x 12 x 2-inches)
TIME: 30 minutes prep and 45 minutes baking

¼ cup coconut, unsweetened

5 cups pineapple, fresh, diced

¼ cup brown sugar

⅓ cup unbleached white pastry flour

2 teaspoons vanilla

Topping

⅓ cup whole wheat pastry flour (or unbleached white flour)

¾ cup rolled oats

¼ cup brown sugar

⅓ cup walnuts, chopped

¼ teaspoon ginger powder

¼ cup butter spread, unrefined corn oil or canola oil

1. Combine the coconut, pineapple, brown sugar, flour, and vanilla.

2. Pour mixture into a lightly-oiled 10 x 12 x 2-inch pan.

3. Spread the topping evenly over the pineapple mixture.

4. Bake in a preheated oven at 375°F for about 45 minutes, or until the top is crispy and the fruit mixture is bubbly. Cool for about 10 minutes. Serve warm or cold. You may wish to serve this dessert with a non-dairy ice cream of your choice.

Topping: Combine the dry ingredients in a small bowl. Cut in the corn oil and mix until it reaches the consistency of a coarse meal.

Dry Cooked Apple Pear Winter Compote

Sautéing uses the concentrated flavored liquid from the fruits to intensify the flavor. Keeping the lid on after cooking enables the dried fruits to absorb the liquid from fresh fruits. Any combination of fruits can be used but the ratio of fresh watery fruits to dry needs to be maintained (for example, bananas would not work in place of pears). This compote makes an excellent winter Napoleon hot or cold.

YIELD: 4 servings
TIME: 20 minutes prep and 20 minutes cooking

2 large apples (about 2 cups) peeled, cored and diced or sliced

2 large pears (about 2 cups) peeled, cored and diced or sliced

2 tablespoons red wine for flavor

1 cup dried apricots

½ cup sweetened dried cranberries

¼ cup sugar

¾ teaspoon cinnamon powder

⅛ teaspoon clove powder

½ teaspoon allspice powder

1. Peel and core apples and pears and cut into large pieces. Place fresh fruit in saucepan with wine, dried fruit, sugar, and spices. Turn heat to medium. Bring mixture to a simmer and stir.

2. Let simmer for about 8 minutes, occasionally stirring the fruits. Remove from stove, place lid on pot and let set for 15 minutes.

3. When cool the fruit will be moist with no liquid in the pan. Serve hot or cold.

NANCY'S PEACH PIE

I call this pie Nancy's because I created it for my wife and it is one of her favorite pies.

YIELD: 8 to 10 Servings (one 10-inch pie)
TIME: 32 minutes and 45 minutes baking

1 recipe Basic Pie Crust (page 336)
6 cups sliced frozen peaches or blanched, peeled, pitted and sliced fresh peaches
½ cup white sugar
3 tablespoons arrowroot powder
2 tablespoons lemon juice
¼ teaspoon salt
⅛ teaspoon mace, ground, optional
¼ teaspoon cinnamon

Polynesian Crisp

1. Preheat oven to 375°F.

2. Prepare and roll out pie dough to ¹⁄₁₆ inch thick and lay in a 10-inch pie pan. Roll out another piece for top of pie.

3. In a large mixing bowl, mix peaches, sugar, arrowroot powder, lemon juice, salt, mace, and cinnamon. Pour filling into pie pan, wet the edges of dough with water or syrup of choice, cover top of pie with second piece of dough, and pinch to seal top and bottom crust. Punch holes in top crust to release steam.

4. Bake in oven for 35 to 45 minutes or until golden brown and filling is bubbling. Remove from oven, let cool to warm/room temperature and serve.

NOTE: The filling will seem heaping full but condenses in the baking process.

*If using the Gluten-Free Crust (page 336), prepare two times the recipe. Roll out pie crust on plastic wrap using rice flour to roll crust. Using plastic wrap to lift the crust, flip it into pie shell and trim. Next, roll out pie top on plastic wrap and flip onto top of pie after filling it. Seal pie crust top to pie crust bottom. Cut hole in top of crust to let steam out and bake.

VARIATION: *Peach Rhubarb Pie*

Exchange 2 cups of the sliced peaches for 2 cups sliced rhubarb (approximately 3 stalks). Continue with recipe.

VARIATION: *Peach Blueberry Pie*

Exchange 2 cups of the sliced peaches for 2 cups of blueberries. Continue with recipe.

Chocolate Cake

This cake has many variables and is one of my old standbys in dairyless, eggless cakes. Carob powder can be substituted for cocoa powder if you want to make a carob cake. Also see White Cake (page 358) and its yellow cake variation.

YIELD: one 8-inch cake, or 8 ⅓ cup each cupcakes (2 ¾ cups batter)
TIME: 10 minutes prep and 20 minutes baking

1 cup unbleached all-purpose white flour
¼ cup whole wheat
1 ⅛ cups sugar
6 tablespoons unsweetened cocoa powder
2 teaspoons baking powder
½ teaspoon salt
1 cup water, room temperature
2 teaspoons vanilla extract
6 tablespoons warm palm shortening, sunflower oil, or warm butter spread

1. Preheat the oven to 350°F. Oil and flour an 8-inch round cake pan (preferably spring form) or an 8-inch round pan.

2. Mix the two flours, sugar, cocoa, baking powder, and salt with a hand whip to evenly blend ingredients together.

3. Add the water, vanilla, and oil. Mix until all dry ingredients are blended together well. Use a spatula to scrape down the sides if necessary.

4. Place in oven and bake for about 30 minutes, or until the cake springs back with a gentle touch in center of the cake. Cool on a rack completely to room temperature.

VARIATION: *Carob Cake*

Use the same amount of carob in place of cocoa powder.

VARIATION: *Cupcakes (for Chocolate, Carob, White, or Yellow Cake)*

Place 8 cupcake liners in a muffin or cupcake tin and spray with oil. Portion ⅓ cup batter into each tin. In a preheated 350°F oven, bake the cupcakes for about 20 minutes or until the muffin springs back with a light touch to the center.

VARIATION: *"Ice Cream" Cake*

1 carob or chocolate cake (made according to the recipe on left)
7 cups non-dairy vanilla or chocolate ice cream
1 cup hazelnut butter
1 ½ cup Chocolate Ganache Icing (page 328)

1. Freeze the cake. Then slice it in half horizontally. Line a cake pan with a large piece of plastic wrap. Place one layer of the cake inside the pan.

2. Beat frozen ice cream and nut butter just until it is soft enough to spread. Spread it over the first layer of the cake. Add the second layer of cake on top and gently press to fill in the gaps between the layers. Freeze the cake completely.

3. Heat the ganache icing to about 95°F. Pour over the frozen cake and spread the icing as necessary. Refreeze the cake. Remove from the freezer about 5 minutes before serving.

APPLE KANTEN CAKE

Kanten cakes are extremely versatile. A basic kanten cake consists of a single layer cake, about one inch tall, spread with a thin layer of pastry cream; then arrange fresh or stewed fruit on the cake, pour a semi-set kanten (agar) over the entire cake, and chill the cake until the kanten gels completely.

You can use any type of cake, pastry cream (or almond butter), fruit, and fruit juice with the kanten. You can also top the finished cake with any sauce, such as a sabayon or fruit sauce, if you wish. Here is one recipe for a kanten cake, along with a variation. The variations are limitless.

YIELD: 6 servings (one 10-inch cake)
TIME: 15 minutes prep, 20 minutes to cool, and 2 to 3 hours for cake to set

2 cups apple juice

2 cups apricot juice or nectar (or 4 cups orange juice)

2 tablespoons barley malt syrup

1 to 2 teaspoons agar powder (or 4 to 5 teaspoons agar flakes)

2 cups apples, peeled and thinly sliced (or canned sliced apples thoroughly drained)*

1 Chocolate Cake (page 356), made in a 10-inch spring form pan (use half the cake recipe)

¾ cup Vanilla Pastry Cream (page 321) or almond butter

1. Pour apple juice, apricot juice, and barley malt syrup into 2 quart pot. Bring to a simmer and add agar flakes. Let simmer for about 5 to 10 minutes or until agar is dissolved—no glassy specks in juice. Set aside.

2. Steam the apples until they are tender but still firm. Or open canned apples and drain.

3. The chocolate cake should be about 1 inch tall. (If 2 or more inches tall, split into two layers, reserving one layer for another use.)

4. Spread a thin layer of pastry cream on the carob cake and place it in a 10-inch spring form pan. Arrange the cooked apples over the cake. When the kanten is semi-set, pour it over the cake. Refrigerate until the kanten is set completely.

5. To serve, release the pan spring. Slide a spatula around the sides of the cake. After removing the pan sides, loosen the cake from the pan bottom. Carefully transfer the cake onto a serving plate. (You may instead serve the cake directly from the spring form pan.)

6. Serve slices of the kanten cake with a sabayon sauce if you wish.

Apple Kanten Cake

White Cake

YIELD: one 8-inch cake, 8 ⅓ cup each cupcakes, or 2¾ cups batter
TIME: 10 minutes prep and 20 minutes baking

1 ¼ cups unbleached all-purpose white flour

¾ cup sugar

2 teaspoons baking powder

½ teaspoon salt

2 tablespoons Golden Flax Meal

1 cup water, room temperature

2 teaspoons vanilla extract

¼ cup warm palm shortening or warm butter spread or canola oil

VARIATION: *Yellow Cake*

1/16 teaspoon annatto added to water before adding to dry ingredients.

1. Preheat the oven to 350°F. Oil and flour an 8-inch round cake pan (preferably spring form) or an 8 x 8 square pan.

2. Mix the flour, sugar, flax meal, baking powder, and salt with a hand whip to evenly blend ingredients together.

3. Add the water, vanilla, and oil or warm butter spread. Mix until all dry ingredients are blended together well. Use a spatula to scrape down the sides if necessary.

4. Place in oven and bake for about 30 minutes, or until the cake springs back with a gentle touch in center of the cake. Cool on a rack completely to room temperature.

Chocolate Fudge Brownie

YIELD: 8 Servings
TIME: 15 minutes prep and 25 to 30 minutes to bake

½ cup whole-wheat bread flour

½ cup unbleached white bread flour

⅞ cup sugar

⅓ cup cocoa powder

½ teaspoon baking soda

12 ounces vegan chocolate chips (1 package)

½ teaspoon salt

½ cup soy milk

1 ½ teaspoons cider vinegar

1 ½ teaspoons vanilla extract

½ of 12.3 ounce package silken tofu (firm or extra firm)

1. Preheat oven to 350 °F.

2. Stir together the two flours, sugar, cocoa, baking soda, chocolate chips, and salt in a large mixing bowl.

3. Pour soy milk, vinegar, and vanilla, and add tofu into a food processor or blender until completely smooth.

4. Add the tofu mixture to the dry ingredients using a paddle until the mixture is evenly dispersed.

5. Spread into a nonstick or oil-floured sprayed 10 x 6 inch baking pan and bake until the top springs back when pressed lightly in the center, about 20 to 25 minutes, and depending on oven, could be up to 35 minutes.

6. Remove from the oven and allow cooling in the pan until cool or room temperature.

OPTION: Spread a thin layer of warmed raspberry jelly and glaze with Chocolate Ganache Icing (page 328) and serve.

MINCE "WHEAT MEAT" PIE

YIELD: 5 cups filling (serves 8)
TIME: 35 minutes prep and 45 minutes baking

1 recipe Basic Pie Crust (page 336)

1 tablespoon canola oil

½ cup onions, ¼-inch diced

¾ teaspoon salt

2 cups water

1 ½ cups seitan, ground (packed)

1 cup apple, Granny Smith, peeled, cored, and chopped

1 cup currants, raisins, dry apricots (single or any mix of these fruits)

¼ cup walnuts, roasted and chopped

½ cup sugar

2 tablespoons almond butter or nut butter of choice

2 ½ teaspoons cinnamon

1 ½ teaspoons allspice

¼ teaspoon cloves, ground

2 tablespoons arrowroot dissolved in 2 tablespoons cool water

2 tablespoons lemon juice

2 tablespoons rum, light

1. Preheat oven to 375°F.

2. Prepare pie crust as directed in the recipe.

3. In a 10-inch frying pan, sauté the onions and salt in the oil over medium heat for 5 minutes.

4. Add water, seitan, apple, currents, walnuts, sugar, almond butter, cinnamon, allspice, and cloves. Bring to a simmer and cook for 20 minutes.

5. Add the arrowroot mixture, stirring constantly. Continue to cook for 3 minutes or until the mixture is thickened.

6. Remove the pan from the heat and add the lemon juice and the rum. Transfer the filling to a covered container and refrigerate it until it is cool. When ready, pour the filling into the prepared pie shell and cover it with the second crust, sealing the edges well and making slits in the top to allow steam to escape during baking.

7. Place the pie in the preheated oven for 45 minutes, or until the pie crust is lightly browned and the filling is slightly bubbling. Remove the pie from the oven and cool it on a wire rack. Serve as desired.

JAMAICAN FLOATING ISLE

This recipe is a spin-off from the original Hungarian dessert of Russian origin called the Floating Isle. It is traditionally made by whipping 6 egg whites with a pinch of salt, Kirschwasser, a little cornstarch, and sugar until light and firm. The egg meringue is then portioned and poached in milk with sugar and vanilla and flipped with a spoon to poach the opposite side.

For the meringue, I went with another light dessert similar to a soufflé in the French meaning of the word to "puff up." The puffed rice is like the egg whites (aerated) and is bound with through osmosis with the Coconut Whipped Cream Topping (page 345). The topping is easy to make and should be prepared, formed, and served as close to service time as possible (within 30 minutes to 1 hour) for maximum effect. The crispiness of the rice gives a pleasant texture to this creamy dessert.

YIELD: 6 portions
TIME: 25 minutes prep and 15 minutes assembling

The Island

¼ cup coconut, toasted
2 cups Coconut Whipped Cream Topping (page 345)*
1 teaspoon vanilla extract
1 ½ cup puffed rice

Jamaican Fruit Crème Glacé

2 cups Vanilla Pastry Cream (page 321)
½ cup fresh pineapple, finely chopped
½ cup fresh mango, freshly chopped
½ cup fresh strawberries, finely chopped
2 teaspoons lemon juice
4 teaspoons rum (optional)

NOTE: If making fruit mixture and serving immediately, it will be necessary to thin out the fruit/pastry cream mixture with no more than 2 teaspoons water or 1 tablespoon of coconut milk. If serving the following day, the pastry cream will be thinned out from the fruit's moisture.

1. Add vanilla to whipping cream and whip until light and fluffy.

2. Fold (gently mix) coconut and puffed rice into whipping cream.

3. Use canola oil to lightly oil a half cup and portion ½ cup mix, pressing gently into ½ cup mold.

4. Unmold immediately onto a lightly oiled plate until firm and full. Repeat 4 times. Cover and refrigerate.

5. Prep fruits (peel, and chop fine).

6. Mix fruits, lemon juice, rum, and pastry cream together. Let set for 5 minutes in refrigerator. If the cream is too thick, thin to the consistency of a light cream with 2 to 3 teaspoons coconut milk.

7. Portion Crème Glacé equally onto 4 dessert plates. Lay one of the Islands on plate and sauce evenly, pour onto plates, garnish with caramel sauce or fruit coulis. Place soufflé on the sauce in the center of the plate.

NOTE: Use about a tablespoon of the fruit mixture as a garnish on the island or dappled on top of glacé for color. Candied ginger is an excellent complement to this dessert.

*OPTION: For a lighter option use commercial vegan whipped topping.

LEMON CHEESECAKE WITH RASPBERRY COULIS

Cheesecake is about as decadent as dessert comes. This vegan cheesecakes could be defined as decadent health, a term used by those who want it both ways, decadent and healthy. Remember the nuts, their health benefits and fat content to protein ratio? This recipe is where health and decadence merge. Delicately sweet with a mild lemon flavor and a rich creamy texture. Decadent, vegan and gluten free.

YIELD: 6 to 8 servings (one 9-inch cake), 4 cups filling (8-inch pan/ring will work and cake will be higher)
TIME: 20 minutes prep time and 8 hours minimum refrigeration

1 prepared Gluten-Free Crust (page 336)

Lemon Cheesecake Filling

2 x 12.3 ounce packages firm silken tofu, drained (24.6 ounces)
½ cup sugar
10 ounces cashews, raw (whole or pieces)
¼ cup lemon zest
⅛ cup unsalted vegan butter spread
2 teaspoons vanilla extract

Garnish

8 sliced fresh strawberries
½ cup Raspberry Coulis (page 326)

Vegan Cheesecake

1. Preheat oven to 375°F.

2. Prepare Gluten-Free Crust and press evenly into 8-inch spring form cake tin. Bake 10 to 15 minutes or until crust is firm to touch.

3. Use a gallon blender with a strong motor and blend tofu, sugar, cashews, lemon zest, butter spread, and vanilla together until a smooth cream develops with no grit.

4. Pour the mixture on ring and place in refrigerator for at least 8 hours to let set (osmosis to create the texture).

5. Unmold and slice into desired portions. Garnish with strawberries and Raspberry Coulis.

VARIATION: *Vanilla Cheesecake*

Remove lemon zest and add additional 2 to 4 teaspoons of vanilla extract.

CHOCOLATE CHEESECAKE

The reason the chocolate cheesecake takes less time to set is two-fold. First, the osmosis occurs quicker in chocolate and second, the chocolate becomes hard immediately upon cooling.

YIELD: Serves 6 to 8 portions (one 9-inch cake)
TIME: 20 minutes prep and 2 hours to set

Chocolate Couscous Crust

¾ cup pecans

2 ½ cups water

1 ½ cups Sucanat

¼ cup cocoa

1 cup couscous

1 tablespoon vanilla extract

Chocolate Cream Filling

1 (10 ounce) package semi-sweet chocolate chips

2 (10 ½ ounce) packages firm silken tofu, at room temperature

3 tablespoons agave or maple syrup

1. Roast the pecans at 300°F for about 30 minutes. Remove from oven and cool. Grind the roasted pecans in a food processor for 5 to 10 seconds. They should have the consistency of a coarse meal.

2. In a medium saucepan, stir together the water, Sucanat, cocoa, and couscous. Bring to a simmer and cook until thickened (5 to 10 minutes). Add the vanilla and stir well. Spread the mixture into a 9-inch spring form pan. Sprinkle ¼ cup of the roasted pecan meal over the couscous cake.

3. Make the Chocolate Cream Filling. Melt the chocolate chips in a small saucepan over low heat, stirring constantly. Transfer to a blender, add the tofu and maple syrup, and blend until smooth.

4. Pour the filling over the couscous crust and top with the remaining pecan meal. Refrigerate the cake until it is set (about 2 hours). Serve cold.

NOTE: It is best to use heavier sweeteners with cocoa or chocolate, because these ingredients are bitter. Sucanat, maple syrup, and agave nectar are examples of heavy sweeteners. Use lighter sweeteners, such as rice syrup, barley malt, or fruit juice with carob, because carob is already somewhat sweet.

VARIATION: *Chocolate Fudge Cream Filling*

YIELD: 4 cups filling

1 ounce semi-sweet chocolate chips
(11 ounces total)

Omit agave or maple syrup and use:

½ cup sugar

½ cup cocoa powder

2 teaspoons vanilla

2 tablespoons vegan butter spread, optional

1. Melt chocolate chips in microwave in 20 second increments. Melt butter separately, if using.

2. Place all ingredients in blender starting with tofu, then sugar and cocoa powder, and finally the melted chocolate and butter spread.

3. Blend until smooth. Deposit on the couscous or a baked gluten-free crust.

*CRUST VARIATION: Use precooked Gluten-Free Crust (page 336) in place of the couscous base.

rant

STRAWBERRY-LEMON NAPOLEONS

These Napoleons are modern interpretations of a dessert classic. They are light, delicately flavored, and absolutely beautiful. You can use Short Dough Skins or phyllo pastry for the crisp layers. Peaches, raspberries, blueberries, pears, fruit compote, bananas, figs, and a variety of fruits can be used in place of strawberries.

YIELD: 4 servings
TIME: 30 minutes

1 ½ cups Lemon Crème Anglaise (page 323)
1 tablespoon canola oil
12 Short Dough Skins (4-inch squares) (page 339)
½ cup sugar
2 cups quartered fresh strawberries
4 teaspoons lemon juice
1 tablespoon powdered sugar for garnish
4 sprigs fresh mint to garnish top of Napoleon (optional)
¼ cup Raspberry Coulis (page 326) to drizzle on plate (optional)

Prepare short dough skins cutting into 4-inch squares. Transfer the skins to a paper towel-lined plate. Lightly sprinkle with some of the sugar.

Strawberry Mixture

In a medium-sized mixing bowl, add the strawberries, lemon juice, and the remaining sugar. Mix well.

To assemble each Napoleon:

Spoon 1 teaspoon of the lemon cream in the center of a dessert plate and top with the short dough skin—sugar side up. Cover the short dough skin with ¼ cup of strawberries, 2 tablespoons of the Anglaise and another short dough skin. Repeat the layers, ending with a third short dough skin.

Sprinkle the top of the Napoleons and the plate with powdered sugar, and serve. Garnishing options, such as candied ginger and fresh mint, are plentiful.

SECOND VEGAN OPTION: Use phyllo dough instead of short dough skin. Oil each of 6 layers of phyllo and stack. Cut into 4-inch squares and bake in a 250°F oven until lightly brown. Remove from oven and immediately remove from baking sheet or it will over bake. Sprinkle with sugar.

Strawberry-Lemon Napoleon

STREUSEL TOPPED FRESH MANGO PIE

This gluten-free and vegan pie has many fresh fruit options.

YIELD: 8 to 10 servings (One 12-inch pie in torte pan)
TIME: 30 minutes prep and 40 minutes assembly and bake time

1 Gluten-Free Crust (page 336)

Cinnamon Streusel

YIELD: 2 ¼ cups
TIME: 10 minutes

1 cup white rice flour
¼ cup medium to fine ground almond meal (or roasted walnut meal)
¼ cup golden flax meal (dark flax meal will work)
4 tablespoons sugar
1 teaspoon cinnamon
¼ teaspoon salt
6 tablespoons palm shortening (or non-hydrogenated shortening)

1. In a mixing bowl with a paddle, mix white rice flour, almond meal, flax meal, sugar, cinnamon, and salt together until evenly dispersed.

2. Add shortening and mix on medium speed until mixture is crumbly and immediately stop mixing.

Mango Pie Filling

3 tablespoons brown rice flour
6 tablespoons sugar
¼ teaspoon cinnamon
2 large ripe mangos, (about 4 cups), diced
1 tablespoon lemon juice

1. Mix rice flour, sugar, and cinnamon together. Add lemon juice and berries to mangos and blend with a spoon. Add rice flour mixture to mangos and mix well.

2. Place gluten-free crust in pie tin. Bake in pre-heated 375° oven for 8 minutes.

3. Remove from oven, pour filling in pan and spread evenly. Sprinkle Cinnamon Streusel mix on pie filling.

4. Bake in a pre-heated 375°F oven for 35 minutes or until baked (160 degrees F. in center of torte). Remove and cool.

OPTIONS: ¼ cup elderberries or ¼ cup blueberries (can double if you wish) or ½ cup pineapple. Peaches can also replace mangos. If substituting peaches, add 2 tablespoons brown rice flower.

Appendix A

Culinary Speed Scratch & Eco-Cuisine

Soon after I became a vegan chef I realized the cuisine had not been developed within the foodservice industry and the unique and staple vegan foods were not available in foodservice distribution channels. Two challenges emerged when I began to cook for conventions—the crucial issues of labor costs and the food costs of special ingredients which defined any classical or modern form of innovative vegan cuisine. Controlling labor was directly related to menu dynamics and/or building vegan entrées around existing restaurant inventory. The second was creating a line of vegan ingredients, specifically proteins and pastries that could be built into the foodservice operation. Bringing the basic vegan staples into foodservice channels can only happen with the emergence of consumer demand. But first the products had to be developed.

I thought I could contribute to solving this challenge by developing a menu concept-driven line of vegan products and make them more accessible to both professional chefs and home cooks. This would both support the chefs/cooks and contribute to the cuisine. I started when very few vegan food products could be found in the marketplace. Since then, I have developed the Eco-Cuisine line and been privileged to assist chefs and cooks nationally and internationally in developing their vegan skill sets and menus. This year I've consulted and/or taught at several international events and on cruise lines educating chefs in vegan cooking techniques, sharing my philosophy, and teaching speed scratch cooking with Eco-Cuisine's products. Global interest in vegan cuisine is rising and raising the bar on consumers' expectations. This book and these speed scratch products are here to help the chef meet those expectations.

Eco-Cuisine products are the only vegan speed scratch menu concept-driven line of foodservice products in the United States. The speed scratch products are also part of the Certified Vegetarian Cook (CVC) program for professional chefs and why I give them a brief spot at the back of the book. Chefs should be aware of these innovative vegan foodservice options.

In 1980 when I started traveling the US as a guest banquet chef to consult, write, and cook vegan menus for conventions, the chefs' major critique of the cuisine was that it was labor intensive and the foods exceptionally expensive. I saw the challenge and knew the solution was a line of dry basic speed scratch mixes that require minimum skill and reduce labor and food cost. I began developing the products. Dry mixes cost less, can be used for multiple recipe applications, and reduce inventory and expensive specialty ingredient costs. The products can mirror/create a vegan version of any ground beef, chicken, muffin, or cookie on any menu, delivering on taste and nutrition while reducing cost. My intent was and is to make Eco-Cuisine mixes a way to bring accessible vegan foods to foodservice operators.

Eco-Cuisine has extensive recipes for each product and videos demonstrating the products on YouTube and recipes on eco-cuisine.com. What is presented here is a brief introduction to the products and a collection of recipes for use in every kitchen to make cooking vegan easy and the food a pleasurable dining experience.

Defining Speed Scratch

When researching the term speed scratch, I learned of two types of speed scratch ingredients. One is processed and partially or fully cooked (prepared) individual ingredients (dry, canned, or frozen). The second is partially assembled recipe mixes or components such as dry bakery mixes, batters, and, in vegetarian cuisine, dry protein mixes.

The first type of speed scratch is thousands of years old, with food history filled with small and large scale commercial production of items like olive oil, wine, tofu, and miso. Closer to our time, two hundred years ago the Lewis and Clark Expedition carried dried soup, definitely created through a natural production method.

The second form is culinary speed scratch, ingredients that are partially assembled for more complex recipes, a form of mostly twentieth-century kitchen innovation designed to save time and money. Cake mixes came into existence with the P. Duff & Sons Ginger Bread Mix in the 1930s. In 1948 Pillsbury Cake Mix emerged and in the 1970s Betty Crocker's Hamburger Helper. These are examples of culinary speed scratch mixes that are sub-components of

recipes and do not include all the ingredients used in the recipes.

Culinary speed scratch presented through Eco-Cuisine helps to keep labor and/or production cost down both in foodservice and home kitchens and enables cooks to increase production with less effort and labor. It enhances menu innovation at a time when the cost of labor is increasing, especially among skilled culinarians. It was designed to reduce the daily routine of food preparation, like scaling out ingredients to make a cake mix, and allows the baker to spend a little of the time saved, for example, to creatively work with the mix to make a variety of desserts, not just cakes, without compromising the quality of the recipe. Chefs recognize the necessity to balance scratch cooking with speed scratch cooking to reduce labor and meet production deadlines. Chefs are always fighting the clock. It is the nature of our business. And speed scratch products help us meet those challenges.

Culinary Speed Scratch

Culinary speed scratch is a version of scratch cooking or baking in which the core food ingredients are manufactured into a mix that becomes the basic ingredient for a number of recipes. The mix can be savory or pastry and has to be a sub-component of a number of recipe applications. Vegan culinary speed scratch products are used by the cook with a variety of cooking techniques and ingredients to create an infinite array of recipes or menu items from one dry blended, refrigerated, or frozen ingredient. They require culinary creativity and a variety of cooking or baking skills to develop the unique recipes and are one of the most effective means of integrating vegan into any menu in the home or restaurant kitchen.

Vegan culinary speed scratch mixes include:

- ○ Broth powders or concentrates to either replace or enhance stocks, broths, soups, and sauces

- ○ Dry blended protein mixes (instant dry bean burrito or hummus mixes), beef, sausage, chicken analogues, and seitan

- ○ Instant plain dry beans, textured soy proteins, instant grains, and dry sea vegetables

- ○ Basic dry blended bakery mixes (cakes, scones, brownies, cookies, muffins, biscotti) that can be used to make a variety of flavors with a variety of recipe applications

- ○ Instant soy puddings, pastry creams, and whipping creams

Vegan speed scratch ingredients include:

- ○ Canned ingredients (tomatoes, pickles, sauerkraut, and beans)

- ○ Frozen and dried prepared vegetables and fruits

- ○ Refrigerated tofu, soy milk, tempeh, and miso

- ○ Frozen vegan meat analogues

A vegan beef-style base concentrate or broth powder is a culinary speed scratch component. The ingredient can be used in a vegan sauce, burger, or loaf, infused into tofu, or used as a breading. A vegan beef-style flavored sauce, frozen or in a pouch, is not a culinary speed scratch component because it is prepared to serve as is.

A speed scratch product isn't a finished product. A vegan frozen burger isn't a speed scratch product, even though a cook can dress it out with a variety of condiments giving it a variety of names. A vegan dry ground beef mix that can be used to make a variety of burgers, meat loaf, and Bolognese sauce is a speed scratch mix. A basic muffin mix that can be used to make a variety of flavored muffins, coffee cakes, quick breads or bread pudding is also a speed scratch mix.

Vegan Integration into Foodservice

One way to integrate vegan products into the foodservice industry is through vegan culinary speed scratch. Vegan culinary speed scratch ingredients are unique in that they save on both labor and food costs while delivering on taste, menu innovation, and nutrition. The ingredients or basic mixes are menu concept driven, meaning each product can be plugged into specific menus instead of creating excessive additional inventory and labor around the vegan menu. Culinary speed scratch is new, innovative, and essential to everyone who has to carve out time to cook at home and for professional cooks challenged to keep labor cost down while delivering enticing vegan menus. It is the new form of scratch cooking joining the best of both scratch cooking with food science and fresh wholesome ingredients into twenty-first century cooking. Just as vegan cuisine is entering into its culinary renaissance, so too is speed scratch cooking entering into its renaissance to bring us back to cooking again.

Eco-Cuisine Special Features

Eco-Cuisine's vegan culinary speed scratch products line and concept is the first and only of its kind, offering the professional chef and the home cook less labor, lower food cost, and wonderful taste. The speed scratch concept is available to both foodservice professionals and retail consumers online.

Speed scratch proteins are designed to be infused with different flavors, vegetables, whole grains, and beans using different cooking techniques. It is like starting with a raw piece of meat from which the cook has unlimited options versus starting with a processed piece of meat, such as a sausage link, which limits the cooking techniques and recipe application options.

Dry mixes offer considerably more menu diversity compared to frozen vegan proteins. The high-protein powder can become a cold cut, meatball, chili, cutlet, roast, or loaf and the flavor can be customized to an original recipe or ethnic cuisine, or to mirror a popular item off the restaurant menu or a family favorite. The mixes allow the culinary professional or home cook the ability to be creative in a broader menu spectrum as shown in the recipe applications with dry blends. It allows the chef to innovatively cook with the protein.

Another difference between frozen vegetarian protein and dry mixes is the fat option. Frozen vegetarian proteins put through the extrusion process have little or no fat. Part of the pleasure of the entrée is enjoying the healthy but delicious protein. In dry protein mixes the cook can control the type of oil being used and the amount. Oil adds lubricity or richness to the protein, especially with vegan proteins because they tend to be dry. The oxymoron of dry mixes is they are generally moister and richer in oil because the cook controls those factors through the preparation technique and recipe application. Remember that vegan proteins, if too dry, can be rehydrated.

A listing of culinary speed scratch products is in the ingredient brands and distribution resource section in Appendix B. For more detailed information on these products, contact the companies directly. Retail consumers may have more speed scratch product options than are offered to professional cooks.

Here is a quick summary of the advantages of Eco-Cuisine speed scratch products:

- Eco-Cuisine's products are unique in that they save on both labor and food costs while delivering on taste, nutrition, and menu/product innovation.

- Eco-Cuisine created a menu concept driven speed scratch line of vegetarian basic dry blended proteins and bakery mixes to enable cooks and bakers to efficiently prepare fresh innovative healthy dining menus at their onsite kitchen.

- The mixes are *menu concept driven,* meaning each Eco-Cuisine product can be plugged into specific menus versus creating menus and inventory around the product. For example, any chicken item on the menu can be replaced with Eco-Cuisine's Reduced Sodium "Chicken Style" Quick Mix and "Chicken Style" Broth to form a cutlet, a roast, or a nugget.

○ As dry mixes they *reduce food cost by approximately 50 percent* for the same product in frozen form. As dry mixes they do not require freezer space, and the mixes have a two-year shelf life. The cook can control food cost by using recipe applications with higher yields.

○ *Minimum culinary skill* is needed to produce the products. Apprentice cooks and bakers can produce these products. *Minimum labor is needed* to produce the products. Approximately 20 to 30 percent less labor is needed for speed scratch compared to cooking/baking from scratch.

○ The mixes are "speed scratch mixes" in that they combine the speed of working with pre-mixes (savory or sweet) with the creativity of cooking and baking from scratch.

○ *Basic mixes allow for diverse recipe applications enabling the professional culinarian to be creative, developing signature menu items* to keep patrons interested in their foodservice operation.

○ *Additional nutritional density can be built into the mixes* with whole food ingredients (For example, fresh or dried fruits for bakery and fresh vegetables and whole grains for savory). The basic mixes were developed as vegan products for operational purposes so a chef can cover all categories of vegetarians with one menu.

○ All of the prepared culinary speed scratch proteins and bakery products are freeze/thaw stable.

NOTE: Tofu or tempeh can be substituted for the chicken recipes in this section as can the chicken analogue be used in place of tofu or tempeh recipes depending on the recipe applications.

Seitan can be made from scratch if you have the time (page 276) or from the mix in this section. It is an ancient protein that emerged into the analogues with the emergence of the instant Seitan Quick Mix and commercial ready to eat products. Tempeh, chicken analogue, and tofu can be used in place of seitan. Any of the grain loaves, shepherd's pies, or burger recipes in this book are interactive with the Ground Beef Style Quick Mix.

Eco-Cuisine Culinary Speed Scratch Products

Eco-Cuisine® Reduced Sodium "Ground Beef Style" Quick Mix

Vegan Salisbury Steak

VARIATION: *Salisbury Burger*

American-Style Meat Loaf

VARIATION: *American Barley Loaf*

"Beef-Style" Bolognese Sauce

VARIATION: *Bolognese Sauce with Roasted or Grilled Eggplant*

VARIATION: *Bolognese Sauce with Mostaccioli*

Italian Meatballs

Eco-Cuisine® Reduced Sodium "Chicken Style" Quick Mix

Chicken & Pot Roast/Steam Methods

Asian BBQ Chicken with Caramelized Onions on a Bun

VARIATION: *Asian BBQ Seitan*

VARIATION: *Asian BBQ Tempeh*

Vegan "Chicken-Style" Piccata

"Chicken-Style" Protein

VARIATION: *Chicken Piccata with Cannellini Beans*

VARIATION: *Cannellini Beans Piccata with Pine Nuts*

Chicken Le Coq au Vin (Chicken with Wine)

VARIATION: *Chicken-Style Le Coq au Vin with White Kidney Beans*

VARIATION: *Navy Beans au Vin with Roasted Pecans*

Thanksgiving Day Vegan Chicken

Vegan Chicken Cranberry Salad

Eco-Cuisine® Reduced Sodium "Sausage Style" Quick Mix

Basic "Sausage-Style" Patties

Italian "Sausage-Style" for Pizza

Eco-Cuisine® "Beef Style" Seitan Quick Mix

Sauté Method

Single Steam Method

Eco-Cuisine® Basic Chocolate Brownie Mix

Basic Brownie

Texture Options

Basic Firm Textured Chocolate Brownie

VARIATION: *Walnut Brownie*

Vegan Chocolate Cake

Eco-Cuisine® Basic Muffin and Pancake Mix

Basic Muffins

Basic Pancakes

Cranberry-Orange Streusel Coffee Cake

Eco-Cuisine Streusel

Eco-Cuisine® Basic Cookie Mix

Basic Cookies

VARIATION: *Chocolate Chip Cookie*

Date-Coconut Cookie Bar

Eco-Cuisine® Basic English Scone Mix

Basic English Scone

English Cranberry-Ginger Scone

Italian Pistachio Biscotti

Eco-Cuisine® Instant Soy Pudding Mix

Instant Vanilla Soy Pudding

VARIATION: *Chocolate Pudding*

Also Available
Eco-Cuisine® Seasonings

Eco-Cuisine Reduced Sodium "Beef Style" Broth Mix

Eco-Cuisine Reduced Sodium "Chicken Style" Broth Mix

For use in sauces, soups, entrées, side dishes, and tofu pâtés.

Eco-Cuisine® Reduced Sodium "Ground Beef Style" Quick Mix

The vegan ground beef style quick mix is one of a new generation of protein-concentrated meat analogues for foodservice operators. It is every chef's dream—very easy to prepare with infinite room for creativity and can be prepared with minimum skill and labor cost. While it saves money on labor and food cost, it offers maximum menu recipe applications ranging from burgers, meatballs, meat loaf, lasagna, chili, and stuffed peppers to simple burrito fillings.

VEGAN SALISBURY STEAK

YIELD: 6 (4-ounce) steaks (approximately 1 ½ pounds)
TIME: 15 minutes prep and 20 minutes cooking

6 ounces Eco-Cuisine® Reduced Sodium "Ground Beef Style" Quick Mix
2 ounces Eco-Cuisine® Reduced Sodium "Chicken Style" Quick Mix
2 teaspoons Eco-Cuisine® Reduced Sodium "Beef Style" Broth Powder
¼ cup canola oil
½ cup peeled and diced onions
½ cup fresh finely diced mushrooms
1 tablespoon minced garlic
½ teaspoon ground black pepper
1 ¼ cups water

1. Preheat oven to 350°F.
2. Mix together the ground beef-style and chicken-style proteins and broth powder.
3. Add oil and preheat a large (3- or 4-quart) pan on medium heat. Add onions, mushrooms, garlic, and pepper. Sauté until onions are transparent.
4. Add hot water and mix until thoroughly mixed.
5. Remove from heat and add protein mixture. Stir until the dry mixture is fully hydrated with wet ingredients. Let sit for 10 minutes.
6. Form into steaks. The easiest way is to scoop mixture onto an oiled surface or parchment paper–lined pan using a 3 ½ ounce scoop and flatten with a spatula to ¼ to ⅜ inch thick. With hands form into an oval shape. Lightly oil each steak to prevent them from sticking to the pan.
7. In a preheated and lightly oiled sauté pan on medium-low heat, sauté steaks for 3 to 5 minutes or until lightly browned. Flip steaks and repeat procedure. When brown, put in roasting pan with ¼ cup water, cover, and bake for 20 minutes. Check steaks; if they're not firm to touch, cover and bake another 10 minutes.

OPTION: When brown, add ¼ cup water to pan, cover and continue cooking until water has evaporated. Touch steak and if firm to touch, it is cooked. If not, add another ¼ cup water and repeat procedure. Let steaks cool for 10 to 15 minutes for protein to set. If steaks are too cool, steam, sauté, broil, or grill to reheat. Serve with Salisbury Steak-Style Sauce (page 212).

VARIATION: *Salisbury Burger*

When formed with scoop, flatten to ¼ inch thick in a round shape and follow the same directions to precook the burgers. Or you can form and steam the burgers for 10 to 15 minutes until firm, cool, refrigerate or freeze until ready to use.

AMERICAN-STYLE MEAT LOAF

YIELD: Approximately 7 (4-ounce) servings (approximately 1 ¾ pounds meat loaf)
TIME: 20 minutes prep and 45 minutes cooking

6 ounces Eco-Cuisine® Reduced Sodium "Ground Beef Style" Quick Mix

2 ounces Eco-Cuisine® Reduced Sodium "Chicken Style" Quick Mix

2 teaspoons Eco-Cuisine® Reduced Sodium "Beef Style" Broth Powder

¼ cup canola oil

½ cup peeled and diced onions

½ cup shredded carrots

1 tablespoon minced garlic

½ tablespoon dry chopped basil

½ teaspoon ground black pepper

1 ½ cups water

¼ cup ketchup

1. Preheat oven to 350°F.

2. Mix together ground beef and chicken proteins and broth powder

3. In a preheated, large (3- or 4-quart) pan on medium heat, add oil and onions, carrots, garlic, basil, and pepper. Sauté until onions are transparent.

4. Add hot water and ketchup and mix until evenly mixed.

5. Remove from heat and add protein mixture. Stir until the dry mixture is rehydrated into wet ingredients.

6. Lightly oil a large loaf pan and pack mixture evenly into the pan. Cover with aluminum foil, but do not let foil touch loaf. Place in preheated oven and bake for approximately 30 to 45 minutes or until the internal temperature reaches 160°F. The bake time could be less than 30 minutes, depending on how hot the mixture is when placed in the oven.

NOTE: The mixture will be soft when removed from the oven. Flip loaf pan upside down onto cutting board, letting it sit for at least 25 minutes to cool and to set the protein so it becomes firmer. Slice and serve or containerize and refrigerate until needed. If the loaf is too cool when ready to slice, flip back into loaf pan, cover, and bake another 10 minutes, or cover and steam or microwave for about 1 minute.

VARIATION: *American Barley Loaf*

Follow steps 1 and 2 for American-Style Meat Loaf. Add 1 cup cooked moist barley to the dry protein mixes and let sit for 15 minutes. Then proceed with steps 3, 4, 5, and 6.

"BEEF-STYLE" BOLOGNESE SAUCE

YIELD: 8 servings (6 cups)
TIME: 15 minutes prep and 25 minutes cooking

3 tablespoons extra-virgin olive oil (or canola oil)

¼ cup diced white onions

1 teaspoon minced garlic

1 teaspoon dry chopped basil

2 bay leaves

2 teaspoons dry Italian seasoning blend

¼ teaspoon salt or to taste

¼ teaspoon black pepper or to taste

2 tablespoons white wine (or water)

2 tablespoons tomato paste

2 cups water

3 ¼ cups diced tomatoes, unseasoned

1 tablespoon fresh, chopped parsley

3 tablespoons Eco-Cuisine® Reduced Sodium "Beef-Style" Broth Powder

5 ounces Eco-Cuisine® Reduced Sodium "Ground Beef-Style" Quick Mix

Heat oil in medium stock pot, add onions, garlic, dry basil, bay leaf, and Italian spice herbs, salt, and pepper, and cook until soft (about 5 to 8 minutes). Add wine and tomato paste; stir well and cook 1 to 2 minutes to allow some wine to cook off and tomato paste to caramelize a little. Add water, tomatoes, parsley, broth powder, and ground beef style dry mix and stir well. Bring to a simmer, lower heat and slowly simmer for 45 minutes; stirring every 10 minutes; do not allow to stick or scorch. Taste sauce to ensure that texture is soft and fully rehydrated. If sauce becomes too thick, a small amount of water may be added; but this should be a very rich and meaty sauce.

SERVING SUGGESTION: Cook 1 pound of dry ziti al dente; toss with sauce and cook in pan for 1 minute; top with vegan parmesan.

VARIATION: *Bolognese Sauce with Roasted or Grilled Eggplant*

This is an authentic version of Bolognese Sauce recipe using the Reduced Sodium "Ground Beef Style" Quick Mix with eggplant, a unique ingredient that gives the sauce a soft texture and additional flavor.

1 ½ cups grilled or roasted eggplant, about ¼ inch diced

Stir diced eggplant into Bolognese Sauce, and let cook on low heat for about 5 minutes, occasionally stirring the sauce if it's not in a commercial steam kettle.

VARIATION: *Bolognese Sauce with Mostaccioli*

YIELD: 4 servings
TIME: 15 minutes prep and 30 minutes cooking

2 ½ cups Bolognese Sauce

2 ½ cups cooked mostaccioli pasta

¾ cup vegan shredded mozzarella

Heat Bolognese Sauce in saucepan until simmering. Add cooked pasta and stir. Heat to a simmer or until hot. Mix in ½ cup shredded mozzarella. Serve in four equal portions. Garnish with remaining cheese, and serve.

OPTION: Garnish with parsley and/or serve a side of Tuscan Vegetable Sauté (page 191).

ITALIAN MEATBALLS

YIELD: 12 meatballs (1.1 ounces each/use #40 scoop)
TIME: 15 minutes prep and 10 to 20 minutes cooking
(including 10 minutes under broiler)

4 ounces Eco-Cuisine® Reduced Sodium
"Ground Beef Style" Quick Mix
1 ounce Eco-Cuisine® Reduced Sodium
"Chicken Style" Quick Mix
1 ounce finely diced onions
1 ⅛ teaspoons Italian seasoning
⅛ teaspoon ground black pepper
1 teaspoon fresh minced garlic
1 ½ tablespoons olive oil
1 ¼ cups water

1. Mix ground beef-style mix with chicken-style mix and set aside for 10 minutes to allow the proteins to hydrate. (This will allow the mixture to become firm enough to scoop out in one ounce meatballs.)

2. Sauté onions, Italian seasoning, black pepper, and garlic in oil until onions are translucent. Remove from heat and add water and protein mixture. Mix to incorporate and set aside for 5 minutes.

3. Scoop out as meatballs, cover and steam for 15 minutes. The meatballs can be served immediately but best to let them rest for 5 to 10 minutes before serving.

OPTION: Preheat 10 to 14 inch sauté pan with lid on medium heat. Lightly oil pan and meatballs. Place meatballs in pan. Let sauté for about 1 to 2 minutes to lightly brown and then steam following step three.

Eco-Cuisine® Reduced Sodium "Chicken Style" Quick Mix

Eco-Cuisine® Reduced Sodium "Chicken Style" Quick Mix can replace chicken wherever it is used on your menu. By simply adding water and oil to the basic mix (plus any desired combination of savory flavoring ingredients, precooked whole grains, and/or beans), then mixing, forming, and cooking, the result is a reduced-fat and reduced-sodium, plant-based meat substitute with the rich flavor, texture, and color of cooked chicken. Applications include cold cuts, chicken loaves, burgers, cacciatore, piccata, à la king, stuffed "breast," pistachio crusted, and more. The variations are limited only by the chef's creativity. This product is freeze/thaw stable when prepared and has a shelf life of 5 to 7 days when cooked and properly refrigerated.

CHICKEN & POT ROAST/STEAM METHODS

YIELD: 11 (3-ounce) servings
TIME: 20 minutes prep and 20 minutes cooking

1 pound Eco-Cuisine® Reduced Sodium
"Chicken Style" Quick Mix
4 teaspoons Eco-Cuisine® Reduced Sodium
"Chicken Style" Broth Powder (optional)
2 ¼ cups water
½ cup canola oil

Mix protein and broth powder until evenly dispersed. Add water and ¼ cup of oil. Mix for 2 to 3 minutes on low speed with a paddle. Form into a roll and equally divide into 4 pieces. Form each piece into a 1-inch thick large rectangular shape. Pour ¼ cup oil into a large sauté pan on medium heat. Place 4 "chicken" pieces in the pan and immediately flip so both sides are coated with oil. Sauté side one until golden brown, 3 to 5 minutes. Flip and when second side is browned, immediately remove from heat.

TO POT ROAST THE CHICKEN PROTEIN: Place on a wire rack in a roasting pan with ¼ inch water in pan. (Water level must be below the rack holding the protein.) Cover and cook in a preheated 375°F oven for about 20 minutes or until protein is firm or reaches 160°F internally.

TO STEAM: Place the protein in an oiled shallow steam pan. Cover with plastic and place in a commercial steamer. Steam for 20 minutes or until protein reaches 170–180°F. Remove and set aside until ready to use.

ASIAN BBQ CHICKEN WITH CARAMELIZED ONIONS ON A BUN

Use a BBQ sauce with a smoked flavor.

YIELD: 4 servings (¾ cup each)
TIME: 10 minutes prep and 20 minutes cooking

To Caramelize Onions

3 tablespoons canola oil
1 cup peeled and thinly sliced yellow onions
⅛ teaspoon salt
1 teaspoon fresh, minced garlic
½ teaspoon roasted sesame oil (optional)

To a preheated sauté pan on medium high heat, add the oil, onions, salt, and garlic. Sauté while occasionally stirring until onions are caramelized (lightly brown). Remove from heat.

To Barbecue "Chicken"

1 ½ cups (8 ounces) precooked Eco-Cuisine® Reduced Sodium "Chicken Style" Quick Mix, sliced approximately ⅛ inch or thinner (the final product is like shredded or pulled pork—there is only a semblance to slices).
¾ cup Asian BBQ Sauce (page 235) or commercial BBQ sauce
¼ cup water
¼ cup thinly sliced scallions (optional)

1. To the sautéed onion and garlic mixture, immediately add chicken, BBQ sauce, and water, stir ingredients together, and return to heat, reducing to medium low. Cook 10 minutes or until simmering.

2. Remove from heat. Stir in scallions. If steaming, place in steam pan, cover with plastic wrap and steam for 10 to 15 minutes. Remove and serve. If not steaming, pour 2 tablespoons water into mixture, cover sauté pan, use a low heat and cook for 8 to 10 minutes or until hot. Adjust seasoning to taste.

NOTE: Because the "chicken" is sliced thin, it requires less stirring to give the chicken a pulled pork effect and it will immediately absorb the BBQ flavor.

VARIATION: *Asian BBQ Seitan*

In place of "chicken," substitute thinly sliced seitan.

VARIATION: *Asian BBQ Tempeh*

In place of "chicken," substitute ⅛-inch-thin sliced tempeh (smoked if possible).

OPTION: Use a commercial barbecue sauce of your choice or your favorite recipe. You may have to increase the amount of barbecue sauce used depending on the flavor concentration.

VEGAN "CHICKEN-STYLE" PICCATA

YIELD: 8 (3-ounce) servings
TIME: 30 minutes prep and 20 minutes cooking

Chicken-Style Cutlet Protein
¾ pound Eco-Cuisine® Reduced Sodium "Chicken Style" Quick Mix

1 ½ cups water

3 tablespoons canola or extra-virgin olive oil

6 tablespoons flour

4 tablespoons olive oil

2 cups Piccata Sauce (page 237)

3 tablespoons capers

¼ teaspoon salt (optional)

1. Pour chicken-style dry mix, water, and oil into a mixing bowl. Mix with spoon by hand or with a paddle on slow speed for about one minute to rehydrate. Mix on slow speed for about 2 to 3 minutes or until it forms a dough.

2. Form into a roll, and cut into 8 (¼-inch thick) raw cutlets (3 ounces each).

3. Dredge the cutlets in the flour and set aside.

4. Heat the oil in a tilt fryer or large sauté pan over medium heat. Add cutlets and cook for about 2 to 4 minutes, or until brown.

Turn and cook for 2 to 4 minutes, or until the second side is browned. Transfer the cooked cutlets to a plate that is lined with paper towels to absorb any excess oil.

5. Add the Piccata Sauce to the pan along with the capers and salt and heat over medium-low heat. Serve the chicken-style cutlets hot with at least ¼ cup of sauce.

VARIATION: *Chicken Piccata with Cannellini Beans*

Use 1 ¼ pounds diced chicken-style protein and 1 ¼ pounds cannelloni, fava, or other bean of your choice.

VARIATION: *Cannellini Beans Piccata with Pine Nuts*

Use 2 ½ pounds of cooked and drained beans in place of chicken and include 2 to 3 ounces (½ cup) roasted pine nuts.

CHICKEN LE COQ AU VIN (CHICKEN WITH WINE)

The original recipe for Le Coq au Vin calls for diced salt pork. A hint of smoke flavor is a delicious vegan alternative. I have used Vegan "Beef Style" Broth Powder in place of "Chicken Style" broth powder. It is an excellent secondary option.

YIELD: 6 servings (3 cups sauce) or ½ cup sauce per 3 ounces protein
TIME: 20 minutes prep and 20 minutes cooking

Savory Red Wine Sauce
4 tablespoons safflower or canola oil

½ pound shiitake or button mushrooms, quartered

1 cup baby pearl onions or diced fresh onions

2 teaspoons fresh, minced garlic

½ teaspoon dried thyme

1 bay leaf

⅛ teaspoon ground black pepper

5 tablespoons unbleached white flour

1 ¼ cups water

¼ cup Eco-Cuisine® Reduced Sodium "Beef Style" Broth Powder (option to add more for a stronger flavor)

1 cup cabernet or red wine

1/16 teaspoon liquid smoke flavor (optional)

1. Heat sauté pan on medium heat and add oil, mushrooms, bay leaf, and onions. While occasionally stirring, sauté on medium high heat for about 5 minutes or until the onions are caramelized. Add the garlic, thyme, and pepper and continually stir for about 1 minute to sauté the garlic without burning it.

2. Mix in flour and cook another 3 minutes while stirring to lightly brown the roux. Add water and broth powder and mix until evenly dispersed and sauce thickens. Slowly mix wine into sauce and let cook on low heat for about 15 minutes. If sauce becomes too thick, add water to thin.

Chicken-Style Le Coq au Vin Protein
YIELD: 6 (3-ounce) servings
TIME: 10 minutes prep and 15 minutes cooking

1 ⅛ cups water (for "Chicken Style" mix)

2 tablespoons canola oil

8 ounces Eco-Cuisine® Reduced Sodium "Chicken Style" Quick Mix

¼ cup unbleached white flour

¼ cup water (for cooking protein)

1. Add 1 ⅛ cups water and 2 tablespoons oil to chicken-style protein, mix for about 2 minutes to form into a protein dough.

2. Form into a roll and cut into 6 equal slices. Flatten each into a ⅜-inch cutlet.

3. Dredge cutlets in flour and sauté on medium-low heat until lightly brown. Flip and do the same. Add ¼ cup water to sauté pan, cover and let cook on simmer (medium-low heat) until water has evaporated (about 6 to 10 minutes).

4. Remove from heat. When finished, the protein should be firm to the touch as would be real chicken meat.

NOTE: Lay protein on a plate of cooked rice of your choice or Whipped Squash Potatoes with Rosemary (page 185). Pour ¼ cup sauce over the bottom half of the protein. Tuscan Vegetable Sauté (page 191) is a complementary side dish.

VARIATION: *Chicken-Style Le Coq au Vin with White Kidney Beans*

Use 1 cup beans and 10 ounces diced "Chicken Style" Quick Mix. Note: Prepare and set aside half of the cooked protein for future use.

VARIATION: *Navy Beans au Vin with Roasted Pecans*

Use 1 ½ cups cooked, drained navy beans instead of protein recipe and 3 ounces or ¾ cup roasted pecans.

THANKSGIVING DAY VEGAN CHICKEN

YIELD: 8 servings (1 medium loaf)
TIME: 35 minute preparation and 60 minutes baking

¾ pound Eco-Cuisine® Reduced Sodium "Chicken-Style" Quick Mix
1 ¼ cups water
3 tablespoons oil
2 cups Sage Dressing (page 260)

1. In a mixer or mixing bowl, combine the mix, water, and oil with a large spoon or with a mixing paddle. Mix until blended on medium speed (about 1 minute). Rest a few minutes to allow the protein mixture to absorb the water becoming firmer and easier to handle.

2. Roll out horizontally the width of the pan and vertically 4 times the height of 8 ½ x 4 x 2 ¾ inch oiled loaf pan. Center rolled-out protein over pan vertically and gently press into pan.

3. Place Sage Dressing in loaf pan and flip both vertical ends to center of loaf, seal, cover with foil and steam or bake in 350°F oven with steam heat, conventional oven, or steamer. Note: Any method will work but moist heat is generally the best option for vegan meat analogues.

4. For the option of a roll instead of a loaf, cut 2 (15–inch-long) pieces of plastic wrap and overlap each piece horizontally on a kitchen countertop. Remove the protein from the mixer and place at the center of the plastic on the countertop. Spread with wet hands into a 13 by 7-inch wide piece of protein on the plastic wrap. Place the dressing down the center of the piece.

5. Seal the edges and ends and roll tightly into a log. Next, roll in aluminum foil, gently twist ends to seal. Steam for about 45 minutes or until the internal temperature reaches 170°F.

VEGAN CHICKEN CRANBERRY SALAD

YIELD: 3 servings (1 ½ cups)
TIME: 10 minutes

1 ½ cups prepared Eco-Cuisine® Reduced Sodium "Chicken Style" Quick Mix and cut into strips or diced
½ cup sweetened dried cranberries
¼ cup sliced scallions
½ cup vegan commercial mayonnaise or Soy Mayonnaise (page 154)
⅛ teaspoon nutmeg
¼ teaspoon celery seed (optional), or 2 tablespoons fresh finely diced celery (optional)

Mix together all ingredients, cool, and serve.

Eco-Cuisine® Reduced Sodium "Sausage Style" Quick Mix

Applications include sausage "meat" balls, sausage links, loaves, or patties and are limited only by the chef's creativity. The Eco-Cuisine® Reduced Sodium "Sausage Style" Quick Mix has a basic sausage flavor profile, which can be modified to a breakfast sausage, Italian sausage, or any flavor or application desired by the end user. The sausage is freeze/thaw stable once cooked and has a shelf life of 5 to 7 days under refrigeration under ideal conditions (when cooked and stored as directed). This sausage mix makes an exceptional pizza topping that can be placed raw on a pizza and baked like traditional sausage on a pizza.

BASIC "SAUSAGE-STYLE" PATTIES

YIELD: 10 (2-ounce) patties
TIME: 10 minutes prep and 15 to 20 minutes cooking

6 ounces Eco-Cuisine® Reduced Sodium "Sausage Style" Quick Mix
2 ounces Eco-Cuisine® Reduced Sodium "Chicken Style" Quick Mix
2 teaspoons sausage seasoning* (optional)
1 ½ cups hot water
2 tablespoons canola oil

1. Place quick mixes into a bowl with sausage seasoning. Mix ingredients together.

2. Add hot water and oil. Mix with spoon by hand or with a paddle on slow speed for about one minute to rehydrate.

*Use any type of sodium-free or low sodium sausage seasoning.

NOTE: The "Chicken Style" Quick Mix gives the Breakfast "Sausage Style" Patties additional binding for robust handling of the patties on the grill. Immediately after steaming, the texture will be softer. Once cooled and reheated (such as grilled, etc.) the sausage patties will have a strong, pork-like texture and flavor.

ITALIAN "SAUSAGE-STYLE" FOR PIZZA

If you are making pizza and want a vegan sausage protein that is exceptional, here is your recipe.

YIELD: 6 cups Italian Pizza Sausage
TIME: 10 minutes prep and 30 minutes to rehydrate

1 pound Eco-Cuisine® Reduced Sodium "Sausage Style" Quick Mix
6 tablespoons Italian spice blend
1 tablespoon ground fennel
1 tablespoon granulated garlic
5 ½ cups hot water
½ cup canola or olive oil

1. In a mixing bowl, combine sausage mix, spice blend, fennel, and garlic. Add hot water and mix into protein until evenly dispersed (about 1 minute). Next, add oil and mix until evenly distributed. Let sit for half an hour to rehydrate (using hot water will speed the process).

2. Mix again to ensure even distribution of the ingredients. Place in dollops on the pizza, and bake according to pizza instructions.

Eco-Cuisine® "Beef Style" Seitan Quick Mix

The traditional labor-intensive method of making seitan was introduced earlier in "Seitan Method I" on page 276, where you'll also find an entire recipe section. Eco-Cuisine® "Beef Style" Seitan Quick Mix as a culinary speed scratch product cuts about 90 percent of the labor in making seitan. Make it from scratch and you will see my point. The quick mix is different from traditional seitan in that it has three different plant proteins: gluten flour, flax meal, and whole wheat flour. The preparation technique presented below is an easy cooking method, and the end product works well in the recipes presented in the entrées section.

What is also unique about the quick mix versus making seitan from scratch is with the quick mix the cook can add any spice blend, grains, etc., to the seitan, infusing it with an array of flavors and textures. Once prepared the protein will keep about 1 week in the refrigerator if properly handled and stored. It is freeze/thaw stable.

SAUTÉ METHOD

YIELD: approximately 2 ½ pounds
TIME: 15 minutes prep and 35 to 40 minutes cooking

1 pound Eco-Cuisine® "Beef Style" Seitan Quick Mix

¾ teaspoon garlic powder

¼ teaspoon ground ginger

1 cup + 3 tablespoons water

⅓ cup tamari or soy sauce

⅓ cup canola oil for sautéing

1. Mix the vegan "Beef Style" Seitan Quick Mix with garlic, ginger, water, and tamari into a dough. Place dough on cutting board and cut into ⅛-inch slices.

2. Heat oil on medium heat. In tilt fryer or flat grill, fry pieces of seitan until lightly browned on both sides, about 5 minutes total. Immediately transfer seitan to 2 to 4 quart stockpot already filled with 1 pint ice and 1 quart ice water.

3. When all seitan has been cooked and shocked in ice water, transfer stockpot to burner. Cover seitan with 1 inch of water. Bring to a simmer for 25 minutes, let cool, and refrigerate until ready to use.

Cooking Notes for Seitan Dry Mix

↻ Avoid high heat as it will burn the seitan before it cooks through or cause it to "set" in its spongy state.

↻ Once the seitan expands when sautéing, don't cook it any longer than 30 to 45 seconds or the gluten will "set" in its spongy state.

↻ Shocking immediately after the seitan begins to expand will cause it to constrict, creating the desired firm texture.

SINGLE STEAM METHOD

YIELD: 2 pounds
TIME: 10 minutes prep and 35 to 45 minutes steaming

1 pound Eco-Cuisine® "Beef Style" Seitan Quick Mix

1 ¾ cups room temperature water

5 ½ tablespoons tamari or soy sauce

¾ teaspoon granulated garlic

½ teaspoon ginger powder

1. Mix water, tamari or soy sauce, granulated garlic, and ginger powder together in mixing bowl, preferably with a paddle or dough hook. Add the Beef Style Seitan Quick Mix to the seasoned water solution. Mix for about 4 minutes, or until a dough is formed.

2. Preheat vegetable steamer with water about ½ inch below perforated pan (water will

expand and if it touches seitan could cause it to become soggy). Oil a perforated vegetable steamer insert. Hand rub seitan with oil and firmly press into pan and cover with vegetables steamer lid. Steam seitan until the center reaches 180° or about 35 minutes. Check water about 10 minutes into steaming and add more water if necessary to avoid total evaporation of water. Check and steam more if necessary.

3. When seitan is fully cooked, place in a blast chiller or in ice water to cool and set the protein. This will cause the seitan to contract.

NOTE: Another technique is to form seitan rolls about 2 ½ inches in diameter. DO NOT OIL THE ROLLS as it will not allow the plastic wrap to adhere to the seitan. Tightly wrap in plastic wrap, and then in aluminum foil twisting the ends to form a chub and hold seal. Place in same vegetable steamer and steam until reaches 180°F. The seitan will be firmer, absorbing additional moisture and flavor when cooked in moist heat.

ALSO NOTE: If the seitan isn't completely cooked in the center when cooled, slice ½-inch thick slices to make steaks, steam to 180°, and blast chill or refrigerate until cool. Use as needed in recipes. Seitan can be re-cooked and refrigerated or frozen several times without any negative textural effects.

Eco-Cuisine® Culinary Speed Scratch Bakery Mixes

These mixes were primarily created for those in the foodservice industry who don't have the option (labor, equipment, inventory storage space, a pastry chef, a baker, or a committed pastry shop in their kitchen) to bake from scratch. These easy-to-use mixes reduce inventory management while increasing pastry and dessert diversity with just one bakery mix. This line of mixes is called "Basic" because each product is like a blank canvas for even an inexperienced baker to be minimally innovative while creating a consistent pastry. For experienced pastry chefs the sky is the limit with Eco-Cuisine's basic speed scratch bakery mixes. Here are a few of the bakery mixes with basic applications and some labor-saving recipes.

Eco-Cuisine® Basic Chocolate Brownie Mix

This brownie won the Gold Medal in the International Culinary Olympics in 1996 and is low fat without any icing. It is what I call a "midrange" brownie, between a cake and a fudge brownie. See the recipe below on how to change the texture.

BASIC BROWNIE BAKING TECHNIQUES

○ *Do not overmix.* When first mixed, the batter may seem stiff. Once it sets for a few minutes and the sugars break down, the batter will soften.

○ *Cool before cutting.* The vegan brownie must cool before cutting to create clean slices of brownie. It is optimal to freeze the brownies before cutting to obtain a clean cut in portioning.

○ *Creativity encouraged.* Nuts, chocolate chips, black cherries, etc., can be added for different flavors and textures. It will take strong ingredients to stand up to the rich chocolate flavor of the brownie.

BASIC BROWNIE

YIELD: 12 (2-ounce) servings
TIME: 5 minutes prep and 15 minutes baking

1 pound Eco-Cuisine® Basic Chocolate Brownie Mix
1 cup water
1 tablespoon vanilla extract

1. Preheat oven to 350°F.
2. Place chocolate brownie mix and flour in a mixing bowl. Add water and vanilla and mix with spoon until evenly dispersed and dry mix is fully rehydrated (don't overmix).
3. Pour batter into an oiled and floured (unless no-stick surface is used) baking pan (10 ¼ x 6 ½ x 1 ¼ inches). Bake for approximately 15 to 20 minutes, or until the center springs back when gently pressed.

OPTIONS: Add 1 ounce sugar per pound of mix for a fudgier brownie.

Add 2 ounces flour per pound of mix for a cakier brownie.

BASIC FIRM TEXTURED CHOCOLATE BROWNIE

This brownie is the overall best vegan application for serving as a simple brownie. It maintains its rich chocolate flavor while making it very easy to handle. The firm texture makes for an improved dining experience and ease of handling.

YIELD: 12 (2-ounce) servings
TIME: 5 minutes prep and 15 minutes baking

1 pound Eco-Cuisine® Basic Chocolate Brownie Mix
2 ounces white flour
1 cup water
4 teaspoons vanilla extract

1. Preheat oven to 350°F.
2. Place chocolate brownie mix and flour in a 2- to 3-quart mixing bowl. Add water and vanilla and mix with large spoon until evenly dispersed (don't overmix).
3. Pour batter into an oiled and floured (unless no-stick surface is used) brownie baking pan (10 ¼ x 6 ½ x 1 ¼ inches).
4. Bake for approximately 15 to 20 minutes, or until the center springs back when gently pressed.

VARIATION: *Walnut Brownie*

Add 4 ounces chopped walnuts with flour to brownie mix.

VEGAN CHOCOLATE CAKE

This recipe is an example of how culinary speed scratch bakery mixes can work in tandem to create a totally different product.

YIELD: 12 (2-ounce) servings
TIME: 5 minutes prep and 15 minutes baking

14 ounces Eco-Cuisine® Chocolate Brownie Mix
3 ounces Eco-Cuisine® Basic Muffin Mix
1 cup water
4 teaspoons canola oil
1 tablespoon vanilla extract

1. Preheat oven to 350°F.

2. Place chocolate brownie and basic muffin dry mixes in a mixing bowl and blend for 30 seconds on low speed.

3. Add water, oil, and vanilla and mix until evenly dispersed.

4. Pour batter into an oiled and floured (unless no-stick surface is used) baking pan (10 ¼ x 6 ½ x 1 ¼ inches).

5. Bake for approximately 20 to 25 minutes, until the center springs back when gently pressed.

Eco-Cuisine® Basic Muffin and Pancake Mix

Eco-Cuisine's all-natural basic muffin and pancake dry mix has infinite muffin variations including cranberry orange, chocolate chip pecan, bran, and banana. Other applications include coffee cake, cobbler topping, quick breads, pineapple upside down cake, jelly rolls, and different pancakes. The bakery products have a shelf life of 3 to 5 days if properly stored.

BASIC MUFFINS

YIELD: 8 (3 ½-ounce) muffins
TIME: 5 minutes prep and 20 minutes baking

1 pound Eco-Cuisine® Basic Muffin and Pancake Mix
¼ cup oil
1 ½ cups water
1 tablespoon vanilla extract

1. In a mixing bowl, combine the basic muffin dry mix, water, and vanilla. Blend until evenly dispersed.

2. Place ⅓ cup batter in each cup of a silicone paper-lined or oiled muffin tin and bake at 375°F for 15 minutes or until golden brown and completely baked. Cool and serve.

BASIC PANCAKES

YIELD: 4 servings (2 pancakes each)
TIME: 5 minutes prep and 10 to 15 minutes cooking

1 ¼ cups Eco-Cuisine® Basic Muffin and Pancake Mix
1 tablespoon cornstarch
1 ⅛ cups (18 tablespoons) water
2 tablespoons sunflower or canola oil
1 ½ teaspoons vanilla extract

1. In a mixing bowl, combine basic muffin mix and cornstarch. Mix until starch is evenly dispersed in muffin mix.

2. Add water, oil, and vanilla and mix until batter is formed and all dries are hydrated.

3. Oil and heat sauté pan or griddle to medium heat. Spoon about ⅓ cup batter onto oiled pan for each pancake and cook until pancake begins to show bubbles. Flip and cook until pancake is firm to touch.

4. Pancakes can be served immediately but they have better texture when left to sit for about 5 to 10 minutes.

CRANBERRY-ORANGE STREUSEL COFFEE CAKE

YIELD: 8 (4-ounce) servings
TIME: 10 minutes prep and 20 minutes baking

1 pound Eco-Cuisine® Basic Muffin and Pancake Mix
3 tablespoons palm shortening
¾ cup dried, sweetened cranberries
½ teaspoon cinnamon
1 ½ cups orange juice
½ teaspoon lemon extract
1 cup Eco-Cuisine Streusel

1. Preheat oven to 375°F.

2. Oil and flour a 10 ¼ x 6 ½ x 1 ¼-inch pan or a 9-inch round cake pan.

3. In a mixing bowl, combine the muffin mix and shortening. Mix with a paddle until the shortening is evenly dispersed (similar to cutting shortening into flour for a pie dough).

4. Add dried cranberries and cinnamon and mix until the berries are evenly coated with dry mixture and the cinnamon is evenly mixed into muffin mix.

5. Add orange juice and lemon extract; mix long enough to integrate dry and wet ingredients.

6. Pour batter into the prepared pan. Top with vegan streusel (see recipe below).

7. Bake in preheated oven for 20 to 25 minutes, or until golden brown and completely baked. Cool and serve.

Eco-Cuisine Streusel

1 pound Eco-Cuisine® Basic Muffin and Pancake Mix
1 cup sweetened flaked coconut
¾ cup palm shortening

1. Mix ingredients together with a paddle until shortening is evenly cut into the muffin mix.

2. Sprinkle desired quantity over muffins and bake according to recipe.

Eco-Cuisine® Basic Cookie Mix

This basic mix was designed to make cookies and cookie bars. The cookie bar is very forgiving in terms of scaling and baking. The cookie isn't. So the foodservice professional or passionate cook has options. Any creative cookie variation may be made by adding a variety of flavors, dried fruits, or nuts to the basic mix. This includes cookies and bars such as chocolate chip, pecan, coconut, oatmeal raisin, or Genoa (fruit cake type) cookie bars which are much easier to make. Genoa cookie bars are an exceptional vegan option for a delicious Christmas fruit cake style pastry.

BASIC COOKIES

The basic cookie mix can be baked into plain sugar cookies for those who want a simple dessert.

YIELD: 12 cookies using #40 scoop (about 2 ½ tablespoon portions)
TIME: 10 minutes prep and 10 minutes baking

1 pound Eco-Cuisine® Basic Cookie Mix
5 tablespoons canola oil
7 tablespoons water
2 teaspoons vanilla extract

1. Put oil with cookie mix in a mixing bowl. Using a paddle, mix for 5 minutes on low speed.

2. Add water and vanilla and mix on low speed. Scrape the sides of the bowl after about 1 minute then continue mixing until blended.

3. Use a #40 (1 ¾-inch diameter) scoop to portion dough onto lightly oiled baking sheet and press with your wet hand to about ¼ inch thick.

4. Bake at 375°F 7 to 9 minutes or until completely baked or firm to touch (springs back).

VARIATION: *Chocolate Chip Cookie*

Add 2 ½ ounces vegan chocolate chips to the dry mix with oil.

DATE-COCONUT COOKIE BAR

YIELD: 12 servings (2 ounces each)
TIME: 10 minutes prep time and 25 minutes baking

1 pound Eco-Cuisine® Basic Cookie Mix
5 tablespoons canola oil
⅛ teaspoon salt
1 cup chopped pitted dates* (about 6 ounces by weight)
1 cup shredded sweetened coconut
⅝ cup (10 tablespoons) water
4 teaspoons vanilla extract

1. Preheat oven to 350°F.

2. In a large mixing bowl, combine cookie mix, oil, and salt until evenly dispersed.

3. Add dates and coconut and evenly mix.

4. Combine water and vanilla and add to dry ingredient mixture. Mix until a soft dough is formed.

5. Oil and flour a 10 ¼ x 6 ½ x 1 ¼-inch brownie pan. Spread batter evenly in pan using wet hands to prevent it from sticking to hands. Press evenly into pan.

6. Bake in oven for approximately 25 minutes or until lightly browned. Remove from oven and cool on a rack.

*****NOTE:** Ingredient weight varies depending on the density of the ingredient. For instance the volume of a cup of (dense) pound cake will be less than a cup of (light) angel food cake.

Eco-Cuisine® Basic English Scone Mix

I contacted and worked with the United Kingdom bakery industry to attain and develop a vegan version of the original English scone, which is a semisweet biscuit. In the United States the scone has been modified with numerous versions that are quite sweet. The Eco-Cuisine Basic Scone Mix has infinite flavor variations with spices, nuts, and fruits. It can also be used to make Italian biscotti. It can be served for breakfast, snack, or dessert. I have also used the scone as a cheesecake crust.

BASIC ENGLISH SCONE

YIELD: 16 scones
TIME: 15 minutes prep and 10 minutes baking

1 pound Eco-Cuisine® Basic Scone Mix
½ cup (4 ounces) palm shortening or vegan butter spread
¾ cup water or soy milk
1 tablespoon vanilla extract

1. Preheat oven to 400°F.
2. In a mixing bowl, combine the scone mix and palm shortening. Mix with a paddle until the shortening is evenly cut or integrated into the mix.
3. Add milk and vanilla and mix long enough to integrate the dry and wet ingredients.
4. Divide dough into two equal pieces about ¼- to ⅜-inch thick. Roll one piece of dough on a floured surface into a round. To make 8 triangular scones, cut the round in quarters,

then each of those in half. Repeat process with second piece of dough.

5. Bake in preheated oven for 10 minutes, or until golden brown and completely baked. Cool and serve.

ENGLISH CRANBERRY-GINGER SCONE

YIELD: 16 scones
TIME: 15 minutes prep and 10 minutes baking

1 pound Eco-Cuisine® Basic Scone Mix
½ cup (4 ounces) palm shortening or vegan butter spread
½ cup chopped dried sweetened cranberries
½ cup chopped candied ginger
¾ cup water
2 tablespoons lemon extract

1. Preheat oven to 400°F.
2. In a mixing bowl, combine the scone mix and shortening. Mix with a paddle until the shortening is evenly dispersed.
3. Add cranberries and ginger and mix until evenly dispersed.
4. Add water and lemon extract and mix long enough to integrate dry and wet ingredients.
5. Divide dough into two equal pieces. Roll one piece of dough on a floured surface into a round. To make 8 triangular scones, cut the round in quarters, then each of those in half. Repeat process with second piece of dough.
6. Bake in preheated oven for 10 minutes, or until golden brown and completely baked. Cool and serve.

ITALIAN PISTACHIO BISCOTTI

Biscotti are first baked as a raw product until completely baked. Then they are sliced and baked at a low temperature to dry the biscuit. I think of biscotti as the Italian version of the English scone.

YIELD: 18 biscotti
TIME: 15 minutes prep and 30 minutes baking

1 pound Eco-Cuisine® Basic Scone Mix
½ cup (4 ounces) palm shortening or vegan butter spread
½ cup coarsely chopped pistachio nuts
2 tablespoons ground fennel
¾ cup water
1 tablespoon vanilla extract

1. Preheat oven to 400°F.

2. Pour scone mix, shortening, pistachios, and fennel into a mixing bowl and use a paddle to mix. On medium speed mix for 3 to 5 minutes until the shortening is evenly cut into the dry mix. Add water and vanilla and mix on medium speed for about 1 minute or until a dough is formed.

3. On a lightly floured surface, form the dough into a 14-inch long x 4-inch wide oval loaf. Place on oiled baking sheet pan.

4. Bake in preheated oven for 20 minutes. Remove from the oven and let cool for 10 to 15 minutes. Reduce oven temperature to 300°F.

5. Slice the loaf into ½-inch thick pieces and lay on same baking sheet. Bake for an additional 25 minutes. Remove from oven. Let sit until cool. Store in sealed container until ready to serve.

Eco-Cuisine® Instant Soy Pudding Mix

The versatile Eco-Cuisine Instant Soy Pudding Mix flavor is delicate enough to complement added flavors like chocolate, lemon, etc. By adding oil and water, the basic dry mix becomes a great tasting, nutritious pudding that is low fat. Substituting soy milk for the water makes for a richer pudding. Numerous culinary applications include pastry cream for pie fillings, icings, mousses, cream cake/tort fillings, parfaits, classical desserts, and rice puddings.

INSTANT VANILLA SOY PUDDING

YIELD: 12 (½ cup) servings
TIME: 10 minutes

1 pound Eco-Cuisine® Instant Soy Pudding Mix
6 cups water or 7 cups soy milk
½ cup canola oil

Pour 6 cups water into medium mixing bowl. Add Instant Soy Pudding mix and stir with paddle on medium speed for 2 to 3 minutes (or mix by hand until smooth and creamy). Stop mixer and add oil, then continue mixing for another 1 to 2 minutes on medium speed to develop the pudding's smooth texture and delicate flavor. Serve immediately, or chill or heat as desired.

VARIATION: *Chocolate Pudding*

Add 1½ cups cocoa powder and 1 cup sugar to pudding dry mix. Using a wire whisk, stir until the cocoa is evenly mixed into the dry mix. Then follow the directions for making the basic pudding mix.

Appendix B

Distributor/ Retailer Resource List
for Vegan Ingredients

The list of natural vegan foodservice and retail options is extensive. This section looks at foodservice distribution and vegan ingredients available at the distributor and retail level. Most medium to large cities in the United States have a natural foods retail store and nationwide distributor services are available to foodservice customers.

All major foodservice distributors have at least a minimal amount of vegan and natural products, and the larger ones use third-party logistics. The following distributor and product list includes some foodservice terms and will assist in your ingredient sourcing. Also included at the end are some smallwares bakery equipment.

Distributor Services

For professional chefs with foodservice operations, many options exist through broadline distributors. Also check in with your regional distributor to compare prices with national distributors. Regional distributors may pay a little less or more for a product but often have a significantly lower operating cost and quite often beat the national distributors on total price. If you don't have a primary vendor contract with a broadline distributor, you most likely pay a higher price that regional distributors may be able to beat. Many food companies, if they sell a brand as a dry product or ingredient, ship direct. Visiting their websites will present you with more information on the company's products and purchasing options. With rare, if any, exception, all companies have a website.

Two Different Food Categories

The two different food categories in both foodservice and retail food distribution are conventional foods and natural/organic foods. Many conventional foodservice distribution companies now carry natural, organic, and vegetarian food products and some natural foods distributors cross dock products for broadline distributors.

Some Distribution/FoodService Terms

What Is a Broadline Distributor? In foodservice language a broadline distributor supplies a large variety of food products to many different accounts. A specialty distributor handles a certain segment or a narrow part of the market and fulfills accounts with different special needs.

What Is "Third-Party Logistics"? Essentially it is the third leg of a logistical transaction to move product from distribution to the customer when the distributor who sells the product does not inventory it. The customer orders the product(s) from the distributor, and the distributor passes the purchase order onto an independent warehouse that ships the order to the customer. The third party invoices the distributor and the distributor invoices the customer with both the third party and distributor adding their profit margins onto the product(s).

Why Do Broadline Distributors Have a Direct Ship Program? The primary reason is because the distributor has insufficient sales to merit inventorying (storing or warehousing) the products. Most distributors want to sell at least five cases of a product per week to justify inventorying the product. When sales are sufficient, the distributor will stock the product.

Pricing

Whether professional chef or home cook, look for the competitive price point. Large distributors are not necessarily the least expensive nor the smaller companies more expensive. It is all relative to their pricing structure.

Conventional Distributors

Here is the online address for the top 50 conventional broadline foodservice distributors in the United States. You can choose one from the list that is in your demographic area. **(foodservice.com/foodshow/foodservice_distributors.cfm)**

Natural and Vegan Product Distributors

KeHE is a large specialty distributor in the United States with nine distribution centers in the U.S. and three in Canada. **(kehe.com/Suppliers/Distribution.aspx)**

Companies That Sell Vegan Products Direct to Retail Customers or Third-Party Logistics through Broadline Distributors

Med Diet Foodservice Express is a third party logistics company that drop ships products for retail customers. You can order online through their storefront with your credit card. The company sells specialty food items for diabetics, gluten intolerance, vegan, and many other special dietary needs. **(med-diet.com)**

Food Service Express, a subsidiary of Med Diet, sells products directly to foodservice customers or through third party logistics national foodservice distributors that have an account with a broadline distributor. Note: Eco-Cuisine's products are available through both companies by direct ship. **(foodserviceexpress.com)**

Other Retail Customer Options

Retail customers have many options to procure natural vegan products at their local natural foods stores or through online storefronts. Go to your local natural foods store, websites such as Med Diet, or the branded companies that ship direct.

Companies That Ship Vegan Products Direct

Many natural food companies ship vegan products directly to the retail customer. These include:

Great Eastern Sun	**Frontier Natural Products Coop**	**Eco-Cuisine**
(great-eastern-sun.com)	(frontiercoop.com)	(eco-cuisine.com)
(828) 665-7790	(800) 669-3275	(303) 402-0289

Both Great Eastern Sun and Frontier Natural Foods are generous donors to the American Natural Foods (ANF) nonprofit program.

Vegan Ingredients

We are currently blessed with a good number of vegan ingredients available to us in today's marketplace. I have listed the ingredients I often use. I have also noted when any of these manufacturers or suppliers are donors to the nonprofit American National Foods programs and projects.

Vegan Dairy-Free Soy Products

Follow Your Heart Vegan Cheeses: *Follow Your Heart* is a generous donor to the American Natural Foods Certified Vegetarian Cook (CVC) program. I have used their Veganaise mayonnaise since they started producing it—superb! All of their cheeses taste good in recipes, and they melt in dry heat (in pizza oven or under broiler). The vegan cream cheese is an exceptional substitute where cream cheese is needed. **(followyourheart.com) (888) 394-3949**

Vegan Mayonnaise

Original Veganaise Soy Mayonnaise

Vegan Cheeses and Sour Creams

Vegan Gourmet Mozzarella Shreds	Vegan Sour Cream
Vegan Gourmet Cheddar Shreds	Vegan Gourmet Sour Cream
Vegan Gourmet Cream Cheese	

Vegan Salad Dressings

Vegan Thousand Island Dressing	Original Balsamic Vinegar Dressing

Whipped "Cream" Toppings

Rich's Whip Topping/Rich's Products Corporation: *Rich's* is a generous donor to the American Natural Foods Certified Vegetarian Cook (CVC) program. Rich's offers foodservice clients its Rich® Non-Dairy Whipped Topping, a one quart frozen soy whipped topping. The vegan topping may include high fructose corn syrup and trans fats. I make a rare exception here for this vegan product that isn't 100 percent natural. It is for those who are into healthy vegan cuisine and flexible for special occasions. Consumer products are listed on their consumer site. (**richsfoodservice.com** *also* **richs.com**) **(716) 878-8000**

Soy Milk & Butter Spreads

Earth Balance is a very generous and major donor to the American Natural Foods Certified Vegetarian Cook (CVC) program. Their trans fat-free butter spreads are an exceptional vegan substitute for butter. Their vegan soy mayonnaise is also and exceptional product. (**earthbalancenatural.com**) **(201) 421-3970**

Earth Balance Butter Spreads

Original Buttery Spread	Olive Oil Buttery Spread	Vegan Soy Mayonnaise	Organic Coconut Spread

WhiteWave Foods Company is a generous donor to the American Natural Foods Certified Vegetarian Cook (CVC) program. Their soy milks are available in retail and foodservice operations. (**whitewave.com**) **(303) 635-4000**

White Wave Original Soy Milk—for dessert recipes	Silk Unsweetened Organic Soymilk—for savories and desserts	Silk Chocolate Soymilk

Instant Soy Milk Powder

Now Foods: Organic instant soy milk powder is provided by Now Foods. (**nowfoods.com**)

Coconut Milk, Butter, & Oil

Simply Asia Food Thai Kitchen Coconut Milk: Unsweetened coconut milk—13.66-ounce can. This product of Thailand is a white coconut milk that contains guar gum and water to emulsify the oil to the liquid. (**thaikitchen.com**)

MaraNatha Foods: Coconut Butter comes in 15 ounce bottles and contains coconut pulp which will burn in sautéing. It is recommended for baking or moist (i.e., boiling) low temperature cooking to prevent the pulp from burning. (**maranathafoods.com**)

Tropical Traditions, Inc.: Coconut Oil is pure coconut oil available in a variety of high quality option from extra virgin to organic. Coconut oil is pure oil and can be used like drawn butter (pure butter oil with no milk solids that burn at high heat like coconut pulp in coconut butter). Comes in 32-ounce jar, 1, and 5-gallon pails and available in some regions of the country and nationally by online ordering. (**tropicaltraditions.com**)

Vegan Proteins

Canned Beans

Bush Brothers & Company is a generous and major donor to the American Natural Foods Certified Vegetarian Cook (CVC) program. Their canned beans were used in the recipes in the development of the CVC program and in the recipe testing for this cookbook. As a progressive company, Bush Brothers continues to explore ways to build beans into foodservice menus and into the American diet. Their reduced sodium beans are an example of Bush Brothers' continuing effort to improve the nutritional quality of their products. Bush's Best beans are available in retail stores nationwide and from major foodservice distribution companies.

Bush's Best beans are packed in cases of six #10 cans for foodservice and 16-ounce cans in the retail market. Their canned bean varieties include but are not limited to

Black Bean	Kidney Bean	Navy (or Great Northern) Bean
Pinto Bean	Garbanzo Bean	Cannellini Bean (white kidney bean)

One half-cup serving of reduced sodium Bush's Best beans has about 240 mg sodium. The same quantity of full sodium beans has 450 mg sodium (19% of RDA). Note: Rinsing full sodium beans will give you about the same sodium level as unrinsed reduced sodium beans. (**bushbeans.com**) (**800**) **590-3797**

Dry Beans

A wide range of dry beans is available through all foodservice distribution channels and retail stores. For the unique kinds of beans, see Indian Harvest (**inharvest.com**) in their grains, nuts, and seeds section.

Instant Dry Beans

Commercial instant dry bean mixes are flavored bean mixes with extended but limited recipe applications. Add water and oil, mix and serve. These mixes can be used in soups, pâtés, pasta salads, etc. Refried beans in pinto and black bean options are the most common options.

Frontier Natural Products: sells instant pinto and black bean flakes. (More information in specialty seasonings section at **frontiercoop.com**.)

Textured Vegetable Protein (TVP)

The primary protein available to both foodservice and retail customers, TVP is cooked soy beans from which the oil is extracted leaving the soy protein, which is extruded and dried. It comes in many forms from flake to ground and caramel colored to an off-white tan color.

TVP is available at some retail natural foods stores, Whole Foods stores, Bob's Red Mill (on-line at **bobsredmill.com** and retail), and **amazon.com. Foodservicedirect.com** is also an online source for TVP in foodservice packs. Check with your local foodservice distributor for regional options.

Frozen Beans

Edamame—Frozen Green Soy Beans (shelled or in shell) are available in most supermarkets, natural health food stores, and broadline distributors. There are a variety of retail brands to choose from and your foodservice distributor either has or can easily bring in a foodservice pack including edamame succotash (corn and edamame).

Tofu

Many regional private label brands are regionally manufactured for the major supermarket chains (natural and mainstream). Distributors generally work with regional brands unless they carry a national brand. I recommend extra firm water-packed tofu for savory foods. Today tofu is available in almost, if not all, major supermarket chains and foodservice distributors.

Mori Nu Silken Tofu from Morinaga Nutritional Foods, Inc.: The tofu that I recommend and is available nationally is Mori Nu Silken Tofu. Again, the extra firm is recommended. It is the only one I use in my desserts.

Silken Tofu comes in soft, firm, and extra firm and is packed in 12 units weighing 12.3 ounces for foodservice and individual units for retail. Note: Because of its aseptic packaging, Mori Nu Silken Tofu does not have to be refrigerated. It is a superior product for use in desserts, hollandaise-type sauces, and dessert-type sauces. **(morinu.com) (310) 787-0200**

Instant Dry Vegan Analogues

Eco-Cuisine, Inc.: Eco-Cuisine is a major sponsor of the ANF and the Certified Vegetarian Cook program. It is the first vegetarian foodservice company to develop vegan dry mixes for both savory and pastry with applications using the speed scratch menu-concept format. Its products are designed to be integrated into the foodservice operator's existing menu versus creating specialty menus.

Eco-Cuisine savory products include:

Eco-Cuisine® Reduced Sodium "Ground Beef Style" Quick Mix (10 pounds)	Eco-Cuisine® Reduced Sodium "Sausage Style" Quick Mix (10 pounds)
Eco-Cuisine® Reduced Sodium "Chicken Style" Quick Mix (10 pounds)	Eco-Cuisine® Seitan Quick Mix (10 pounds)
	Eco-Cuisine® Chicken and Beef Style Broths

To explore several options for both foodservice operators and retail customers to order Eco-Cuisine's mixes, please contact Eco-Cuisine via e-mail to ron@eco-cuisine.com. Eco-Cuisine's website and on YouTube offers training videos demonstrating how to prepare the different types of proteins. **(eco-cuisine.com) (303) 402-0289**

Refrigerated & Frozen Vegan Proteins and Analogues

Many refrigerated and frozen vegan proteins are available in both foodservice and retail with significantly more in the retail sector. Several companies also manufacture tempeh in the United States and sell it frozen or refrigerated.

Turtle Island Foods: Tempeh and meat analogues are available in several forms with grains and/or sea vegetables added to them for nutritional value and innovative new ways of presenting tempeh. Turtle Island Foods under its Tofurky label offers an Organic Five Grain Tempeh, and Organic Soy Tempeh (traditional), plus several marinated tempehs which I recommend for menu innovation. I generally work with plain tempeh. Turtle Island's hot dog has a firm texture and good flavor. The company is well known for its Thanksgiving Tofurky Roll and it also has a burger and roast. All of their products are either organic or non-GMO.

Tofurky Tempeh	Tofurky Hot Dogs	Deli Slices (for sandwiches)
Kielbasa	Italian Sausage	

(tofurky.com) (541) 386-7766

Gardein Protein International offers many frozen prepared and ready-to-heat-and-serve proteins/meals that don't require preparation beyond heating or applying them as a cooked protein to a recipe. They also have a foodservice line. Their proteins are designed for easy implementation into menu development. The proteins are used in fully developed menus.

Frozen Beef Strips	Frozen Chicken Strips	Burgers

Retail website **(gardein.com/products)**

Foodservice website **(gardein.com/food-service) (877) 305-6777**

Grains, Nuts, & Seeds

Bob's Red Mill sells many unique flours and grains including Vital Wheat Gluten (75 percent to 80 percent protein) from the endosperm of the wheat berry, Almond Meal/Flour, Golden Flaxseed Meal, and a number of bean flours. Some specialties are gluten-free ingredients, mixes, and Xanthan Gum Powder which is used as a stabilizer in gluten-free foods and salad dressings. **(bobsredmill.com/flours-meals) (503) 654-3215**

Nuts

Nuts are readily available in both foodservice packs through foodservice distributors and retail in bulk and 1-pound packages. Raw, unprocessed or plain (with no salt or other seasoning) is the way I purchase nuts in general. That leaves me with an infinite array of options. My preference for almonds is blanched (skin removed) to give me a wider array of options to use in recipes.

In Harvest offers an extensive line of whole grains and beans, including some unique ancient grains. They generally have several varieties of many grains and a line of heirloom lentils and beans along with some specialty pastas. In Harvest products are available through foodservice distribution channels, in retail (bulk bins and retail packages), and direct ship. Specialty products include:

Black Beluga Lentils	Green Wheat Freekeh	Moroccan Couscous
French Green Lentils	Bamboo Rice	Red Quinoa
Red Lentils	Arborio Rice	Black Quinoa
Green Flageolet Beans	White Israeli Couscous	Wheat Berries
Giant Peruvian Lima Beans	Whole Wheat Israeli Couscous	Bulgur Wheat
Butterscotch Calypso Beans	Black Barley	White Barley

(inharvest.com) (800) 346-7032

Specialty Seasonings

Edward and Sons offers the Wizard's Worcestershire Sauce, available in both vegan organic and nonorganic versions. **(edwardandsons.com) (805) 684-8500**

Frontier Natural Products Co-op is donor to the American Natural Foods CVC program. Frontier bakery flavors, spices, and herbs are used almost exclusively by the ANF and Eco-Cuisine. Frontier's extensive line of ethnic spice blends includes both organic and conventional options. They also offer high-quality bulk teas (some organic) and a few soy products (plain and seasoned TVPs of which "Bac-uns" are used sparingly in salads due to its high sodium content). Frontier also sells vegan chicken, beef, and vegetable broths and offers spices and seasonings from A-Z, grilling seasonings, seasoning blends, gourmet pepper seasonings, gourmet salts, seafood seasonings, soup mixes, sauce mixes, and salt-free seasonings. **(frontiercoop. com) (800) 346-7032**

Great Eastern Sun is a donor to the ANF and CVC program. Their products are available through natural foods retail stores and through direct ship from their website. Great Eastern Sun® misos, which need to be refrigerated after opening, are the gold standard of misos. These include:

Miso Master® Organic
Traditional Miso

Miso Master® Organic
Mellow White Miso

Miso Master® Organic
Traditional Red

Miso Emperor's Kitchen® are Asian condiments offered by Great Eastern Sun including:

Emperor's Kitchen® Kosher
Traditional Umeboshi
Vinegar

Emperor's Kitchen®
Mirin Stir-Fry Sauce

Emperor's Kitchen® Organic
Toasted Sesame Oil

Their products are available through natural foods distribution channels, retail stores, and direct ship. **(great-eastern-sun.com) (828) 665-7790**

Sea Vegetables

Great Eastern Sun: In addition to its top grade misos, Great Eastern Sun also sells high-quality sea vegetables:

Emerald Cove® Organic
Pacific Sushi Nori

Emerald Cove® Silver Grade
Ready to Use Wakame

Emerald Cove® Silver Pacific
Kombu

Emerald Cove® Silver Pacific
Grade Arame

Atlantic Mariculture
Organic Canadian Dulse

(great-eastern-sun.com) (828) 665-7790

Agar (Agar Agar) Flakes and Powder

Retail natural foods stores may carry agar ingredients, and I suggest that you check to see if they carry it and at what cost. Agar products are available online.

○ Frontier Coop sells agar powder online in one-pound bags. (**frontiercoop.com**)

○ *Now Foods* now sells agar powder online and it may be available in some natural foods retail stores. (**nowfoods.com/Agar-Powder-2oz.htm**)

○ **Amazon.com** also sells agar powder and flakes.

Bakery Ingredients

Sweeteners

Frontier Coop: Stevia powder is available in 1 pound bulk packs from Frontier Coop. Stevia is a sweetening ingredient that I have not fully addressed in *The Classical Vegetarian Cookbook* since it is more known as a sugar-free special diet ingredient. It is a vegan product that is many more times sweeter than sucrose, and easily used in beverages. (**frontiercoop.com**)

Great Eastern Sun: In addition to its outstanding misos and excellent sea vegetables, Great Eastern Sun also offers:

Sweet Cloud® Organic Kosher Brown Rice Syrup

Sweet Cloud® Organic Barley Malt Syrup

(**great-eastern-sun.com**)

Wholesome Sweeteners, Inc.

Wholesome Sweeteners, Inc. provides the foodservice industry and the retail customer with Fair Trade Certified™ organic and natural sweeteners and syrups. Many of the sugars are in foodservice and industrial pack sizes. All sweeteners are in retail packs.

Organic Blue Agave Syrup	Organic Powdered Sugar
Organic Molasses Syrup	Organic Coconut Palm Sugar
Organic Pancake Syrup	Organic Sucanat
Natural Cane Sugar	Organic Turbino
Light Brown Sugar	Organic Dark Brown Sugar

(**wholesomesweeteners.com**) (**800) 680-1896**

Bakery Flavors & Items

Frontier Natural Coop: This ANF donor also carries many natural bakery flavors including butterscotch, cherry, lemon, mint, orange, and vanilla. Frontier ships their products direct. (**frontiernatural.com**)

Liquid Lecithin is a derivative extract of soybeans and used as an emulsifier option in the pastry technique section. Sold by **amazon.com**.

Eco-Cuisine, Inc. offers a complete line of basic bakery speed scratch mixes. Each mix has multiple applications to make a wide variety of muffins or cookies. A little muffin mix added to brownie mix makes a superb vegan chocolate cake. Instant soy pudding mix added to the muffin mix with bread cubes makes a superb vegan bread pudding. The mixes are available to foodservice and retail customers online.

Basic Brownie   Basic Muffin   Instant Soy Pudding Mix

Basic Cookie   Basic English Scones

(eco-cuisine.com)

Global Sugar Art: This website is essentially about pastry decorating, icing decorations, bakery mixes, and pastry equipment. It is a good general site for those serious about working with pastry. **(globalsugarart.com) (800) 420-6088**

Smallwares Bakery Equipment for Retail Customers

Camerons Products is a generous donor to the ANF's CVC program. Camerons Products sells stovetop smokers, chips, and a variety of smoking equipment for both foodservice and domestic use. I use their stovetop smoker and chips exclusively. **(cameronsproducts.com) (888) 563-0227**

Hamilton Beach Brands, Inc.: I use the commercial (foodservice model) Hamilton Beach Blender in the ANF's recipe development. Their blenders have the power necessary to immediately turn a nut into a cream without stressing out the motor. I use it to make vegan cheeses, ice creams, and sauces. The blender almost effortlessly rises to the culinary task at hand. Their website offers both commercial foodservice and retail domestic options. **(commercial.hamiltonbeach.com or hamiltonbeach.com) (800) 572-3331· USA, Canada**

Recommended Resources

The books I recommend in this section are a personal sampling of the resources I use in sourcing recipes and understanding nutrition and the philosophy of cuisine. For the professional and everyday cook, it is a rich mix of cuisine history, technique, health, science, and philosophy. While the Internet offers infinite resources to search out recipes of every ethnicity and category, there often is no clue to authenticity and no opportunity for deeper understanding. Many of the books listed here are classics and should be part of every chef and food lover's culinary education.

While several titles may be out of print and available only through specialty retailers, most of these books should be available in most culinary school libraries and possibly in some public libraries, and all are worthwhile investments for your own bookshelf. Some of these titles are available in revised editions. I've included the well-worn editions that are in my own library.

Many of these books are not vegetarian. I consider them a springboard to ideas for continued development of classical vegetarian cuisine as we explore new ingredients and remain committed to taste and health.

The Masters

Cooking for Kings: The Life of Antonin Carême—the First Celebrity Chef Ian Kelly. Walker & Company, September 2003, hardcover, 288 pages, ISBN: 978-1-9040-9520-0

Auguste Escoffier: Memories of My Life Translated by Laurence Escoffier. Wiley and Sons, 1996, hardcover, 272 pages, ISBN: 978-0-4712-8803-9

Escoffier's Basic Elements of Fine Cookery A. Escoffier. Crescent Books, Inc., New York, 1941, 148 pages, Library of Congress Card number: 66-22655

The Escoffier Cookbook: A Guide to the Fine Art of French Cuisine August Escoffier. Crown Publishing, Inc., New York, 2000, revised edition, 923 pages, ISBN: 978-0-5175-0662-2

Classical and Modern French Techniques

The Great Book of French Cuisine. Henri-Paul Pellaprat. World Publishing Company, New York, 1971, Library of Congress Catalogue card number: 78-162570

La Technique: An Illustrated Guide to the Fundamental Techniques of Cooking. Jacques Pepin. Time Books, 1976, 476 pages, ISBN 0-8129-0610-1

The New Larousse Gastronomique. Prosper Montagne. Crown Publishers, Inc., New York, 1988, 1,064 pages, ISBN 978-0-517-53137-2

The Roux Brothers on Patisserie: Pastries and Desserts from 3 Star Master Chefs. Michel and Albert Roux. Simon & Schuster, 1986, 256 pages, ISBN 978-0-13-783382-2

American Voices

Joy of Cooking: The American Household Classic Newly Revised and Expanded with over 4500 Recipes and 1000 Informative Illustrations. Irma S. Rombauer and Marion Rombauer Becker. Bobbs-Merrill Company, Inc., 1975, 915 pages, ISBN: 0-02-604570-2

The Art of Eating (50th Anniversary Edition). M.F.K. Fisher. Houghton Mifflin, 2004, 784 pages, ISBN: 978-0-7645-4261-9

Health

Food Is Your Best Medicine. Henry G. Bieler, MD. Random House, New York, 1965, 256 pages, ISBN: 978-03944-25337

Vegetarianism

The Heretic's Feast: A History of Vegetarianism. Colin Spencer. University Press of New England, 1996, 402 pages, ISBN: 978-0874517099

The New Becoming Vegetarian: The Essential Guide to a Healthy Vegetarian Diet Vesanto Melina, RD, and Brenda Davis, RD. Healthy Living Publications, Summertown, Tennessee, 2003, 373 pages, ISBN: 978-1570671449

French Gourmet Vegetarian Cookbook. Rosine Claire with introduction by Hans Holzer. Celestial Arts, Millbrae, California, 1975, 106 pages, ISBN 978-0-8998-7058-7

Lord Krishna's Cuisine: The Art of Indian Vegetarian Cooking. Yamuna Devi. Dutton, New York, 1987, 816 pages, ISBN: 978-0525245643

Salads

Main Course Salads: Creative Salads that Satisfy. Donna Rodnitzky. Avery Books, New York, 1999, 256 pages, ISBN: 978 0-89529-928-4

Macrobiotic Lifestyle

The Book of Macrobiotics: The Universal Way of Health and Happiness. Michio Kushi. Japan Publications, Inc., 1997, ISBN 0-87040-381-8

Cooking with Japanese Foods: A Guide to the Traditional Natural Foods of Japan. Jan and John Belleme. Talman Company, 1986, 220 pages, ISBN: 978-0-936184-04-3

The Sweet Life: Natural Macrobiotic Desserts. Marcea Weber. Japan Publications, 1980, 176 pages, ISBN 978-0-87040-493-8

Science and Philosophy

On Food and Cooking: The Science and Lore of the Kitchen. Harold McGee. Charles Scribner's Sons, New York, 2004, 896 pages, ISBN: 978-0684800011

The Omnivore's Dilemma: A Natural History of Four Meals. Michael Pollan. Penguin Press, New York, 2006, 450 pages, ISBN: 978-159420-082-3

Nutrition—Amino Acids

Livestrong.com/article/426939-essential-amino-acids-in-vegetables

Vegetarian Resource Group (vrg.org)

A great resource for all things vegetarian and vegan. The article "Humans are Omnivores" by John McArdle, Ph.D., can be found on this site at the link: vrg.org/nutshell/omni.htm

About Chef Ron Pickarski

After spending his teenage years working in his parents' diner and later training as a certified meat cutter, Ron Pickarski became a progressive chef in the art of translating classical French and modern cuisine into vegan cuisine using plant-based natural and/or organic ingredients. For Chef Ron, vegetarianism is its own cuisine, with vegan ingredients creating a new emerging cuisine for the twenty-first century.

In 1978, Chef Ron decided that the world stage of the International Culinary Olympics (IKA) would be a viable event to give vegetarian cuisine a contemporary and upscale image. From 1980 to 1996, he led his American Natural Foods team to win seven medals (gold, silver, and bronze) as the first chef in the IKA history to use only vegan plant-based foods. He is the first vegetarian chef to be certified as an Executive Chef by the American Culinary Federation.

Culinary educator and innovator, dedicated to bringing the finest vegan cuisine into both restaurants and home kitchens, Chef Ron is the founder of Eco-Cuisine, integrating a new interpretation of classical and modern vegan cuisine for today's health-driven and taste-conscious consumer with specialty "speed scratch" products designed to support chefs and cooks at all levels. Chef Ron also trains other chefs throughout the United States and internationally and translates for vegan cuisine the classical techniques established by master chefs such as Antonin Carême and August Escoffier. Chef Ron is also the president of American Natural Foods, a nonprofit dedicated to supporting vegan culinary education and the American Natural Foods Culinary Olympic Team.

The Classical Vegetarian Cookbook for Professional Chefs and Inspired Cooks represents a lifetime of recipes, culinary techniques, and a bounty of specialized information for the new art of vegan cuisine. With thanks to past masters and today's culinary innovations, Chef Ron is helping to transform the way we eat.

Eco-Cuisine

After completing twenty years of Culinary Olympic competition, Chef Ron's goal was to translate what he and his team accomplished at the IKA into American foodservice operations. He founded Eco-Cuisine, Inc. in 1991, a culinary vegan/ vegetarian company to bring classical and modern interpretations of vegan cuisine into the U.S. foodservice industry. Eco-Cuisine food products can be found nationally in restaurants and kitchens. The company's speed scratch products and services allow him to act on his belief that vegetarianism is an innovative twenty-first century cuisine that works with minimum skill, labor, and food cost.

Chef Ron passionately pursues the latest in food science technology and the culinary arts, specializing in the research and development of all-natural speed scratch vegan or vegetarian savory and dessert food products that are tasty and nutrient dense. From his decades in professional kitchens, he understands the chef's challenge to match great tasting cuisine with the need for cost effectiveness, ease of production, and proper nutrition.

For more information on Eco-Cuisine, visit eco-cuisine.com

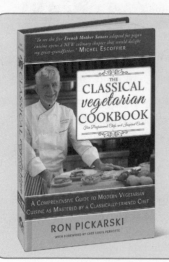

Eco-Cuisine is a major supporter of the American Natural Foods (ANF) 501 (c) 3 nonprofit and the Certified Vegetarian Cook (CVC) program.

Purchasing this book directly from Eco-Cuisine enables it to assist and support the ANF and CVC.

Order the book online at the ECO-CUISINE.COM storefront to help support the ANF, CVC, and its vegetarian education programs.

Certified Vegetarian Cook Program

Through the nonprofit American Natural Foods, Chef Ron is currently developing the first vegan vegetarian core competency culinary skills certification program. The Certified Vegetarian Cook (CVC) program is a vegan culinary educational platform that will offer specialized training online and in person for professional chefs and culinary students. *The Classical Vegetarian Cookbook for Professional Chefs and Inspired Cooks* is a distillation of the CVC certification program.

For more information on the CVC, visit americannaturalfoods.org or eco-cuisine.com.

Index